Rationing Health Care

Hard Choices and Unavoidable Trade-offs

D1826855

Rationing Health Care

Hard Choices and Unavoidable Trade-offs

André den Exter and Martin Buijsen (eds.)

Maklu
Antwerpen | Apeldoorn | Portland

Rationing Health Care
Hard Choices and Unavoidable Trade-offs
André den Exter and Martin Buijsen (eds.)
Antwerpen | Apeldoorn | Portland
Maklu
2012

250 pag. – 24 x 16 cm
ISBN 978-90-466-0525-7
D/2012/1997/44
NUR 824

Maklu- Publishers
Somersstraat 13/15, 2018 Antwerpen, Belgium, info@maklu.be
Koninginnelaan 96, 7315 EB Apeldoorn, The Netherlands, info@maklu.nl
www.maklu.eu

USA & Canada
International Specialized Book Services
920 NE 58th Ave., Suite 300, Portland, OR 97213-3786, orders@isbs.com, www.isbs.com

Contents

ECONOMICS

Preface

In most OECD countries, health care spending is outpacing economic growth, witness the fact that it amounted to an average 7 percent of the gross domestic product in 2002 versus 9 persent in 2008; further rise was expected in 2009.[1] This phenomenon is largely ascribed to innovation in health care technologies and ageing of the population claiming medical care. Both factors will continue to push up health spending in the near future. Under these circumstances, health care rationing is (expected to be) the central policy issue. So, the "R" word has cropped up again – although one may claim that the item has never disappeared from the policy agenda since the introduction of the famous 'Oregon Health Plan (1989).'[2] healthcare rationing has never disappeared from the policy agenda. Others, however, would perhaps claim that rationing is no policy or clinical issue, at least not in their country.[3]

Part of the rationing problem is disagreement about its meaning. How to define health care rationing? Traditionally, the term 'rationing' refers to the distribution of scarce resources during wartime, but in fact the term applies to any time a scarce good or service will be denied or delayed. Still, there are many notions of health care rationing, which differ in several ways.[4] First, they may differ according to whether the rationing is explicit or not, as it is argued that rationing includes only conscious decisions taken at an administrative level that make a service unavailable to some people.[5] Or – in contrast – non-explicit mechanisms, such as allocating goods by the free market, may be classified as rationing.[6] Second, they may differ as to the scarcity of resources. Some maintain that a resource must be absolutely scarce for its distribution to qualify as rationing (e.g., organs); whereas others think that rationing also includes the allocation of non-scarce resources (e.g., expensive medicines).[7] Third, they may differ on whether rationing involves only limits on medical necessary services, or involves limits on any beneficial services.[8] In our view

---

[1]   OECD, *Health: Key Tables from OECD*, OECD 2011 (accessed on April 13, 2011).

[2]   The essence of the Oregon rationing approach was based on budget control through explicit rationing of services. It represented a striking contrast both to the well-established practice of implicitly rationing medical care in the United States by income and insurance coverage, and to the somewhat less visible resource allocation decisions made by health policy makers and professionals in other countries. See L Jacobs, Th Marmor, J Oberlander, 'The Oregon Health Plan and the Political Paradox of Rationing: What Advocates and Critics Have Claimed and What Oregon Did' (1999) 1 *JHPPL* 162.

[3]   JA Califano, 'Rationing' Health Care: The Unnecessary Solution' (1992) 5 *University of Pennsylvania Law Review* 1592-38.

[4]   PA Ubel, SD Goold, 'Rationing' Health Care, Not all definitions are created equal, Commentary 158 (1998) Feb 9 *Arch. Intern Med* 210.

[5]   RH Brook, KN Lohr, 'Will we need to ration effective health care?', (1986) Fall *Issues Sci Tech* 68-77, quoted by Ubel (note 4) 210.

[6]   MA Hall, The problems with rule-based rationing 19 *J Med Philos* 1994:315-332.

[7]   ibid note 2.

[8]   DC Hadorn, RH Brook, 'The health care resources allocation debate: defining our terms' (1991) 266 *JAMA*: 3328-3331; AS Relman, Is rationing inevitable? (1990) 322 *N Engl J Med* (NEJM) 1809-1810.

Reinhardt's broad notion of health care rationing is the most adequate: the use of any mechanism – price or non-price – to deny individuals access to beneficial health care.[9] The *use* of such a selection mechanism implies painful choices of scarce goods and services, emphasizing the "moral significance" of these decisions, which notion is absent from the general phrase "allocation or distribution of resources".[10] The painful outcomes of rationing decisions cause controversy in society and therefore, rationing has a negative connotation. We would like to argue that rationing can even be perceived as fair, provided the decision-making process is fully transparent and public, and the arguments are rationally explained to those who are denied health care. These requirements give rationing its moral legitimacy, or what Fleck describes as the process of "rational democratic deliberation".[11]

'The Importance of being Earnest'

In the rationing debate, most authors favour explicit rationing for reasons of accountability (e.g., *Newdick, Syrett* and *Flood*), or transparency and democratic decision-making (*Fleck*). In contrast, implicit rationing on a micro level occurs in a sub rosa world: decisions are based on imperfect information, distorted inter-pretations of evidence on effectiveness, and hidden cost concerns.[12] From a legal perspective, implicit rationing can also be rejected since it violates a basic notion of health law: the principle of informed consent. Traditionally, consent has been interpreted as a moral and legal condition to legitimize any medical intervention. Patients are expected to give consent on the basis of objective information from the responsible health professional prior to treatment.[13] Absent or insufficient information makes consent invalid and can be considered as a violation of the fundamental right of bodily integrity and the autonomy principle.[14] Moreover, in international law, providing informed consent is fundamental to a person's right to health care, i.e. informed decision-making on the available and accessible health care services of good quality.[15]

---

[9]   U Reinhardt, 'Rationing Health Care: What It Is, What it Is Not, and Why We Cannot Avoid It' in S Altman and U Reinhardt (eds) *Strategic Choices for a Changing Health Care System* (Health Administration Press, Chicago 1996) 63-99, quoted by LM Fleck, *Just Caring Health Care Rationing and Democratic Deliberation* (OUP 2009) 405.

[10]   Fleck (note 4) 211. Nonetheless, we agree with Ubel that also allocation decisions involve tragic choices, and can be just or unjust like rationing.

[11]   Fleck (note 9) ch. 5.

[12]   JR Fox, 'A sub rosa world: Medicare and the cost of new technology' (2011) 3-4 *Int J Healthcare Technology and Management* 321-332.

[13]   The doctrine of informed consent is historically rooted in both common law and civil law coun-tries, and developed by landmark cases such as *Canterbury v. Spence*, Circuit Court of Appeals for DC (US 1972) setting the "reasonable man" standard for informed consent; ECrtHR *Keenan v. the United Kingdom*, no. 27229/95; ECrtHR *Herczegfalvy v Austria*, no. 10533/83.

[14]   E.g., ECrtHR *K.H v. Slovakia*, no. 32881/04; *M.A.K. and R.K. v UK*, no. 45901/05.

[15]   United Nations, Report of the Special Rapporteur on the right of everyone to the enjoyment of the highest attainable standard of physical and mental health. 'Right to everyone to the enjoyment of the highest attainable standard of physical and mental health', UN General Assembly Doc A/64/272. 10 August 2009: 6.

As a general rule, the duty to inform covers information about the purpose and nature of treatment or research, (side) effects, possible risks, and alternative treatment options. The scope of information may vary by patient, however, depending on characteristics such as age, co-occurring diseases, high or low risk intervention, language skills, etcetera. To conclude, respecting informed consent therefore requires full information about all treatment options "in order to weigh up the necessity or usefulness of the medical intervention against its risk and the discomfort or pain it will cause".[16] The less knowledgeable, docile patient is withheld this information in the case of implicit rationing. In the legal doctrine, withholding information can only be justified in the so-termed 'therapeutic exception', i.e. when it is in the patient's health interest. But courts are unlikely to accept such a claim in case information is withheld for non-therapeutic reasons. Consequently, nondisclosure of a beneficial treatment option based on economic rather than strictly medical grounds may increase the risk of medical disciplinary and malpractice litigation.[17] Fear of litigation as a counterargument for nondisclosure is not legitimate as it is rather based on the health provider's self-interest. Taking the right to health care seriously, both state and non state parties, such as health professionals, would be obliged to respect and protect this right, i.e. to abstain from implicit bedside rationing.

Rationing at the Court

Nonetheless, fear of litigation in case of explicit rationing is not unfounded. On several occasions applicants have successfully challenged the denial of necessary medicines or treatment by local health trusts or health financiers, for example the refusal to provide Herceptin in *Rogers v Swindon NHS Primary Care Trust* (UK),[18] and the refusal to fund in vitro fertilization treatment in *Cameron v Nova Scotia* (Canada).[19] But in general, the judiciary has been reluctant to overturn rulings of decision-making bodies on health care rationing, therefore accepting their margin of appreciation. Instead of considering the substance of the decision, courts have been more comfortable in challenging the decision-making *proce Marketization dure*.[20] This is a procedure that requires the highest degree of transparency of decision-making, or 'clarity about how priorities are set'.[21] Since adequate rationales

---

[16]   Convention for the protection of Human Rights and dignity of human beings with regard to the application of biology and medicine: Convention on Human Rights and Biomedicine (ETS No 164). Explanatory report para 35.

[17]   Though in practice, no such malpractice cases have been found. Some reasonable speculations are possible such as the patient remains simply unaware of alternative treatment options, and when it concerns low-income and less knowledgeable patients the high costs of malpractice litigation.

[18]   As discussed by Keith Syrett in his contribution 'NICE and the problem of 'postcode prescribing' in the English National Health Service, chapter 7.

[19]   In: CF Flood and I Essajee, 'Setting limits on Health Care: Challenges in and out of the Courtroom in Canada and Down-under', chapter 9.

[20]   Flood and Essajee ibid, also C Newdick, 'Re-balancing the Rationing Debate: Tackling the tensions between individual and community rights', chapter 8.

[21]   Daniels and Sabin, chapter 1.

for the political priorities are absent, there is the danger of arbitrariness, which is the main reason to initiate lawsuits.

Towards fair and just rationing decisions

According to Fleck, the focus on procedural justice – thus the plea for explaining rationing decision-making based on evidence, reasons and principles – is in itself not sufficient. Democratic deliberation in health care rationing and priority-setting is need to make fair and just rationing decisions, as Fleck argues.[22] Whereas Daniels thinks the deliberate process of independent 'citizens panels' is futile, Fleck strongly believes it is essential to "having an outcome that is self-constructed and self-imposed by the deliberative group". This would help ensure the outcome is just and legitimate.[23] Given that we are critical about the practical implications, we nevertheless support Fleck's idea of broad public deliberation organized by a NICE-like entity creating a broad range of rationing protocols.

Triggering the rationing debate, 'Rationing Health Care – Hard Choices and Unavoidable Trade-offs' is aimed at achieving fair and just rationing decisions. The debate remains unresolved – but the strength of the book is that each chapter analyses the rationing debate from a different perspective in search of a reasonable solution.

Rotterdam, 2012

André den Exter
Martin Buijsen

---

[22]   L Fleck, 'Just caring: In defense of the role of democratic deliberation in health care rationing and priority-setting', chapter 2.
[23]   ibid.

Chapter I

Accountability for Reasonable Priority Setting

Norman Daniels and James Sabin

1. The problem: ethical disagreement about priorities in health

Many health policy decisions involve setting priorities for the use of resources in meeting health needs. Such decisions often rest on ethical considerations, and reasonable people may disagree about them. These ethical disagreements about priorities raise questions about the legitimacy and fairness of the decisions that are made.

Such decisions are pervasive in health policy. In the context of individual medical care, questions that often attract attention include coverage decisions for a new technology or limits in public or private insurance schemes. These might take place at a national level, as in the case of the National Institute for Health and Clinical Excellence (NICE) recommendations to the NHS in the UK about a specific intervention or as in Israel's decisions about which new interventions to include among a list of candidates for addition to its "basket' of benefits, or when the FDA in the U.S. approves a drug and it is then available within Medicare and Medicaid by legal requirements, or in private insurance schemes by contractual arrangement. They might also take place within a specific local health authority or purchasing agent, as in the UK or Sweden or in a particular private insurance scheme in the U.S.

But priority setting about medical care is not just about new health technology assessments. It includes decisions about how a hospital or local health authority uses its budget to meet competing health needs in the population it serves. And, in the context of public health, as in health and safety regulation, priority-setting decisions may involve investing in risk reduction for one group versus another at varying cost and intrusiveness.

Where such decisions are made, they create winners and losers. Some people are benefited by them and others and are not. These conflicting interests and claims contribute to the disagreement about specific priorities.

One form that ethical controversy takes when priorities are set is whether to maximize aggregate health in a population or to address concerns about health disparities. Both are key goals of health policy, and sometimes they conflict. We have strong ethical reasons to pursue both goals, and much controversy surrounds what trade-offs in those goals are ethically acceptable in specific contexts. Some theories may emphasize one goal over the other – as utilitarianism arguably does by favoring maximizing aggregate population health, but other theories may support a complex blend of both, as in some liberal egalitarian approaches.[1]

Other disagreements involve tension between the compassionate use of unproven technologies and careful stewardship of resources,[2] controversy about the use of a treatment/enhancement distinction as a rough guide to priorities in health policy, or tension between identified and statistical victims.[3] Sometimes one side of these disagreements reflects a health maximizing strategy (e.g. stewardship may be aimed at more cost-effective care), but sometimes not (e.g., if there are the same numbers of identified and statistical victims but there is a preference for the former).

The shared feature of all these disagreements is that we lack consensus on ethical principles that can resolve these disputes.[4] If we had such consensus, our disagreements would take the form of controversy about how they should be applied, including controversy about the facts of the context. Unfortunately, the controversy is deeper. As a result, the controversies about priority setting raise hard questions about both legitimacy (who has the moral authority to make these decisions, and how should they be made) and fairness (are the decisions fair to the different parties with conflicting health needs and the claims they can base on them?).

To illustrate the pervasiveness and depth of the ethical disagreements, we shall argue in Sections 2 that existing economic tools aimed at helping with priority setting fall short of addressing important distributive issues and that people hold defendable attitudes toward distribution that differ from the maximizing assumptions in these tools. In Section 3 we suggest we need a fair deliberative process that holds decision-makers accountable for the reasonableness of their decisions. The main idea is an appeal to a notion of pure procedural justice: in the absence of prior agreement on principles to resolve disputes, the outcomes of a fair process count as fair outcomes.[5] Though the proposed process faces some important objections, described in Section 4, we conclude it not only enhances the legitimacy of contested decisions but also yields fair decisions, even if convincing arguments later compel us to modify our views about their fairness (The fairness of the outcomes is thus defeasible). This approach has varied applications, and there has been varied up-take of them in different places, less in the U.S. than elsewhere. Some of these applications are briefly described in Section 5. Further research is needed to establish the merits of the approach.

---

[1]   N Daniels, *Just Health: Meeting Health Needs Fairly* (CUP 2008).
[2]   N Daniels, JE Sabin, *Setting Limits Fairly: Learning to Share Resources for Health* (2nd edn, OUP 2008), chapter 5.
[3]   N Daniels, 'Reasonable Disagreement about Identified vs Statistical Victims' (2012) 1 *Hastings Center Report* 35-45.
[4]   N Daniels, JE Sabin, 'Limits to Health Care: Fair Procedures, Democratic Deliberating, and the Legitimacy Problem for Insurers' (1997) 26 (40) *Philosophy and Public Affairs* 202-50.
[5]   ibid.

2. The Limitations of Key Economic Tools

Comparative Effectiveness Research (CER) and cost effectiveness analysis (CEA) have important applications for guiding priority-setting decisions. Nevertheless, both kinds of tools fall short of being able to address important questions about distribution and value that many priority-setting decisions must address. Both tools provide important inputs into a broader deliberative process, but they do not substitute for it.

In the U.S., the Patient Protection and Affordable Care Act[6] promotes CER for the information it gives about alternative interventions, but the legislation bars CER from playing a role in coverage decisions, an unfortunate concession to the politics surrounding limit setting in the U.S. (Public officials in the U.S. resist acknowledging the need for limits, and candidates for public office score points by accusing their opponents of 'rationing.' Arguably, the effect is to distract attention from limit-setting by insurers.) A typical use of CER compares the effectiveness of two interventions (drugs, procedures, or even two methods of delivery), but in the U.S. context, it largely avoids considerations of cost. Obviously, if there is only one effective treatment for a condition, CER tells us nothing useful. Similarly, it tells us nothing about whether a more effective intervention is worth its extra cost. And CER cannot help us compare the outcomes of interventions across different disease conditions, since it uses no measure of health that permits such a comparison of effectiveness. Accordingly, there are many questions facing decision-makers about resource allocation in health care that cannot be answered by this approach, even if it can help us avoid investments in things that do not work or that offer no improvement over other interventions.

In Germany, however, CER is combined with an economic analysis that takes cost into consideration and that allows the calculation of "efficiency frontiers" for different classes of drugs.[7] To calculate an efficiency frontier, the effect of each drug in a class in producing some health outcome is plotted against its cost, and the curve is the efficiency frontier for that class of drugs. It is then possible to project from the performance of drugs in a specific class to see if a new intervention in that class yields an improvement in effectiveness at a price that makes it more or less efficient than what is projected from the existing efficiency frontier. This use of CER allows German decision-makers to negotiate about the price of treatments, rejecting payments that yield inefficient improvements. The assumption in Germany is that every intervention that has greater effectiveness can be covered, but only at the appropriate price. Still, the German use of CER cannot make comparisons across diseases, and so it allows great differences in efficiency across conditions.

---

[6]   Patient Protection and Affordability Act (PPACA) 2010. Pub.L. 111-148, 124 Stat. 119, to be codified as amended at scattered sections of the Internal Revenue Code and in 42 U.S.C.

[7]   JJ Caro and others, 'The efficiency frontier approach to economic evaluation of health-care interventions' (2010) 19 (10) *Health Econ* 1117-27, Article first published online: 2010 June 24.

Cost Effectiveness Analysis (CEA) aims for greater scope. It deploys a common unit for measuring health outcomes, either a disability-adjusted life year (DALY) or a quality adjusted life year (QALY). This unit purports to combine duration with quality, permitting us to compare health states across a broad range of disease conditions. In doing a CEA, we construct a ratio (the incremental cost effectiveness ratio or ICER) of the change in costs that results from the new intervention with the change in health effects (as measured by QALYs or DALYs. This allows us to calculate the cost per QALY (or DALY) and arrive at a general efficiency measure for a broad range of interventions for different conditions.

Critics have noted problematic ethical assumptions in both the construction of the health adjusted life year measures and the use of CEA.[8] To see some of these problems, consider the following table:

Rationing Problem	CEA	FAIRNESS
Priorities	No priority to worst off	Some priority to worst off
Aggregation	Any aggregation is OK	Some aggregations OK
Best Outcomes/ Fair Chances	Best Outcomes	Fair Chances

CEA systematically departs from judgments many people will make about what is fair. The priorities problem asks how much priority we should give to people who are worse off. By constructing a unit of health effectiveness, such as the QALY, CEA assumes this unit has the same value whoever gets it or wherever it goes in a life ("A QALY is a QALY" is the slogan). But intuitively many people think that a unit of health is worth more if someone who is relatively worse off (sicker) gets it rather than someone who is better off (less sick).[9] At the same time, people generally do not think we should give complete priority to those who are worse off. We may be able to do very little for them, so giving them complete priority means we would have to forego doing a lot more good for others. Few would defend creating a bottomless pit out of those unfortunate enough to be the worst off.

Similarly, CEA assumes that we should aggregate even very small benefits so that if enough people get small benefits it outweighs giving significant benefits to a few. But intuitively, most people think some benefits are trivial goods that should not be aggregated to outweigh significant benefits to a few.[10] Curing a lot of colds, for example, does not outweigh saving a life.

Finally, CEA favors putting resources where we get a best outcome, whereas people intuitively favor giving people a fair (if not equal) chance at a benefit. Locating an HIV/AIDS treatment clinic in an urban area may save more lives than reaching

---

[8]   E Nord, *Cost-Value Analysis in Health Care: Making sense out of QALY's* (CUP 1999); D Brock, 'Ethical Issues in the Use of Cost Effectiveness Analysis for the Prioritization of Health Care Resources' in G Khusfh (ed) *Bioethics: A Philosophical Overview* (Kluwer Publishers 2004).

[9]   D Brock, 'Priority to the Worst Off in Health Care Resource Prioritization' in M Battin, R Rhodes and A Silvers (eds) *Medicine and Social Justice* (OUP 2002) 362-372.

[10]   F Kamm, 'The Choice Between People, Commonsense Morality, and Doctors' (1993) 1 *Bioethics* 255-71.

out to a rural area, but in doing so we may deny many people a fair chance at a significant benefit.[11]

In all three of these cases, CEA favors a maximizing strategy, whereas people making judgments about fairness are generally willing to sacrifice some aggregate population health in order to treat people fairly. In each case, whether it is giving some priority to those who are worse off, viewing some benefits as not worth aggregating, or giving people fair chances at some benefit, fairness deviates from the health maximization that CEA favors. Yet we lack agreement on principles that tells us how to trade off goals of maximization and fairness in these cases.

Determining priorities primarily by seeing whether an intervention achieves some cost/QALY standard is adopting a health maximization approach. Such an approach will depart from widely held judgments about fairness. Thus NICE in the UK has had to modify its initially more rigid practice of approving new interventions only if they met a cost/QALY standard in the face of recommendations from its Citizen's Council. This Council, intended to reflect representative social and ethical judgments of a people in the UK, has proposed relaxing NICE's threshold in a variety of cases where judgments about fairness differed from concerns about health maximization. The judgments of the Citizen's Council in this regard are consistent with what the social science literature suggests are widely held views in a range of cultures and contexts.[12]

3. Accountability for Reasonableness: A Proposal

The problem, as we have described it, is that priority-setting decisions are often ethically controversial, and this raises questions about their legitimacy and fairness. In addition, the main analytic tools we have to aid decision-making, comparative effectiveness research and cost effectiveness analysis, either address only limited questions or adopt controversial approaches that ignore important distributive issues. These tools conflict with widely held views about what is equitable or fair. At the same time, we lack agreement on principles fine-grained enough to tell us what is fair in these cases. Because we lack agreement on principles, we shall argue that we need to rely on a form of procedural justice to arrive at decisions we can regard as legitimate and fair. Before making that argument, however, it is worth briefly considering some alternative views.

Despite our characterization of the problem, some may think issues of legitimacy and possibly of fairness are at least already addressed in either of two ways. The

---

11   N Daniels, *How to Achieve Fair Distribution of ARTs in "3 by 5": Fair Process and legitimacy in Patient Selection.* (World Health Organization/UNAIDS 2004).
12   P Dolan and others, 'QALY Maximization and People's Preferences: A Methodological Review of the Literature' (2005) 14 *Health Economics* 197-208; P Menzel and others, 'Toward a Broader View of Values in Cost-effectiveness Analysis in Health Care' (1999) 29 (3) *Hastings Center Report* 7-15; E Nord (note 8); PA Ubel, J Richardson, JL Pinto Prades, 'Life saving treatments and disabilities: Are all QALYs created equal?' (1999) 15 *International Journal of Technology Assessment in Health Care* 738-748; PA Ubel, J Baron, DA Asch, 'Preference for equity as a framing effect' (2001) 21 *Medical Decision Making* 180-189.

first approach is a market argument: at least where decisions are made by private insurance schemes, as in much of the health care delivered in the U.S., it might be claimed that people who buy such insurance express implicit consent to the limits involved in priority-setting decisions these insurers make. The claim is that consent to these limits means issues of legitimacy are clearly settled and, arguably, fairness is not at issue since we freely gave informed consent to them and they are therefore not unfair to us.

This argument fails both in theory and in practice.[13] Even if enrollment in an insurance scheme constituted freely given consent, half of all Americans getting employer-based insurance have no choice of plans and so are not freely consenting to one among alternative mechanisms for setting priorities. Basically, the only health insurance they can afford is the plan their employer provides to them, and their employer is in general not their fiduciary agent, bound to pursue the workers' best interests. In practice, then, the argument does not work for many people. But even in theory it is problematic: people lack real information about such priority setting when they enroll in a health insurance scheme, and they cannot exit from plans and seek alternatives easily when they realize a plan may not meet their needs, as they can when their family's needs outgrow what a given car can meet (too many children) and they sell it to buy another. Even if they could exit a plan and enter another, the market offers them few real options and so may fail to meet their needs or market preferences.

A more promising argument may be that the authority democratically delegated to agencies that manage our health systems mean decisions have at least the legitimacy of other democratically authorized decisions. Since we rely on a representative, democratic political process to make decisions in the face of many ethical disagreements about policy, it is arguably fair, and at least no more problematic than similar decisions that devolve to appropriately delegated authorities. One problem, however, for standard democratic decision-making is that it often rests on the simple aggregation of preferences,[14] and few people want to accept that process as determining what counts as ethically right. A racist policy that has popular support from a majority is not thereby the right policy to pursue. In moral deliberation, in contrast, we aim to evaluate the weight that reasons should receive; we do not simply aggregate the preferences people have. This suggests that we need a process that is more deliberative than a simple aggregative democratic vote; such a process can supplement and improve, even if not replace, broader democratic processes that we hope may become more deliberative. The deliberation that the process encourages is intended to emphasize ethical reasoning about what we should count as fair. (Maybe if some existing public procedures that were intended to be deliberative worked better, they would suffice; in any case, what we propose draws on features of process that are widely believed to be necessary to assure proper deliberations.)

---

13   Daniels and Sabin (note 4).
14   J Cohen, 'Procedure and Substance in Deliberative Democracy' in S Benhabib (ed) *Democracy and Difference: Changing Boundaries of the Political* (Princeton Univ. Press 1996) 95-119.

Key elements of fair deliberative process will involve at least four conditions: 1) Publicity, specifically, transparency about the grounds for decisions; 2) Relevance, rationales that rely on reasons that all can accept as relevant to meeting health needs fairly (by "all" we mean people who are affected by a decision and who seek mutually justifiable grounds for such decisions); 3) Revisability, including procedures for revising decisions in light of new evidence and arguments and other challenges to them; 4) Enforcement, meaning assurance that the conditions 1-3 are met. Together these elements assure "accountability for reasonableness."[15]

A fair process requires publicity about the reasons and rationales that play a part in decisions. There must be no secrets where justice is involved, for people should not be expected to accept decisions that affect their well being unless they are aware of the grounds for those decisions. This broader transparency about rationales is a hallmark of fair process. Fair process also involves constraints on reasons. Fair minded people -those who seek mutually justifiable grounds for cooperation - must agree that the reasons, evidence, and rationales are relevant to meeting population health needs fairly, the shared goal of deliberation. One important way to make sure that there is a real deliberation about relevant reasons is to include a range of stakeholders in the deliberative process. Such stakeholders should not be token "lay" people who may be intimidated by others; they should be supported so they can clearly express their views about relevant reasons. Including an appropriate range of stakeholders does not make a process more democratic (for they are not elected representatives of the public), but it can improve the quality of the deliberation, provided the process is managed so that it is not simply a lobbying exercise by people who are not really seeking relevant reasons. Fair process also requires opportunities to challenge and revise decisions in light of the kinds of considerations all stakeholders may raise. There should be a mechanism for appeals of decisions by those affected by them.

Accountability for reasonableness makes it possible to educate all stakeholders about deliberation about fair decisions under resource constraints. It facilitates social learning about limits. It connects decision making in healthcare institutions to broader, more fundamental democratic deliberative processes.

Accountability for reasonableness also occupies a middle ground in the debate between those calling for "explicit" and "implicit" rationing. Like implicit approaches, it does not require that principles for rationing be made explicit ahead of time. But, like explicit approaches, it does call for transparency about reasoning that fair minded people can eventually agree is relevant. Since we may not be able to construct principles that yield fair decisions ahead of time, we need a process that allows us to develop those reasons over time as we face real cases. The social learning that this approach facilitates provides our best prospect of achieving agreement over sharing medical and other health resources fairly.

Since there are various levels at which priority-setting decisions are made - national, state, health authority, hospital, health plan - it will be necessary to adapt

---

[15]   Daniels and Sabin (note 2, 4).

a fair, deliberative process to the institutional level and type of decision being made. One size will not fit all. Even the four general conditions described are not intended to be exhaustive, and some flexibility in applying them may be needed. For example, including a range of stakeholders in the process in general increases the quality of decisions and may increase the "buy-in" that results, enhancing legitimacy and acceptability. But such inclusion may not fit all contexts -indeed, it may be so far from what is legally required in, say, U.S. law regarding private insurance schemes, that demanding it would make the approach unrealizable given the obstacles to such inclusion by many organizations. Better to rely on transparency to accomplish some of what stakeholder involvement might achieve than make it a requirement regardless of the legal context.

4. Problems with Accountability for Reasonableness

In this brief essay, we cannot do justice to many of the objections that have been made to this approach, but we shall briefly consider four.

First, does the approach actually yield decisions we should view as fair and not simply as legitimate?[16] Following Rawls's discussion, we can distinguish two main forms of procedural justice. In pure procedural justice, we lack prior agreement on a relevant principle for determining just outcomes, and we accept the outcome of a fair process as fair. Rawls offers gambling as an example: we accept the outcome of an unfettered spin of the roulette wheel as fair. In contrast, criminal trials constitute an example of impure procedural justice, since we have prior agreement on a relevant principle: convict all and only the guilty. We determine who the guilty are through trials that pit adversaries against each other but are judged by neutral parties. If we later find conclusive evidence that someone we found guilty in a trial is innocent (say through DNA evidence), then we should overturn the trial result.

Since we lack prior agreement on distributive principles specific enough to yield outcomes to decisions about allocating health care resources, the proposed process has some resemblance to pure procedural justice. On this view we have no basis for denying fairness to the outcome of a fair process. But the situation differs in two important ways from Rawls's example of gambling. Unlike gambling we should reject outcomes that violate requirements of justice, say about non-discrimination. Further, again unlike the case of gambling, we can imagine arriving at a philosophically persuasive view about how to solve the priorities problem or any of the other unsolved rationing problems. Such a view might "defeat" decisions about fairness arrived at through the process. The "defeasible" fairness that results is the most we can claim for the outcome of our fair process - it is as fair as we can determine, given everything we know and believe.

Second, why think we can arrive with more confidence at an account of fair process than we can arrive at an account of fair outcomes?[17] It may well turn out to

---

16   Dan Brock has urged this objection in conversations with one of us (ND).
17   Marc Roberts and Michael Reich have urged this objection in conversations with one of us (ND).

be the case that we cannot arrive at a widely acceptable account of a fair deliberative process and that we are in the same fix as we are with regard to contested substantive decisions. Indeed, skepticism is often warranted about the many ways a process can be captured by parties who subvert its intended role as a form of procedural justice. On the other hand, many societies succeed in finding agreement about fair procedures in the face of ongoing substantive disagreements. In short the worry is real, but there are many instances where the search for a fair process that is widely acceptable succeeds. There is to be sure no guarantee it always will.

Third, accountability for reasonableness may yield different answers for cases that seem similar, violating a principle of formal justice that like cases be treated alike. We discuss this issue elsewhere:[18] a fair process can yield different conclusions when considerations that all see as relevant are given different weight in two applications of a process that meets the conditions of accountability for reasonableness. It does not follow that such a result violates any formal principle of justice, for two cases, however similar they seem, are not being judged the same way if the reasons that play a relevant role in deciding them are given different weights by different groups involved in the two procedures. The rationales explain why the groups treat the cases differently, and so the different outcome is not arbitrary.

Still, how tolerable such differences are, for example, between different districts or health authorities in a health system, may be depend on differences in their political culture. If the belief is that a national health system, such as the NHS in the UK, cannot accept such "postal code variations" in decisions, then a uniform decision may have to be made for the whole system. Achieving uniform decisions was one of the central rationales for setting up NICE in the UK. If, however, the system has a more federalist structure, intended to reflect locally distinct beliefs, including those about fair treatment when using scarce resources, then variation might be an acceptable result. Whether the variation in outcomes is a problem, then, depends on judgments about how uniform treatment must be in a health system, and those judgments may vary without one view being right and the other clearly wrong.

Finally, is there any evidence that accountability for reasonableness achieves better outcomes? Most of the studies done to date on this approach to priority setting simply accept the theoretical rationale for the framework, ask if the decision-making in that context complies with the conditions, and sometimes proposes how to secure better compliance. But a different kind of empirical evidence is needed if the goal is to show that accountability for reasonableness improves outcomes in some way. Producing such evidence is difficult for quite distinct reasons. First, we would need proper comparison cases - cases where there is good compliance with the conditions and cases where the approach is not implemented. If other factors can be controlled for, we may find an appropriate comparison in a before and after study of the use of the fair process (but then baseline measures are needed). Getting such cases is difficult. Second, we would need good measures of the ways in which

---

[18]   Daniels and Sabin (note 2).

outcomes are better. Given that one of the reasons for the approach is that we lack consensus on principles for what counts as a fair outcome, how can we tell that the decisions are more fair? We lack an independent measure of fairness against which to measure change. We might argue that some accounts of greater equity in health outcomes should be used to measure fairness, but that assumes we can determine what counts as equitable in these cases. We might think that legitimacy is easier to find a measure for: we might be able to find out the attitudes of people affected by the decisions, or even those making them, to see if they judge it to be more legitimate. But finding indicators of legitimacy is itself complex. For example, we might think that greater acceptability would mean fewer appeals of decisions. But how active the appeals process is may depend on how legitimate it is believed to be – people may appeal only if they trust the process to yield reasonable outcomes.

This empirical challenge to accountability for reasonableness is a serious problem: it is hard to persuade people who might, for largely theoretical reasons, be interested in using it to actually adapt it to their needs, which requires a resource investment in it, if we cannot point to evidence that it improves the situation. Practical people are going to ask whether "it works," and answering that question requires evidence we do not have.

5. *Applications of Accountability for Reasonableness*

Despite this lack of empirical evidence, accountability for reasonableness has had enough theoretical appeal to motivate significant use of it. We shall begin by describing briefly some of these uses, and then we shall try to explain why these uses primarily occur outside the U.S, where the approach was developed. We conclude by noting some further contexts where this approach to priority setting may be of use.

Until very recently, NICE in the UK had the assignment of making recommendations to the NHS in England and Wales about coverage for new interventions (exactly what its role will be under the new Conservative-Liberal government coalition is less clear). Its main tool was, as noted earlier, to invoke a cost-effectiveness threshold: interventions whose cost per QALY is below 20,000 pounds per QALY are routinely covered, and those above 30,000 pounds per QALY are rarely covered, but those in the 20-30,000 pound per QALY range are deliberated about more carefully. Because this threshold seemed an unacceptably inflexible standard to some, the Citizen's Council, a group of representative lay-people who deliberate about issues a few times a year for 2-3 days at a time, proposed some forms of flexibility in the standard, such as allowing life extending treatments to meet a less demanding standard. The Citizens Council has deliberated about a variety of social and ethical issues, and some of its recommendations regarding them have been adopted by NICE as features of its policy toward recommendations. The Director of NICE, Sir Michael Rawlins, cites accountability for reasonableness as the inspiration for this kind of stakeholder input into ethical issues.[19] In addition, NICE's recommendations are fully transparent, with all evidence and rationales available on its website. Further, there is provision for reconsidering decisions in light of new evidence and arguments. In short, NICE arguably meets or comes close to meeting the conditions that are central to accountability for reasonableness.

Other examples of the influence of this approach can be found elsewhere in Europe. For example, the Swedes are engaged in a process of identifying and possibly replacing the least valuable 10% of services offered in its health systems.[20] The exercise is carried out in local districts, which engage in a highly transparent process that involves a broad range of stakeholders. The Norwegians began to emphasize the importance of fair, deliberative process as opposed to "principles" nearly a decade ago.[21] And the WHO gave some recognition to the approach in its Ethical Guidelines for anti-retroviral treatment.[22]

There have also been some experiments using the approach in middle and low income developing countries. In Mexico, toward the end of Julio Frenk's administration as Secretary of Health, a manual was developed for a fair process for incrementally adding coverage to the catastrophic insurance plan that was part of Mexico's new Seguro Popular. The manual explicitly embodied accountability for reasonableness. Though implementation of the manual was suspended in the next administration, perhaps because it required more transparency and stakeholder involvement than was comfortable for the leadership in the Mexican system, there is current interest in using it to make decisions about the formulary in IMMS, the Mexican social security health plan.

There has also been some experimentation with accountability for reasonableness in three low-income African countries. An EU sponsored project (REACT) in Tanzania, Kenya, and Zambia, for example, examined the acceptability of the central ideas in the approach in the context of district health management plans.[23] In Tanzania, improvements were noted in the degree to which stakeholders were involved in some deliberations and in the amount of transparency that surrounded district-level plans. But downward constraints from budgets and planning at higher

19   MD Rawlins, 'Pharmacopolitics and Deliberative Democracy' (2005) 5 (5) *Clinical Medicine* 471-75.

20   S Waldau, L Lindholm, and AH Wiechel, 'Priority Setting in Practice: Participants Opinions on Vertical and Horizontal Priority Setting for Reallocation' (2010)96 *Health Policy* 245-54. Epub 2010 Mar 12.

21   S Holm, 'Developments in the Nordic Countries – Goodbye to the Simple Solutions' in A Coulter and C Ham (eds), *The Global Challenge of Health Care Rationing* (Open Univ. Press 2000) 29-37.

22   World Health Organization (WHO) 2004. *Guidance on Ethics and Equitable Access to HIV Treatment and Care*. Geneva: World Health Organization. Available at: http://www.who.int/ (accessed 26 July 2011).

23   J Byskov, 'Accountable Priority Setting for Trust in Health Systems' Paper presented at the Global Ministerial Forum on Research for Health, 2008 Nov 17-19, Bamako, Bali. Available at: http://www.reactforhealth.net/ (accessed 26 July 2011).

national levels meant there were significant departures from the conditions central to accountability for reasonableness as well.[24]

In contrast to the theoretical appeal accountability for reasonableness has had in this range of low, middle and high income countries, it has had little up-take in the land of its birth. The approach was originally developed to improve the legitimacy and fairness of priority setting decisions in private, managed care health plans in the U.S. – possibly a hardest case for the approach. Initially there was some interest in having the approach adopted within the accreditation system for such health plans, but health plans were fearful of the exposure to more transparency and possibly to litigation. We have argued that the relative lack of interest in this approach derives from several sources in the U.S: a highly fragmented system in which public and private agencies do not want to be identified as the source of any limits to care; a political culture that has hidden from the need for priority-setting (evidence for which comes from the devastating force the mention of "death panels" had in the debate about U.S. health reform); and a strong, vested interest in the private sector that aims to deflect attention away from the many ways it sets limits to care and to hide behind the view that all "medically necessary" care is available to any insured person in need.[25] Unfortunately, even with the recent U.S. health reforms, there remains an explicit policy of avoiding the kind of deliberation about limit setting that is essential to defining an effective and cost-effective benefit package.

We conclude by noting three applications of the approach that have not been implemented. Health policy not only aims at population health improvement in the aggregate but also at the reduction of health inequalities, especially ethically problematic ones such as those that derive from socio-economic status, race, gender, or various policies of social exclusion. But even when a health inequality is clearly one we judge to be unfair or unjust, devoting resources to reducing it encounters the rationing problems we noted earlier. For example, knowing that we could do something to improve the health of those whose health is likely to have been harmed by an unfair distribution of the socially controllable factors that affect health may involve tradeoffs against efforts to improve the health of those equally badly off and to whom we have obligations even if their health states are not the result of social injustice. Since reasonable people will disagree about how those trade-offs should be made, accountability for reasonable priority setting is arguably appropriate.

A second application that invites implementation is using accountability for reasonableness to supplement human rights-based approaches to health. Sofia Gruskin and one of us (ND) have argued that a human rights framework does not yield judgments about priorities – right claims are not prioritized across rights or

---

S Maluka and others, 'Improving District Level Health Planning and Priority Setting in Tanzania through Implementing Accountability for Reasonableness Framework: Perceptions of Stakeholders' (2010a) 10 *BMC Health Serv Res* 322; S Maluka and others, 'Decentralized Health Care Priority-Setting in Tanzania: Evaluating against the Accountability for Reasonableness Framework' (2010b) 71 (4) *Soc Sci Med* 751-9.

25   Daniels and Sabin (note 4).

even within them.[26] One consequence of this is that the priorities among programs improving health that human rights advocates negotiate with government officials fail to provide adequate rationales for the priorities that result. This lack of clarity about how priorities are set adds vagueness to the notion that rights to health or health care are to be "progressively realized." Given the commitment of the human rights framework to transparency, to involvement of stakeholders, and to government accountability for goals and targets, there is a natural fit between accountability for reasonableness and the human rights approach to health.

Finally, other pervasive disagreements that affect resource allocation can be addressed by holding decision-makers accountable for the reasonableness of decisions they make. For example, some philosophers, economists, and others have criticized policies that give some priority to rescuing "identified victims" over "statistical" ones, arguing that statistical lives are still lives that deserve equal respect and attention. This prioritization is pervasive in many contexts that protect people against risks to safety and health. Some social science literature suggests that the factor the attitude that people express in these contexts is a concern about the concentration of risk-identified victims have risk fully concentrated in them, whereas statistical victims are parts of larger populations that face smaller individual risks. If, however, concentration of risk can be morally relevant to consider in some contexts,[27] then different people may reasonably assign it different weights. This pervasive problem is therefore one that invites an application of accountability for reasonableness.

We conclude by emphasizing an earlier point: the main arguments so far for accountability for reasonableness are theoretical justifications of why the conditions can enhance legitimacy and improve fairness. But policy makers are practical people and they demand and deserve some empirical evidence that this approach "works," where what counts as "working" is both hard to specify and harder to operationalize and measure. That is the task still facing those who are moved by the theoretical rationale: show the process improves decision-making in relevant ways.

---

[26]   S Gruskin, N Daniels, 'Justice and Human Rights: Priority Setting and Fair Deliberative Process' (2008) 98 (9) *American Journal of Public Health* 1573-77.
[27]   Daniels (note 3).

Chapter II

Just Caring: In Defense of the Role of Democratic Deliberation in Health Care Rationing and Priority-setting

Leonard M. Fleck

I have written extensively about what I refer to as the 'Just Caring' problem: What does it mean to be a 'just' and 'caring' society when we have only limited resources to meet virtually unlimited health care needs?[1] Money is what is limited, either the funds taxpayers are willing to see used for meeting health care needs or the money they would be willing to spend from their own pockets to meet their health care needs. Health care needs are virtually unlimited for all the reasons Daniel Callahan has identified, in particular, the fact that every new technology creates "needs" related to that technology.[2] For example, in the United States in 1970 there was no need for bypass surgery because bypass surgery had not been invented. In 2010 we did about 400,000 bypass surgeries at $70,000 each and 1.2 million coronary angioplasties at $40,000 each. That represents aggregate annual costs of about $76 billion. When one considers all the advances that have occurred in medicine over the past forty years it is easier to understand how total national health care spending went from $26 billion in 1960 [5.2% of GDP] to $2.6 trillion in 2010 [17.6% of GDP] with projections to 2019 of $4.5 trillion [about 19.3% of expected GDP].[3] This is not a trend that can continue indefinitely because it threatens to crowd out other equally important social spending.

Demographic forces will worsen the trend that technological forces in health care have set in motion. In both the United States and Europe we have populations that are rapidly aging out. In the United States in 2011 about 13% of our population is over age sixty-five, roughly 40 million individuals. It is expected that number will increase to almost 80 million by 2030, roughly 21% of our population then. These numbers are of great significance because in 2009 the 13% of our population over age sixty-five consumed about 35% of all the health dollars spent then, about $850 billion. This would be a problem if medical technology were frozen at its 2010 levels. That, of course, is practically and politically impossible. Instead, we can confidently expect the stream of costly life-prolonging technologies to advance unabated, and with equal confidence we can expect our future elderly selves to demand these new

---

[1]   Leonard Fleck, *Just Caring: Health Care Rationing and Democratic Deliberation* (OUP 2009).

[2]   Daniel Callahan, *What Kind of Life: The Limits of Medical Progress* (Simon and Schuster 1990), chapter 2; see also his more recent volume *Taming the Beloved Beast: How Medical Technology Costs are Destroying Our Health Care System* (Princeton University Press 2009).

[3]   CJ Truffer and others, 'Health Spending Projections Through 2019: The Recession's Impact Continues' (2010) 29 *Health Affairs* 522-29.

interventions for ourselves rather than being satisfied with less costly and more modest interventions from 2010. We can also confidently predict that the "burden of chronic illness" (and related costs) will continue to increase for the elderly in coming decades. This is because many of our life-prolonging technologies, such as cardiac care, have been successful in prolonging the lives of elderly individuals, thereby permitting them to experience a growing number of chronic degenerative disorders, such as arthritis, various cancers, and Alzheimer's along with heart failure.[4] Also, a spate of recent articles in surgery journals document a dramatic increase in the willingness of surgeons to perform complex surgeries in hyper-elderly patients, surgeries that rarely would have been contemplated fifteen years ago.[5]

The practical implication of the "Just Caring" problem is that the need for health care rationing is unavoidable. That is, not all health care needs can be met. Consequently, choices need to be made and priorities must be set among health care needs. The ethical question is: How can that be done fairly and justly? We have no reason to believe that either the normal operations of the market (governed by ability to pay) or normal policymaking processes (governed by interest group power) will yield outcomes that are just. Of course, in order to make such judgments we would have to have a well justified and highly determinate conception of health care justice. I have argued elsewhere that we do not have such a conception of health care justice.[6] To be clear, I am not a moral skeptic. We do have some widely shared understandings of health care justice, or, as Rawls would say, considered judgments of health care justice.[7] But these shared understandings are not adequate to address the very complex problems of health care justice posed by the problems of health care rationing today. I argue instead that we need to call upon processes of rational democratic deliberation to yield just judgments regarding many health care rationing problems.

In the first part of this essay I review the background circumstances related to the problems of health care rationing and priority-setting that generate the need for rational democratic deliberation as a mechanism for addressing those

---

[4]   JL Wolff and others, 'Prevalence, Expenditures, and Complications of Multiple Chronic Conditions in the Elderly' (2002) 162 *Archives of Internal Medicine* 2269-76. The article points out that 82% of Medicare beneficiaries had one or more chronic conditions and 65% had multiple chronic conditions. A more recent study is represented by T Lehnert, 'Review: Health Care Utilization and Costs of Elderly Persons with Multiple chronic Conditions' (2011) 68 *Medical Care Research Review* 387-420.

[5]   G Speziale and others, 'Operative and Middle Term Results of Cardiac Surgery in Nonagenarians: A Bridge Toward Routine Practice' (2010) 121 *Circulation* 208-13; CR Bridges and others, 'Cardiac Surgery in Nonagenarians and Centenarians' (2003) 197 *Journal of the American College of Surgery* 347-56; MD Bachetta and others, 'Outcomes of Cardiac Surgery in Nonagenarians: A 10-Year Experience' (2003) 75 *Annals of Thoracic Surgery* 1215-20.

[6]   See Fleck (note 1) chapter 4.

[7]   John Rawls himself has very little to say about justice in relation to health care. But an important notion for him is that of 'considered ethical judgments.' One might think of these as the basic building blocks of our moral experience. They are judgments about which there is wide agreement as a result of considerable public ethical discussion, much as we have seen over the past forty years as the core of our understanding of medical ethics has become settled through a process Rawls refers to as 'reflective equilibrium.' See J Rawls, *A Theory of Justice* (HUP 1971) 47-53.

problems. In part two of this essay I review the arguments I have offered in defense of the moral legitimacy and utility of rational democratic deliberative processes for addressing specific problems of health care rationing. I also explain what I take to be the morally necessary features of a democratic deliberative process that is capable of yielding just health care rationing judgments. In the third part of this essay I consider a number of substantial objections to relying upon democratic deliberation to yield either *just or legitimate* health care rationing judgments and I respond to those objections. My twofold goal is to show the moral and political legitimacy of rational democratic deliberation in addressing the problems of health care rationing and priority-setting, and, in addition, to show that this approach is morally and politically preferable to any feasible alternative. In the final portion of this essay I offer a brief practical conclusion.

1. *Rational Democratic Deliberation: Background Circumstances*

No doubt some health care rationing problems do not require our invoking democratic deliberative processes for their resolution. We have sufficiently shared considered judgments of health care justice that yield a reasonable resolution. Imagine, for example, a "last bed in the ICU" problem. Two individuals need that bed for survival. They are roughly the same age, say, fifty-five years old. One of these individuals is doomed to die by virtue of their medical problems within the month. Access to the ICU bed will assure him that extra month of life. This individual has excellent health insurance. The other individual also needs access to the ICU bed for survival. That access will assure him complete recovery and an indefinite life expectancy, perhaps twenty or more years of life. This individual has no health insurance and no ability to pay the $100,000 worth of care he will require.[8] If the ICU director simply awarded the bed to the fully insured individual because that individual was fully insured, I am certain there would be wide agreement that this was unjust.

Perhaps the relevant moral judgment would be formulated this way: "No one should be able to buy access to scarce life-sustaining health care at the expense of another who had equal need for that care." A Rawlsian "veil of ignorance" experiment would seem to affirm this judgment. We imagine an individual behind a veil of ignorance (not knowing which of these two individuals he might be) and we ask that individual who should be awarded access to that last ICU bed. It is very hard to imagine anyone not choosing the uninsured individual with the much better recovery prospects for both utilitarian and moderately egalitarian sorts of reasons.

In contrast to this first scenario we can imagine another "last bed in the ICU" scenario in which the two individuals are fifty-three [Patient A] and fifty-five [Patient B] years old. Both will die shortly without access to the ICU bed; insurance status is not an issue. The difference between them is that patient A's

---

8   Europeans readers will see this as very much an American problem. In 2011 the United States has about 50 million individuals without health insurance. The Obama Administration hopes to reduce that number by 32 million through its reform efforts.

overall medical circumstances are such that he will still die after two years, no matter how successful his stay in the ICU is, while patient B has a predicted life expectancy of ten years. Who has the stronger just claim to that last bed in the ICU? Utilitarian considerations would be morally persuasive and favor Patient B, but egalitarian considerations would speak in favor of flipping a coin (or some other randomizing method) to determine who would get that last ICU bed. As nearly as I can judge, we could go either way and the outcome would be "just enough", as long as that was a consistent policy that we adopted. Neither of these justice-oriented approaches is clearly rationally and morally superior to the other. This is the sort of situation in which a rational democratic deliberative process should be employed for purposes of establishing a preferred policy that by virtue of that process would be both just and legitimate. The outcome is *just* because the options being considered are both presumptively just. The process is *legitimate* because it is a public, transparent, unbiased, deliberative (non-manipulative) process that results in a rationing policy that is *self-imposed* rather than being imposed by some powerful group on a less powerful group. It takes little reflection for individuals engaged in this process to realize that their future possible self could be either "A" or "B". Participants in this deliberative process are making a choice for their own future possible self.

The above example is about rationing with regard to medical resources that are *absolutely* scarce. That sort of scenario is uncommon. The more common rationing scenarios today are about *fiscal* scarcity, limitations with regard to the amount of money available for meeting an unlimited range of health care needs.[9] These scenarios are considerably more complex, morally and politically speaking, because of the fungibility of money. An ICU bed is an ICU bed and nothing else. But dollars or euros can be used to purchase an infinite variety of health care resources to meet an equally heterogeneous range of health care needs. What this means in practice is that any particular rationing decision, such as denying a left ventricular assist devices costing $200,000 to patients with advanced Alzheimer's disease (and end-stage heart failure), will be open to apparently justified moral criticism because there will be some reasonable considered judgment of health care justice that would support that criticism. In this particular case appeal might be made to the claim that this represents unjust discrimination against a class of persons with disabilities.

But if virtually all rationing decisions could be ethically challenged and undermined in this way the practical consequence would be that no rationing decision would be just. Accepting this implication would have the following practical consequences: (1) We assert that all forms of health care rationing are unjust, but we understand that the need for health care rationing is inescapable, so we simply allow all manner of non-moral factors (interest group power) to determine what

---

[9]　Haavi Morreim has introduced into the health care rationing literature this distinction between absolute scarcity and fiscal scarcity. See her *Balancing Act: The New Medical Ethics of Medicine's New Economics* (Kluwer Academic Publishers 1991).

specific rationing decisions will prevail in practice. Or (2) we assert that all forms of rationing are unjust (the "tragic choices" argument of Calabresi and Bobbitt), but we recognize that health care costs must be constrained, so we claim that all our efforts to control health care costs will be through economic mechanisms aimed at getting rid of waste and inefficiency or through putting in place incentives to consumers that will motivate them to make more prudent (cost-effective) choices of care for themselves.[10] What this means in practice is that we rely upon hidden or invisible forms of health care rationing (disguised as economic efficiency) to achieve our cost control goals. Thus, economically less well off individuals will often be forced by their economic circumstances to deny themselves needed health care because they cannot afford the co-pays designed (allegedly) to make them "more prudent" purchasers. In some cases those self-denials will have fatal consequences. But those deaths (typically premature) will not generate any moral outrage, much less public notice, because they will appear to be "natural deaths." It is in that respect that rationing and the injustice are invisible.

The problem with invisible forms of rationing is that all manner of gross injustices can be hidden from critical public scrutiny and reform, contrary to the publicity condition," which Rawls argues ought to be the core of any morally acceptable conception of justice.[11] Of course, advocates for various forms of invisible rationing will not be troubled by this criticism because they contend all visible forms of rationing are unjust as well, but social peace can be more readily maintained if we rely upon invisible rationing practices.[12] I have criticized this view at length in chapter three of my book.[13] I will not repeat those criticisms here. Instead, what I want to call attention to is the inadequacy of any of our conceptions of health care justice to address satisfactorily the micro-problems of health care rationing.

Part of the problem is that we have multiple conceptions of health care justice (strongly egalitarian,[14] fair equality of opportunity egalitarian,[15] welfare egalitarian,[16] resource egalitarian,[17] luck egalitarian or responsibility-sensitive egalitarian,[18]

---

[10] See G Calabresi and P Bobbitt, *Tragic Choices* (W.W. Norton and Company 1978). This has been a very influential volume. The basic thesis of this book is that we cannot avoid tragic choices with regard to a broad range of social economic problems. A tragic choice is one in which we are condemned to violate some deep central social value no matter what we choose. The problem of "pricing human life" is one such broad set of problems, as when we set limits to what we are willing to spend for highway safety or for prolonging the lives of individuals doomed to die. Consequently, they argue that society (and decision-makers responsible for making such choices) are "better off" if the choices are hidden from public view. In that way the violation of those values is publicly invisible, and consequently, is less likely to threaten the fabric of society (so they argue).

[11] John Rawls, *Political Liberalism* (Columbia University Press 1993) 47-88.

[12] See Calabresi and Bobbitt (note 10) 17-50.

[13] Fleck (note 1) chapter 3.

[14] John Harris, *The Value of Life* (Routledge and Kegan Paul, London 1985) 87-110; Robert Veatch, *The Foundations of Justice: Why the Retarded and the Rest of Us Have Claims to Equality* (OUP 1986).

[15] Norman Daniels, *Just Health: Meeting Health Needs Fairly* (CUP 2008).

[16] GA Cohen, *Rescuing Justice and Equality* (HUP 2008).

[17] Ronald Dworkin, *Sovereign Virtue: The Theory and Practice of Equality* (HUP 2000).

[18] Shlomi Segall, *Health, Luck, and Justice* (Princeton University Press 2010).

capabilities egalitarian,[19] sufficientarian,[20] prioritarian,[21] utilitarian of various stripes[22] and libertarian[23]), all of which can yield relevant and reasonable justice judgments in very specific rationing contexts, but all of which can come into conflict with one another in those specific contexts. Further, we do not have any meta-theory of health care justice that can fairly and reliably adjudicate those conflicts. The result, as noted above, is that every rationing judgment we might be inclined to make will appear to be unjust from the perspective of some alternate conception of health care justice. In addition, Rawls has called our attention to the "burdens of judgment," all those niggling details and complexities in the real world that get in the way of our making easy and obvious moral judgments on which we can all agree, resulting instead in moral pluralism and multiple opportunities for reasonable disagreement.[24] Of course in some circumstances such disagreement is both morally tolerable and practically feasible. But in other circumstances, such as many situations requiring just rationing decisions, we must have common practices and policies rooted in roughly shared moral understandings. This is what we would hope to achieve through suitably structured rational democratic deliberation.

Consider the following example. Individuals at risk for disturbances in the rhythm of the heart are very likely to die suddenly. We now have a device that can be implanted in the chest cavity that can sense a potentially fatal arrhythmia and shock a heart back into a normal rhythm. This is known as an Implantable Cardioverter Defibrillator [ICD]. The cost of this device and the surgery needed to implant it is about $40,000. This is not an unreasonable cost for a device that can save a life otherwise lost prematurely. In 2010 in the United States we implanted about 200,000 of these devices at a cost of about $8 billion. What raises the rationing issue with regard to these devices is that 81% of them never fired over a five-year period of time, which is when a battery would need to be replaced at a cost of $20,000.[25] *Prima facie* this appears to be a substantial waste of limited health care resources, and consequently, a reasonable place for a rationing decision.

The medical fact is that we have no perfect way of identifying that 81% of patients who realize no benefit from these devices over a five-year period of time. But we do have a T-wave alternans test that can be used to identify at least 33% of

---

19   Amartya Sen, *The Idea of Justice* (HUP 2009).
20   Madison Powers and Ruth Faded, *Social Justice: The Moral Foundations of Public Health and Health Policy* (OUP 2006).
21   Richard Arneson, 'Luck Egalitarianism and Prioritarianism' (2000) 110 *Ethics* 339-49.
22   David Eddy, *Clinical Decision Making: From Theory to Practice* (Jones and Bartlett 1996) chapters 13-26.
23   H Tristram Engelhardt, *The Foundations of Bioethics* (2nd ed, OUP 1996) 375-410.
24   Rawls (note 11) 54-8.
25   A Gehi and others, 'Primary Prophylaxis with the Implantable Cardioverter-Defibrillator: The Need for Improved Risk Stratification' (2005) 294 *JAMA* 958-60; S Al-Khatib and others, 'Clinical and Economic Implications of the Multicenter Automatic Defibrillator Implantation Trial-II' (2005) 142 *Annals of Internal Medicine* 593-600.

those patients who will not benefit from this device over the next two years.[26] That represents 70,000 individuals and savings of about $2.8 billion. However, that test is 98.7% accurate, which means it gets it wrong 1.3% of the time, which means 800 patients will die of a fatal arrhythmia that could have been prevented if they had had this device implanted. So the cost of achieving the savings of $2.8 billion will be 800 deaths that could have been prevented if we chose to forego using the T-wave alternans test. Does this loss of life represent an injustice? Of course, if this preventable loss of life bothered our conscience we could instead seek the same savings by denying funding to rheumatoid arthritis patients for the very costly drugs that would reduce their very painful symptoms by 70%.[27] No one would die as a result of that denial. However, anyone familiar with the suffering that these patients would endure without those drugs should surely have a conscience that would suffer as well. We can easily imagine dozens of other possible rationing decisions we could make, each of which would be aimed at saving $2.8 billion. But each of those potential choices could provoke roughly equally strong objections that those choices too were unacceptably unjust in some specific respects. What should we conclude?

2. *Rational Democratic Deliberation: Its Structure and Scope*

If we take seriously the "Just Caring" problem, then we accept the fact that the need for health care rationing is inescapable. We do not have the option of making no rationing decisions at all. If we accept the idea that rationing is inescapable, then we ought to want those decisions to be made fairly and to yield "just enough" outcomes. But if our analysis above is correct, then none of our philosophic conceptions of health care justice will be capable of yielding sufficiently just and justified rationing judgments in the range of complex circumstances provided by the real world. The alternative we propose is reliance upon fair and inclusive processes of rational democratic deliberation to yield rationing judgments that are legitimate enough and just enough.

There is some number of ways in which this deliberative process might be instantiated in the real world. We can pass over those details for now. The primary virtue of the deliberative process is that through this public conversation we identify and legitimate rationing protocols that we are willing to impose upon our future possible selves. We might imagine virtually everyone never wanting any rationing decisions being imposed on any of their future possible selves, which is why politicians avoid like the plague any discussion of health care rationing. However, these very same individuals as currently healthy individuals want both reduced health insurance premiums for privately provided plans as well as reduced taxes that fund our Medicare and Medicaid programs.

---

[26]   DM Bloomfield and others, 'Micro-Volt T-Wave Alternans and the Risk of Death or Sustained Ventricular Arrhythmias in Patients with Left Ventricular Dysfunction' (2006) 47 *Journal of the American College of Cardiology* 456-63.

[27]   A Kavanaugh, 'Economic Issues with New Rheumatologic Therapeutics' (2007) 19 *Current Opinion in Rheumatology* 272-76.

Americans have a tendency to look for villains who are responsible for our social problems. If health care costs are out of control, then this must be the fault of greedy lawyers and greedy doctors and greedy hospital administrators and greedy insurance executives and obsequious politicians. Such assertions are reflective of disingenuousness at best. The various types of individuals being disparaged are by and large doing what we want, or, more accurately, being responsive to what we claim are urgent needs. David Eddy and Uwe Reinhardt have both pointed out that the phenomenon we are dealing with is really an internal conflict within each of us.[28] As healthy individuals we want reduced health care costs (taxes and insurance premiums that we pay as healthy individuals), but as sick individuals, especially as individuals faced with a life-threatening medical problem, we want every possible dollar spent to address our health needs (and we want others to be the source of those dollars), no matter how remote the chance that those dollars will buy very much in the way of effective health care. This is what drives us at present to purchase these extraordinarily costly cancer drugs for $100,000 or more that will yield only extra weeks or extra months of life.[29]

What we really have here is a classic instance of the "tragedy of the commons."[30] This is precisely the sort of problem that cannot be solved by individuals as individuals. A Hobbesian monarch could dictate a solution, but we would have no reason to believe such a resolution would be (or would be accepted as) either just or legitimate. A solution has to emerge from those who have created the problem in the first place, all of us, as payers and as patients. A well constructed, rational democratic deliberative process is the mechanism through which shared judgments of health care justice can be constructed in relation to specific rationing proposals. The three features of this process that give it moral legitimacy are *impartiality, reciprocity*, and reliance on *public reason*.[31]

Critics might wonder how we could possibly have a public conversation that embodied the kind of impartiality that is necessary for fair and reasonable moral judgments. We imagine everyone having their own health interests and arguing vigorously for resource allocations that would favor their interests at the expense of others. However, the fact of the matter is that at any point in time the vast majority

[28]   Eddy (note 22) 110-20; Uwe Reinhardt, 'Rationing Health Care: What It Is, What It Is Not, and Why We Cannot Avoid It' in S Altman and U Reinhardt, *Strategic Choices for a Changing Health Care System* (Health Administration Press 1996) 63-99.

[29]   T Fojo and C Grady, 'How Much is Life Worth: Cetuximab, Non-Small Cell Lung Cancer, and the $440 Billion Question' (2009) 101 *Journal of the National Cancer Institute* 1044-48.

[30]   Garrett Hardin, 'Tragedy of the Commons' (1968) 162 *Science* 1243-48.

[31]   There is now a very large literature on rational democratic deliberation. I list here some of the major writers whose views have shaped my own perspective in this regard. James Bohman, *Public Deliberation: Pluralism, Complexity, and Democracy* (MIT Press 1996); James Bohman and William Rehg (eds), *Deliberative Democracy: Essays on Reason and Politics* (MIT Press 1997); Joshua Cohen, *Philosophy, Politics, Democracy* (HUP 2009); James Fishkin and Peter Laslett (eds), *Debating Deliberative Democracy* (Blackwell 2003); Amy Gutmann and Dennis Thompson, *Why Deliberative Democracy?* (Princeton University Press 2004); Amy Gutmann and Dennis Thompson, *Democracy and Disagreement: Why Moral Conflict Cannot be Avoided in Politics and What Should be Done about It* (HUP 1996); Henry Richardson, *Democratic Autonomy: Public Reasoning About the Ends of Policy* (OUP 2002); IM Young, *Inclusive Democracy* (OUP 2000).

of us are perfectly healthy. We know that we will not remain that way until the day we die, and we know that medicine can do much today to prevent a premature death. The medical reality is that very few of us know what we might be afflicted with that could threaten our health and put us at risk for premature death. We are, in effect, behind a practical "Rawlsian veil of ignorance." This gives us a substantial capacity for making rationing judgments through this deliberative process that are suitably impartial.

Again, a critic might point out that many of us have friends and loved ones that might be suffering from some particular disease. This could corrupt our capacity for impartiality as we would be tempted to advocate for policies that would direct more resources toward them or else spare them specific denials of care required by a particular rationing judgment. But presumably in the course of a deliberative conversation such an individual would be reminded of all her other friends and loved ones who are healthy now but vulnerable to some range of other medical problems for which adequate resources must be allocated. Moreover, the choices that must be made are *policy* choices that will apply to everyone in comparable medical circumstances, not just my friends and loved ones with cancer or heart disease or Parkinson's and so on.

I might have a brother with advanced kidney cancer. He might have run out of all the standard medical therapies used to address earlier stages of his cancer. The only thing left is a drug that costs $100,000 and that is likely to offer him only extra weeks of life (though some more fortunate patients, perhaps 5% of all such patients, might benefit with an extra year of life for reasons that are medically obscure). I do not want him to be denied that drug because he cannot afford it. I want that drug paid for from social resources. What kind of justice-relevant reasons can I give to my fellow deliberators to persuade them that they ought to endorse funding this drug for end-stage kidney cancer patients?

I cannot simply say that this is my brother. Every kidney cancer patient is someone's friend or family member. At the very least this would imply that we would have to fund access to that drug for all 14,000 kidney cancer patients who die each year in the United States. But are there any morally compelling reasons for saying that kidney cancer deserves special allocative attention, that is, more in the way of resources than any other cancer? I cannot imagine what such reasons might be. If the drug we had in mind yielded on average five extra years of life for kidney cancer patients and there was no other drug with a comparable degree of effectiveness for any other cancer, then that would represent a reasonable justification for special allocative attention to that drug. But the fact of the matter is that no such drug exists for any of these advanced cancers.

The thirty or so cancer drugs now on the market that have costs in the range of $50,000 to $130,000 for a course of treatment generally offer only extra weeks or months of life.[32] What this implies, morally speaking, is that if we were to agree to fund this kidney cancer drug, we would have to fund all these other comparably

---

[32]   Fojo and Grady (note 29).

costly and comparably marginally beneficial cancer drugs for the 560,000 cancer patients who die each year in the United States. All our deliberators will have friends and relatives with all these other cancers. Moral consistency, reciprocity and impartiality would all require that commitment, which would have annual costs of about $60 billion. However, the economic implications are even broader than that. If we are willing to spend $100,000 for a 5% chance of an extra year of life, then we are saying that extra year of life is worth $2 million. But it is impossible to imagine that this would be true only of kidney cancer patients. Again, moral consistency and reciprocity would require us to say that our policy would pay for any drug or other medical intervention that could offer an otherwise terminally ill individual an extra year of life for less than $2 million (or for some portion of a year of life and a proportional share of that $2 million).

A commitment such as this would have huge cost implications for both taxpayers and insurance premium payers. However, these are precisely the sorts of escalating health costs that generated widespread demands for controlling health costs. We can imagine that our deliberators would have agreed at the beginning of the process that a specific fraction of GDP would be devoted to meeting health care needs at social expense. If that were the case, and if there were now a potential commitment of up to $2 million for the last year of life for any terminally ill individual, this would likely distort very significantly our capacity to meet a very broad range of non-terminal health care needs. What would we imagine would be the morally compelling reasons that deliberators could offer one another to justify such an allocative distortion?

Someone might be tempted to invoke the "Rule of Rescue," the idea that (1) we ought to rescue imperiled individuals (the Chilean miners in 2010) if we have the capacity to do so and (2) the cost of the rescue should not count as a good reason for refusing to rescue.[33] But this rule is reasonable only when the number of individuals to be rescued is relatively small. In the United States in 2010 we had about 2.5 million individuals who died. If each of those individuals had a just claim to $100,000 worth of health care that could give them a few extra weeks or extra months of life, that would represent a potential expenditure of $250 billion. What kind of health care needs would our younger, healthier deliberators in the present be willing to leave unmet in order to provide this magnitude of resources for their future possible terminally ill selves? The very asking of the question illuminates its irrationality. Would we give up funding something as ordinary and as mundane as primary care visits, some of which might identify a serious but effectively treatable symptom that left untreated would result in a fatal outcome? It would be small comfort for such an unfortunate individual that they could be provided with an "extra year of life" for $100,000 when they could have had twenty more years of life if $200 had been spent for that foregone primary care visit that would have identified a treatable cancer.

The point of the prior example is that we are capable of achieving collective agreement regarding a broad range of health care priorities for reasons that reflect

---

[33]   J McKie and J Richardson, 'The Rule Of Rescue' (2003) 56 *Social Science and Medicine* 2407-19.

both prudence and justice. As rational and just (impartial and committed to reciprocity) deliberators we would want to maximize the number of high-quality life years that could be saved for whatever funds were available for meeting overall health care needs. This general commitment would protect our own rational self interests as well as those of our loved ones. It might appear from this example that the conversation among our deliberators is a straightforward utilitarian conversation. But we have no reason to believe that would necessarily be the case. The following example will illustrate that claim (and the broader claim that multiple conceptions of health care justice would be integral to this conversation).

A small number of children are born each year with a genetic disorder known as Pompe Disease. It is an enzyme deficiency disorder that results in a complete loss of muscular function.[34] The early-onset version of this disorder results in death before the age of one. But since 2006 we have had a drug, Myozyme, which can successfully replace that missing enzyme, thereby forestalling death indefinitely. That drug costs $100,000 per year for an infant but will rise in cost to $400,000 per year for an adult. If our deliberators were pure utilitarians, this drug would not be funded and these children would be allowed to die because the cost of getting these children to age twenty would be about $5 million each. However, we would have morally compelling reasons for funding this drug because this drug seems to be extraordinarily effective in correcting the deficiency and giving these children an open-ended high quality life expectancy. We may justifiably regard this as a reasonable application of the Rule of Rescue. This is exactly what is not true with regard to the cancer drugs used with cancer patients in the end-stages of their disease.

What I have been trying to illustrate with these examples is what a rational democratic deliberative process might look like in practice. Some might believe that what I am advocating for is utterly utopian. It can certainly appear that way if we think about the vituperation and disrespect and dishonesty and rigid ideology that have characterized the abortion debates in the United States as well as a number of other highly partisan policy debates of late. The debates we need to have about health care cost control are vulnerable to those same social failings, as Sarah Palin's invocation of the rhetoric of "death panels" perfectly illustrates. The lesson we need to learn is that honest and productive democratic deliberation needs to occur outside the forums of partisan politics.

I think I have had some success in conducting a large number of community dialogues about morally and politically controversial issues without the rancor that seems so pervasive today.[35] Apart from some reminders about mutual respect at the beginning of these social conversations the technique that I have found effective in creating a productive open-minded mindset among deliberators is articulating a problem for them that they would all recognize as their problem and articulating that

---

[34] For a basic description of Pompe disease see: http://ghr.nlm.nih.gov/ keywords: pompe disease (accessed 9 April 2011).

[35] Leonard Fleck, 'Creating Public Conversation About Behavioral Genetics' in Erik Parens and others (eds) *Wrestling with Behavioral Genetics: Science, Ethics, and Public Conversation* (Johns Hopkins University Press 2006) 257-85.

problem in a way that left virtually every deliberator in a state of internal puzzlement. The internal puzzlement dissipates any motivation to "take sides" because none of the sides is especially appealing. In discussions about health care rationing some individuals will always enter the discussions thinking that human life is priceless, that we ought to be willing to spend whatever amount of money it might take to save or prolong a life if we have the medical capacity to do so. But if the practical implications of that position are drawn out with sufficient vividness and sufficient detail, then advocates for that view quickly find that they are not willing to give up the resources necessary to make their view a reality, nor are they willing to live with the grossly distorted health care priorities that would result if that view were made real in the context of limited budgets. Once deliberators have been drawn into that internal state of puzzlement ideological commitments dissolve and individuals are more willing to engage in a cooperative problem-solving inquiry rather than seeing others as political adversaries seeking "a win for their side."

3. Rational democratic Deliberation: Objections and Responses

In what I have written so far I have suggested that the deliberative process as I envision it would yield just rationing judgments. But Daniels has raised a two-part objection to this conclusion.[36] He asks whether the deliberative process can some-times "get it wrong," endorse as just what is really a product of a widely accepted social prejudice of some sort. If this is a real possibility, then how do we know with respect to any particular deliverance of democratic deliberation that the decision is really just as opposed to being only apparently just and really unjust? If we have no way of identifying such moral flaws in the outcomes of the deliberative process, then the deliberative process is not morally trustworthy. On the other hand, if we do have the moral resources and moral norms for identifying such flawed outcomes, then the deliberative process is otiose. That is, we can use those moral resources and moral norms to assess proposed rationing policies directly without the extra bother of a complex democratic deliberative process.

The response I would give to these concerns is that the deliberative process needs conversational boundaries, what I have referred to metaphorically as "constitutional principles of health care justice."[37] In the United States a legislative body may enact a law through the appropriate legislative process, but the law may be struck down as illegitimate by the US Supreme Court if it is judged that the law violates one or more provisions of our constitution. The constitution serves as a check on situationally provoked outrageous social passions that seek legitimacy through being established as law. The constitution can fail in practice as an ultimate safeguard of justice since it is ultimately reliant upon the integrity and wisdom of its authorized (formally and informally) interpreters. Nevertheless, it is all we have. If those interpreters fail in their responsibilities, then all we can hope is that with the passage of time

---

36   Norman Daniels, 'Rationing Fairly: Programmatic Considerations' (1993) 7 *Bioethics* 224-33.
37   Fleck (note 1) chapter 5.

social critics and prophets will generate the political will to correct those failings. The same will be true with regard to the democratic deliberations I see as being necessary to the creation of just policies for health care rationing.

Part of the role of philosophers will be to continue to articulate and refine what I refer to as constitutional principles of health care justice that will mark out the space of legitimate democratic deliberation. Again, what we need to keep in mind is that the options that are legitimately available for democratic deliberation with regard to any very specific rationing problem are options that are prima facie "just enough." That is, we can confidently judge that each deliberative option is "not unjust." Each deliberative option has some number of reasonable justice-relevant considerations that would speak in its favor and no violations of constitutional principles of health care justice that would speak against it.

In the early 1990s, for example, some health insurance companies proposed putting a $200 limit on the amount of care they would pay for that was related to HIV/AIDS. This would obviously have the potential for saving a lot of money, but just as obviously it represents gross discrimination, a violation of the rights of such patients to equal concern and respect (which may be thought of as one constitutional principle of health care justice). So a proposal such as this would not be entitled to deliberative effort.

Let us briefly consider a more sophisticated kind of proposal. Again, we will have in mind HIV/AIDS patients whom we can think of in the present. Prior to 1996 when protease inhibitors were introduced into the medical armamentarium AIDS patients who began to experience various immunodeficiency disorders as a result of their CD4 count falling below 200 cells per cubic millimeter of blood had a life expectancy of about two years. But the protease inhibitors (and later the fusion inhibitors) changed all that because these drugs in various combinations have blocked the replicating capacity of the virus and have helped to restore the integrity of the immune systems of these patients. These patients can now look forward to twenty or more years of life that they otherwise would have been denied. But the cost of the protease inhibitors is about $20,000 per year, and that annual cost rises to $35,000 when fusion inhibitors must be added to the mix to contain the virus. Individuals on these drugs for more than twenty years would incur health care costs in excess of half a million dollars. Eventually it is likely the virus will mutate in a way that defeats all viable drug combinations. Individuals will then be faced with the terminal phase of the disease, which, depending upon the particular immunocompromised disorders with which they might be faced, could result in last-year-of-life costs in excess of $100,000.

Given this scenario, one can imagine someone proposing a rationing protocol somewhat like the following: As soon as it is medically possible to confidently judge that an AIDS patient has less than a 20% chance of surviving another year then only comfort care will be provided to that patient at social expense (no more aggressive life-sustaining care). We can imagine the following justification being proposed in support of this rationing protocol. We have only limited resources to meet virtually unlimited health care needs. We have already provided these patients far in excess of a half a million dollars worth of health care. That care was both just and justified because those drugs have been so effective in prolonging a large number of high quality life-years. But the additional life that might be provided these patients in a terminal phase is much diminished in quality and much more costly than care that could be provided to other patients with these saved resources.

This sort of rationale has clear moral plausibility about it, which suggests that it ought to be an object of democratic deliberation. But it also has some objectionable discriminatory features about it. What we can imagine, however, is that those features would provoke some important democratic moral reflection. More specifically, that reflection might take this form: It does not seem to be the case that only AIDS patients are costly consumers of health care resources in the relatively earlier stages of what is likely ultimately to be a terminal outcome. Many cancer and cardiac and kidney patients, to name just a few, are in roughly the same circumstances. The highest costs for the care of all these patients seem to be in the end-stages of their disease where it also seems the least good is accomplished. So perhaps what we ought to consider is formulating a much broader rationing protocol regarding reasonable end-of-life costs, especially in circumstances where society has been very responsive to such patients by providing costly resources in earlier stages of the disease process when those resources could do much more good. We would not abandon these patients, but we would limit our care to palliation.

These brief comments represent only a crude approximation of the much more complex deliberations that would have to occur in genuine democratic deliberation. But they do illustrate how it would be possible to eliminate the potentially unjust discrimination that seemed to be part of the original proposal. Further, this seems to be an appropriate response to the concerns contained in Daniels' objection to the deliberative process and its ability to deliver just health care rationing judgments reliably. There are resources within a well-constructed deliberative process for correcting what might be regarded as a morally flawed proposal initially.

The transparency of the deliberative process itself and the consistent require-ment for appropriate justice-relevant reason-giving to justify any specific rationing proposal serve as adequate internal resources for maintaining the moral integrity of the deliberative process. Further, what I refer to as the constitutional principles of health care justice are themselves internal to the deliberative process. In this regard there is no need for appeal to external norms to assess either the legitimacy or the justness of the outcomes of this process. The justness of the process reflects fair terms of cooperation constructed through the deliberative process.

Again, I remind the reader that the object of this deliberative process with regard to any specific rationing problem will be multiple possible rationing options that all appear to be "just enough" because one or more reasonable considerations of health care justice offer *prima facie* justification for them. Further, in the final analysis after considerable deliberative effort it might well be the case that no particular rationing option for that situation is unequivocally superior. However, it needs to be added that this is not something that can be typically known *prior* to the deliberative process itself. In this regard then, contrary to Daniels, the deliberative process is not otiose.

The deliberative process is essential to having an outcome that is self-constructed and self-imposed by the deliberative group. This is what helps to assure (as much as is practically possible) that the outcome is just and legitimate and stable. HIV/AIDS patients can accept with dignity and respect the end-of-life rationing proposal articulated above because they have the understanding that the end-of-life resources saved through this rationing protocol will be redirected to providing less costly and more effective life-prolonging care at an earlier stage in the disease process where such gains can be more appreciated by the patients themselves. Further, the revised and expanded rationing protocol itself does not target unfairly (and disrespectfully) any particular social group or disease group; rather, it reflects a suitable degree of impartiality in application that facilitates its being accepted with equanimity by all who might be directly affected as a result of future health circumstances.

Other critics have contended that the deliberative process is otiose for other reasons. They contend that the deliberative process I imagine occurring within a large deliberative group can just as readily occur within the mind of a reflective individual.[38] That is, we have to imagine that individual considering the various options with respect to a particular rationing problem, assessing those options thoroughly from a health care justice perspective, and identifying the option that is most just. If each individual in our society commits to such thoughtful internal reflection, then we will all agree regarding the most just rationing option and there will be no need for collective deliberative effort. However, this proposal is flawed in at least three respects.

(1) This internal deliberation proposal assumes a capacity for omniscience and omni-compassion that is far beyond anything realistically human. (2) It assumes the existence of some moral metric of health care justice that, if rigorously applied, will yield clear and convincing judgments of health care justice with regard to any rationing problem. Some may argue that cost-effectiveness is that moral metric, that if we just "do the math" we will all arrive at the same answer.[39] That is, we always ought to allocate health care resources in such a way as to purchase the greatest amount of health benefits for the least cost. But this view assumes we would all measure health benefits in the same way, say, in terms of Quality Adjusted Life Years [QALYs]. We have no reason to believe such an understanding of health benefits is either realistic or desirable (though I want to be clear that in some limited range of circumstances a QALY methodology is useful and morally relevant).[40] Further, this is fundamentally a utilitarian or maximization strategy that will often not yield a sufficiently just judgment, as my earlier example of Pompe disease was intended to illustrate. (3) This internal reflection view assumes that moral pluralism is fundamentally wrong, that there is some unity of moral reason such that for any just rationing or just allocation problem the uniquely correct answer is rationally determinable. However, we have little reason to believe this is true, as our earlier

38   Robert Goodin, *Reflective Democracy* (OUP 2003).
39   Eddy (note 22).
40   I agree with Peter Ubel on this point. See Peter Ubel, *Pricing Life: Why It's Time for Health Care Rationing* (MIT Press 2000).

discussion of reasonable conceptions of health care justice and the "burdens of judgment" was intended to suggest. What we find very often in practice is that reasonable persons will end up reasonably disagreeing, despite the most careful and honest reflection by each of them. If what we need in practice with regard to a specific rationing problem is a single agreed upon rationing protocol, then we need the deliberative process to bring that about, not just internal reflection by individuals. If we were to imagine that the deliberative process was no more than an exchange of personal judgments among the deliberators, then we would have no reason to hope that such a process was worth the effort or that it would yield judgments that were either socially just or socially legitimate. But if we imagine the process as one of mutual education (something useful and essential for less than omniscient democratic citizens) and mutual willingness to labor with others to construct fair rationing protocols for a specific rationing problem, then we have good reason to believe that such a process can achieve what individual reflection cannot achieve.

Another criticism of democratic deliberative approaches to health care rationing is that citizens are fundamentally ignorant, especially with regard to the complexities of our health care system. Consequently, any judgments that they make will be grievously flawed as a result of being so uninformed and misinformed. The suggested alternative is that we ought to turn to the relevant experts to take responsibility for formulating the rationing protocols necessary to address specific rationing problems. But the obvious critical question is: Which experts would we call upon? Would we call upon economists? Or health care administrators? Or health policy analysts? Or experts responsible for creating various health care technologies? Or physicians from various areas of specialization? No doubt all this expertise is necessary and relevant to making social choices that are both informed and fair with regard to various health care rationing challenges. I have no doubt that democratic deliberators ought to have access to this expertise. But it is far from obvious that any of these disciplinary or professional sources of expertise have the capacity to resolve the challenge of conflicting value perspectives that are integral to the rationing problem. Who should decide which balancing of justice-relevant considerations is most appropriate for making a reasonable rationing judgment in specific circumstances? If it is morally important that just rationing decisions be self-imposed, then having some mix of experts make these choices will not yield that result.

It will seem obvious to many that physicians have both the relevant expertise and the relevant value commitments for making rationing decisions that are fair and medically reasonable. But the critical question that needs to be raised pertains to which physicians ought to have that responsibility. Are we talking about physicians at the bedside responsible for the individual patient in that bed? Or are we talking about physicians in various areas of specialization who should be responsible for making policy decisions (remote from individual patients) regarding specific rationing circumstances? Both options raise substantial moral problems.

For physicians at the bedside denying their patients what from a social point of view is judged to be marginally beneficial non-costworthy health care will feel very much like disloyalty to the best interests of that patient and corruption of their own integrity as physicians.[41] But if those physicians give patients "whatever they want and demand," no matter what the cost to the health care system and no matter how small and remote the likelihood of benefit, then we either end up with no cost control or random injustices throughout the health care system as different physicians in the same clinical circumstances make very different allocation decisions for all manner of idiosyncratic reasons.

The physician loyalty problem can be avoided if responsibility for making rationing decisions is handed over to groups of physicians representing various areas of medical specialization remote from any individual patient. However, the most likely outcome of such a process would be that professional self interest would corrupt the justness or the reasonableness of any rationing protocol that might emerge from such a process. One survey of oncologists, for example, showed that they believed that cancer drugs with a cost of $300,000 per QALY ought to be provided to their patients at social expense.[42] The basic problem here is that these medical specialists cannot be placed behind a "veil of ignorance" in the real world to achieve a suitably impartial perspective because they are very mindful of their own professional interests. As we have already shown, however, healthy democratic citizens will be largely ignorant of their future possible health care needs and, consequently, can achieve the impartiality that will elude physician specialists.

What we need with regard to the rationing problem are fair and reasonable rationing *policies*. We rely upon legislators, as representatives of democratic citizens, and formal legislative processes to effect policies democratically that will bind all of us. Those policies will always be less than perfectly just, but that will also be true of the democratic deliberative processes for which I advocate. So why, a critic will ask, should we invest all this effort in democratic deliberation when we are already paying legislators to do this job? There are several responses to this objection.

The largest problem is that interest group politics is the dominant mechanism by which policies are legitimated in the legislative process. Interest group politics is about relative political power, not justice. The language of justice is no more than useful manipulative rhetoric in the policymaking process. It is not just a matter of getting outcomes that are non-ideally "just enough." Too often the outcomes are seriously unjust. Moreover, in the typical legislative process it is too often the case that inflammatory rhetoric subverts reason. Partisanship subverts the common good. And when health care cost control is the object of specific policies endorsed

---

41   Probably the most vocal proponent of this view is Norman Levinsky, 'The Doctor's Master' (1984) 311 *New England Journal of Medicine* 1573-75.

42   E Nadler, B Eckhart, P Neumann, 'Do Oncologists Believe New Cancer Drugs Offer Good Value?' (2006) 11 *The Oncologist* 90-95; PJ Neumann and others, 'Cancer Therapy Costs Influence Treatment: A National Survey of Oncologists' (2010) 29 *Health Affairs* 196-202; LE Schnipper and others, 'Value and Cancer Care: Toward an Equitable Future' (2010) 16 *Clinical Cancer Research* 6004-08.

through the legislative process it will typically be the case that costs are controlled through invisible forms of rationing with their hidden injustices.[43] By way of contrast, as already noted, the deliberative process I have outlined is essentially immune to interest group politics. Deliberative individuals, whether healthy or somewhat unhealthy, have no good reason for aligning themselves with any particular health care interest group and allowing their deliberative judgment to be skewed or corrupted. Their ignorance about their future health needs permits the kind of impartiality that is absent from the normal policymaking process. Likewise, inflammatory and manipulative rhetoric have no practical value in the deliberative process because such rhetoric assumes that some deliberators already know the correct answer to specific rationing challenges and they just need to persuade everyone else to adopt their perspective. But if initial efforts to induce internal puzzlement have been successful, then intellectual humility rather than intellectual arrogance will shape the deliberative process.

Someone could argue that the deliberative process might be immune to interest group politics *as things are now*, but the genetic revolution is likely to change all that in the very near future. Specifically, it is expected that by the year 2013 we will have a $1000 genome test, a test that will give a complete readout of the genome of any individual. The implication is that individuals would then know where their own future health interests would lie, and consequently, they would become very self-interested lobbyists in the deliberative process for those interests. However, such a view would be a very simplistic view of what such genetic information would mean to more thoughtful individuals.

Some genes (very few in practice) determine the health destiny of an individual. Huntington's would be an obvious example. But the vast majority of genes linked to particular medical disorders represent vulnerabilities and probabilities, often depending upon a large and largely unknown range of non-genetic environmental variables that will determine whether or not that vulnerability becomes an actuality. Among the environmental variables, of course, are my own health choices. Knowing my own genetic vulnerabilities should motivate me to take control of health-related factors within my control. That kind of self interest would serve equally well a common interest. Apart from that, the fact of the matter is that a scan of my entire genome would likely reveal multiple health vulnerabilities, which would be sufficient to protect my capacity to make suitably impartial judgments regarding rationing protocols and priorities for our overall health care system.

Again, as I discussed in another essay of mine, much medical research today is revealing that individuals may respond very differently for genetic reasons to

---

[43] In the United States recent policy discussions in Congress have focused on controlling health care costs by, for example, raising the age of eligibility for Medicare to sixty-seven rather than sixty-five. This would clearly save the federal government money. But the practical reality is that the costs for those two years would be shifted to the elderly, some of whom might be able to manage those costs, others of whom would deny themselves needed health care. That is an example of invisible rationing.

some of these extraordinarily expensive cancer drugs mentioned earlier.[44] Thus, research in the past has reported that the average gain in life expectancy for some of these $100,000 cancer drugs is measurable in weeks or months. More recent research, however, is showing that some individuals with a favorable genotype are very positive responders to some of these drugs.[45] They might gain two or more years of additional life with their terminal cancer from one of these drugs while other individuals gain only the average and still others might not even achieve that average, perhaps because of their genotype. A medical situation such as this does raise some enormously difficult rationing issues, especially from the perspective of an egalitarian conception of health care justice.

If we imagine, for example, that only 7% of a group of end-stage patients have the "most favorable" genotype for a positive response to one of these cancer drugs (and they gain 2.5 extra years of life on average from this drug), while the next genotype represents 11% of patients (and they gain on average eight extra months of life), and 62% of patients gain only two extra months of life on average and the remainder seem to experience no gain at all, then which of these groups should be denied access to this drug at social expense? If we tease this out in cost-effectiveness terms, then the cost per QALY for the first group is about $40,000 (roughly the same amount we spend to save a life-year for an HIV/AIDS patient). But the cost per QALY for the second group would be about $150,000 and the cost per QALY for the third group would be $600,000. Would we have a more just outcome if either all the cancer patients needing this drug received it or if none of them received it? Or does justice require that at least the first group receive that drug because we already spend $35,000 per QALY for HIV/AIDS patients and about $67,000 per QALY for dialysis patients?

I am not going to try to propose any resolution to the above questions. This is the sort of challenge for which we need our rational democratic deliberative process. Again, some readers may focus attention on the fact that individuals with that most favorable genotype may now have strong self interest in becoming advocates for funding that cancer drug for themselves. That, however, is a misreading of the relevant genetic and social facts. What the reader must imagine, if they take themselves to be that favored individual, is that they have this knowledge of their genetic endowment at age thirty when they are perfectly healthy. That genetic fact about themselves would then have little practical or intellectual relevance because they would not actually be afflicted with that cancer at that time. And it might well be the case that that cancer is itself not something to which they are genetically vulnerable. Further, they might well have other genetic facts about themselves that would result in very favorable responses to some expensive drugs and much less favorable responses to other drugs for other medical conditions. Such likely facts

---

[44]   Leonard Fleck, 'Personalized Medicine's Ragged Edge' (2010) 40 *The Hastings Center Report* 16-18.

[45]   BP Schneider and others, 'Association of Vascular Endothelial Growth Factor and Vascular En-dothelial Growth Factor Receptor-2 Genetic Polymorphisms with Outcome in a Trial of Paclitaxel Compared with Paclitaxel Plus Bevacizumab in Advanced Breast Cancer: ECOG 2100' (2008) 26 *Journal of Clinical Oncology* 4672-78.

re-establish a suitable degree of ignorance regarding their future possible health needs and their future possible capacity to respond to the therapies that might be available in the future.

4. Conclusion

We have one final concern that needs to be addressed. As things are now in the United States, any outcome from the deliberative process I envision that would seek to put in place just and reasonable rationing protocols for our Medicare program or for some form of national health insurance would need to be formally ratified by Congress. But if this were the case, nothing would protect just and reasonable rationing protocols from being corrupted by the normal legislative process and the interest group politics integral to that process. *That* would make the democratic deliberative process I envision otiose. If the integrity of the outcome of the deliberative process cannot be protected, then there is little point to the process. Hence, one of the recommendations I would make is that the deliberative process must be independent of Congress and interest group politics.

What we find in Britain in the form of the National Institute of Clinical Excellence [NICE] is the sort of entity I have in mind that we would have to create in the United States.[46] This is not something entirely foreign to our political culture. We have institutions such as the Federal Reserve Board that has the kind of political independence that is required to protect the integrity of their decisions from the politics and political passions of the moment. So Congress would have to create a NICE-like entity with that same degree of independence from Congress. That NICE-like entity would have two main responsibilities. First, it would do as impartially as possible the research needed to establish the effectiveness and cost-effectiveness of most of the interventions that are part of medicine today, but especially new and costly interventions, such as the cancer drugs to which I have alluded or devices like the artificial heart, now in clinical testing. Of course, few interventions are either effective or ineffective. There are degrees of effectiveness and those degrees would often be related to various sub-types of patients with a particular diagnosis. This type of information is critical to making fair and reasonable rationing decisions. Second, this NICE-like entity would have the capacity to organize and manage a broad national democratic deliberative process responsible for creating a broad range of rationing protocols for specific medical circumstances. This entity would have responsibility both for creating the deliberative materials that would help to ensure an adequately informed deliberative process and for training the preceptors responsible for facilitating these conversations in hundreds of local venues. If we imagine such a broad dispersal of the deliberative process, then we need also

---

[46] MD Rawlins and AJ Culyer, 'National Institute for Clinical Excellence and Its Value Judgments,' (2004) 329 *BMJ* (July 24) 327-29; K Claxton and AJ Culyer, 'Wickedness or Folly? The Ethics of NICE's Decisions' (2007) 32 *Journal of Medical Ethics* 462-64; AR Mason and MF Drummond, 'Public Funding for New Cancer Drugs: Is NICE Getting Nastier?' (2009) 45 *European Journal of Cancer* 1188-92.

imagine that those somewhat diffuse deliberative results would have to be assessed and integrated and legitimated by the Board of this NICE-like entity.

In conclusion, the process of rational democratic deliberation as I have described and defended it will not yield perfectly just or flawless rationing protocols. No institution or process will yield that outcome. I have only argued that there are good justice-relevant reasons for endorsing this approach to health care rationing and priority-setting over any other feasible alternative if we want health care rationing protocols that are "just enough," stable, and legitimate.

Chapter III

Rationing and the Disabled: Several Proposals

Frances M. Kamm

In this chapter I will first critically examine some recently published views of Peter Singer about rationing scarce health care resources, in particular to the disabled. For purposes of comparison, I will then briefly summarize some alternative proposals about rationing and the disabled I have made in greater detail in earlier work. This will lead me to also compare my proposals to some of those more recently made by Dan Brock. Hopefully, distilling the essence of making my proposals will make them more accessible, and comparing them with other proposals will show the need for distinctions they draw. Finally, I shall point to some concerns raised by those proposals.[1] Throughout, the discussion focuses on resources that are not under personal control and that it is impermissible to distribute according to purely personal preferences. I shall be particularly concerned with whether favoring the nondisabled over the disabled in distributing scarce resources involves invidious discrimination, mistakenly focuses on maximizing health benefits, or exhibits no moral fault at all.

1. *Singer*

Singer is concerned with maximizing health benefits per dollar spent using a QALY measure.[2] For example, he thinks a teenager should be saved rather than an 85 year old person because we can expect much more future life from the teenager than from the old person. In response, it should be pointed out that this is also true if we compare a teenager with a 50 year old. If we think the 50 year old should not

---

[1] My remarks on Singer are in response to his "Why We Must Ration Health Care" (*N.Y. Times Magazine*, July 19, 2009). All references to Singer are to that article, which he wrote while the Obama health care proposals were being discussed. A short extract of my discussion of Singer was published as a Letter to the Editor of the *N.Y. Times Magazine* August 13, 2009. My remarks on Brock are in response to his "Cost-Effectiveness and Disability Discrimination," *Economics and Philosophy* 25 (2009) 27–47. All references to Brock are to this article. I am grateful for comments to audiences at the Conference on Rationing, Erasmus University, Rotterdam, Dec. 2010, at the Bioethics Colloquium, New York University, April 2011, and at the Department of Clinical Bioethics, NIH June 2011. The chapter also appears in N Eyal, S Hurst, O Nordheim, and D Wikler (eds), *Health Inequality: Ethics and Measurement* (OUP, forthcoming) and I am grateful to the editors of that volume for additional comments.

[2] The QALY, which multiplies years of life times quality, was invented by Richard Zeckhauser who also thinks we should allocate health resources to maximize QALYs per dollar. It is not clear why Singer favors maximizing health benefits rather than all benefits. Prima facie, the latter standard could imply saving the rich, beautiful and productive rather than those who lack such good traits.

be disfavored relative to the teenager, it may be because sometimes persons have a right to certain types of health care independent of whether this maximizes health benefits per dollar.

On the other hand, suppose that the teenager could be saved for fewer good years than the 85 year old. It might be argued that we should still save the teenager because she would die having had much less life overall than the older person if she is not helped. Helping the person who will have had much less life overall if not aided so that she improves to some significant degree might also be relevant to how to allocate resources, not just maximizing expected health benefits per dollar. This is related to giving priority to the worse off.

Singer also considers how to compare the health benefit achieved in saving one person's life with curing a serious condition that, nonetheless, does not threaten another person's life (e.g. quadriplegia). He argues that the way to think about this question is to consider the trade-off each person would reasonably make in his own life between life years lived and quality of life. For example, if every person (already disabled or not) would be indifferent between living ten years as a quadriplegic and living five years nondisabled, this would indicate that people take living as a quadriplegic to be half as good as living nondisabled. Singer thinks that such data would show that using our resources to cure two quadriplegics is just as good as saving someone else's life, provided the life expectancy of all three people if helped would be the same (for example, ten years).[3] His reasoning (which he does not spell out but that I shall now try to supply) seems to be that if someone would give up five out of ten years of his own life rather than be quadriplegic, that would justify curing one person's quadriplegia rather than saving someone else's life for five years. Since there are two people whose quadriplegia we can cure, the combined benefit of curing both, he thinks, is equal to saving the life of another person who would live for ten years.

There are several problems with this conclusion and the reasoning that leads to it, I think. First, in the tradeoff between quality and quantity that a person might make in his own life, it is that person who benefits from the tradeoff. When we make tradeoffs between different people, the people who get the improved quality of life are not the same people who suffer the loss of more life years. Rather, we are imposing the loss of life on another person who does not benefit for the sake of benefiting others. This raises different moral issues than the trade off within one life, I think.[4]

---

[3]   He says: "How can we compare saving a person's life with, say, making it possible for someone who was confined to bed to return to an active life... One common method is to describe medical conditions to people – let's say being a quadriplegic – and tell them that they can choose between 10 years in that condition or a smaller number of years without it...If most...have difficulty deciding between 5 years of nondisabled life or 10 years with quadriplegia, then they are, in effect, assessing life with quadriplegia as half as good as nondisabled life...(These are hypothetical figures....) If that judgment represents a rough average across the population, we might conclude that restoring to nondisabled life two people who would otherwise be quadriplegics is equivalent in value to saving the life of one person, provided the life expectancies of all involved are similar."

[4]   On why this might be so, see my "Should You Save This Child? Gibbard on Intuitions, Contractualism, and Strains of Commitment" a comment on Allan Gibbard's Tanner Lectures, published in Gibbard's *Reconciling Our Aims* (OUP 2008).

Second, the conclusion that curing two quadriplegics who would live for 10 years anyway is equal to saving someone else who would otherwise die, so that he can live for ten additional years depends on aggregating (adding up) the benefit to two people to weigh against the loss of the benefit of having his life saved for ten years to the third person. However, calculating total health benefits produced by aggregating smaller benefits to a greater number of people can be problematic. For example, suppose the trade-off test within one person's life showed that a small disability (e.g. a damaged ankle) made life only 95% as good as a nondisabled life. Then a person would rather have 9 ½ years without the small disability than ten years with it. On Singer's view, this implies both that we should cure one person's small disability rather than save someone who would otherwise die so he can live for an additional ½ year[5] and that we should cure small disabilities in twenty one people rather than save someone who would otherwise die so that he then live for ten years. This is the sort of reasoning that led to the discredited rationing plan in Oregon many years ago in which resources were to be allocated to cap many people's teeth rather than save a few people's lives. It can lead us to deny significant help to people who will be the worst off (and badly off in absolute terms) because they will die if they are not helped in order to help many who are disabled only in a small way and so not very badly off.[6]

To see a third problem, notice that Singer's way of reasoning is independent of the particular values found through intrapersonal tradeoffs of quality and quantity of life. Suppose people who are severely paralyzed would trade off only a few days of life in order to live without their disability. This result in a tradeoff between quality and quantity of life would imply that their disability has only a slightly lower value than nondisability. Taking this data, Singer's method of reasoning implies that we just need a much larger number of people who could be cured of severe paralysis in order to compensate for not saving someone who would go on to live for ten years. A particular problem to which this case gives rise is that the conclusion to which Singer's method leads may now seem reasonable. That is, it may be said that curing thousands of severely paralyzed people is indeed to be preferred to saving one person so that he can go on to live for an additional ten years. Aggregating benefits across people seems to give the right answer here. However, if we agree with this conclusion, it is probably because we are assuming that severe paralysis makes for a type of life that is very bad

---

[5] Such a rescue is different from deciding when someone is, for example, twenty whether to allocate resources in such a way that he lives to 60 ½ rather than 60. I discuss this distinction briefly in "Aggregation, Allocating Scarce Resources, and the Disabled," in *Social Philosophy and Policy*, 26 (Winter 2009).

[6] In general, Singer believes that it could be morally correct to aggregate small benefits to many people each of whom is not badly off and produce a large overall benefit, rather than provide a significant benefit to prevent someone else from being much worse off. So while he is known for his views on the duty to save people from famine, his theoretical position actually implies that it could be morally preferable to save many from headaches rather than save a few from death. For this and other criticisms of Singer's views see my "Faminine Ethics," in D Jamieson (ed), *Singer and His Critics* (Blackwells 1999) which somewhat revised is also Chapter 13 in my *Intricate Ethics* (OUP 2007).

for each person by contrast with nondisability and, hence, that someone would trade much more than a few days of life in order to be unparalyzed. But Singer's reasoning implies that such a low value need not be attached to the paralysis in order for curing the many paralyzed people to outweigh saving the life. And this is why his reasoning is problematic.

Finally, Singer argues that if we accept that disability can make a person's life less good healthwise, other things equal, and we want to maximize the health benefits we get with our resources, we should save the life of a nondisabled person rather than someone whose disability cannot be cured, other things equal. The only alternative to this, he says, is to deny that disability per se makes someone's life not as good health-wise, and to say *that* would have the unpalatable implication that there is no reason to allocate resources to cure or prevent disabilities.[7] (Notice, in Singer's defense, that saying that "a life is not as good with a disability" in the sense that the quality of life for the person goes down does not itself imply that the person herself is not as good as or not worth as much as a nondisabled person.)

I have argued that there is another alternative that does not deny that disability makes life significantly worse for a person, other things equal, and yet does not lead to Singer's conclusions about allocation: We should recognize that a consideration can give us a reason to do something in one context but not another. For example, having a paralyzed finger can make life not as good in a small way, holding other factors constant. This can give us some reason to try to cure this condition while also recognizing that, when it comes to deciding whose life to save, it is an irrelevant consideration that one person has a paralyzed finger and another person does not. The additional admitted good of a nonparalyzed finger in the life of one person is what I called an "irrelevant good" when deciding whose life to save, and so equal

---

[7] It is sometimes argued that people who are not disabled mistakenly believe that becoming severely disabled is very bad. This is because, it is said, they are poor predictors of how unhappy they would be if they were disabled, as shown by the fact that the disabled are as happy as the nondisabled due to adaptation and various protective psychological mechanisms (even including self deception). These points are made by Timothy Wilson in his *Strangers to Ourselves* (HUP 2004). However, there are disturbing implications of basing rationing decisions on these findings, in addition to not allocating funds to cure disabilities. Suppose many people come to an emergency room with severe headaches that will last several hours. At the same time, someone else comes in with a spinal injury that will paralyze his legs if surgery is not done right away. Should we treat all the headaches or do the surgery if we cannot do both? Suppose that we can predict that someone will quickly adapt to paralysis but the people with severe headaches cannot adapt to them. If experienced well-being were all that mattered, we should cure the headaches. This is the wrong conclusion, I believe. This is an indication that experienced well-being and accurate predictions about it are not all that matters in rationing decisions. The fact that people can adapt to, and deceive themselves about, a bad condition does not mean that we should not prevent the bad condition. (In this connection, it is interesting to note that Daniel Kahneman, who reports that disfigured people's "daily mood" is the same as nondisfigured people's, also reports that the disfigured people themselves want to have the disfigurement removed) mentioned in his "Evolving Notions of Well-Being," a lecture in the Mind, Brain, and Behavior Distinguished Lecture Series, Harvard University, April 17, 2008.

chances should be given to each. It is not necessarily irrelevant when deciding whether to spend dollars on a curative treatment for finger paralysis.[8]

This explanation suggests that it is not the judgment that disability can make an outcome worse that has to go; it is the judgment that we should always maximize health outcomes with our resources that has to go.

It may be clear that small differences in victims, like a paralyzed finger, should not affect who is chosen for a life saving resource. But what is the explanation of this irrelevance? Here is a possible explanation: in a two-person contest for a scarce life saving resource, either person would get the greater part of the best possible outcome that can be gotten by someone (i.e., a worthwhile life whether with or without a paralyzed finger). It is also the case that the alternative for each to being saved would be very bad (death), and each wants to be the one to survive. It is crucial to this explanation that we are dealing with separate persons and that we think that from a moral point of view their different perspectives on an outcome (Viz. each cares who survives) should matter to what we should do. Otherwise, it would be clear that we should maximize QALYS. This is what we would do if we had a choice with respect to one person of merely saving his life or saving his life and also unparalyzing his finger, holding costs constant.

But what of larger disabilities that bring down quality of life as far as .5 or somewhat below, so that it is not true that either person would get the greater part of the best possible outcome that can be gotten by someone? I have suggested at least two grounds for why we should still give equal chances for a life saving procedure to the disabled and nondisabled. Importantly, neither ground depends on the view that a disabled life is as good for someone as a nondisabled one, other things equal. First, each person can get what it is most important that people have, namely a worthwhile life and each wants to be the one to survive (Call this the Moral Importance Ground). Second, when one's only option is to have a life at .5, it may be reasonable to *care about* keeping it as much as it would be reasonable to care about keeping a life rated at 1. (Call this the Only Option Ground.) Note that this is consistent with its being reasonable to *care to have* the life rated at 1 rather .5 and even its being reasonable to risk death to get it, were this possible. This implies that it could be reasonable to risk death to get a life at 1 about which it will not be reasonable to care once one has it any more than one should care about the life one has now (at .5). All this may seem puzzling, yet I think it is true. Neither of these

---

8   This explanation and others I am about to describe are presented in greater detail in "Deciding Whom to Help, the Principle of Irrelevant Goods and Health-Adjusted Life Years," (1999), unpublished but circulated as a working paper of the Center for Population Studies, Harvard University; "Deciding Whom to Help, Health-Adjusted Life Years, and Disabilities," a revision of the working paper, published in S Anand, F Peters, and A Sen (eds), *Public Health, Ethics, and Equity* (OUP 2004); "Aggregation, Allocating Scarce Resources, and the Disabled," in *Social Philosophy and Policy* 26 (Winter 2009) 148-197 and a slightly different, longer version, "Disability, Discrimination, and Irrelevant Goods," in K Brownlee and A Cureton (eds), *Disability and Disadvantage* (OUP 2009) 260-318. I shall refer to these papers in the text by their dates or as "unpublished" only when some point is present in one version but not in another. I earlier discussed the Principle of Irrelevant Goods in my *Morality, Mortality*, vol 1 (OUP 1993).

grounds applies when quality of life rating falls very low (e.g. coma) and I will not consider such cases here.

But now imagine two nondisabled patients. One could live for 20 years if he had a scarce life-saving surgery and the other could live for 5 years. The Importance and Only Option Grounds also seem to imply that it would be wrong to favor the person who would live much longer. If we disagree, we will need an argument that distinguishes allowing significant differences in length of life to count in rationing decisions while significant differences in quality do not. One suggestion I have made is that we distinguish between the "type" of person someone is, constituted by the qualitative features of his life, and how long any type of life goes on. Respect for persons might often require ignoring types when rationing but not big differences in how long any given type will persist. (Call this the Respect Ground).

In sum, using quality of life considerations and comparing and aggregating benefits across different people, at least in the manner Singer recommends, in order to determine how good a health outcome is, often seems to be the wrong way to ration scarce resources. It is important to realize that we might be able to think seriously about how to allocate scarce resources among different people--and even be willing to endorse rationing--without necessarily reaching all of Singer's conclusions.

It is also worth pointing out (2009)[9] that in *cases not involving life and death* decisions (such as treating gastritis with a scarce resource), arguably it need not matter whether we treat the disabled or nondisabled even if we, like Singer, were only concerned with how much good health there will be in an outcome overall. This is because if a scarce treatment for gastritis is equally effective in a disabled or a nondisabled person, both people will continue to exist and the same improvement in the gastritis will occur whomever we treat. Using abbreviation makes this clear, where "cure gastritis" is C, P is "paralyzed person" and U "unparalyzed person." If we treat P so that we have P(C), U is still alive (unlike a case where we do not treat his life-threatening illness in order to save P), albeit with gastritis, and P(C) + U(– C) contains as much good as P(– C) + U(C), only distributed differently. It is true that there is no "perfect specimen" in the outcome if the nondisabled person is not treated – no U(C) – but medicine is not concerned with producing perfect specimens. (Of course, it might be a good reason to give the cure for gastritis to someone who will already have the problem of paralysis to deal with, rather than treat someone who has no such additional problem. This concern for the person who would be worse off is, arguably, independent of concern for the amount of good in the outcome overall, unless we think there is diminishing marginal utility of a gastritis cure to the nondisabled, which seems unlikely.)

---

[9]   See note 5: 160, 169-70.

2. *Proposals for Counting Disability*

While I have provided some possible reasons for ignoring many quality of life differences in rationing, in earlier work I have also suggested additional reasons why taking account of such differences sometimes does not involve the particular problem of invidious discrimination. This is so even if taking account of the differences raises the *different* problem of giving too much weight to what should be irrelevant goods, and even if favoring the nondisabled over the disabled for scarce life saving resources sometimes does involve invidious discrimination. Consider some of the arguments for this view when deciding whether to treat someone just recently seriously paralyzed or, instead, some unparalyzed person.[10] One argument focuses on cases where there are multiple causes of a condition such as paralysis. This condition gives us a reason to treat a specific illness with a scarce resource. For example, suppose we are equally able to treat two patients for a specific illness that causes both paralysis and pain, but we are most concerned with the illness because it causes paralysis. However, there is another cause of paralysis in one of the patients that we cannot treat. We can refer to such cases as "condition similarity cases."[11] I argued that there would be good reason not to treat the patient who will still be paralyzed due to the other cause even though our treatment against the specific illness is equally effective in both patients. It seems that it is better to get rid of both pain and paralysis than to just get rid of the lesser problem of pain. Hence, it may be permissible to leave the unavoidably paralyzed person with pain and treat pain and paralysis in the other person.

I also argued that we should distinguish treating a person differently on the basis of (a) disability as a component of someone's life, making him a certain type of person, versus (b) disability as a cause of other bad effects in the person's life. So when the presence of a disability has the causal effect of interfering with treatment of another condition (e.g., we cannot perform heart surgery as well because of paralysis) there might be no objectionable discrimination in providing treatment to a nondisabled person instead (2009). (This is consistent with there possibly being objectionable failure to prioritize the worse off.) Also, counting differences in life expectancy caused by the disability in deciding whom to help need not involve invidious discrimination if it is permissible to count an otherwise-caused difference in life expectancy.[12] Similarly, it can be permissible and non-discriminatory to take into account obstacles to treatment that arises from not having a disability (e.g., we cannot perform heart surgery as well because someone has two legs rather than one). Or if nondisability reduced life expectancy, this may be taken into account consistent with nondiscrimination. Hence, someone's undeserved disability can

---

10   I deal with the recently paralyzed to factor out the relevance for rationing decisions of one candidate having had a worse life in the past than another candidate. See my *Morality, Mortality* vol. 1 for a theory of rationing that takes into account different pasts in candidates for a scarce resources.

11   See note 5: 172. There I called it "Treatment Similarity."

12   See my "Deciding Whom to Help, Health-Adjusted Life Years, and Disabilities," p. 240.

sometimes determine that he suffers a further loss (his life), without this involving objectionable discrimination. This is what I called "linkage."[13]

I further distinguished between (1) producing a better outcome in one patient than in another by (what I call) "piggybacking" on the good property a patient already has or *will have* but that we do not, per se, produce, and (ii) producing a better outcome in one patient than in another by causally producing the additional good property. For example, I discussed what I called "Switch Cases" (1999, 2004) (See Figure 1, where "⇒" signifies causing paralysis or nonparalysis and "→" signifies absence of such a causal role, all in cases where we would cause the saving of life of any person we treat.) In all three cases, two people compete for a scarce life-saving treatment. The difference is only in the impact on paraplegia.

	Case 1	Case 2	Case 3
Person one	P⇒U	U⇒P	P→U
Person two	P→P	U→U	U→P

FIGURE 1

In case 1, two paraplegic people are up for a scarce lifesaving treatment but in the first person the treatment, as a side effect, will undo the paralysis (i.e., P⇒U). In Case 2, two unparalyzed people are up for a scarce lifesaving treatment but in the first person the treatment, as a side effect, will cause paraplegia (i.e., U⇒P). (Case 3 will be discussed below.) In Case 1, if we choose to save the paralyzed person whom we cause to become unparalyzed, we do not merely get a better outcome by saving an already unparalyzed person or one who will become unparalyzed independently of our specific paralysis cure. Rather, we get a better outcome by saving a person and unparalyzing him. I argued that this different causal route to *the same better* outcome might make a moral difference to whether it is permissible to decide not to save a person who will remain paralyzed. That is, it might be permissible not to give a person who will remain paralyzed an equal chance to be saved relative to another person whom we can save *and* unparalyze. This is so even if it is impermissible not to give a person who will remain paralyzed an equal chance relative to another person whom we can save but whose being unparalyzed, per se, is not due to our efforts. This moral difference is not taken account of by those like Singer who claim that all that matters is how good the outcome is (i.e., that the person we save be unparalyzed). Nor is it taken account of by those who claim that deciding whom to save on the basis of whether they will be disabled always involves objectionable discrimination. (This is so even if we assume, for the sake of argument, that favoring U→U over P→P involves invidious discrimination and not just giving too much importance to maximizing QALYs.) To capture these results, I described the following principle:

---

[13]   Brock refers to "Kamm's Nonlinkage Principle" (p. 35) to describe the view that linkage might be morally objectionable in general, but he does not note that I specifically rejected this view. See note 12: 240. I discuss this further in note 5: 171-2.

The Causative Principle: It may be morally permissible to take account of large differences in QALYs if and only if we cause them (1999, 2004).[14]

But how can we justify there being a difference between a better outcome *achieved* by piggybacking and one achieved by causing? Perhaps we have greater entitlement to decide on the grounds that a better outcome will come about (i.e., there will be a nonparalyzed person in existence rather than a different paralyzed person) if we cause the nonparalysis rather than piggyback on this property by saving a person already unparalyzed. This entitlement could weigh against other factors pulling in another direction. (Similarly, we might be entitled to avoid causing something bad like paralysis in U⇒P rather than piggybacking on it as in P→P, in Case 2.)

I argued that the Causative Principle could not simply be subsumed under what I called the Treatment Aim Principle (2009).[15] The latter is the view that if our treatment for a particular problem would be equally effective in a narrow sense (e.g. cure heart failure) in either a disabled or nondisabled patient, each should have an equal chance for the treatment. This is a common justification for giving equal chances for a scarce life saving drug to a disabled and nondisabled person. However, the Treatment Aim Principle also implies that if treatment outcome in a narrow sense would be different, we might permissibly decide to treat the patient who gets the better outcome. One reason I gave for not subsuming the Causative Principle under the Treatment Aim Principle is that if a treatment aimed at curing heart failure unexpectedly cures or causes paralysis, as in the Switch Cases, this would ordinarily be considered a side effect of treatment, not part of the narrow sense of effectiveness of the heart treatment. By contrast, the Switch Cases and the Causative Principle are intended to suggest that the good or bad *side effect* we cause might also be relevant to deciding how to allocate the scarce life saving resource. I did note (2009)[16] that we might modify the Treatment Aim Principle, so that it would take account of side effects in determining the effectiveness of treatments. (However, this would be a wide rather than narrow sense of equally-effective treatment.) I also noted that if a drug's good side effect were consistently present in many patients, one might come to consider the drug as a treatment for two different problems, either together or alone (even though it was not developed with this in mind). If the drug were considered a treatment for two problems *at once*, its effectiveness might be judged, even in a narrow sense, by whether it cured both problems rather than just one.

The important point, I argued, is that sometimes having a causal role in making someone disabled or nondisabled might be a ground for deciding whether to treat someone with a scarce resource for a completely different problem, such as heart disease, without this involving objectionable discrimination. This could be true

---

[14]   In note 12. I discuss Switch Cases and the Causative Principle on p. 238.
[15]   In note 5: 178.
[16]   ibid 179.

regardless of whether having this causal role means that our treatment is more effective for the different problem per se.

In sum, I argued that even those who disagree with Singer and think that picking U→U instead of P→P is objectionably discriminatory could agree with the following: There is no objectionable discrimination in taking disability into account when (1) our treatment causes or cures it, (2) the disability affects treatment, (3) the disability causes further bad effects such as reduced life span, and (4) the disability is similar to the effects of an illness we are specifically trying to treat.

However, even if these four reasons for distinguising people do not involve objectionable discrimination, attending to them may involve giving too much weight from a moral point of view to differences in outcome. That is, some differences in outcome may still be "morally irrelevant goods" in certain contexts. For example, given that life itself is at stake for either candidate for the scarce resource and each wants to be the one to live, the fact that taking account of a minor difference in outcome that we cause did not involve objectionable discrimination per se need not show that taking account of it is morally permissible. Hence, I suggested, objections to not treating the disabled in many contexts may have to rest on violating a principle of irrelevant goods rather than a claim of improper discrimination.[17]

3. Brock on Equally-effective treatment

The distinction I drew between the Causative Principle and the Treatment Aim Principle are relevant to evaluating some recent views of Dan Brock's on rationing and the disabled. By contrast to Singer, Brock suggests that we accept a narrow notion of equally-effective treatment. It is a "treatment specific" understanding of effectiveness (p. 41). He considers the case of heart surgery. Brock says that surgery which fixes heart valves can be equally successful in each of two people even though we can predict that one person will live for ten years and another will live for one year, because the second will be executed within the year (p. 41). The measure of success of the surgery on this account is how well the valves are fixed, independent of how long the person goes on to live. Similarly, he says, "specific medical treatments are developed for specific medical conditions and their effectiveness is determined by how well they correct that condition" (p. 41). This implies that if a treatment designed to remove an impairment does so entirely in one person (even for a limited time, before she is executed) but only partially in someone else, the treatment is more effective in the first person.

Given this narrow notion of treatment effectiveness, it is theoretically possible for a paralyzed person to have just as successful a heart surgery as a nonparalyzed person. Hence, contrary to what Singer suggests, Brock thinks that if surgery must be rationed, there is no reason to favor the nondisabled person. Indeed, it could be objectionably discriminatory not to give equal chances for surgery to each.

---

[17]   In note 12: 242.

My concern is whether Brock's narrow notion of treatment effectiveness is consistent with some other claims that he goes on to make. This is where the discussion of my earlier work is relevant. *First*, in discussing a case of hip replacement, he says "...a pre-existing disability in effect often acts as a co-morbidity that makes treatment less effective in improving a patient's health-related quality of life. Patients with COPD, for example, have substantial limitations in mobility and ability to carry out a variety of activities requiring physical exertion; this would reduce the benefit they would otherwise receive from an intervention like a hip replacement, which is also intended to restore mobility and ability to carry out physical activities" (p. 30). If we were to decide not to treat the COPD patient for these reasons, Brock says it would be a "form of discrimination [that] seems less morally problematic because it is based on an arguably relevant and defensible difference in treatment effectiveness, although that difference in effectiveness is caused by a pre-existing disability" (p. 41-2).

What Brock means here is *not* that the hip cannot be replaced as successfully because the COPD makes surgery more difficult. Rather Brock is here considering that the disabled person *will get less out of what the new hip is meant to help provide (e.g. mobility)*. But this does not seem to involve use of a narrow notion of treatment effectiveness for it considers what further benefits someone gets from a treatment in judging how effective the treatment is. This is a wider notion of treatment effectiveness. If we used this wider notion, then if one person got more out of heart valve surgery because he got more of what it is was supposed to provide than someone else (e.g. longer life), then the first person's heart treatment would be judged more effective. This seems contrary to what Brock originally claimed to be the correct understanding of surgery that would fix each person's heart to the same degree.

Second, Brock considers a hypothetical case considered by a government agency using the Americans with Disabilities Act (ADA). In that case, two people are imagined to have sustained life-threatening injuries in a car accident that also left them unable to walk (p. 29). We can save each person's life but a cure for the disability only works in one of the people. The agency argued that automatically saving the person who could also be made nondisabled would be objectionable discrimination according to the ADA. One reason given for this conclusion was that judging an unparalyzed life to be better than a paralyzed life, other things equal, was itself discriminatory. This reason seems wrong for, as Singer noted, it is because we think an unparalyzed life is better for someone than a paralyzed life, other things equal, that we try to cure and prevent paralysis in cases where there is no conflict for a scarce resource. Dong so is not thought to involve an objectionable discriminatory judgment.[18] The agency also suggested that choosing to save the unparalyzed life implies that one thought the life of a paralyzed person was not worth

---

[18] It is possible that there is a different reason for in general trying to cure and prevent paralysis, namely a life with the disability is harder even if not less good. It could be supererogatory to require that people lead the harder life even if it were no less good. But it is also not objectionably discriminatory to judge that the paralyzed life is harder. For the "supererogation argument" see my "Disability, Discrimination, and Irrelevant Goods."

as much. Brock thinks this complaint fails to distinguish between the equal worth of a person and the unequal worth of the contents of that person's life. Apparently, he thinks the latter can be relevant to allocation decisions consistent with respect for the equal worth of persons.

Brock's positive view about the hypothetical case considered by the government agency is that our treatment will be more effective if it both saves a life *and* cures a disability incurred in the accident. Therefore, it is not objectionable discrimination to save the person who will not be disabled.[19] Notice that we are probably considering this to be a case in which we are *aiming* to reverse all the damage – life threatening as well as disability causing – that has occurred in the accident. Hence, we are probably not conceiving of this as a case in which a treatment that is aimed only at saving someone's life also has a *foreseen but unusual side effect* of curing his disability, as in my Switch Cases.[20] Indeed in the government's case, there may be two treatments, one is life-saving and will work on each person equally well in the narrow sense. Another is a disability-curing treatment that will work on only one person. Suppose we are concerned not with whom we can treat most effectively (as Brock puts it), but with whom *a treatment* will be most effective. Then the question becomes whether we should choose one of the patients to get a life-saving treatment that works equally well in either patient just because another treatment we have is effective curing disability only in him? But loss of life is the most pressing concern (and length of the expected survival is not said to be different). So it seems that the narrow standard of treatment effectiveness implies, as it would imply in my Switch Cases, that we should ignore whether we can cure a disability in deciding whom to save.

Third, Brock says that if a treatment for an unrelated condition (such as heart disease) causes a disability (such as paralysis) in one person but not another, as it did in my Switch Case 2, the treatment is less effective in the first person, other things equal.[21] However, the idea of unequal effectiveness that Brock employs here seems inconsistent with his original, narrower notion of treatment effectiveness. For if a treatment's causing disability counted against its narrow effectiveness, so should its causing reduced life span in one patient but not another. This limits the

---

[19]   He says, "The fifth form of discrimination is where a particular treatment is less effective in some kinds of patients than in another kind, leaving the first kind disabled, but not due to any background conditions of pre-existing disability. This case seems simply to be a difference in treatment effectiveness, with disability entering the picture for some patients but not others only as a result of the treatment" (p. 41). This quote probably applies to both cases in which treatment does not cure disability acquired in an accident (as in the text) and where it actually causes a disability (as in my second Switch Case).

[20]   In my Switch Case that involves life saving and a cure of disability in one patient but not another, the disability was recently acquired in both patients, but independently of the life threatening illness. When I first wrote about the Switch Case in "Deciding Whom to Help, the Principle of Irrelevant Goods and Health-Adjusted Life Years" I did not know about the hypothetical case considered by the government agency and its analysis of the case. Indeed, Brock informed me of it as a way of criticizing my conclusion that curing disability could matter morally in the Switch Cases. He seems to have changed his position on this.

[21]   Although Brock cites "Deciding Whom to Help, Health-Adjusted life Years, and Disabilities" in his article, he does not mention the discussion in that article of the Switch Cases.

scope of Brock's view that we should not consider how long a patient survives after a life-saving treatment in deciding on treatment effectiveness. (p. 41). Further, if a drug for heart disease caused paralysis, on the narrow view of treatment effectiveness we would presumably consider it a bad *side effect* of the drug, just as if it caused dandruff; causing a bad side effect is not an indication of a less effective treatment for heart disease. We might seek another drug that treated the heart disease as *effectively* but without the bad side effect, but we would not describe this as seeking a more effective treatment, in a narrow sense, for heart disease.

It is only if we adopt a wide notion of treatment effectiveness that good or bad side effects will speak against treatment being equally effective in different people. Hence, it does not seem that the narrow standard implies that we should prefer to save the person in whom the treatment does not produce or does cure a disability. (This issue arises, in part, because Brock introduces the narrow notion of treatment effectiveness in conjunction with the `idea that "specific medical treatments are *developed* for specific medical conditions." So it seems that it is only the condition for which the treatments are developed that matters for deciding whether effective treatment is present. Focusing on development for specific medical conditions, if this means specific illnesses, will also raise problems if we consider cases where "condition similarity" due to different illnesses (as described earlier) exists, or where a patient will be treated successfully for heart disease but soon die of liver failure anyway.)

Brock himself specifically qualifies his conclusions based on the narrow notion of treatment effectiveness, saying that they hold "unless attending to treatment effectiveness is ruled out on other moral grounds" (p. 42). Still, I think that Brock does not correctly draw out the implications of the narrow conception of treatment effectiveness that he favors. Furthermore, the correct implications of the conception are often inconsistent with what seem to be the correct views about possible nondiscriminatory handling of cases. Hence, we have reason not to always rely on such a narrow notion in deciding whether allocating scarce resources is or is not invidiously discriminatory.

4. *Problems with the Causative Principle and Ideas of Discrimination*

Having distinguished the Causative Principle from a narrow treatment effectiveness view, I want to discuss some problems I have elsewhere raised for the Causative Principle. The problems show that, despite avoiding some of the problems raised by the narrow treatment effectiveness view that principle fails. Moreover, some of its failings involve (other) forms invidious discrimination.

(i) Recall that the Causative Principle states that it may be morally permissible to take account of large differences in QALYS if and only if we cause them (rather than piggyback on them). Consider a case where we must choose whether to give a life-saving scarce drug to an unparalyzed person who will remain unparalyzed because we do not affect this property of his in any way (U→U) or, instead, to a recently paralyzed person in whom the life saving drug has the side effect of unparalyzing him (P⇒U), where "⇒" indicates our causal role in treating paralysis. (This case involves the second person in Case 2 and the first person in Case 1, Figure 1.) In this case, our causal role is greater in the originally paralyzed person than in the originally unparalyzed person. Yet, I believe, it would be morally wrong and even invidiously discriminatory to make this factor relevant in deciding whom to help. This is because both people will be unparalyzed in the outcome and there is no difference in their past lives that would imply that one person will have lived a much worse life overall if he is not helped to live on. That is, suppose we endorse some morally acceptable role for the Causative Principle (on the basis of cases where the choice is between giving a scarce life-saving drug to P who will remain P and P whom our treatment can make U, as in Case 1). Then we may make the wrong decision and, it seems, even an invidiously-discriminating one, in some cases. This is so if we choose to aid the person on whom we have a much greater positive causal effect, in cases where the candidates' outcomes are the same. (Brock does not consider such cases and the problems they raise in his discussion of our greater impact on one patient than another. I shall comment on this further below.)[22]

In response to such same-outcome cases, I suggested that a mark invidious discrimination may be that we hold it for or against someone in a contest for a scarce resource that he is disabled or nondisabled when we did not cause those states in him. In cases where the outcomes for both patients would be U, if we count it in favor of one person that we would cause his being U, we will really be holding it *against* the other person that he would be U rather than P independently of anything we do.[23] This is because it is his being and remaining U that makes it true that we cannot have a causative role in producing U in him. Hence, sometimes if we want not to be engaged in invidious discrimination against either the disabled *or* the nondisabled, we should *not* attend to the causative role of our treatment. (The same may hold when we must decide between saving U⇒P and P→P. The fact that our causative effect is negative in one person but not the other can be irrelevant if the outcome is the same. This is so even though we would be harming one of the people, especially since depriving him of a chance for the procedure that paralyzes him would result in a worse effect for him, namely death.) This is why I suggested that we should move beyond the simple Causative Principle (and also beyond seeing where our treatment narrowly construed is most causally effective). Hence, in deciding how to allocate a scarce resource, insofar as we are concerned with quality in outcome and assume that invidious discrimination can occur when we piggyback, we should focus on whether we would cause a significantly *better* or worse outcome in one patient than in another.[24]

---

[22] I raised this issue in note 12: 239-40.

[23] A full discussion of this point would have to consider as an exception the idea of giving priority to the worse off paralyzed person because her past and the past of the unparalyzed persons are very different. I owe this point to Carlos Soto.

[24] For a more detailed discussion of this, see note 5. In moving beyond the simple Causative Principle, I introduced another principle, the Principle of Irrelevant (Type) Identity. I omit discussion of it here to avoid unnecessarily complicating matters. Elizabeth Pike has suggested that in same outcome cases not involving life and death, we *should* attend to our causative role. For example,

This solution to the problem raised by the simple Causative Principle for same outcome cases helps refine the idea of invidious discrimination.[25] As suggested by what I have said above, I do not think that judging paralysis to be worse than nonparalysis, other things equal, is itself an instance of an invidiously discriminatory value judgment. Now suppose it is sometimes not invidiously discriminatory to differentiate candidates for a scarce resource on the basis of the expected presence or absence of disabilities when our treatment for some other condition would cause or cure the disabilities. Then we also cannot conceive of invidious discrimination as taking account of someone's disability when this will lead to a worse outcome for him (e.g., he loses his chance for a scarce resource for another medical problem). But one sense of invidious discrimination seems to involve doing what holds someone's disabled or nondisabled state against or in favor of him just because our treatment does not cause the state *when outcomes are the same*. Finally, we have been supposing that someone believes that invidious discrimination occurs in attending to differences in outcome when they come about through piggybacking, yet he also thinks this is not true when the same difference is caused by us (as in the Switch Cases). Putting all this together, we get a conception of discrimination that seems to involve holding someone's abled or disabled state against or in favor of him in a contest for a life saving resource when our treatment does not cause the difference, quite generally, that is, whether outcomes are different or the same. (One exception is when the disabled state is similar to the condition that gives us reason to try to treat an illness with our scarce resource.)

(ii) Another problem with emphasizing whether our treatment causes or cures disability is the threat of intransitivities:[26] Suppose we may sometimes take account of how we causally affect disabilities when deciding how to allocate scarce resources. Then it may be morally permissible to treat $P \Rightarrow U$ and $U \rightarrow U$ differently when they are each in contests for resources with someone who is $P \rightarrow P$. That is, $P \Rightarrow U$ may be preferred to $P \rightarrow P$ without invidious discrimination, but if we assume the view that taking account of piggybacked disability is wrongly discriminatory, $U \rightarrow U$ may not be preferred to $P \rightarrow P$. Yet, it was argued above that $P \Rightarrow U$ and $U \rightarrow U$ should be treated as equals in a contest between them alone for a scarce resource. So individuals who are equals in a pairwise comparison behave differently when they are compared pairwise with a third party ($P \rightarrow P$). This gives rise to the (apparent)

---

suppose that we could treat either P or U for gastritis. U would remain U if he is treated but the drug for gastritis would also have the side effect of making P unparalyzed. Surely, she says, we should give the drug to P, for then the person who remains U will still be alive and U, albeit with gastritis, and we will both cure gastritis in someone and produce another unparalyzed person. I agree that in this case we should give the treatment to P. However, this case shows that it is not enough to focus on just the outcomes for the competitors for a scarce resource in order to know whether we will have produced the same outcome whomever we treat. For if we treat U instead of P, we will have a world in which there is still a paralyzed person (P) whereas if we treat P we will reduce the number of paralyzed people and cure the same amount of gastritis. Hence our overall outcome will be *different* depending on whom we treat.

[25] I discuss this in note 12: 238-9.

[26] This was discussed in note 12: 242, n. 13. Further discussion of this is in "Aggregation, Allocating Scarce Resources, and the Disabled."

threat of intransitivity and the problem of whom we should select when all three of these individuals are present at once. (It also implies that it is being held against someone that he was U without our assistance since he fares worse relative to P than someone who began as P and whom we would *make* U. To avoid this problem, we could just settle for avoiding invidious nondiscrimination, as I described it above, in pairwise comparisons only.)

More specifically the problem of (apparent) intransitivity can be put as follows, where ">" is "preferred without invidious discrimination": (1) P⇒U > P→P; (2) P→P = U→U; and yet (3) – (P⇒U > U→U).[27] Brock does not speak to this issue because, as I noted earlier, he does not deal with cases where our causative role in helping (or harming) one person would lead to the same outcome for both patients. That is, Brock's discussion considers the comparisons in (1) and (2), but not the comparison involved in (3). This may be why he does not notice that (1) and (2) imply what seems to be untrue, namely that P⇒U > U→U.[28]

What should we do when all three individuals (i.e., P→P, U→U, and P⇒U) are in competition for the same life saving scarce resource? When all three are present, I suggested (2009) that it would not involve invidious discrimination to select one of the people who would have the best outcome. We could reason in the following way: PP could be eliminated from the contest by P⇒U, and so not have to be directly compared with U→U. Then we can give equal chances to P⇒U and U→U. (There will be no cycling.) The underlying view is that we are morally permitted to seek a significantly better outcome, and follow a path in decision-making that leads us there, so long as our path to this end is not invidiously discriminatory and no other relevant moral principle is violated.[29]

iii. Let me present a third problem I have discussed. I think it is a problem for those opposed to taking account of disability and nondisability in allocating life saving scarce resources when P→P and U→U, but who nevertheless think that significant differences in life expectancy – whether they come about through our causation or piggybacking – *should* sometimes matter in allocation decisions. Suppose candidate A for a life-saving treatment will live for one year and B for 6 years, and this is a reason to select B. Suppose A is nondisabled and B was recently severely paralyzed. Other things equal, if we do not give the treatment to B, we would be holding his disability against him. Suppose B receives the treatment and subsequently wishes to take advantage of a new surgery that will unparalyze him though it reduces his life expectancy to slightly over one year. (I called this a Switch and Reduce Case.) He wants to do this because, let us suppose, it is a reasonable intrapersonal trade off to exchange six years of severely paralyzed life for slightly

---

[27] Also, P⇒U = UU, and U→U = P→P, yet – (P⇒U = PP).

[28] Perhaps there is another reason for his not seeing this problem. It is possible that a treatment that did more for one patient than another should (as in (3)) still be considered equally effective in a wide sense in both, and so not grounds for permissibly preferring one patient. This is because the treatment equally deals with *all* the problems each patient had, even if the nondisabled patient has fewer problems. It would be just as *effective* in a wide sense though it did not literally *affect* as much.

[29] A round-robin procedure would lead to the same result, according to Peter Graham.

more than one year of nondisabled life. In fact, it makes him better off. With the Switch and Reduce surgery, B would be almost identical to the way A was; the difference in length of life expected (a few months) would presumably be morally irrelevant in an interpersonal choice of whose life to save. Had B's prospects earlier been nearly identical to A's, the objection we raised to the simple Causative Principle implies that we should have given them equal chances for the life saving resource. Even if at the time of allocating the scarce treatment we only knew that B would have the Switch and Reduce surgery were his life to be saved, it seems we should have given A and B equal chances. Might it be that if we select B over A because he will live for six years, we should elicit a promise that he will not have the later surgery so that the five additional years of life that gave us a reason to deprive A of his chance will come about? Limiting B's options subsequent to his selection would imply that there are moral reasons for his having to make decisions only about his own life from the same perspective that led to him rather than someone else being alive. (This would be even clearer if A would have been preferred over B (with a life expectancy of slightly over one year) because A had a significantly longer life expectancy than 1 year).

Further, suppose that at the time of the choice with A we could have saved B in two different ways: (i) so that he will live for 6 years paralyzed or (ii) so that we switch him to being unparalyzed with a life span of slightly more than 1 year. Then if B chose Switch and Reduce option (ii), it seems that equal chances should have been given to A and B. Hence, if at the time of selecting a candidate, B chose the life-saving procedure (ii) that was better for him intrapersonally, he would eliminate the superior chances to live relative to A that he would have had if he chose to be P for six years.[30]

The problem in these cases arises because we are refusing to allow the same tradeoff between quality and quantity of life interpersonally that we (are assuming) is reasonable intrapersonally. Such a tradeoff interpersonally (we are assuming) would make six years P in B equal to one year U in A. One ground for not allowing quality/quantity tradeoffs interpersonally was suggested earlier: When all one can have is a life with severe P, it may be reasonable to care about one year with such a life as much as someone else cares about one year with U (2004, 2009). However, we are also allowing the reasonableness of bringing about the intrapersonal tradeoff between a long life with severe P and a shorter one with U when this can be done. That is, someone who reasonably cares maximally for a year with severe P when it is all he can have, can consistently care to be U for even much less time, when that is an option. As a result of these two moves, B's P life lasting for 6 years is judged better *interpersonally* than A's U life lasting for 1, and yet B's U life for slightly more

---

[30]   A similar issue arises if B who would be P for 6 years confronts C who would be P for 6 years, when only B has the option of another life saving treatment that would result in this being U for 1 1/8 years. Suppose the latter is his preferable option. Should B be deprived of his equal chance simply because he selects a better intrapersonal option that we would cause? It seems so, because giving him an equal chance with A would involve counting the length of someone's life differently depending on whether she was U or P.

than one year, which would *intrapersonally* be better than the better interpersonal option, is not judged better *interpersonally* than A's year.

These cases may remind us of what Thomas Scanlon famously emphasized, that intrapersonal tradeoffs that are adequately reasonable for an individual to make can lack moral relevance from an interpersonal point of view. He described someone (call him Joe) who had a claim on us for food to meet his nutritional needs but for whom it was more important to build a monument to his god than to eat. Scanlon claimed that Joe would have no claim on us to provide him with funds to build the monument instead of spending the same amount for his food. Now suppose that our money is scarce and both Joe and Alice have an equal claim on us for food. The amount we can purchase is the minimum necessary for survival and so there is no point dividing it between them. Then if other things are equal between them, we should give each a maximal equal chance for food. However, if Joe will sell the food we give him to get supplies to build the monument to his god, then, presumably, he should lose his equal chance for the food. His not unreasonable intrapersonal tradeoff would not have a legitimate interpersonal role in his retaining an equal chance with Alice for food. This would be true, even if Alice had the same preference ranking that Joe had but would not be able to act on it with her food supply.[31]

---

[31] For Scanlon's case, see his "Preference and Urgency," *The Journal of Philosophy* 72(19) 655-69. Thomas Nagel reminded me of the relevance of Scanlon's case for my discussion of the Switch-and-Reduce Cases. Suppose, however, that Joe used money of his own on monument building and this left him without money for his food. It seems unlikely that Scanlon would think that Joe now had no claim on us to provide him with food. (Perhaps he would not even think that Joe had a weaker claim on food than someone else whose hunger was not the result of having spent his money on this other project.) This raises many interesting issues about the specificity of the use of our aid (after all, Joe will eat the food we give him) and also about responsibility for one's condition.

Chapter IV

What do theories of social justice have to say about health care rationing? Well-being, sufficiency and explicit age-rationing[1]

Carina Fourie

1. Introduction

It is commonly accepted that theories of social justice provide only limited guidance on health care rationing decisions. Broad theories of justice, such as John Rawls's justice-as-fairness, may tell us how to regulate society's main political, social and economic institutions fairly but they cannot, at least it is often believed, provide us with specific guidance or fine-grained principles for allocating health care resources.[2] Subsequently, theories of justice may not be able to help us to determine how to ration health care resources, for example, in helping us to choose between new treatments or public health initiatives when resources are scarce. Although there is much truth to this – particularly as broader theories of social justice usually do not aim to answer such specific allocation decisions – we should take care not to under-estimate the significance of situating health care decision-making within the ethical framework provided by a broad theory of justice.

In this chapter, I identify four potential tests, embedded in a broad theory of justice, which can be used to assess the fairness of health care rationing decisions. These are the tests for 1. sufficiency, 2. multiple determinants, 3. multiple dimensions, and 4. moral urgency. To uncover the tests and to illustrate the guidance they provide, I discuss them in application to a specific dispute over health care resource rationing: the debate about the justice of explicit age-based rationing. I extract these tests from a

---

[1]   I would like to thank audiences at the Ethics Centre at the University of Zurich, the Fifth International Conference on Applied Ethics at Hokkaido University and the International Conference on Health Care Rationing at Erasmus University for the opportunity to present and develop drafts of this paper. I am particularly grateful to Norman Daniels, Urs Marti, Johan Rochel and Antoinette Scherz for comments and questions that have helped me to improve this paper. I am pleased to acknowledge the funding from the Swiss National Science Foundation (SNSF) which has made this paper possible, as well as funding from the URPP Ethics Programme at the University of Zurich, and the Center for Applied Ethics and Philosophy at Hokkaido University. I would also like to thank Neil Roughley and Anton Leist for developing the broader project of which this paper forms a part.

[2]   N Daniels, *Just health: Meeting Health Needs Fairly* (CUP 2008) 24-25.

multifaceted, broad theory of justice developed by Madison Powers and Ruth Faden, 'the well-being sufficiency approach' (or simply, 'well-being approach', for short).[3]

One of the most important contributions that the well-being approach can make to the debate on health care rationing is that it unifies a number of disparate understandings of justice under one theory. Situating divergent claims about what is fair within a multifaceted and broader notion of social justice can 1. help us understand how such divergent claims can each be seen to represent justice, at least in some form, and 2. provide greater moral guidance for a number of rationing decisions.

Including this introduction, the chapter is divided into 5 sections. In the second section, I identify a problem with the way in which the justice of health care rationing is often discussed, the problem of narrow justice associated with a direct approach. In the third section, I discuss an alternative to approaching justice narrowly, the well-being approach. In the fourth section, I apply the well-being approach in the form of four tests for justice to the debate about whether we should explicitly prioritise health care resources for younger people as a matter of justice. Finally, I consider two objections to the way in which I apply the well-being approach to age-rationing, specifically, and health care allocation, generally: (1) the prudential lifespan objection and (2) the separate spheres objection, respectively.

2. The problem with a direct approach to the justice of health care resource allocation

We can distinguish between two substantive approaches[4] to determining the justice of health care resource rationing, the direct and the indirect approaches.[5] The direct approach makes judgements about the justice of particular rationing allocation decisions primarily or exclusively by considering the influence that a particular

---

[3]   M Powers and R Faden, *Social Justice: the Moral Foundations of Public Health and Health Policy* (OUP 2006).

[4]   A substantive approach can be contrasted to a procedural approach. Literature on the ethics of health care includes both substantive and procedural approaches, where a substantive approach provides actual guidance or principles on what is fair, e.g. it presents an idea of what a fair allocation of health care resources would be. In contrast, a procedural approach establishes how to go about determining guidance or health care policy fairly, without taking a stand on what the outcome of the procedure should be (usually within certain ethical boundaries). For more on procedural approaches, see L Fleck 'Just caring: Oregon, Health Care Rationing, and Informed Democratic Deliberation' (1994) *Journal of Medicine and Philosophy* 19, 367; N Daniels and JE Sabin *Setting limits fairly* (OUP 2002); N Daniels (2008) 103. Although procedural approaches are often presented as a solution to problems associated with substantive approaches – for example, with the lack of consensus associated with conceptions of justice – these two approaches are not mutually exclusive. In this paper, although I elucidate a substantive approach, this does not imply any particular stance on procedural approaches, although by emphasising a particular substantive approach and claiming that it does indeed provide moral guidance on rationing, I clearly distance myself from claims that substantive approaches *cannot* be constructive for health care policy.

[5]   I borrow the terms direct and indirect from Fabienne Peter, who describes a direct approach as one which sees justice in health or health care as limited to achieving particular distributions of health outcomes, such as distributions which maximise total aggregate welfare or prioritise care for the worse off. F Peter, 'Health Equity and Social Justice' in S Anand, F Peter and A Sen (eds), *Public Health, Ethics, and Equity* (OUP 2004).

principle of health care allocation will have on health, either of an individual or a population group.[6] This approach usually does not consider how the allocation of health care fits into a broader framework of social justice. At least partially, this means that it tends not to consider how the allocation of health care may influence other aspects relevant to justice, besides health, nor does it consider how other social goods, besides health care, influence health. This is problematic for at least two primary reasons.

A first problem with the direct approach is that it appears to ignore the significance of the need for 'background justice'. It is questionable if we can ever achieve justice by simply aiming for justice in each separate policy sphere or in terms of each social good understood in isolation, such as health and education. John Rawls argues that justice cannot be maintained solely by rules that govern particular transactions or isolated cases, even if these rules guarantee that the transactions are free and fair. Justice requires that the background structure or institutions of society, such as the constitution and the design of the economy, are fair, and not merely that isolated principles in particular decision spheres are fair.[7] Applied to health care specifically, one could argue (although Rawls notoriously neglects health and health care) that principles of justice should apply, foremost, to the design of the health care system rather than to particular allocation decisions.

Although it is undoubtedly true that background justice is necessary for achieving a just society, this should not however imply that health care allocation will be entirely unjust without a fundamental change in the entire health care system of a society, or perhaps even in the design of its economy, constitution, legal system and other institutions. Practically, health care rationing decisions cannot wait for background justice to be put in place. In order to reach decisions in health care, we need to be able to set aside broader unresolved problems of justice, and to isolate and resolve local, nonideal health care allocation problems. If we are not able to do so, we would "risk always having to advocate revolutionary change in order to solve any social problem".[8] Perhaps it is ultimately correct that no actual, real world society is genuinely just and that in order to become just, fundamental change is required, however, in reality, we must be able to develop and maintain social policies that are at least 'more or less' just. Health care policy-makers should thus not be deterred from considering the justice of health care allocation, even if this allocation does not occur within an ultimately and ideally just health care system or society.

The second problem with the direct approach – a problem that is more significant for this paper – is that it presents a narrow notion of the justice of health care. As I

---

[6]   You are particularly likely to adopt a direct approach if you are convinced by a 'separate spheres' approach to justice. In section 4, I assess the claim that health care (or health) should be considered as a sphere separate from other dimensions of justice and consider its relevance for my application of the well-being approach to explicit age-based rationing.

[7]   J Rawls, *Political Liberalism* (Columbia University Press 1993) 265-269; *A Theory of Justice* (rv edn OUP 1999) Section 14, 73-78.

[8]   L Fleck, 'DRGs: Justice and the Invisible Rationing of Health Care Resources' (1987) *The Journal of Medicine and Philosophy* 165, 168.

will argue, it does so by primarily only considering the influence of health care on health, rather than also considering other determinants of well-being and the other dimensions of well-being that health care can influence, By ignoring other aspects of justice, what can then seem to be a just rationing decision could actually lead to injustice. In section 4, I will illustrate these claims when I consider the problem posed by explicit age-based rationing in-depth.

In contrast to the direct approach, an indirect approach starts with a broad notion of justice which determines how the basic institutions of society should be organised in order to achieve a fair allocation of primary social goods. This broad theory can then be used to shape and constrain specific allocation decisions, such as health care rationing, and the justice of rationing can then be understood within the context of an overall fair allocation of social goods. This approach is not without its challenges. Primarily, it is questionable whether a broad theory of social justice can provide substantive guidance on specific rationing decisions. Norman Daniels claims that theories of justice are often too general and indeterminate to provide advice on fine-grained principles for health care resource allocation.[9] For example, he highlights two common theoretical approaches to rationing: 1. giving priority to the worst off or 2. maximising overall health benefit.[10] He points out that while most people reject extreme versions of these views, there is broad sympathy with more moderate, combined versions. Broad theories of justice, however, cannot help us to find a balance between these views: "Once we abandon either extreme position, we are in an area where general principles give no guidance".[11] This is not a *fault* of theories of justice – they are generally not intended to answer such specific allocation decisions but rather to guide the design of basic institutions and their overall influence on the distribution of social goods. They are thus not designed to answer these very specific questions of what can be called 'local' justice.

Considering problems with both approaches, and if we want our health care resource allocation policies to be fair, what should be done? What may be needed are specific guidelines about the justice of health and health care, which are able to provide detailed direction for particular and nonideal allocation decisions, but which would also be informed by and consistent with a broader theory of justice. Such an approach would avoid the problems associated with narrow justice, in other words with isolating health care from other aspects of justice. Although I do not aim to present a comprehensive set of such specific guidelines in this paper, I do aim to demonstrate how a particular broad theory of justice can be used to set up and constrain guidelines for specific rationing problems. In doing so, I aim to illustrate how adopting an exclusively direct approach to health care justice is too narrow and, in being so, a supposedly fair means of rationing health care could actually create injustices. Although a broad theory of justice may lack some ability

---

[9] N Daniels and JE Sabin (note 4); N Daniels (note 4) 103-139.
[10] Daniels (note 4) 103-108.
[11] ibid 106.

to give us specific answers, it is important to establish precisely what guidance it can give us, and indeed, as I aim to show in this paper, precisely by considering justice beyond merely the influence of health care on health it can provide us with substantial guidance on certain rationing decisions.

3. The 'sufficient well-being approach': using a multifaceted notion of justice for health care rationing

Madison Powers and Ruth Faden have developed a nonideal theory of social justice, what we can refer to as the 'sufficient well-being approach'.[12] In contrast to narrow approaches to the justice of health care, their theory is a multi-faceted, broad theory of justice. It identifies numerous constitutive dimensions of well-being which are shaped by multiple, often overlapping social determinants. It identifies (at least) six constitutive dimensions of well-being: 1. health, 2. personal security, 3. reasoning, 4. respect, 5. attachment and 6. self-determination. Social determinants of well-being could include health care, education, occupational hazards, income and opportunities for jobs and leisure although the dimensions of well-being are often also determinants of each other. For example, anxiety about personal security or systematic failures in respect through racism may negatively impact on health.[13]

In terms of assessing injustice, there are two aspects to the approach. Firstly, it is an injustice when any social determinant causes a lack of sufficiency in any dimension of well-being; sufficiency means that everyone should have 'enough' to live a good life. The positive aim of justice is to achieve sufficiency in each dimension of well-being: "a life substantially lacking in any one is a life seriously deficient in what it is reasonable for anyone to want, whatever else they want. Each is thus a separate indicator of a decent life which it is the job of justice to facilitate".[14] However, secondly, multiple determinants and multiple dimensions of well-being mean that the moral urgency with which we should address injustices can vary. Powers and Faden consider four scenarios as the basis for providing a framework for assessing moral urgency. I have represented these scenarios in Table 1 below.

---

12   Powers and Faden, (note 3) 37, acknowledge an "intellectual debt" to the capabilities approach of Amartya Sen and Martha Nussbaum, however, they explain that their theory differs in a number of ways from a capabilities approach.

13   It is not within the scope of my paper to *defend* Powers and Faden's conception of justice. For the purposes of this paper, I merely describe and extend their theory to demonstrate how it applies to a particular problem of health care rationing, and to contrast this to a narrow approach to justice. Of course, their theory will indeed require justification and it would need to address a number of objections, such as for example, the objections often raised against sufficientarian theories of justice (see, for example, P Casal, 'Why sufficiency is not enough' (2007) 117 *Ethics* 296, for a clarification and criticism of the notion of sufficiency).

14   Powers and Faden (note 3) 6.

1. One social determinant affects one dimension of well-being E.g. A lack of adequate medical care influences health	
2. Overlapping determinants affect one dimension E.g. Increased exposure to occupational hazards and a lack of adequate medical care influence health	
3. One determinant affects several dimensions E.g. A lack of adequate medical care influences health, reasoning, self-determination	
4. Overlapping determinants affect several dimensions E.g. A lack of adequate medical care, education, job opportunities, income influence health, reasoning, self-determination, respect and attachment	

TABLE 1: *The moral urgency of injustices according to the well-being approach*

The well-being approach demands that we should be concerned with rectifying any injustices, which means that scenarios 1-4 are all of concern. However, we may need to be particularly concerned by scenarios 2-3, while scenario 4 is the most urgent. We need to be particularly vigilant when overlapping determinants threaten one dimension of well-being, as in scenario 2 where a combination of increased exposure to hazards and a lack of adequate medical care threaten sufficiency of health. We also need increased vigilance when one determinant threatens multiple dimensions, as in scenario 3, where a lack of adequate medical care could influence health, reasoning and self-determination. The assumption is that in both these scenarios, well-being is often more likely to be affected or it is likely to be more seriously affected than in scenario 1.

The greatest urgency, however, is to address scenarios represented by 4 where a number of social determinants systematically threaten sufficiency in a number of dimensions of well-being. In these kinds of cases, multiple failures in multiple dimensions reinforce each other and trigger cascading and interactive effects across well-being. Think of a child who grows up in an impoverished family – a lack of education, adequate nutrition, greater exposure to environmental toxins and the lack of adequate access to health care could affect health, reasoning (in other words, cognitive reasoning abilities such as attention, learning and memory) and self-determination (our ability to shape our lives, at least to some extent). In turn, the effects on reasoning further compound and effect self-determination, and failures in both these dimensions cause further failures in terms of health. The lack of sufficiency in reasoning and self-determination also affect her ability to take up opportunities for education and jobs at a later age, which in turn only reinforce the failure of sufficiency at numerous dimensions of well-being. In scenarios like these, continuous and reinforcing threats to well-being are set in motion. Furthermore, as Powers and Faden highlight, if these failures occur in childhood they may be irreversible – health or reasoning affected at an early age may lock in certain disadvantages, which can never be overcome, no matter what opportunities are offered later on in life.[15]

---

15   Powers and Faden (note 3) 77-8. Their emphasis on the importance of achieving sufficiency (for the basis of) of well-being in childhood could be said to provide some indication that prioritising resources for children above anyone else could be justified. I do not consider this claim within

Additionally, the well-being approach recognises that justice is a function not only of formal institutions and the ways in which they distribute social goods but also of social structure (Powers and Faden refer to this as the nondistributive side of justice). The idea is that justice is not merely about the way in which material social goods or services such as income and health care are distributed. Justice is also concerned with the way in which social structure, including formal institutions but also intersubjective relationships and people's everyday interactions and attitudes towards each other, shape lives. Consider, for example, 'attachment' as a dimension of well-being. Bonds of attachment include love and friendship "as well as a sense of solidarity or fellow-feeling with others in one's community".[16] A sense of solidarity is not solely about the distribution of material goods and services – we could have a perfectly fair distribution of material goods and still not achieve a sense of solidarity in society, as this feeling of affiliation is likely to be partially dependent on the nature of the relationships people have with each other and on their everyday interaction and attitudes.

As a broad theory of justice, the well-being approach, is not geared towards establishing fine-grained allocative principles. Rather its aim is to describe how social institutions and social structure should be set up in order to achieve justice. On many decisions about the allocation of social goods, including many decisions about health care rationing, it will be silent. However, Powers and Faden claim, I believe rightly, that their approach provides greater moral guidance for health and health care decision-making than is often granted to theories of justice. They provide examples of how it does so including, briefly, a discussion of the age-rationing debate.[17] However, I think we can examine the application of their theory to the age-rationing debate more systematically and in greater detail. In the next section, I consider four tests for the justice of rationing decisions that I believe we can elicit from the well-being approach and consider its application to the debate on age-rationing.

4. The sufficient well-being approach in practice: tests for the justice of health care allocation and the age-rationing debate

In section 2, I discussed what I referred to as a narrow understanding of justice. Putting this problem into a specific context will help us to elaborate on the potential solution offered by the well-being approach and to understand more particularly what kind of moral guidance it can offer in terms of health care rationing. I think we can usefully apply the discussion thus far to the debate about explicit age-rationing.

---

the scope of this paper as it is substantially different from the claims made by advocates of explicit age-based rationing who emphasise the importance of prioritising resources for younger people over older people or those who have lived to a sufficient age. The argument from explicit age-based rationing is not defended on the basis of achieving sufficiency in well-being from an early age, and indeed, as it is likely to defend prioritising resources for 40 year olds, for example, over 80 year olds, it could not be justified on this basis.

[16]   ibid 2.
[17]   ibid 162-7.

However, I must qualify my interest in using age-rationing as an example – for the purposes of this paper, I use it to illustrate how the well-being approach can provide moral guidance for rationing decisions as part of a unifying and systematic theory of justice. I thus do not discuss age-rationing, per se, comprehensively.

Age is frequently discussed as a possible criterion for rationing scarce health care resources. The main point of controversy is whether we should give priority to those who are younger at the expense, at least under certain circumstances, of older people. Many theorists and practitioners claim that younger people should be given priority for health care resources over older people *as a matter of justice*.[18] We can call prioritising resources for younger people, explicit age-based rationing (in short, simply age-rationing). This can be contrasted to tacit age-based rationing, which might prioritise health care for younger people but not because of age *per se*, but, for example, because younger people are likely to have a greater amount of life-years ahead of them and thus the outcome of treating them, as opposed to older people, often results in greater health benefits overall. This paper is only concerned with *direct* age-rationing and thus only where age, in of itself, is used to determine allocation. As an example of how explicit age-rationing might apply, advocates suggest that in decisions about which new treatments to fund, quality-adjusted life-years (QALYs) should be modified so that more value is given to the life-years of a younger person than an older person.[19]

One of the reasons put forward to defend explicit age-rationing is that individuals who would otherwise die young have had less of an opportunity for life-years than those who would die at an older age, and thus those who are younger need the health care resource more.[20] However, critics claim that prioritising health care resources in this way would actually be an injustice. For example, they claim that health resources should in fact be allocated on the basis of urgency – how soon you will die if you do not receive treatment or how bad your quality of life will be.[21]

---

[18]   In the case of the fair innings argument, there is a cut-off point at which someone has lived a 'fair innings' – a sufficient amount of time. See, for example, A Williams, 'Intergenerational Equity: an Exploration of the "Fair Innings"' Argument (1987) *Health Economics* 117. However, for some theorists priority should be given to anyone who has had less life-years or has had less of an opportunity for life-years, thus simply being 'younger' (whether that means you are 20 years old or 60) rather than having reached a certain age threshold is morally relevant. See, for example, F Kamm, *Morality, Mortality Volume 1: Death and Whom to Save from It* (OUP 1993) 233-267.

[19]   K Kappel and P Sandøe, 'QALYs, Age and Fairness' (1992) *Bioethics* 297. In this paper, I will be concerned with these types of decisions, in other words, macro- or meso-allocation decisions about, for example, whether certain treatments should be funded or whether QALYs should be adjusted according to age, rather than about micro-allocation decisions where a choice needs to be made between individual patients.

[20]   I have emphasised that my treatment of the age-rationing debate is not comprehensive. This means that I do not aim to represent and assess all of the primary arguments for and against age-based rationing. I should, however, highlight that while one particularly well-known argument – Norman Daniels' prudential lifespan approach – is not mentioned here, I do consider Daniels' argument in section 5.1 as an objection to my application of the well-being approach (*Am I My Parent's Keeper: An Essay on Justice Between Young and Old* (OUP 1988); 2008 161-190).

[21]   See Kamm (note 18) 233-267, for a detailed discussion of the distinction between need and different kinds of urgency. For his challenges to prioritising health care resources for younger people, see J Harris, 'Does Justice Require That We Be Ageist?' (1994) *Bioethics* 74.

Persuasive arguments on both sides may convince us that this is a deep moral disagreement, which cannot be resolved through theory. It may be tempting to abandon theory for guidance in this case and to rely solely on consulting public opinion or procedural justice as a means to determine how much of a role age should play in rationing decisions. However, I think this would be discarding theory too quickly. Part of the problem with many arguments about age-rationing is that they use narrow understandings of justice, which only consider justice in terms of the influence of health care on health or one aspect of health and they are seldom contextualised within a broader theory of justice. Reference might be made to a general theory as justification for age-rationing decisions – for example, equality of opportunity for life-years is often defended with reference to justice understood as the equal opportunity for welfare.[22] However, usually little consideration is given to the interaction between this particular allocative principle and the broader theory. For example, firstly, there is a lack of explanation as to how indeed this age-rationing policy fits into a theory of equal opportunity for welfare. After all, equal opportunity for welfare in of itself does not necessarily imply that we should ration health care resources according to years lived, but rather according to the welfare or opportunities for welfare of the years lived. In this case, one could justify giving preference for resources to older people who suffer chronic mental health conditions, over mentally healthy younger people.[23] Secondly, the influence of age-rationing on other aspects of justice besides the distribution of health care, such as respect, social stigma and marginalisation, which I will discuss in greater detail in the multiple-dimensions test, and which at least have the potential to affect equality of opportunity for welfare, tends to be ignored.

In contrast, the well-being approach, places the justice of health care within the framework of a broader theory of social justice, and does not consider the influence of health care on health solely. As an example of how this approach can provide a framework for decision-making, I consider how it can be used to develop four tests for the justice of rationing decisions and apply these tests to the problem of explicit age-rationing.[24] These tests are:

1. the sufficiency test;
2. the multiple-determinants test;
3. the multiple-dimensions test; and
4. the moral-urgency test.

---

[22] RM Veatch, 'How Age Should Matter: Justice as the Basis for Limiting Care to the Elderly' in H Kuhse and P Singer (eds), *Bioethics: An Anthology*. (2nd edn, Blackwell 2006) 443.

[23] For an extended analysis of the conflict between welfare and age-rationing, see D Waring, 'Adequate Conscious Life and Age-Related Need: FM Kamm's Approach to Patient Selection' (2004) *Bioethics* 234.

[24] I think the tests of justice I have identified are over-simplifications of the density and complexity of the well-being approach, however, in order to demonstrate how the approach can be applied to a specific problem within the context of this paper, we may need to simplify.

The sufficiency test

As health is one dimension of well-being, justice could be said to require, among other things, distributive principle/s which aim to help individuals achieve a sufficient level of health. As health care is a socially distributed good which influences health (although as I will discuss later, by far not the only determinant of health and indeed perhaps not the most significant), justice should include fair principles for the allocation of health care resources, including guidance for prioritising health care resources which will indicate how it should be allocated when there are not enough resources to satisfy all legitimate claims for health care (in other words, when it needs to be rationed). A first test that a principle for health care allocation would need to pass is whether it contributes to achieving sufficiency in health as one particular dimension of justice.

Different principles could help to achieve sufficiency in health. When it comes to this specific dimension of justice, and this specific determinant of this dimension, we could have numerous options in terms of what is fair. As long as this principle helps to achieve sufficiency in health through the allocation of health care resources, it will pass the first test for the justice of allocation. Whichever principles pass this test could be considered to be candidates for allocating health care. Here, if there are competing views, and as long as the additional tests discussed below are also passed, then the well-being approach *may not be able to offer us any further guidance* and we would have to look to other reasons or methodologies for making more specific decisions and choosing between principles.

What the well-being approach does consider according to this test – i.e. how to distribute one social good in terms of trying to achieve justice in health – matches the narrow way in which justice is often assessed. The well-being approach, on this level, can account for the fact that there appear to be many principles for allocating health care that seem appropriately fair.

However, instead of leaving the disagreement at this level, the well-being approach can offer greater moral guidance by providing additional tests for the justice of particular principles. This is especially important as a principle may seem adequate in the effort to achieve sufficiency of health, but it could threaten well-being in other ways. In these cases, we might then have to discard a principle which at least, prima facie, and according to this first test, seems to be required or at least permitted by justice.

It seems that the age-rationing debate may be an example here. If viewed only at the level of this first test of justice, the well-being approach might be used to defend explicit age-rationing. Consider two principles for health care rationing. The first allocates health care resources according to urgency and refuses to distinguish between people, directly, according to age. The second allocates health care resources in such a way that priority is given to younger people, for example, by age-weighting QALYs. If we judged these two principles only according to whether or not they helped to achieve sufficiency in health, we could make a case for preferring explicit age-rationing in order to strive to achieve sufficiency in lifespan. In other words, we can say that we should prefer it if many people lived until a sufficient age, until they have had what has come to be called a 'fair innings' (however this may be defined – where to draw the line is clearly contentious) rather than that some live much longer, while others live much shorter lives.

Does the well-being approach support explicit age-rationing? Even considered only according to this first test, support for explicit age-rationing is limited. A principle of explicit age-rationing may seem defensible when we consider life-saving treatment – if we prioritise this kind of treatment for younger people we may help to achieve *sufficiency of lifespan*. However, sufficiency of health cannot mean sufficiency in lifespan alone – health consists of other significant aspects such as quality, and not merely length, of life. Thus if our aim is to achieve sufficiency in health we need to achieve more than merely sufficiency in lifespan. Consider for example, good mental health or pain relief as aspects of sufficiency of health. In these cases, explicit age-rationing is not justified – we may want to ration lifesaving treatment in a way that prioritises younger people but it seems wrong to think that justice demands that we should give younger people priority when it comes to pain relief, for example.[25] The argument we considered in favour of age-rationing considers that older people have lived a sufficient amount of years – which may be relevant when we are considering policies which influence how the opportunity for life-years is to be further distributed, but it is not relevant to many other aspects of health care.

Thus far the well-being approach appears consistent with support for age-based rationing when it comes to lifesaving treatment. However, before we can state this conclusively we need to judge this form of rationing according to the additional tests of fairness, and these may call the justice of age-rationing into question more substantively.

The multiple-determinants test

Each dimension of well-being will have numerous determinants that have significant effects on its development. The justice of an allocative principle must be considered within this context as we may find that once we no longer consider it in isolation the interplay between determinants may make us question whether it is indeed just, or whether it is indeed necessary to bring about sufficiency in health. According to the multiple-determinants test, a principle which aims at sufficiency in one dimension of well-being must be analysed to determine what effect it has on sufficiency in the light of how other determinants could also influence sufficiency.

In terms of health, much attention has been drawn recently to the many social determinants of health (besides health care). Not only have low income, low social status and reduced autonomy in one's job, for example, been shown to be correlated with ill health, health seems to follow a social gradient where each relative position in a social hierarchy is correlated to a corresponding level of health, in which the higher your position in the hierarchy, the better your health is likely to be.[26] The

---

[25] Powers and Faden (note 3) 164-5.
[26] See, for example, R Wilkinson, *Unhealthy Societies: The Afflictions of Inequality* (Routledge 1996); M Marmot, *Status Syndrome: How Your Social Standing Directly Affects Your Health* (Bloomsbury 2005); M Marmot and R Wilkinson (eds), *Social Determinants of Health* (2nd edn, OUP 2006).

theory is that these are actually determinants of health (rather than merely, as some would argue, the effects of health).[27]

The social determinants of health could challenge the need for funding health care at all – *for any age group*. Gopal Sreenivasan, for example, has argued that the social determinants of health seem to play such a strong role in determining life expectancy and health care seems to play such a trivial role, that an argument from the equal opportunity for welfare should actually recommend that we spend public money on determinants of health other than health care.[28] Even if this is true (and it is likely to require greater empirical support), there could be other reasons for providing universal health care besides sufficiency in lifespan. However, these claims about the significance of the social determinants of health could raise an empirical problem with age-rationing. Would it indeed achieve what it sets out to achieve? In other words, will it provide individuals with the opportunity to live a sufficiently long life? If health care is not a primary contributor to lifespan, then denying older people health care resources in favour of younger people seems pointless, and if indeed, denying older people health care could marginalise older people and threaten sufficiency in other dimensions of well-being, as I argue in the next section, then we would be causing injustices in certain dimensions of well-being without helping to achieve sufficiency in another dimension. If we consider the justice of age-rationing according to the multiple determinants test, a challenge is raised as to whether this form of rationing actually sets out to achieve what it aims to achieve, sufficiency in one aspect of health. This is by no means a conclusive criticism of age-rationing – more research is necessary to consider the impact that health care and other determinants of health actually have on lifespan. However, considering that age-rationing seems, at best, only relevant to sufficiency of lifespan, rather than other aspects of health, and that it may actually not even contribute greatly to achieving sufficiency of lifespan, the well-being approach raises some serious challenges for this form of rationing. In contrast, a narrow approach to justice, which focuses only on health care as a determinant of health, may miss this point entirely.

The multiple-dimensions test

A further test that an allocative principle would have to pass is a check in terms of its influence on dimensions of well-being other than the dimension for which it aims to achieve sufficiency. As health is only one dimension of well-being and as justice, according to the well-being approach, requires that we should be concerned with achieving sufficiency in all of the essential dimensions of well-being, it would be remiss not to consider how particular allocative decisions influence the other dimensions of well-being. Principles which help achieve sufficiency for one dimension may be all very well, but such principles must be brought into question if they threaten sufficiency in other dimensions of justice in the process.

---

[27] Marmot and Wilkinson (note 26).
[28] G Sreenivasan, 'Health Care and Equality of Opportunity' (2007) 37 *The Hastings Center Report* 21.

It is at this level that we can really see how the well-being approach manages to systematically and consistently incorporate a number of seemingly conflicting intuitions and principles of justice into one unified theory. Narrow approaches to justice tend to have an either/or approach here: either *this* principle for allocation is just or *this* conflicting principle is just, or perhaps some combination of the two is just. On the other hand, the well-being approach could claim that while on one level, considered in terms of one dimension or one determinant, particular allocative principles are fair, when considered in relation to other dimensions, they are not fair. We are not talking about two different kinds of justice here – rather we are talking about different dimensions of justice, which may conflict but which can be understood within the context of one unified conception of broader justice.

The multiple-dimensions test is particularly pertinent for age-rationing. While allocating health care according to age might seem fair in terms of the sufficiency of health (when we consider lifesaving treatment), it could undermine other dimensions of well-being. This could lead to a failure of sufficiency in these other dimensions and in turn, the interplay between dimensions of well-being and the cascading effects of the influence of certain determinants of well-being could result in further or reinforced threats to well-being, including health itself. The argument could look something like this: if we ration health care in such a way that people who are older are denied health care or, at least, have low priority in terms of receiving health care resources, two dimensions of well-being could be threatened: respect and attachment. Respect includes (1) being treated by others as a dignified moral being "deserving of equal moral concern" and (2) having self-respect, seeing oneself as "the moral equal of others".[29] Denying older people resources because of age would marginalise and devalue them, making them feel as if they are second-class citizens and thus being treated as if they do not deserve equal concern. As our self-respect is closely connected to respect from others, marginalisation could also impact on older people's self-respect, thus threatening respect further. The dimension of attachment – which includes a sense of solidarity with one's community – could also be threatened, as health care policies that marginalise older people could affect trust and co-operation between age-groups. In turn, explicit age-rationing could have a cascading effect on well-being: the stigma, anxiety and lack of trust that result from knowledge of age-rationing policies and from the failures in respect and attachment may even have a detrimental effect on older people's health.[30]

---

[29]   Powers and Faden (note 3) 22.

[30]   Although more empirical research is necessary, there is some evidence that social exclusion or marginalization can negatively impact on health. See, for example, M Shaw and others, 'Poverty, Social Exclusion and Minorities' in M Marmot and R Wilkinson (note 26). There is also a suspicion that chronic anxiety (which could be caused by stigma and exclusion) negatively impacts on health. See, for example, E Brunner and M Marmot, 'Social Organization, Stress and Health' in M Marmot and R Wilkinson (note 26) and P C Strike and A Steptoe, 'Psychosocial Factors in the Development of Coronary Artery Disease' (2004) 46 *Progress in Cardiovascular Diseases* 337. However, the evidence for the influence of anxiety on health is inconsistent: H Kuper and others, 'Systematic Review of Prospective Cohort Studies of Psychosocial Factors in the Etiology and Prognosis of Coronary Heart Disease' (2002) 2 *Seminars in Vascular Medicine* 267. There is also a lack of standardization as to what the terms 'social exclusion' and 'anxiety' might mean. This means

After applying the third test for justice, we now have a conflict. On the one hand, we aim to achieve sufficiency of health. Explicit age-rationing could be defended as one possible means for achieving one part (sufficiency of lifespan) of one determinant (health care) of one dimension of well-being (health). On the other hand, using explicit age-rationing to try to achieve sufficiency of health may lead to threats to several other dimensions of well-being, including, through the interaction and complex causal relationship between determinants and dimensions of well-being, health itself. Powers and Faden do not make explicit how conflicts between dimensions of justice should be weighed against each other. They do, however, directly refer to explicit age-rationing, and claim that it is ruled out, among other reasons, because it threatens well-being in terms of respect and attachment.[31] The question we need to understand more fully however is why injustices that lead from age-rationing outweigh the potential injustice of some younger people not achieving sufficiency of lifespan.

We can start to approach this question by considering the way in which the well-being approach ranks the moral urgency of different cases.

The moral urgency test

An additional test of justice implied by the well-being approach is one that compares the moral urgency of inequalities or injustices. It needs to be emphasised that this is an instance of *non-ideal justice.* Justice, according to the well-being approach, means achieving sufficiency in each of the dimensions of well-being. In the case we are considering, it seems that sufficiency cannot be achieved in each dimension of well-being. Justice then, as it should be, cannot be achieved. Under these circumstances, there will inevitably be some unfairness. What we are looking for here is not 'full' justice, as we would expect it under ideal circumstances, but something of a second-best. However, this does not mean that there are no better or worse answers in terms of justice – although we cannot achieve 'full' justice we can try to aim for what seems to be the fairest solution considering the circumstances.

In section 3, I described the framework that can be used for assessing the urgency of injustices. The framework implied four levels of moral urgency, and we can use these levels as a guide to compare conflicting injustices. At the most basic level, injustices occur where one determinant (such as health care) threatens one dimension of well-being (health), and in which there are no other causes of or consequences for justice. At the second and third level, greater moral scrutiny is required for situations where more than one determinant threatens a single dimension of well-being, or where one determinant threatens more than one dimension. The implication, one might be tempted to argue, is that these latter cases at these levels, outweigh the former at the first, most basic, level-cases where there is one failure due to one determinant are outweighed by cases where one determinant is

---

that research will require more precise definitions of these terms. See, for example, Morgan and others, 'Social Exclusion and Mental Health: Conceptual and Methodological Review' (2007) 191 *British Journal of Psychiatry* 477, on the different ways in which social exclusion has been defined.

[31] Powers and Faden (note 3) 162.

under extreme threat or where many dimensions are under threat. I think this gives us *some* guidance about which injustices we should be more or less concerned about, and it *could* be used to weigh up options where principles for achieving sufficiency clash. However, it definitely cannot provide us with any straight-forward answers, and indeed it shows that there is some challenge to articulating how to determine what is morally more urgent if we are only comparing the first three levels.

Clearly, the number of dimensions of well-being threatened must play *some* role: "If deprivation in one essential dimension of well-being below a level of sufficiency is unjust, deprivations of still more dimensions of well-being below sufficiency levels are additional injustices creating particular moral urgency".[32] Furthermore, the degree to which sufficiency is threatened is also relevant – a dimension is more likely to fall below sufficiency, or it will fall more severely below the level of sufficiency if it is severely threatened and particularly if it is threatened by more than one determinant. However, these cannot give us precise and fixed rules on how to establish moral urgency. This is the case for several reasons.

Firstly, it will not always be clear that the choice made should favour cases where more than one dimension is under threat or where a dimension is under threat from numerous determinants. In other words, it is not clear that injustices at the second and third levels should necessarily outweigh injustices at the first level. What if we have to choose between cases where one dimension is affected so gravely (even if by only one determinant) that it would be extremely difficult to rectify in comparison to cases where two dimensions only just drop below the level of sufficiency? In this example it is not clear that we should choose to favour two dimensions of well-being over one: we could make a case to claim that it would be morally more urgent to ensure that individuals do not fall so far below the threshold for sufficiency that it would be extremely challenging to help them to ever achieve sufficiency in this dimension.

Secondly, there is something contingent about claiming that it is the *number* of dimensions that are morally relevant considering that which dimensions we should include and how many to include are open to debate. Consider, for example, that Martha Nussbaum originally identified 'affiliation' as a central capability which included both respect and attachment.[33] Powers and Faden, however, have split her category of 'affiliation' to create two categories, 'respect' and 'attachment'. If we were judging the severity of an injustice according to the *number* of dimensions, Nussbaum's theory would then give us a different answer, in terms of moral urgency, to Powers and Faden's theory, although it is not clear why this is a moral difference rather than merely a difference of definition.[34] There could even be a danger here of adjusting or choosing dimensions of justice purely to suit particular policy preferences. The primary point is that guidance from the second and third

---

[32] ibid 67.

[33] M Nussbaum, *Women and Human Development: The Capabilities Approach* (CUP 2000) 78-80.

[34] I am not saying that it is impossible to show that we should indeed include both respect and attachment as separate capabilities or dimensions of well-being but rather that we need to be careful about claims which relate to the quantity of dimensions that are affected.

levels of moral urgency, at least as described here, may not be able to provide us with a clear answer for how to weigh up injustices against the first level of moral urgency. Indeed, this seems to be why Powers and Faden claim these scenarios are subject to greater moral scrutiny, rather than claiming that they are indeed necessarily morally more urgent.[35] If we aim to use the well-being approach to provide substantial moral guidance to health care decision-making, this is at least one aspect that will require greater analysis – it seems that more work needs to be done to try to clarify how and why trade-offs should be made when these conflicts of injustice occur.

However, these inconclusive considerations do not exhaust what the well-being approach can tell us about moral urgency. The fourth and most severe level of moral urgency implied by the well-being approach gives us clearer answers. In these cases, systematic and multiple overlapping determinants threaten multiple dimensions, which in turn reinforce or worsen failures of sufficiency, or threaten new dimensions of well-being. These kinds of cases identify who is most disadvantaged in society. Although identifying these cases will not necessarily help us with developing specific principles for the allocation of particular goods, such as health care, they can provide guidance in terms of assessing and selecting allocative principles. For example, we could argue that principles for health care allocation should, at the least, not compound the disadvantage of those who are worst off. It is for this reason that Powers and Faden, for example, rejected targeted screening for the groups at greatest risk groups of HIV/AIDS.[36] As these groups tended to be primarily women of colour, who often suffer systematic disadvantage, they believed that targeting them for screening would stigmatise them further. Here a particular rationing policy was rejected on the grounds that it would interfere with respect and attachment – two dimensions of well-being already under systematic threat for the group in question. The good that the rationing policy could do for sufficiency of health seems to be outweighed on the grounds that it is morally more urgent to counteract the multiple and systematic threats to well-being suffered by the most disadvantaged than to achieve the most cost-effective outcome in terms of this particular health policy. Considering that systematic disadvantage and exclusion may impact negatively on health, as mentioned in the previous section, one could even use the indirect threat to health implied by targeted screening as one of the justifications for why it should not be adopted.

Even here, however, the decision made will not necessarily be straight-forward – it is likely, at least under certain circumstances to require interpretation and will probably need to be made on a case-by-case basis. Greater analysis would still need to be given to establish how to make trade-offs. Therefore, for example, we would need to consider whether the amount of individuals under threat makes a difference, and if so, how this should be factored into the trade-off decision. However, unlike the previous considerations about moral urgency, it is clearer that systematic and

---

35   Powers and Faden (note 3) 6.
36   ibid vii-viii.

multiple failures of sufficiency could often be said to outweigh singular threats to one dimension of well-being or more minor threats to a number of dimensions of well-being.

If we consider explicit age-rationing in the context of the test for moral urgency, the well-being approach seems to rule out directly prioritising health care resources for younger people at the expense of older people. There are two ways in which the discussion in this section could be said to lead us to this conclusion but one of these ways is dubious, at least in terms of what we have established here, while the second means is more decisive. The unsatisfactory answer would be that we could weigh up the benefits for health implied by age-rationing against the negative impact that age-rationing would have on more than one dimension of well-being for older people and claim that age-rationing is disallowed as their situation would then fall under the third most urgent level of concern. As I explained, however, it is not definitive that cases where only one dimension is threatened should be dismissed as less urgent than cases where two, or more, are threatened. A more conclusive answer comes from the claim that policies of explicit age-rationing will trigger a cascade of interactive negative effects on the well-being of older people, including failures at respect, attachment and possibly even health itself. What we would be saying is that age-rationing seems to disadvantage older people more than younger people would be disadvantaged if age-rationing is not put in place. One could also argue that where the elderly are indeed already a vulnerable and marginalised group in society, health care policies which marginalise them even further would compound their disadvantage. Here we are not simply comparing the quantity of dimensions under threat, but trying to assess the overall severity of the threat to well-being, including the number of dimensions under threat as well as their influence on creating new threats to well-being, and the additional ways in which the population group in question could be said to be already suffering threats to their well-being.

This does not mean, however, that this claim is not subject to change. If extreme pressure is put on resources due to large numbers of older, retired people in a society, younger people may be more at risk of suffering multiple threats to multiple dimensions well-being. The moral urgency of addressing the disadvantages faced by younger people would increase if their well-being as a group can be seen to be under severe threat. If this does occur, the moral urgency could shift and we could claim that it is morally more urgent to address the threats to sufficiency faced by younger people. Considering trends in declining birth rates and increases in life expectancy, this is an acute threat to justice we should indeed be vigilant about.[37] Subsequently, we can say that although it seems as if the well-being approach would rule out explicit age-based rationing, at least under certain empirical conditions, this does not mean that this is a universal, fixed claim about health care allocation. We would need to continuously monitor whether and how and according to which dimensions of well-being sufficiency is being threatened – what we find, should

---

[37]   Daniels (note 2) 162-4.

influence how we view the moral urgency of principles of allocation. As mentioned previously, however, the social determinants of health challenge the idea that prioritising health care resources for the young will actually make a difference to sufficiency of lifespan, and thus even if we agreed that it was most morally urgent to address the needs of younger individuals for resources, it is not necessarily clear that age-rationing would be an appropriate measure. Thus, the well-being approach may require or be consistent with age-rationing only if younger individuals can be shown to have the most morally urgent needs in terms of sufficiency of well-being *and* if it is clear that age-rationing will indeed help to bring about sufficiency of lifespan.

5. Objections from the lifespan approach and separate spheres argument

In this section, I consider two objections to my description of the well-being approach and its application to age-rationing. The first is an objection specifically to the claims that I have made about the justice of age rationing, while the second is an objection to the way in which the well-being approach ignores the boundaries of distributive spheres.

The prudential lifespan approach

A potential objection to the way in which I have described age-rationing is that I have (unnecessarily) pitted age-groups against each other – this creates the impression that older people are being treated unjustly. Norman Daniels claims, however, that instead of considering the problem of rationing as a conflict between older and younger people, we should adopt a 'lifespan' approach to resource allocation.[38] This means that "We should allocate resources prudently to protect health and thus opportunity at each stage of our lives. The basic idea is that, since we all age, we should take as a model of what is fair between age groups what it is prudent for us to do for ourselves at each stage of life".[39] Under exceptional circumstances, when "Very expensive or very scarce life-extending services can be provided to those who have reached a normal life expectancy only by giving fewer services to the young", direct age-based rationing could be justified. It is fair because people are treated equally across a lifespan – although individuals might be denied resources at an older age, those same individuals would have been given preferential treatment for resources at a younger age. Once one reaches a 'sufficient' age, what Daniels refers to as a normal life expectancy, resources may then be denied to help someone who has not yet reached this age and thus each person's chances of reaching a normal life expectancy are maximized.[40]

Practically, policies based on Daniels' view and that of the well-being approach are unlikely to differ substantially. Daniels claims that age-based rationing would

---

[38] Daniels (note 2) 161-190. See also N Daniels, *Am I My Parents' Keeper?: An Essay on Justice Between the Young and the Old* (OUP 1988) and N Daniels, *Just Health Care* (CUP 1985).

[39] Daniels (note 2) 161-2.

[40] This is fair because it treats all people equally over the course of their lives "and it would benefit them each by maximizing the chances of reaching a normal life expectancy", ibid 179.

only be acceptable under exceptional circumstances when indeed we would be limited to choosing between life-saving treatment for older and younger people. Perhaps under such circumstances the well-being approach would advocate the same age-based rationing – there may be circumstances, I argued in the previous section, where providing younger people with health care resources may seem more morally urgent than providing those resources to older people.

Despite the likelihood that practically these two perspectives on the justice of age-based rationing may be very similar, they have fundamentally different understandings of what is just. As such, Daniels' claims are less strictly an objection to the approach I present here as simply an alternative description of what is just. The problem with Daniels' description from the perspective of the well-being approach is that what is fair should not be described as a matter of how prudent individuals would allocate resources – justice, rather, means sufficiency is achieved in each of at least six objective measures of well-being. The argument I highlighted in section 4 is a claim that respect and attachment will be under threat if older people are denied or are given diminished priority for health care resources. In the light of this claim, whether prudent individuals would agree that they should forego expensive and scarce treatments at an older age is primarily irrelevant. Even if prudent individuals did indeed do so, or more extremely and this is not Daniels' argument, even if individuals actually consented to giving up resources in favour of a younger generation, the state, as a matter of justice, should not institute policies which marginalise older people and which could cause them severe anxiety, thus threatening sufficiency of respect and attachment. In this case, the fact that it may be prudent for me to agree to forego resources at an older age could be considered to be a *pragmatic* solution to the problem of scarce resources – it is not, according to the well-being approach, a fair way of allocating resources.

One could try to turn Daniels' argument into an empirically-based objection to the well-being approach. The claim would then be that because prudent individuals would agree that resources should be spread across their lifespan, and thus they should agree to forego expensive and scarce treatments once they have (at least potentially) benefited from this allocation by reaching a normal life expectancy, they would *not* feel marginalised, and respect and attachment would thus not be under threat from policies of age-rationing. If this were true, then the well-being approach might concede, according to its own description of justice, that age-rationing was indeed fair, at least under certain circumstances. It is not clear to me, however, that this empirical objection is true however. Even if we believed that theoretically prudent individuals under a 'veil of ignorance' were likely to agree to allocate resources in a particular way,[41] this does not mean that in reality, older people would not feel devalued and anxious if the state imposed policies which denied them significant social goods.

---

[41]   Consider Daniels' discussion ibid 173-4, of how we would need to pretend not to know how old we are to avoid bias when considering what a fair health-care insurance policy would be.

Indeed, it seems to me that older people who did not require lifesaving treatment or expensive resources at a younger age are *particularly* likely to feel marginalised due to age-rationing according to Daniels' description of the prudential approach. Although Daniels claims that he is presenting age-rationing in a way that would not pit age groups against each other, in reality, I think this is misleading. Perhaps it is prudent of me to agree that if I 'use up' an allotted fixed sum of resources at a younger age, then I should be denied expensive resources once I have reached a normal life expectancy (it may be prudent but it is still not just, at least not according to the well-being approach). This is entirely different, however, to agreeing that *even if I do not use expensive social resources at a younger age, I should still be denied expensive resources once I have reached a normal life expectancy.* In this case, it seems fair to assume that it would be reasonable to feel aggrieved, even marginalised, by policies that dictated I should be denied health care resources. I may feel so particularly as it seems that in this case it is not a question of spreading resources fairly across my lifespan – rather I am denied resources (that I did not need at a younger age) merely because I am unlucky enough to be in competition for those resources with someone who is younger than I am (more specifically, someone who has not reached a 'normal' life expectancy). Subsequently, I do not agree that Daniels' prudential lifespan approach successfully challenges my description of the well-being approach's stance on age-rationing.

The separate spheres objection

An additional objection to the well-being approach, one could argue, is that it violates a 'separate spheres' approach to justice. Accordingly, justice consists of separate spheres (e.g. health care or health; education) which should each be subject to their own principles of justice rather than being subject to general principles of justice which regulate justice overall.[42] For example, according to this objection, we should determine who is worst off in the sphere of health care by focusing on who has the worst 'health'. Being badly off in other spheres of justice, e.g. respect or education, should not come into play in determining who is badly off in terms of health and thus how health care resources should be distributed. So, for example, when it comes to age-rationing the point is that we should focus only on the sickest or those who have had the least opportunity for life-years, as each of these are relevant to health. The problem then with the well-being sufficiency approach and its application to age-rationing is that it considers justice broadly speaking, and it includes other spheres of justice, in determining the fairness of health care allocation.

The separate spheres objection points to the central difference between considering the justice of health care allocation according to a direct approach or an indirect approach, in other words, to a broad theory of justice. Although a direct approach

---

[42] M Walzer, *Spheres of Justice: A Defense of Pluralism and Equality* (Basic Books 1983); Kamm (note 18); Kamm, 'Deciding Whom to Help, Health-Adjusted Life Years and Disabilities' in S Anand, F Peter and A Sen (eds), *Public Health, Ethics, and Equity* (OUP 2004); D Brock, 'Priority to the Worse Off in Health-Care Resource Prioritization' in R Rhodes, M. P. Battin, and A. Silvers (eds) *Medicine and Social Justice: Essays on the Distribution of Health Care* (OUP 2002).

is not necessarily related to an argument for separate spheres, such an argument could be said to underlie many direct approaches. Thus, according to this argument what I refer to (and criticise), a 'narrow' approach to justice, could simply be seen to be a necessary focus on the separate sphere of health care. As I mentioned with Daniels' prudential lifespan approach, this is not so much an objection to the well-being approach as simply a different (rival) approach to the justice of allocation. We could say that the well-being approach aims to show precisely why we should not use a separate spheres approach. While we may be able to identify somewhat separate spheres (separate dimensions of well-being, e.g. health, and separate determinants of well-being, e.g. health care) we cannot view them exclusively as separate spheres as they influence each other and overlap. It seems no objection to the well-being approach to claim that it should not consider other dimensions of well-being such as respect and attachment, when the reason why the well-being sufficiency approach does consider these is precisely because health care influences them. The point from the well-being approach is that spheres of justice are not entirely separate and thus should not be treated as such.

When considering certain examples, the separate spheres objection seems to have much intuitive force. However, on examination we will find this force presents a problem to certain approaches to health care allocation, such as a utilitarian approach which considers only *total* well-being (meaning different dimensions of well-being are not distinguished), while it does not apply against the well-being approach. For example, if we consider only total well-being when thinking about who is worst off and allow this to determine how we allocate health care resources then those who are worst off overall, such as for example the poor, may be prioritised over people who are much sicker, but who are better off overall. We may in fact exhaust all of our resources on trying to improve the lot of the poor before treating anyone who is actually ill. This seems problematic – although we may be concerned with the poor and alleviating their lot, we tend not to believe that we should focus on the poor at the expense of providing people who are very ill (no matter how badly or well off they are in total) with health care resources. This example has much intuitive force – it seems to support the idea that we should consider only the unhealthy when we think about health care and that we should not consider other ways in which individuals could be worst off. However, this is a mistake – although this example may imply that there is something wrong with considering total well-being (exclusively) when distributing health care resources, it does not follow from this that we should adopt a separate spheres approach to justice.

The well-being sufficiency approach would agree with the separate spheres argument that we should not distribute social goods purely on the basis of who is worst off overall. Justice is defined as achieving sufficiency in *each* of the dimensions of well-being, thus the distribution of social goods is judged according to whether or not it helps or hinders achieving sufficiency in whichever dimensions of well-being it has an influence. Subsequently, the distribution of health care should be considered, not according to who is worst off overall, but rather according to how it influences each dimension of well-being on which it does indeed have an impact.

We may find that achieving sufficiency in some of the dimensions of well-being come into conflict with each other and thus priorities need to be set, e.g. potentially in the case of whether age-based rationing is fair. In these cases we could determine moral urgency according to which distributions of the particular social good in question will lead to greater 'overall' well-being, but only if this is understood according to how sufficiency will be affected for each particular dimension of well-being which could be jeopardised by distribution. It will not consist of merely comparing distributions according to the total well-being they bring about. Powers and Faden emphasise a similar point in their discussion of the separate spheres argument maintaining that while this argument is indeed correct in its claim that certain factors are morally irrelevant, this does not imply that we should then apply a "blanket exclusion of everything but health benefits", as we will then indeed be disregarding a number of morally relevant aspects.[43] Subsequently, it seems that where the separate spheres approach does indeed seem to have a footing, it provides no objection to the well-being approach.

6. Conclusion

Theories of justice are indeed limited in terms of the moral guidance they provide for specific allocative questions such as health care rationing. However, we can under-estimate the guidance which they provide. While the notion of justice is often dealt with narrowly in the health care literature, the well-being approach can provide substantial moral guidance for some aspects of health care rationing precisely *because* it recognises the multifaceted nature of justice. From this approach, we can elicit four tests for the justice of health care allocation. Applied to the debate about age-rationing these tests imply that explicit age-rationing principles for allocation are, on the whole, not just. I do not claim, however, that my discussion of the well-being approach provides a comprehensive solution to the problems posed by an ageing society – this is clearly not the case. However, for the purposes of this paper, the age-rationing debate provides an illuminating example of how a broad theory of justice can provide moral guidance for rationing decisions within a systematic framework for social justice.

---

[43]   Powers and Faden (note 3) 168.

Chapter V

Organ Procurement and Allocation: Tragic Choices and Utilitarian Redefinitions of Death

Jean-Marc Piret

1. Introduction

Who do we save from death if not everybody can be saved? In conflict and catastrophe medicine people have been familiar for a long time (at least since the first World War) with the notion that tragic choices have to be made in situations when the lives of some people can be saved, but sometimes only at the expense of the lives of other people. On the battlefield and on catastrophe sites, where death and severe injuries are omnipresent, medical personnel have to choose whom to save from death first and who is going to be left dying because of the lack of personnel or other medical means. Those with only a small chance of survival are left untreated (except with analgesics if possible) and those whose injuries are not life-threatening will have to wait because priority goes to those with severe injuries and good chances of survival on the condition that they are treated rapidly. 'Triage' as a technique of prioritizing patients for treatment, has become a standard procedure in situations of mass-casualty and constitutes an essential part of any training in battlefield and catastrophe medicine.[1] Because of military imperatives in war-situations the triage rationale is not always to save as many patients as possible or to treat those who were wounded on the battlefield first.[2] In those types of exceptional situations strategic imperatives and consequentialist calculations are sometimes considered to legitimately trump the individualistic principles of Hippocratic medical ethics directed to the well-being of the individual whose medical need should be the only relevant consideration.

Because of the evolution of medical technology, triage, originally occurring only in situations of medical exception, has become more widespread and in some medical disciplines it has even become the normal daily practice. The number of medical treatments that are live-saving or stabilizing the medical condition of the patient but that are not available for everyone in need of them, because of the sophisticated and

---

[1]   See for example the interesting entry 'triage' on Wikipedia.

[2]   In World War II penicillin, which was very scarce, was sometimes given in priority to patients with venereal diseases at the expense of those injured in combat because the former could be sent more rapidly to the battlefield. G Winslow, *Triage and Justice* (Berkeley 1982), cited in V Schmidt (note 3).

expensive medical technology involved or because of other conditions of scarcity, is growing. Sometimes conditions of shortage can be repaired by increasing the numbers of medical personnel or the financial resources for the acquisition of medical technologies. But when this is not possible scarcity becomes structural and the system of prioritizing that designates the patients who will be treated and those who will have to wait (even if this means that they will eventually die) becomes the normal practice.[3] The consequence is that not everything that is medically feasible and that is needed by patients can be provided to them due to the lack of money or because of the lack of sufficient medical resources such as machines for kidney dialysis, intensive care units or organs needed for transplantation. Treatments will then be rationed and some therapies withheld to patients who would otherwise benefit from them.

In such situations of structural medical scarcity physicians are confronted with problems of distributive justice for which their traditional medical deontology, which teaches them to help their patients in the best of their ability (the principle of beneficence) and above all not to harm them (*primum non nocere* – the principle of non-maleficence), was not designed. The scarcity of medical resources compels medical practitioners to ration treatments on the ground of criteria that are (at least partially) non-medical, such as to treat in priority those under a certain age, or even worse, those with sufficient ability to pay, as it is practiced in the US where patients may have to undergo a 'wallet biopsy' (a scrutiny into the patients financial standing) before getting the medical treatment they need. During the eighties doctors in the UK told many of their patients who suffered from renal failure and who were above age 65 that they could not be helped anymore by medicine while in reality they had to be turned away because of insufficient dialysis capacity.[4]

Decisions of medical rationing whereby one patient gets the treatment and another patient who is also in need of it and who would also benefit from it, is dismissed until further notice (which may never come for him), are sometimes concealed behind seemingly medical reasons. This can be the case when a patient is told that the presumed chance that the treatment (for example a transplantation) will be successful is too small, while the real reason for dismissing him is that the treatment will benefit 'more' to another patient (in the given example: the prognosis of how long the transplant will function is better when the organ is transplanted to another patient). The latter criterion is not medical but utilitarian. It does not focus on the well-being of every individual patient, but compares the presumed outcomes of different patients in case a certain medical treatment is carried out. There can be no *medical justification* for the decision that, due to the pursuance of maximization of the aggregated utility of a given quantum of medical resources (for example a pool of organs for transplantation); individual patients are not given the therapy that would benefit to their medical condition.[5] Justification for that kind of decision

---

[3]   Volker H Schmidt, 'Veralltäglichung der Triage' in W Lübbe (ed), *Tödliche Entscheidung. Allokation von Leben und Tod in Zwangslagen* (Paderborn 2004) 77-103.
[4]   ibid 91.
[5]   ibid 95.

is extra-medical and grounded in a consequentialist ethics that puts the aggregated utility of the delivered output of a subdivision of the health care system first in situations where the doctor's duty to prevent and remove harms (the principle of *beneficence*) cannot be applied to every patient in need of a certain therapy.

The question that rises here is whether this decision-making on extra-medical grounds is ethically acceptable and compatible with the legal principle of equal treatment and with the primacy of individual medical need which is central in European health law. Some ethicists think that in situations of crisis such as the growing organ scarcity, the doctor's duty is not only directed to his individual patient, but he has also a responsibility towards the larger group of patients that have a comparable organ failure, for every decision regarding transplantation of this individual patient has consequences for the chances of another patient who is also in need. So the ideal of commutative justice, giving each individual what is due to him, cannot be the exclusive value in a situation of growing shortage and hence considerations of distributive justice, taking into account efforts directed at maximizing the aggregated utility of the actual organ pool, may legitimately interfere with traditional medical ethics.

2. *Legal philosophy, ethics and tragic choices*[6]

Since antiquity philosophy and ethics have struggled with the question of ethical and legal responsibility in extreme situations where the life of some person can only be saved by causing the death of some other person (by letting a person die or omitting to save him). In medieval canon law the view that necessity made the prohibited permissible because necessity knows no law (*neccesitas non habit legem*) was applied in a casuistic manner. Cicero,[7] Lactance,[8] Pufendorf,[9] Kant,[10] Fichte[11] and Anselm Feuerbach[12] all commented on the problem of the 'plank of Carneades': May a shipwrecked sailor who will otherwise drown push off an exhausted colleague from a plank (that can only hold one person) thereby causing the death of the other one in order to save his own life? Should he be punished after being rescued?[13] One

---

[6]   On the problem of tragic choices from a viewpoint of law and economics, cf. Guido Calabresi and Philip Bobbitt, *Tragic Choices, The Conflicts Society Confronts in the Allocation of Tragically Scarce Resources* (Norton & Company 1978).

[7]   Cicero, *De Oficiis* (Walter Miller tr, Loeb edn., HUP 1913) Book III, 90.

[8]   Lactantius, *Divine Institutes*, 5, 17 cf. http://www.newadvent.org/fathers/07015.htm.

[9]   Samuel von Pufendorf, *Über die Pflicht des Menschen und des Bürgers nach dem Gesetz der Natur* (Insel Verlag 1994) chapter 5.

[10] Immanuel Kant, *Metaphysik der Sitten*, ('Anhang zur Einleitung in die Rechtslehre, II: Das Not-recht') *Werke in Zehn Bänden*, W Weischedel Hrsg. (Darmstadt 1983) B.7, 343.

[11] J. G. Fichte *Foundations of Natural Right* Edited by: Frederick Neuhouser, translated by: Michael Baur (CUP 2000) II § 19 I.

[12] Anselm von Feuerbach, *Lehrbuch des gemeinen in Deutschland gültigen peinlichen Rechts* (Goldbach 1997).

[13] Kant (note 10) gives the following answer: 'there can be no *penal law* that would assign the death penalty to someone in a shipwreck who, in order to save his own life, shoves another, whose life is equally in danger, off a plank on which he had saved himself. For the punishment threatened by the law could not be greater than the loss of his own life. A penal law of this sort could not

of the most difficult problems in penal law has always been the question whether a person who causes the death of someone else by saving his own life should be granted an emergency excuse.[14]

But since this classical discussion, many related problems have raised, especially in bioethics. The ethical core of some of these problems has been exemplified in different variations of the so called 'trolley problem'.[15] In this thought experiment a trolley which has gone out of control, is speeding toward five persons tied to the tracks. If the trolley hits them, they will all die. We can switch a button in order to divert the trolley to another track, where it will hit one other person and cause his death. Is it ethically allowed or do we even have an obligation to push the button? Is it better to save five people than only one? In the 'fat man variation' of this thought experiment we can only stop the trolley by pushing a fat man who is standing on a bridge above the tracks.[16] This will kill him but save the five. The difference between the two cases is that in the second case, killing the fat man is an intentional part of the plan to rescue the five while in the first case one does not intend to harm anybody, but unfortunately our intentional act to save the five will have the (non-intended but foreseeable) side-effect of killing the one on the other track.

Allowing to push the button to save the five in the first case would be an application of the Aquinian doctrine of double effect which says that you may act in a way that is good but that also causes some bad side-effects.[17] In contrast with that, pushing the fat man on the tracks is intrinsically wrong even if it will save the lives of the

---

have the effect intended, since a threat of an ill that is still *uncertain* (death by a judicial verdict) cannot outweigh the fear of an ill that is *certain* (drowning). Hence the deed of saving one's life by violence is not to be judged *inculpable* (*inculpabile*) but only as *unpunishable* (*impunibile*)...' Transl. by Mary Gregor (CUP 1991) 235-236. For Kant the act of causing the other shipwrecked's death can not be *justified* but only be *excused* as a side-effect of saving one's life. Joachim Hruschka, 'Rechtfertigungs- und Entschuldigungsgründe: Dass Brett des Carneades bei Gentz und bei Kant' (1991) 138 *Goltdammer's Archiv für Strafrecht* 1-10.

[14] David Cohen, 'The Development of the Modern Doctrine of Necessity: A Comparative Critique' (1985) 4 *Journal for History of Law*; Alexander Aichele, 'Was ist und wozu taugt das Brett des Karneades? Wesen und ursprünglicher Zweck des Paradigmas der europäischen Notrechtslehre' (2003) Vol. 11 *Annual Review of Law and Ethics*; Weyma Lübbe, 'Lebensnotstand – Ende der Normativität? Untersuchung einer Grauzone im Unrecht des Tötens' in W Lübbe (note 3) 104-121. See also the commented bibliography in Lübbe's book.

[15] Philippa Foot, 'The Problem of Abortion and the Doctrine of the Double Effect' in *Virtues and Vices* (OUP 1978); Judith Jarvis Thomson, 'Killing, Letting Die, and the Trolley Problem' (1976) 59 *The Monist* 204-217; see also Bonnie Steinbock & Alastair Norcross (eds), *Killing and Letting Die* (Fordham University Press 1994).

[16] Someone who falls from the bridge will inevitably land on the tracks. The fat man weighs enough to stop the trolley while you don't. So a heroic act of self-sacrifice in order to save the five is not an option. The premises of this version of the thought experiment are that all this is certain and that you know it.

[17] Thomas Aquinas, *Summa Theologiae*, IIa-IIae Q. 64, art. 7. Aquinas underscores the importance of proportionality: the intended good should outweigh the bad side-effect. Later explicitations of the doctrine point out that the bad side-effect may not be an intrinsic part of the plan aiming at the realisation of the intended good. That is why the bad side-effect should result from the realisation of the intended good and not the other way around. Another important point is that the bad side-effect has to be unavoidable when realising the good and that the harm that it will realise should be minimized if possible. For a succinct but relatively thorough discussion (and bibliography) of the doctrine of double effect see *Stanford Encyclopaedia of Philosophy* at http://plato.stanford.edu/

five. The two versions of the trolley problem exemplify the classical distinction in ethical theory between killing and letting die: killing the fat man to save the five is not allowed, letting the one person on the alternative track die as an unavoidable side effect of saving the five is permissible although highly regrettable. Act-utilitarians would disagree with this on the ground that saving the five by pushing the fat man is also justifiable because the sum total of utilities produced by that act is greater than the sum total utilities produced by the alternative act the agent could have performed in its place. But rule utilitarians could oppose that with the argument that in the long run the maximization of the total welfare of society would be served more by a rule that absolutely prohibits killing as a means to achieve some greater good. The rule-utilitarian then would not have prohibited such an act because he thinks that it is intrinsically evil, but because he believes that the prohibition would lead to a better overall outcome in his calculation of utility. Because of that, from a Judeo-Christian as well as from a classical Kantian deontological point of view, consequentialism is not an ethics but a strategy of maximisation of useful consequences and as such it can not found absolute prohibitions or an absolute duty to refrain from certain acts. Consequentialists can always be blackmailed to do something terrible (for example to torture or to kill) in order to prevent something that constitutes even a greater potential harm.[18] Non-consequentialists do not think that we have always a duty to produce the best state of affairs because they determine the rightness or wrongness of an act on the ground of valuings (such as 'intrinsic goodness' or 'evil character') from which may derive categorical obligations or prohibitions trumping the prima facie duty to produce the best overall consequences.

Now consider another version of the trolley problem that makes it relevant for the paradigm of cadaveric organ donation:[19] in this version one can divert the out-of-control trolley speeding toward one person tied to the tracks to another track where it will hit and mutilate an already dead body from a person that accidentally fell from a bridge. Suppose that a doctor declared the person dead, but that for one reason or another he cannot be removed from the tracks. Suppose further that this person filled out a form while being alive stating his wish (possibly based on religious grounds) to be buried intact. Is it permissible or even morally obligatory

---

entries/double-effect/; see also Richard A McCormick and Paul Ramsey (eds) *Doing Evil to Achieve Good* (Loyola University Press 1978).

[18] Robert Spaemann, 'Die slechte Lehre vom guten Zweck' in Weyma Lübbe (note 3) 173-181. Another type of critique was formulated by Bernard Williams, who thinks that consequentialism alienates a person from his moral feelings and from his actions. Consequentialism will always succeed in justifying a bad job by an actor, even when the consequence of refraining from that bad job consists in the actors allowing *someone else* to perform an even worse job. According to Williams consequentialism is indifferent to whether a state of affairs consists in what I do, or is *produced* by what I do or omit. For consequentialists the only thing that matters is the overall outcome of our actions. B Williams, 'A critique of utilitarianism' in JJC Smart and B Williams, *Utilitarianism for & against* (CUP 1973). In that respect see also the debate about the 'ticking time bomb' scenario and the possible consequentialist justification of torture in order to prevent terrorism. David Luban, 'Liberalism, Torture, and the Ticking Bomb' (2005) *Virginia Law Review* 1425-61.

[19] Adam J Kolber, 'A Matter of Priority: Transplanting Organs Preferentially to registered Donors' (Spring 2003) *Rutgers Law Review* 693.

to divert the trolley? The relevant analogy with cadaveric organ donation is that in both situations a life (and in organ donation sometimes more than one) can be saved by violating the integrity of a dead body against the declared will of the deceased. The argument that the excuse of the doctrine of double effect does not work in the example of cadaveric organ donation because there it is the *intention* to use the body parts of the deceased as a means to save the recipients' life (while in the trolley model the dismemberment of the dead body is only an unfortunate and accidental side-effect), is not cogent, but rather a matter of interpretation. For in transplantation medicine the need of the patient is already pre-existing, logically and chronologically. The intention to save him comes first. The use of the dead body of the donor is only a derivative from that pre-existing intention. The body of the deceased is used only as a last resort, as an emergency solution to save the life of the recipient whose life-saving can exclusively be carried through by providing the organ he needs.

Another related compelling question that we already met with in discussing the trolley problems, is whether it is better to save more people. This topic has become notorious in philosophy following the controversial article of John Taurek 'Should the Numbers Count'?[20] Since then, the ongoing debate gave rise to numerous publications.[21] Taurek famously argued that in a situation where we can either help one stranger or many, there is no obligation to save the many because when the many die there is no one who will suffer more of a loss than when the one dies. When the many die, it is worse for each of the individuals who will die but no single individual suffers a summation of losses. To Taurek suffering is not additive because there can be no subject that could experience a summation of sufferings of different persons. That is why numbers don't count when deciding whom to save in situations when not everybody can be saved. Parfit has replied that Taurek assumes that consequentialism is true because he contends that we would be morally obliged to promote the best state of affairs.[22] Only the reason why we are not obliged to save many people rather than one person is because in Taurek's theory we cannot claim that saving the many would be better. But we need not be consequentialists. We might want to prevent what we consider to be morally wrong whatever the circumstances, even if that implies that we do not promote the best state of affairs. For example in cases when saving the many implies that we have to do something that is intrinsically terribly wrong. On the other hand non-consequentialists do not have to be insensitive to consequences. Non-consequentialists have no problems in assuming that there is an obligation to promote the best state of affairs each

---

[20]   John M Taurek, 'Should the Numbers Count?' (1977) 6 *Philosophy & Public Affairs* 293-316.
[21]   Derek Parfit, 'Innumerate Ethics' (1978) 7 *Philosophy & Public Affairs* 285-301; Frances M Kamm, *Morality, Mortality, Vol. I. Death and Whom to Save from It* (OUP 1993); Thomas Scanlon, *What We Owe to Each Other* (HUP 1998); Michael Otsuka, 'Scanlon and the claims of the many versus the one' (2000) 60 *Analysis* 288-293; David T Wasserman and Alan Strudler, 'Can a Nonconsequentialist Count Lives?' (2003) 31 *Philosophy & Public Affairs* 71-94; Paul Dinkin, 'Can a Nonconsequentialist Justify Saving the Greater Number?' (2003) 1 *The London Journal of Philosophy* 4-10.
[22]   Parfit (note 21) 300.

and every time when there is no moral prohibition that is strong enough to trump that obligation.

3. Equity and utility in organ allocation

In transplantation medicine conditions of scarcity due to organ shortage have become chronic and are getting worse every year. Because of the spectacular progress in transplantation techniques and the growing success rate of this medical treatment the numbers of patients who could benefit from this treatment are steadily growing while the supply of organs does not keep up with this expanding demand. All the relevant publications are describing this worsening situation with thousands of patients in need of an organ dying on waiting lists in Western countries. Those patients do not die because we don't know how to treat them, but because many usable organs that could save their lives are buried or burned as a part of the mortal remains of the deceased. Moreover, many patients do not even get the opportunity to enter into a waiting list, or are removed from it, because they are considered to be already too sick to benefit enough from transplantation.

All the organ allocation systems in the Western world trade off between factors such as medical urgency, time spent on the waiting list, blood and tissue compatibility (to reduce the risk of rejection) and the likelihood of success of transplantation. In regard to the last factor it is important that the medical condition of the patient is good enough for transplantation. In the U.S. there is also a preference for allocating organs to recipients that are geographically not too far removed from the donor. This reflects some medical consideration of preserving the quality of the organ but to a certain extend it may also reflect a communitarian reflex: people will be more content if they know that someone of their local community will be helped by a donated organ. This geographical preference conflicts with medical urgency, especially when one takes in consideration the considerable differences in waiting time, not only between States, but also within States between different transplant centres.[23]

Other criteria can also conflict with medical urgency. Young people for instance often have a better prognosis for transplantation success but their need of an organ may be less urgent than that of older patients. From a utilitarian perspective, it is legitimate to discriminate elderly patients because old age is associated

---

[23] The President's Council on Bioethics. Dan Davis and Rebecca Wolitz, A Staff Working and Discussion Paper: The Ethics of Organ Allocation, http://purl.access.gpo.gov/. Davis and Wolitz quote and comment an article by Alan Zarembo that was published in the *Los Angeles Times* on June 11, 2006 under the eloquent title 'Death by Geography'. The article compares the story of two patients who were on the New-York waiting list for a liver transplantation. The first patient (Van Vlack) died in December 2005 after he had waited for more than a decade. The other patient (Evanac) who had been waiting for four years, moved to Florida, where he received a new liver fourteen days later. After having analyzed the relevant data, the newspaper was able to draw the conclusion that 1800 livers (from the total amount of 6121 that were transplanted nationwide) went to patients who were healthier than Van Vlack.

with a worse outcome.[24] What should have priority: the overall utility of a pool of organs for a given population or the urgent medical need of those who are in an alarming medical condition? There may also rise ethical disagreements when it comes to specifying the significance of the different criteria and the respective weight of each of them on allocation decisions. That is why medical deontology and legal rules pointing towards prioritizing the medically urgent cases come into conflict with utilitarian rules directed to maximization of the overall utility of a given organ pool. Utilitarians think that equity should not take precedence in case that this will increase the amount of poor outcomes. Allowing patients with predictably poor chances of recovery after transplantation (for example because they are too poor to afford the immunosuppressive drugs they will be needing) to 'consume' a scarce resource of organs would be a 'betrayal of society' from a utilitarian perspective.[25]

But even when overall utility of the organ allocation system would be our only moral value (which it is not), the allocation-ethical question would not be resolved. For utilitarian ethics does not give us unambiguous answers as to what has priority: saving the greatest number of lives or maximizing the aggregated number of post-transplantation live years? Should we transplant the person who will probably have the most long term use from the organ, even if his medical condition is not urgent, or transplant the person whose life is probably going to be saved for an indeterminate period by the operation? For how much does the loss of a life count as a draw back on the utility scale? Analogous questions rise when we focus on equity in organ allocation. Should we give older people an equal opportunity to be transplanted or should we give younger people an equal chance to grow old?[26]

The core values underlying much of the laws and regulations about organ donation and allocation in Europe and in the U.S. are equity and equality. That means that persons who are in medical need should have an equal opportunity to get access to organ transplantation and that the benefits of the distribution of that scarce medical resource should be equitable.[27] That commitment to equity functions as a corrective on the imperative of maximization of the benefits so that individual need and medical urgency may trump rules that are based on a mere macro-level cost utility analysis. But when one looks more into detail *medical* utility can also affect the conception of equity. Consider the example of two patients in need of a kidney, the first one is waiting for a relatively long time on the list and has a high medical urgency while the second one is a newcomer whose medical situation allows him to wait a little longer. Now let's consider that an available organ is a

---

[24] James Neuberger, 'Should liver transplantations be made available to everyone? The case against' (2003) 163, 16 *Archives of Internal Medicine 1881-1883*.

[25] Raja B Khauli, 'Issues and controversies surrounding organ donation and transplantation: the need for laws that ensure equity and optimal utility of a scarce resource' (1993) *Suffolk University Law Review* 1225.

[26] Davis and Wolitz (note 23) ibid.

[27] Norman Daniels, *Just Health Care* (CUP 1985).

very poor match to the first patient but a perfect match to the second. Would it be equitable to the second patient when the first patient gets the organ, considering that it is not sure that he will survive the operation for a long time given his general medical condition and the degree of mismatch with the transplant? Or should a zero-mismatch also have a 'determinative moral weight that trumps other criteria'?[28] The frequency of these tragic choices in the allocation of organs could be reduced by increasing the number of available transplants.

4. *Organ procurement and the ethics of decision systems.*

In order to reduce the shortage of organs for transplantation, different decision systems have been proposed. Under a decision system of presumed consent, absent an explicit declaration to the contrary a person is treated as if he had given his consent to donate his organs. The biggest advantage of this model lies in the fact that the default is located in a presumed readiness to donate so that staying apathetic will not worsen the organ shortage. Specifying donation as the default presupposes that there is a prima facie duty to donate that can only be declined by an explicit decision. That implies that we have to depart from the traditional ethical view that organ donation is a purely altruistic gift, an act that is *supererogatory*: going beyond what is required by duty and thus something which omitting is not blameworthy. Critics of the presumed consent model have underscored that a strict enforcement of it disrespects the autonomy of those persons who preferred not to donate but for one reason or another failed to formally opt out. That is why some prefer a system of mandated choice that compels each citizen to formulate his choice explicitly in regard to being a donor upon death or not.

One of the most controversial proposals to increase the availability of transplants, was formulated by the British bio ethicist John Harris. He considers that in regard of the terrible and unnecessary tragedy of thousands of patients dying because many usable organs that could save their lives are buried or cremated, all cadaveric organs should be made automatically available to the community.[29] In Harris's opinion not only the friends and relatives of the deceased have interests that his bodily integrity and his will are respected, but the potential organ recipients and their friends and relatives also have a claim, because the use of (one or more) organs of the deceased can possibly save the lives of the recipients. According to Harris the potential damage to the interests of these two parties can be compared and weighed against each other. The cadaver (and potential donor) is dead and past being harmed, so he loses only a posthumous preference and his friends and relatives may be distressed about that. But the potential organ recipient may lose her very life. Mandatory availability would remove the necessity of asking permission

---

[28]   Davis and Wolitz (note 23) ibid.

[29]   John Harris, 'Organ procurement: dead interests, living needs' (2003) 29 *Journal of Medical Ethics* 130-134; John Harris, 'In praise of Unprincipled Ethics', (2003) 29 *Journal of Medical Ethics* 303-306.

to the relatives, which would relieve them in a difficult time of emotional distress. It would also transform cadaveric organs into a class of public goods.

The respect of people's wishes concerning their post-mortem affairs should be limited by reasonable demands of public interests. Harris does not deny that people may have persistent interests after their death but these interests and their posthumous frustration are not 'person affecting'. While the interests of dead people may persist in some way, 'they' don't and consequently 'they' are no longer there to be affected. That is why preventing damage to the interests of living people is more important than not to frustrate people's posthumous interests.[30] According to Harris, who is using Ronald Dworkins terminology, the person affecting interests of the living (in staying alive) 'trump'[31] the non person affecting persistent interests of the dead. These interests of the potential organ recipients equally trump the interests of parents or next of kin of the dead person.

The critique that it is impossible to compare the harms to the living and the harms to the dead, except in some very blurred and intuitive manner,[32] is rejected by Harris because legislators always have to compare the moral importance of different sorts of interests such as the freedom not to wear seat belts in cars with the potential harm caused by car accidents and the cost to the health care system. At this very point, the reflections of Harris become also relevant from the perspective of legal philosophy. The assumption in Harris's theory is that the community has the right to use state power to seize the corpses of its deceased members in order to detach the usable spare parts from the body and allocate them to those living members of the community who need them more. To Harris rights or interests have to be extremely powerful to warrant their upholding at the cost of the lives of others. That's why in Harris's theory it is highly implausible to think that having one's body remain whole after one's death 'is an objective one is entitled to pursue at the cost of other peoples lives', not least because the objective is impossible of achievement due to the natural process of bodily decomposition.

But that leaves the problem unsolved why a person who is not involved in the unfortunate state of affairs that some other person suffers from organ failure, has an obligation to that person. Are we responsible for harming someone if we allow a harmful event to happen that we did not cause but that was within our power to prevent? Does the fact that we allow a harm to happen to someone (especially when we have no kind of relation to that someone other than his being a fellow human being) make us morally responsible for his being harmed even if we did not primarily cause that harm but only refrained from contributing to the prevention of it? For Harris the remediable suffering of others creates obligations to us that get stronger to the extent that the costs to us are little.

---

[30]   John Harris, *Wonderwoman & Superman* (OUP 1992) chapter 5.

[31]   Ronald Dworkin, *Taking Rights Seriously* (HUP 1977).

[32]   CL Hamer, MM Rivlin, 'A stronger policy of organ retrieval from cadaveric donors: some ethical considerations' (2003) 29 *Journal of Medical Ethics* 196-200.

Harris's powerful statements deserve further scrutiny because his proposals (and analogous proposals from others[33] diminish the importance traditionally attributed to the individual autonomy of the person and his freedom of choice and to the freedom of decision of the family after death.

5. Definition of death and maximizing organ procurement

Three ethical and legal principles are guiding the practice of transplantation of vital organs since its inception. The first two principles are not specific for the practice of organ transplantation (although they have important consequences in this context), but are overarching principles in western medicine: the prohibition of active euthanasia and the primacy of informed consent. The third principle is the *dead donor rule*: organ retrieval shall not be carried out until the donor is dead.[34] That implies that the patient shall not be killed by the prelevation of his organs. But when is a person dead? Repeatedly fears have been expressed that patients could be declared dead prematurely in order to 'harvest' their organs or that doctors would possibly do less than they could to save one's life when they know that the dying patient is a donor upon death.

Particularly since the development of critical care medicine, the question raised as to when a patient whose heart and blood flow had been artificially sustained by life support technology but who is in an irreversible coma, could be declared 'dead' in order to retrieve his organs for donation without violating the dead donor rule. At the end of the nineteen sixties some transplant surgeons stood at trial in the U.S., charged with the accusation of causing irreversibly comatose patients' death by removing their vital organs. The solution in order to avoid this in the future was found in a redefinition of death. In 1968 an ad hoc committee of the Harvard Medical School proposed a new definition of death as 'brain-death' which has been adopted in all the countries of the Western world. Patients whose brains no longer functioned could now serve as cadaveric organ donors. The artificial sustainment of their cardiopulmonary function providing oxygenated blood to the organs prevented the cells and tissues to suffer ischemic injury and provided ample time to obtain family consent for donation. Since the adoption and progressive acceptation of brain death, the vast majority of cadaveric organs in the U.S. and Europe have been procured by heart beating donation from brain-dead patients.

Despite this success the debate about 'brain-death' shows that 'death' is not longer an inherently biological fact that can be established with scientific certainty, but also a social construction, as Margareth Lock showed in her superb book.[35] 'Brain

---

[33] See for example Aaron Spital, 'Conscription of Cadaveric Organs for Transplantation: Neglected Again' (June 2003) *Kennedy Institute of Ethics Journal* 169-174; Aaron Spital and Charles A Erin, 'Conscription of cadaveric organs for transplantation: Let's at least talk about it' (2002) 39 *American Journal of Kidney diseases* 611-615.

[34] The exception is living directed donation, but in that case the organs are paired (kidneys) and only one of them will be removed or the excision will concern only a part of an organ (liver, lung).

[35] Margaret Lock, *Twice Dead. Organ Transplants and the Reinvention of Death* (University of California Press 2002).

death, a concept that permits the commodification of body parts for transplant, is an invention of the West.'[36] The brain-dead patient on life support is like a 'living cadaver', a hybrid between a human being and a technological device, breathing, digesting food, urinating and continuing his metabolical activity (in a rare case a brain-dead woman even gave birth to her child), but nevertheless in a doomed condition that can only be prolonged thanks to the ventilator and other life-sustaining technology. However it was clear from the beginning that the profound philosophical and ethical perplexities concerning the border between life and death could not be eliminated by definition. And neither by the progress in our scientific knowledge, because the uncertainties about the border between human life and death are not of such a nature that they can be resolved by collecting more empirical data. They relate to profoundly different understandings of what it means to be a living human being and that is why most of these questions remain until today. Is the 'person' of a brain-dead patient 'dead' while his body is still alive? Or does the person die only when his heart has stopped beating and he no longer breaths, in which case a person with a dead brain on artificial life support should be considered as alive? In the first case the patient is like a living cadaver, stripped of his rights as a member of society, a container of organs in which blood circulation and heart beat are artificially induced and who has to be handled carefully, not for 'him- or herself' (because there is no longer a 'self') but in order to preserve the precious body parts. In the second case we are confronted with a person who has lost consciousness irreversibly and who will die, but who is nevertheless still alive. In that case the process of organ excision in a person who is still on life support is killing that person.

The philosopher Hans Jonas was one of the first who contested the 'new death' as defined by the ad hoc committee of the Harvard Medical School. Jonas underscored that the redefinition of death had been undertaken for two reasons. The first was to introduce a criterion on the basis of which artificial prolongation of life could be judged 'futile' so that it could be discontinued in a legitimate way. Jonas had no problem with this aspect as it provided a criterion to stop all treatment of persons who are in an irreversible condition of loss of consciousness and let them die in dignity. But the second reason, which would have far reaching consequences, was pragmatic, as it was based on the need to 'advance' the declaration of death while keeping the brain-dead body 'alive' by artificially sustaining its cardiovascular circulation in order to preserve the quality of its organs for transplantation.[37] The Harvard commission was pretty open about this underlying utilitarian intent. But Jonas argued that the ethical shift in the redefinition was at least seriously questionable as the excision of organs under the new definition of death would have qualified as 'vivisection' under the old one. Jonas very lucidly identified the undertaking of the Harvard committee as a case of gerrymandering with the border between life

---

[36]   ibid 291.
[37]   Hans Jonas, *Technik, Medizin und Ethik*, (Suhrkamp Verlag 1987), especially para. 10 'Gehirntod und menschliche Organbank: Zur pragmatischen Umdefinierung des Todes' (originally published in English as 'On the redefinition of death (1969) *Daedalus* and 'Against the Stream: Comments on the Definition and Redefinition of Death' in Jonas, *Philosophical Essays* (1974).

and death in order to increase the number of available organs without hurting too much the moral sensibilities of the public.

According to Jonas, because we do not know the exact border between life and death, we should stick to a maximalist definition of death (brain-death plus cardio-vascular arrest) before intruding violently into the body of someone and retrieving organs from it. Although he knew that this battle was lost in advance, Jonas argued that it is ethically unacceptable to artificially prolong the process leading to 'death' under the old definition (in order to harvest organs under optimal conditions) after having decreed a new definition implying that such a robust instrumentalisation of a person's body is harmless because that person is already 'dead' and thus beyond harm. If the person is 'dead', he is no longer a member of the moral and legal community and the prohibition not to kill him becomes meaningless. That is why Jonas interestingly argued that in a situation of irreversible coma, we are confronted with a person who's brain is dead, but who is nevertheless partially alive as long as his pulse, his blood pressure and other vital functions can be sustained. The ethically crucial question then is not whether the patient is already 'dead' but: What should be done to this person who is still a patient, what is his due? According to Jonas the answer should be that it is morally unacceptable to prolong the life of a brainless body. We should let the person die completely and only then retrieve his organs.

In the new definition of death as brain death which locates life and the end of it in the brain, Jonas detects a revival of the dualism between body and 'soul'. The extinction of the brain is equivalent to the departure of the soul; what is left are the 'mortal remains'. But to Jonas the body is equally essential in the constitution of one's identity. 'The body is uniquely the body of this brain and no other, as the brain is uniquely the brain of this body and no other. (...) My identity is the identity of the whole organism, even if the higher functions of personhood are seated in the brain.'[38] The person who is irreversibly unconscious but still breathing and whose heart is still beating, should therefore not be treated as a mere instrument in the treatment of another patient.

After a case of successful resuscitation of a person who had been declared brain-dead, the President's commission established stricter criteria for the uniform determination of death in the U.S., which resulted in a law under that name in 1981.[39] The equivocal Harvard criterion of 'irreversible coma' was replaced by 'whole brain-death' and 'irreversible loss of all brain function, including the brain stem' which was carefully distinguished from a 'persistent vegetative state' in which some parts of the lower brain are still functioning. But the commission adopted this not as a cumulative criterion for the determination of death but as an alternative

---

[38] ibid 139 (German transl. p. 234).

[39] *The Uniform Declaration of Death Act* (UDDA) provides that 'an individual, who has sustained either (1) irreversible cessation of circulatory and respiratory functions, or (2) irreversible cessation of all functions of the entire brain, including the brainstem, is dead. A determination of death must be made in accordance with accepted medical standards.' Neurological criteria for the determination of death have been recognized in all the 50 states, but New York and New Jersey have specific regulations in order to take into account the objections to neurological determinations of death on religious grounds.

to the traditional criterion of irreversible cessation of circulatory and respiratory functions so that the ambiguity persisted as there were still two ways to die. Some philosophers and physicists had also divergent opinions concerning the notion of 'death of the person'. Some argued that the person is dead when the higher brain had stopped functioning and irreversible loss of consciousness had occurred, even if some functioning of the lower brain continued and cardiac or circulatory death had not occurred.

All the perplexities and ambivalences of the concept of brain death are even worsened with the concept of 'neocortical death', put foreward by proponents of increased organ procurement. Patients who are totally brain-dead cannot breath spontaneously and their bodies will for certain die when they are disconnected from the ventilator. But patients whose lower brain continues to function to some extent are sometimes breathing spontaneously although they are considered to be in a state of irreversible unconsciousness. If such patients were to be considered as legally dead, would it be acceptable to take organs for donation from them even when they have previously given their consent? Is our culture prepared to consider patients in a permanent vegetative state who can 'breath without assistance, have sleep-wake cycles and reflexes, and can swallow and yawn' and who could be maintained in that state for years, as dead in order to harvest their organs?[40] What exactly is irreversible loss of consciousness and how certain are we about its diagnosis? And how confident are we with the moral and legal equation between the extinction of consciousness and the death of a person? Is death an event or a process and can it legitimately be reduced to a legal moment in order to facilitate organ retrieval?[41] And should persons who have agreed to be donors upon death (or citizens of countries where a decision system of presumed consent has been adopted) not be informed in detail about the fact that they will not be allowed to die naturally in case that they would suffer irreversible brain damage after a car accident for example? Are people really aware of the fact that in such a situation they will be kept on life support, not because there is any hope for them, but with the exclusive goal of organ retrieval, which will then cause their eventual biological death? All this raises serious concerns about the soundness and validity of the procedures of 'informed consent'.[42]

Several family members of brain-dead patients confirm that brain death followed by donation is not a 'peaceful' death because the patient has to be put on life support

---

[40] M Lock, ibid 349. Lock describes all the consequences of the raw utilitarianism in the debate about anencephalic infants who are born without a cranium and cerebral cortex and who are therefore not considered as living human beings by some authors. Sometimes parents are inclined to donate the organs of their anencephalic child in order to give some significance to their child's life (ibid 354).

[41] ibid 120, 125.

[42] When I recently talked about these issues to a doctor involved with organ excision, I asked him if the potential donors were really aware of all the consequences of their choice, his answer was: 'no, and perhaps luckily not, because if they would, the number of donors would perhaps decrease dramatically'. This kind of well-meaning paternalism is still typifying a big part of the medical world, at least in Europe.

until the organs have been removed from the body. Only after that family mourning can commence. Margaret Lock has shown how different the social constructions of death are in the western world as opposed to Japan. In Japan brain death is not equated to death and mostly patients are only disconnected from the ventilator when the family has accepted the death of their loved one.

6. NHBD procedures and further shifts in the definition of death

The dead donor rule in combination with a definition of death which is twofold and for that reason still ambivalent, raises even more difficulties since there has been a renewed interest during the last twenty years in non heart beating donation (NHBD)[43] in order to obtain more organs. The controversy concerning the 'Pittsburgh protocol' can illustrate this.[44] In 1993 the University of Pittsburgh Medical Centre introduced a protocol for patients who had requested (or their surrogates in case of loss of decision making capacity by the patient) withdrawal of life sustaining treatment. These patients who were not brain dead, were transported to the operating room where the ventilator was disconnected and death be declared after two minutes of cardiac arrest. Thereupon a surgical team standing by would immediately begin with organ retrieval. Critics pointed out that these patients have not suffered irreversible cardiac function as they could be resuscitated after a cardiac arrest of only two minutes and consequently they are not 'dead' according to the legal definition in the UDDA.[45] In the Pittsburgh protocol the word 'irreversible' in the UDDA is not interpreted as signifying 'not possible', but as ethically precluded on the basis of the patient's wish not to be resuscitated. An additional ethical problem is that cardiac arrest is not 100% certain to occur after life support is removed. If the patient starts to breath spontaneously, he will have to be transported again into the ICU. Because of the conflicting interests between intensivists and transplantation surgeons the protocol provides that two different teams of doctors are taking care of the patient and the donor and that the decision to end life-support has to be taken prior to and independently of the decision to donate. Apart from the fact that the intensive care doctors often know of their patient being a donor, this kind of procedural safeguard does not rule out conflicts of interest and implicit pressures as many clinics also depend financially on the success of their transplantation program.[46]

---

[43] In the U.S. NHBD is usually called donation after cardiac or circulatory death (DCD).

[44] American Medical Association, Council on Ethical and Judicial Affairs, Report 4 – I-94 'Ethical Issues in the Procurement of Organs Following Cardiac Death: The Pittsburgh Protocol'.

[45] And neither is the possibility of auto-resuscitation completely excluded after such a short period, some critics contend. J Lynn, 'Are the patients who become organ donors under the Pittsburgh protocol really dead?' (1993) 3 *Kennedy Institute of Ethics Journal* 167-178.

[46] BW Shaw, 'Conflict of interest in the procurement of organs from cadavers following withdrawal of life support' (1993) 3 *Kennedy Institute of Ethics Journal* 179-188; J Frader, 'Non-heart-beating organ donation: personal and institutional conflicts of interest', ibid 189-198; JF Burdick, 'Potential conflicts of interest generated by the use of non-heart-beating cadavers' ibid 199-202. In the U.S. there is also a growing pressure on OPO's to increase the rate of donation and transplantation in hospitals located within their operational area. If they fail to meet the goals they may lose their certification and put at risk the renewal of their contract with Medicare which reimburses some

As Alan Weisbard has argued, the Pittsburgh protocol relied heavily on the traditional principle of double effect and on the distinctions between acts and omissions, between permissible 'allowing to die' and impermissible killings. But it does so in a way that overstretches and instrumentalizes the principle of double effect and the named distinctions in an abusive way and with the actual strategy of obscuring the actor's moral responsibility and to provide a layer of protection from potential legal liability.[47] The presupposition of the argument of double effect in the Pittsburgh protocol is that the patient's death can be the unintended and regrettable but foreseen side-effect of a therapy to relieve pain. Each and every step in the adjustments of respiratory support and administering of medication is meticulously construed as a procedure solely intended to the patient's need of the moment. 'The protocol has only the secondary or 'unintended' (if foreseen) effect of bringing about the patient's (desired) death.'[48] The dying process of the patient is meticulously managed in order to accommodate the needs of transplantation, which may be justified from a utilitarian point of view, but which should not be hypocritically justified as if it were also in the best interest of the dying person. The difference between a permissible allowing to die and a prohibited causing someone's death on purpose became so thin that it was becoming nearly unexisting in the Pittsburgh protocol. Even if one considers legal rules to be 'open textured' the question should be asked whether the exploitation of the ambiguities in the legal definition of death is pushing the dead donor rule over the limit of its reasonable extension.

In order to prevent the risk of warm ischemia causing damage to the organs, the so-called 'transplant community' is moving on a slippery slope in NHBD-procedures, pushing toward a progressive shortening of the waiting time between cardiac arrest and the certification of death, thereby disguising the fact that the procurement process does actually begin before the patient is irreversibly dead.[49] Donors are as dead as necessary to circumvent homicide laws and as alive as possible in order to optimize the quality of the organs. Removing organs from persons who are declared dead, but who are actually in the process of dying, is the consequence of the utilitarian rationale of maximisation of organ procurement in combination with the necessity to circumvent homicide law. The removal of vital organs in NHBD would be the proximate cause of the person's dying at a specific moment, were it not that he had already been declared dead at a previous moment.

---

of the costs related to donation services. 'Requirements for Certification and Designation and Conditions for Coverage: Organ Procurement Organizations' (71 FR 31046, May 31, 2006), see the *Electronic Code of Federal Regulations* on the internet http://law.justia.com/.

[47] Alan C Weisbard: 'A Polemic on Principles: Reflections on the Pittsburgh Protocol' (1993) 3 *Kennedy Institute of Ethics Journal* 217-230.

[48] 'Portrayed in its rawest form, the Pittsburgh protocol envisions wheeling a concededly still living prospective donor into the O.R., prepping the individual's body for subsequent expeditious removal of organs, presiding over a series of events (the 'black box') hopefully culminating in the individual's death (or at least the individual's being 'declared' dead by a new and scientifically unvalidated set of criteria), and finally removing the individual's organs for transplant – all this unless something goes dreadfully wrong, and the patient survives.' ibid 223.

[49] Renée C Fox, 'An Ignoble Form of Cannibalism: Reflections on the Pittsburgh Protocol for Procuring Organs from Non-Heart-Beating Cadavers' (1993) 3 *Kennedy Institute of Ethics Journal* 233.

This 'death by protocol' is described by Renée C. Fox as a 'desolate, profanely *high tech* death' that the patient/donor dies on the operating table, 'beneath operating room lights, amidst masked, growned, and gloved strangers'[50] who are cutting vital organs out of him (her).

But despite of all these critiques addressed at the 'transplant community' in regard to the danger of eroding our basic values in the frensic search for ever more organs, the DDR has been under a permanent attack these last fifteen years. It is becoming more and more obvious that the 'whole-brain' definition of death is untenable because many patients who are currently diagnosed as 'brain-death' do in fact retain some brain function which has to be disregarded as 'not significant' in order to accommodate to the definition of brain death in the UDDA.[51] Some patients have sufficient residual brain function to regulate water balance[52] or secrete hormones, regulate body temperature, digestion, metabolism, immunological reactions and excretion of wastes. Some neurologists argue that we cannot be certain that residual lower brain function is not sufficient to induce a primitive form of consciousness. Another untenable assumption inherent in the concept of brain death is that for a person diagnosed as such, cardiac arrest within a short period is always the necessary outcome.[53]

Once we have accepted gerrymandering with the definition of death for utilitarian reasons we render our concepts inherently unstable and subject to further redefinition whenever utility requires it.[54] And hence several proposals to redefine death once more have been put foreward in order to save the DDR. One of them is the 'higher-brain' definition of death, focusing on the irreversible loss of consciousness.[55] This strategy is willing to preserve the normative rule by extending the significance of the concept 'death' to a larger category of patients on the condition that proper consent has been obtained and existing legal prohibitions have been removed. The functional advantages of this are that we only have to redefine the criteria for brain death (moving from 'whole brain death' to the diagnosis of 'higher brain death') and that homicide laws would not have to be amended in order to protect organ retrievers from being accused of murder.[56] By (once again) fine-tuning our definition of death in that way, anyone who is determined to be a legitimate candidate

---

[50] ibid.

[51] Robert D Truog and Walter M Robinson, 'Role of brain death and the death donor rule in the ethics of organ transplantation' (2003) 31 *Critical Care Medicine,* 2392.

[52] Joanne Lynn & Ronald Cranford, 'The Persisting Complexities in the Determination of Death' in Stuart J. Younger a.o. (eds) *The Definition of Death* (The John Hopkins University Press 1999) 101-114.

[53] D Alan Shewmon, 'Chronic "Brain Death": Meta-analysis and conceptual consequences' (1998) 51 *Neurology* 1538-1545; D Alan Shewmon, 'The Brain and Somatic Integration: Insights into the Standard Biological Rationale for Equating "Brain Death" with Death' (2001) 26 *Journal of Medicine and Philosophy* 457-478.

[54] Robert M Arnold and Stuart J Younger, 'The Dead Donor Rule: Should We Stretch It, Bend It, or Abandon It?' (1993) 3 *Kennedy Institute of Ethics Journal* 267.

[55] See for example Robert M Veatch, 'The whole-brain-oriented concept of death: An outmoded philosophical formulation' (1975) 3 *Journal of Thanatology* 13-30.

[56] Robert M Veatch, 'The Dead Donor Rule: True by Definition' (2003) 1 *American Journal of Bioethics* 10-11.

for organ donation would be dead by stipulative definition. Exceptions to the DDR would thereby be ruled out[57] and the act of extinguishing the remaining quantum of biological life in these legally 'dead' bodies by retrieving vital organs from them, would not be a killing, not even a letting die, but a procedure (based on consent) on a biologically living human body (except for some essential brain-functions) who has lost his/her status as a full member of our legal and moral community.[58] The result would be that more and healthier organs could be harvested at an earlier stage.

7. Should we abandon the dead donor rule?

Some authors prefer another intellectual strategy to reach the same goal (enlarging the pool of available organs). They think that we should abandon the DDR and formulate some carefully tailored criteria under which organ retrieval from patients who are still living would be acceptable. That would require some criteria to identify when a patient's quality of life is so unacceptable and death so imminent that he is past harming and that we may take his organs even before he dies. After all, so the proponents of this approach argue, the consequences of retrieving the organs or not would be likewise death, except that organ procurement may help others.[59] But when exactly is a living person beyond harm? And is the fact that 'informed consent' has been obtained from the patient or his surrogates a justification that is strong enough to reinterpret the principle of non-maleficence (*primum non nocere*) in such a counter-intuitive way that doctors would consider their actions in accordance with this principle even when they cause the dead of a patient by organ retrieval?[60] Proponents argue that abandoning the DDR would also render the carefully orchestrated death in the protocols for NHBD unnecessary. But is this any better? Instead of 'making' the patient legally dead before organ retrieval, this strategy is aimed at making doctors comfortable with the idea that retrieval of vital organs from a living patient under anaesthesia is acceptable because this patient is going to die anyway and the shortening of his life through organ retrieval does not alter or transform the morally relevant cause of the outcome, which is the patient's incurable disease or injury. As the proponents of this approach acknowledge, this would imply the need for a shift in our current legal conceptions of causation. The legal cause of death would have to be defined as the patient's disease just as it is the case when artificial life support is withdrawn.[61] But such a redefinition of

---

[57] ibid.

[58] Robert M Veatch, 'Abandon the Dead Donor Rule or Change the Definition of Death?' (2004) 14 No. 3 *Kennedy Institute of Ethics Journal* 261-276.

[59] ibid 270.

[60] Truog and Robinson (note 51) ibid 2393, believe that in some circumstances 'the harm of dying is sufficiently small that patients or surrogates should be allowed to voluntarily accept it to be able to donate organs. For example, some might say that if they were ever diagnosed as being permanently unconscious they would accept the harm of dying if this would make it possible for them to donate their organs to others. Similarly some patients who are imminently dying might be willing to have their life shortened by a few minutes or hours if this would make donation possible.' Also RD Truog, 'Brain death – too flawed to endure, too ingrained to abandon' (2007) 35 *JLME* 278.

[61] Truog and Robinson (note 51) ibid 2395.

legal causation of death especially tailored to the realm of organ donation could be interpreted as tantamount to defining exceptions to the prohibition on homicide with the consequence of weakening this prohibition and render further exceptions easier in the future.[62]

But to the proponents of abolition of the DDR those arguments are not convincing. They argue that respect for the autonomy and will of the patient should have the primacy. If consent of the surrogates is deemed problematic, organ retrieval could be restricted to those patients who have made appropriate advance directives while they were still competent. As citizens of western countries increasingly have the right to refuse medical treatments, even if this refusal will result in a premature death, why would they not be allowed to become organ donors even if this choice will also speed up the fatal outcome of their underlying pathology?[63]

It seems that the detractors of the DDR as well as those who stick to it agree in one important sense: they both insist that respect for the autonomous will of the patient (or in some cases his surrogates) should play a more important role in regard to the question at what moment organ retrieval would be legitimate. Veatch argues that patients should be allowed to choose their own definition of death within certain limits while the state adopts a conservative default definition of death for all those who did not express their will.[64] For example, would those patients willing to donate organs and who would also refuse continuation of artificial life-sustainment when irreversible coma or PVS occurred, be allowed to be pronounced dead in that situation in order to become donors. Others who would stick to the definition of death as it is formulated in the UDDA would be treated as living until 'whole brain death' or cardio-respiratory death occurred. Veatch hopes that the 'conservatives', who defend the 'whole brain' definition of death, will not be opposed to allowing the 'liberals' who favour 'higher-brain death' to choose that definition for themselves and for those for whom they have decisional authority. Since no one is obligated to become a donor, and no donor would be obligated to donate before he is in a state that he considered to be 'really dead' while he was alive, it could be that such a system of a limited optional definition of one's personal death would meet less resistance with defenders of 'whole brain death' than abandoning the DDR. Abandoning the DDR in order to make donation possible for those who are legally still alive, would almost certainly be considered as an intentional active killing or homicide by the 'conservatives'.[65]

In Donation after Cardiac Death (NHBD) organs are currently removed between 2 and 5 minutes after cardiac arrest. The conservative period of 5 minutes proposed by the (U.S.) Institute Of Medicine was based on neurological insights that within

---

[62]   Veatch warns that abandoning the DDR will have also serious consequences in other fields of the law and render many legislative changes necessary also in insurance and marital law. Veatch (note 58) 271, 273.
[63]   Truog & Robinson (note 51) ibid 2394; Norman Fost, 'Reconsidering the Dead Donor Rule: Is it Important that Organ Donors Be Dead?' (2004) 14 *Kennedy Institute of Ethics Journal* 252.
[64]   Veatch (note 58) 274.
[65]   ibid 275.

that period irreversible whole brain injury will occur. The minimal 2 minutes rule (as adopted in the Pittsburgh Protocol and other similar protocols) is based on the claim that auto resuscitation will not occur after that time although this depends on the specific circumstances of the cardiac arrest, and some controversies between specialists in the field (too complex to understand for the medical lay) do persist.[66] But what was predictable even for an interested lay, is that sooner or later, this 2-5 minutes rule would be violated. In August 2008 the New England Journal of Medicine reported that at Children's Hospital in Denver, between 2004 and 2007, three babies with heart failures received new hearts from three donor babies who had suffered severe brain damage but were not brain-dead.

After the parents had decided to withdraw life-support a 'do not resuscitate' order was signed and consent to let the dying babies become donors was reached. They were transported to the operating room, where life support was discontinued in order to let the babies become non heart beating donors. To minimize their discomfort during the dying process they were also administered pain-killers and sedative drugs (which also suppress the drive to breathe). With two of the babies the doctors waited only for 75 seconds after the heart had stopped before they began with organ retrieval. In NHBD procedures mostly abdominal organs are retrieved because of the very short period that the hearts and lungs stay salvageable after cardiac arrest. And hence in the Denver cases the shortening of the waiting time was judged to be necessary in order to minimize the risk of ischemic damage to the donor hearts. The doctors argued that spontaneous auto-resuscitation in similar circumstances has never been documented after 60 seconds of cardiac arrest. But that conflates a prognosis (which admittedly is pretty sure) with a diagnosis of death which is required by the DDR.

Although artificial resuscitation was legally precluded because it had been formally refused by the parents, the stoppage of the heart was not 'irreversible' in the sense of impossible since the organ was successfully restarted in the recipient. If one takes the word 'irreversible' in the UDDA in its significance of 'not possible' as it was originally intended by the legislator, heart donations and transplantations after cardiac death are impossible. Or to put it the other way around, transplantation of a heart from a donor declared dead according to a cardiac criterion retroactively negates the determination of death.[67] In the current legal situation this means that

[66] See for example Joseph L Verheijde, Mohamed Y Rady and Joan McGregor, 'Recovery of transplantable organs after cardiac or circulatory death: Transforming the paradigm for the ethics of organ donation' (2007) 2:8 *Philosophy, Ethics and Humanities in Medicine*; Sam D Shemie, 'Clarifying the paradigm for the ethics of donation and transplantation: Was "dead" really so clear before organ donation?' http://www.pubmedcentral.nih.gov/; Mohamed Rady, 'Autoresuscitation and organ donation after cardiac death: clarifying misunderstandings about the physiology of human circulation' http://www.peh-med.com/.

[67] James L Bernat, 'The Boundaries of Organ Donation after Circulatory Death' (August 2008) 359 *NEJM* 669-671.

retrieval of the heart from a patient and restarting it in another body, is killing a person by organ removal.[68]

And that is why the Denver case has also been the occasion for those who advocate to abandon the DDR to restate their arguments.[69] Truog and Miller argue that in modern intensive care units the proximate cause of death for many patients lies already in the daily actions of medical doctors, for example when mechanical ventilation is withdrawn. Because it is never 100% certain that the patient will not start to breathe spontaneously, despite his devastating brain injury, those patients regularly get a fair amount of morphine in order to suppress a possible spontaneous breathing reflex. These practices are made compatible with traditional medical ethics by obscuring their real nature by virtue of a set of moral fictions including the understanding that withdrawing life-sustaining treatment allows patients to die but does not 'cause' their dead as the underlying pathology of the patient is the 'real' cause.[70] Because those kind of procedures are daily practice in ICU's they consider the difference with death by organ retrieval as morally insignificant provided that proper informed consent has been obtained and that anaesthesia is administered during the (deadly) operation of the donor. For Miller, Truog and Brock the moral fiction of 'letting a patient die' as a consequence of the withdrawal of artificial life sustainment, is in reality an act of 'justified medical killing'.[71] They argue that the fictional distinction between killing and letting die has become a moral dogma in order to mask that reality because in traditional medical ethics there can be no such thing as 'justified killing'. For Miller, Truog and Brock the ethically relevant distinction in cases of treatment withdrawal is not the obscuring fictional difference between illegitimate acts (killing) and legitimate omissions (letting die through treatment withdrawal) but the question whether or not there has been informed consent by the patient or his surrogate.[72] In their view, given that it is ethical to cause death by treatment withdrawal (provided that consent has been given), it cannot necessarily be unethical to cause the death of that same person by retrieving his vital organs prior to the withdrawal of artificial life sustainment. Under that constraint 'no person would be made dead by vital organ donation who would not otherwise imminently be made dead by withdrawing life-sustaining treatment.'[73] The three authors contend that, provided that anesthesia is maintained during organ extraction and treatment withdrawal, the patient cannot be harmed or wronged by this procedure of making him dead.

---

[68]   Robert M Veatch, 'Donating Hearts after Cardiac Death – Reversing the Irreversible' (August 2008) 359 *NEJM* 673.

[69]   Robert D Truog & Franklin G Miller, 'The Dead Donor Rule and Organ Transplantation' (August 2008) 359 *NEJM* 674-675.

[70]   Franklin G Miller, Robert D Truog, Dan W Brock, 'The Dead Donor Rule: Can it Withstand Critical Scrutiny?' (2010) 35 *Journal of Medicine and Philosophy* 300.

[71]   ibid 304-305.

[72]   ibid 'The consent makes the difference between homicide and legitimate treatment withdrawal, but this ethical and legal difference has nothing to do with the cause of the patient's death, which is the same in both cases.'

[73]   ibid 306.

The first question is whether there is not an ethically significant difference (or at least a difference relevant to our ethical sensibilities) between an 'act' that consists precisely in a decision to discontinue the action of artificially sustaining the life of someone and let him peacefully die on the one hand and a dramatically invasive action (such as cutting out his heart) that will kill him on the other. The second question is whether the weight or the 'reach' of informed consent in our legal and moral culture is strong or wide enough to make it acceptable for doctors to kill a person (even if that person would have died soon anyway) by removing his vital organs. If a patient need not be dead before being a donor of vital organs, where and how would we draw the line? Would it be acceptable to kill legally incompetent human beings with consent of their surrogates for the sake of altruistic organ donation? Or healthy persons with their own consent? The enduring prohibition of active euthanasia and assisted suicide seems to be an indication that this is at least highly questionable.

Robert Truog argues that in cases such as those in Denver, 'all the ethical vectors are lined up in the right direction', so that it would be unethical not to perform the heart transplantations.[74] On the one side you have these dying babies and their parents who are motivated to donate their organs. On the other side you have three other babies whose only chance of survival is to receive these organs (hearts) and yet there is the DDR, which requires that the dying babies first have to be in a condition (dead) wherein their hearts are no longer usable for transplantation for them to be allowed to donate. That is why for Truog the DDR and the question whether the babies are dying or already dead misses the point.[75] But doctor Truog underestimates the ethical values which are embodied in the DDR and the potential danger of changing that rule. As George Annas, a professor of health law and human rights at Boston University underscores, dying people are still persons who have al kinds of subjective rights and the doctors who are taking care of them have obligations towards them.[76] The prognosis that a person is certainly going to die within a short period of time does not give anyone the right to kill that person even if this could save the life of someone else.

One of the striking things when one studies the philosophical and ethical aspects of organ procurement and allocation is the offhandedness of many ethicists in regard to the normative legal framework regulating that process in the U.S. and Europe. Of course the law is not a fetish, it can be criticised and changed, and in so far the candidness of many ethicists in bringing forward all kinds of new arguments and propositions in order to increase the rate of organ

---

[74] See the panel discussion about the Denver cases organised by the New England Journal of Medicine at http://content.nejm.org/.

[75] Robert Veatch, 'Transplanting hearts after death measured by cardiac criteria: The challenge to the dead donor rule" (2010) 35 *Journal of Medicine and Philosophy* 313-329, argues that this type of cases could be solved by further gerrymandering with our definition of death. By redefining death as irreversible loss of circulation in such terms that 'irreversible' includes the intention not to restart the heart within the dying patient. But this begs the question because the actual dying of the patient is precisely due to the stoppage of the heart.

[76] Panel discussion about the Denver cases (note 72) ibid.

procurement is legitimate. But ignoring the law as it is, can also be an indication of a lack of attention to cultural and ethical values embodied in the law and to the deeply rooted normative intuitions of which the law is an expression, especially when there is a consensus on the fundamental principles that lie at the heart of the legal regulations in the field.

Chapter VI

Reproducing Justice: Is There a Good Justification for Equal Access to Fertility Care?

Daniel Sperling

I. Context

Assisted reproductive technologies (ARTs) are modern technologies which help people who for medical or social reasons are unable to conceive or carry a fetus to full term. No doubt, these technologies bring substantial relief to many people and provide new ways through which individuals may become parents. Yet, the social circumstances under which such technologies are regulated, used and provided are not fully explored in the literature. Especially latent are the ways through which ARTs conflict with the principles of formal justice and equality, namely that equal cases should be treated equally.[1] The idea behind this is that one should not make an arbitrary exception on oneself, but rather should apply impartially whatever standards everyone else accepts.[2] In the context of ARTs, this raises a series of questions: What is the relationship between these principles and the legal, ethical or professional duty to provide ARTs, and more specifically fertility care? Do and should the principles of formal justice and equality fully apply to cases involving the use of ARTs? Do ARTs create or guarantee equality in the society or do they make the social gaps deeper, thereby increasing inequality in the society?[3]

There are two major forms through which the principles of justice and equality may apply to ARTs. The first form focuses on the question of whether ARTs should be equally allocated to whoever is in their need, or whether some limitations should be put on the access to these technologies, mainly for the protection of the

---

[1] In this paper I will take the view that any theory of justice is concerned with the value of equality and that these theories vary with regard to the question of what ought to be equalized. See, eg Amartya Sen, *Inequality Reexamined* (HUP 1992).

[2] Gene Outka, 'Social Justice and Equal Access to Health Care' (1974) 2 (1) *The Journal of Religious Ethics* 11, 23.

[3] Judith F Daar 'Accessing Reproductive Technologies: Invisible Barriers, Indelible Harms' (2008) 18 *Berkeley J. Gender L. & Just.* 74; M Crossley, 'Dimensions of Equality in Regulating Assisted Reproductive Technologies' (2005) 9 (2) *The Journal of Gender, Race and Justice* 273; NR 'ART for the Masses? Racial and Ethnic Inequality in Assisted Reproductive Technologies' (2005) 9 (1) *DePaul Journal of Health Care Law* 719-33; G Pennings, 'Distributive Justice in the Allocation of Donor Oocytes' (2001) 18 (2) *Journal of Assisted Reproduction and Genetics* 56; DW Lowry, 'Understanding Reproductive Technologies as a Surveillant Assemblage: Revisions of Power and Technoscience' (2004) 47 (4) *Sociological Perspectives* 357.

welfare of the child.[4] These latter limitations can be framed through the making of relevant distinctions of certain groups of interested parties on the bases of age, marital status, sexual orientation, socio-economic state, etc.[5] Recent discussions in the literature have expanded this list of personal characteristics to also include female obesity and body mass index[6] as well as lifestyle related factors like smoking and alcohol consumption.[7]

In New Zealand, for example, criteria for access to publicly funded ARTs were established in 2000, making only women with a BMI of 18-32 kg/m², aged less than 40 years old and who do not smoke eligible for treatment.[8] In addition, there is also a clinical points system that candidates must meet, which includes factors such as their age, other children at home (<12 years old) and a social score. Single and lesbian women are eligible for scoring if there is a clear biological cause of infertility or after at least 12 cycles of donor insemination with pregnancy of which 6 must be undertaken with an accredited unit. Since 2005, women who meet the criteria in New Zealand, are entitled to a maximum of two cycles of treatment and under the condition that a single embryo transfer is used in the first two embryo transfer cycles in women aged less than 36.[9] Recent empirical studies comparing health systems which include (NZ) and do not include (Australia) criteria for

---

[4] See Emily Jackson, 'Conception and the Irrelevance of the Welfare Principle' (2002) 65 *Modern L. Rev.* 176. In the UK the requirement to take notice of the welfare of the child in the context of fertility care is made by law and professional guidelines. Section 13 (5) of the Human Fertilisation and Embriology Act 1990 reads: "A woman shall not be provided with treatment services unless account has been taken of the welfare of any child who may be born as a result of the treatment (including the need of that child for supportive parenting), and of any other child who may be affected by the birth." For recent developments in the UK law, especially the removal of the "need for a father" requirement from the welfare principle see Rachel Fanton, Susan Heenan and Jane Rees 'Finally Fit for Purpose? The Human Fertilization and Embryology Act 2008' (2010) 32 (3) *Journal of Social Welfare and Family Law* 275. For the professional guidelines see: The Human Fertilisation and Embryology Authority Code of Practice – Division II (Guidance) 2009, 8th ed., available at: http://www.hfea.gov.uk/docs/8th_Code_of_Practice.pdf and National Institute for Clinical Excellence, Assessment and Treatment for People with Fertility Problems (February 2004): http://www.nice.org.uk/nicemedia/.

[5] See e.g. JA Roertson, 'Gay and Lesbian Access to Assisted Reproductive Technologies' (2004) 55 (2) *Case Western Reserve L. Rev.* 323; Daar (note 3) ibid.

[6] Abha Maheshwari, 'Overweight and Obesity in Infertility: Cost and Consequences' (2010) *Human Reproduction* Update; S Pandey, A Maheshwari and S Bhattacharya, 'Should Access to Fertility Treatment be Determined by Female Body Mass Index?' (2010) 25 (4) *Human Reproduction* 815; Anjel Vahratian and Yolanda R Smith, 'Should Access to Fertility-Related Services Be Conditional on Body Mass Index?' (2009) 24 (7) *Human Reproduction* 1532.

[7] W Dondorp and others, 'Lifestyle-Related Factors and Access to Medically Assisted Reproduction' (2010) 25 (3) *Human Reproduction* 578.

[8] CM Farquhar, YA Wang and EA Sullivan, 'A Comparative Analysis of Assisted Reproductive Technology Cycles in Australia and New Zealand 2004-2007' (2010) 25(9) *Human Reproduction* 2281-2289; Anjel Vahratian and Yolanda R Smith,' Should Access to Fertility-Related Services Be Conditional on Body Mass Index?' (2009) 24 (7) *Human Reproduction* 1532; WR Gillett, T Putt and CM Farquhar, 'Prioritising for fertility treatments- the Effect of Excluding Women with a High Body Mass Index' (2006) 113 (10) *BJOG* 1218.

[9] Farquhar and others (note 8) ibid.

fertility treatments suggest that the first resulted in healthier population of women undergoing treatment and better pregnancy outcomes.[10]

The second form of the suggested application of the principles of justice and equality, which I will not discuss in this chapter, focuses on situations occurring after using ARTs. This form centers on the equal distribution of the "outcomes" obtained as a result of ARTs. A frequent scenario includes the situation when one party, usually the male genitor seeks to dispose of or donate a frozen embryo, whereas another party, usually the female genitor, wishes to continue IVF treatment and implant the embryo. The way such a dispute is finally resolved may be the result of an unequal treatment and discrimination on the basis of gender.[11] Another example involves the dilemma of whether to implant a frozen embryo carrying a chromosome responsible for the occurrence of a genetic disease or the sex of the child to be born. To raise such a question, even more so to decide not to implant the embryo and discontinue the IVF treatment may create a serious threat to the principles of justice and equality, especially on the basis of disability and gender.[12]

Very few empirical studies examine the practice of ARTs in light of the principles of justice and equality. Regardless of their small number, these studies reveal a disturbing but well-established phenomenon according to which fertility clinics tend to turn away candidates for IVF and ART on a somewhat arbitrary basis, leading to discriminatory practices.[13] It is also found that in the US for example every fertility clinic has its own screening protocols or uses the common sense of providers to select candidates; the information sought from candidates varies extensively; and the weight which is given to various factors concerning the candidate's personal characteristics differs from one center to another.[14] For example, while all programs inquire about the physical health and age of candidates, 95% of them ask on candidates' marital status, 89% query their mental health, 71% examine their stability of relationship with partner and 52% look at their financial stability. While 33% of fertility programs say they would accept a couple for ART if the woman were addicted to marijuana, 47% of them say they would deny access. More disturbing, some programs report being likely to turn away a candidate with certain personal characteristics, such as sexual orientation or a mental disorder although they do not collect information on these characteristics.[15]

---

[10]   ibid.
[11]   Sally Sheldon, 'Gender Equality and Reproductive Decision-Making' (2004) 12 (3) *Feminist Legal Studies* 303.
[12]   Adrienne Asch, 'Disability Equality and Prenatal Testing: Contradictory or Compatible?' (2002-3) 30 *Fla. St. U. L. Rev.* 315.
[13]   AD Gurmankin, AL Caplan and AM Braveman, 'Screening Practices and Beliefs of Assisted Reproductive Technology Programs' (2005) 83 (1) *Fertility & Sterility* 61; Daniel Sperling Daniel and Yael Simon, Attitudes and Policies Regarding Access to Fertility Care and Assisted Reproductive Technologies in Israel' (2010) 21 *Reproductive Biomedicine* Online 854.
[14]   JE Stern, CP Cramer, A Garrod and RM Green, 'Attitudes on Access to Services at Assisted Reproductive Technology Clinics: Comparisons With Clinic Policy' (2002) 77 (3) *Fertility and Sterility* 537.
[15]   Gurmankin (note 13).

A common phenomenon, which was also observed in the studies, is that providers in most ARTs programs in the US (63%) believe they have the right and responsibility to screen candidates before providing them fertility services. Where clinical guidelines exist, studies show that provider's opinions about access to ART services are even more restrictive than clinical policies.[16]

If the principles of justice and equality should apply to the practice of ARTs, the empirical findings mentioned above would have troubling consequences for ethicists and policy makers that need to be further discussed. I will turn now to examine the question of whether indeed these principles should apply here. Beforehand, I would like to raise some few words on the scope of that question.

To answer whether the principles of justice and equality apply to the use and practice of ARTs (hereinafter "the justice and equality question"), and especially to provision of fertility care one has to consider other perspectives through which such a question and its ethical implications may be addressed. The question of whether people should enjoy equal access to fertility care can be conceptualized in the following four ways. First, is a question of rights. Under this question one should query whether people have a right to (demand) access (to) equal and unlimited fertility care, even at their own expenses.[17] To say that someone has a right to X entails the following three features: a. that someone is entitled to X or that X is due to him, regardless of whether X is desirable for that someone or good in itself; b. that except in rare cases, disentitlement of X leads to a sanction and that failure to provide such a sanction amounts to injustice; c. that the mere fact that infringement of X would maximize utility is not a sufficient reason for disentitlement of X (Buchanan, 2009).[18] If there is a universal[19] right to equal fertility care, such a right can derive from the right to procreation (procreative liberty) or the more general right to access health services. However, both rights suffer from conceptual difficulties. The procreative liberty right was legally developed from abortion, sterilization and contraceptive case decisions and was understood as a negative (liberty/civil-political) right deriving from a person's rights to privacy, autonomy and dignity. It has not been interpreted as imposing any positive duty on the state to allow free and equal access to reproductive care like any other social right.[20] On the other hand, the justifications for a universal right to access health services suffer from substantial difficulties as well. Under Norman Daniels' concept of such a right, which will be discussed *infra*, the right to access health care services involves contingent claims to an array of health-care services protecting fair shares of the opportunity range.

---

[16]   Stern (note 14).

[17]   Daniel Sperling, 'Male and Female He Created Them: Procreative Liberty, Its Conceptual Deficiencies and the Legal Right to Access Fertility Care of Males' (2011) 7 (3) *International Journal of Law in Context* 375-400.

[18]   Allen Buchanan, 'The Right to a Decent Minimum of Health Care' In *Justice and Health Care* (OUP 2009).

[19]   By "universal right" it is meant that one attributes the same right to all persons. For a contrasting position that attaches rights to certain individuals or groups (special right-claims) see Buchanan (note 18) 27.

[20]   Sperling, 2011 (note 17).

Yet, fertility treatment cannot be regarded as medical services devoted to restore normal (physical) functioning or cure disease conditions that necessarily involve a great curtailment of normal opportunity range under such an approach.[21,22] Nor is fertility a necessary condition to bring sufficient autonomy to enable a person to adapt to changing conditions of human life and cope with realities of suffering and death under alternative justifications for the right to access health services.[23] In any event, if people have a right to equal access to fertility care, this does not mean that such a right is absolute and should override any other right (individual or collective) in case of a conflict. It does, however, frame the discussion of the original question concerning the application of the principles of justice and equality in a political and legal context that *prima facie* allows people to make justifiable claims for fertility care under any circumstances.

A second way to address the justice and equality question is to regard it under the situations at stake as involving the question of personal autonomy. According to this perspective, one should ask whether choices of people seeking IVF treatment or fertility care should be respected as part of the ethical principle of autonomy, perhaps the most dominant and acknowledged bioethical principle in Western societies.[24] If, indeed, one's freedom of choice to decide and to establish for herself the life plans she finds most appropriate also includes one's reproductive choices, specifically choices about the means and extent to procreate, then preventing a person from receiving full and equal access to fertility care may contradict this ethical principle.

On the one hand, one can argue that peoples' decisions regarding reproduction and family planning are the most intimate and precious, reflecting important aspects that constitute who the person really is thereby justifying respect for autonomy. Moreover, under relational autonomy, persons are seen as socially embedded and their identities are shaped within the context of social relationship and love.

---

21 Emily Jackson, *Medical Law: Text, cases and materials* (OUP 2006) 47.

22 AV Campbell, 'Defining Core Health Services: the NZ experience' (2005) 9 (3) *Bioethics* 252.

23 One may still argue that under some pro-natalists societies, like Israel the social importance of fertility affects the normal opportunity range of a person and so infertility may be regarded a disease. Daniel Sperling, 'Commanding the "Be Fruitful and Multiply" Directive: Reproductive Law and Policy in Israel' 19 (3) *Cambridge Quarterly of Healthcare Ethics* 363; Daniel Sperling, 'Socializing the Public: Invoking Hannah Arendt's Critique of Modernity to Evaluate Reproductive Technologies' (2012) 15 *Medicine, Healthcare & Philosophy* 53-60. Such a view may also be coherent with Brigit Toebes' minimal notion of health care which includes family planning: Brigit CA Toebes, *The Right to Health as a Human Right in International Law* (Intersentia 1999) 243-89 and section 44 (a) of the UN general comments on the right to the highest attainable standard of health which refers to reproductive and maternal prenatal care: UN Economic and Social Council, The Right to the Highest Attainable Standard of Health E/C.12/2000/4 (General Comments) (11/08/2000), available at: http://www.unhchr.ch/. Another way to justify such a right would be to regard it in par with social definitions of health such as those offered by Peter Davis which defines health as "an ongoing outcome from the continuing process of living life well the latter of which is defined in terms of wealth, relationships, coherence, fitness and adaptability": Peter Davies, 'Between health and illness' (2007) 50 *Perspectives in Biology and Medicine* 444.

24 Tom L Beauchamp and James F Childress, *Principles of Biomedical Ethics* (6th ed OUP 2008).

Procreation and raising children enhances this concept of autonomy.[25] Thirdly, physicians are not in a better position to know what is best for candidates of IVF or their future child than patients themselves so that they are justified in preventing them access to treatment.

On the other hand, one may argue that respect for patient's autonomy relates to medical decision-making and not to situations affecting her overall wellbeing like reproduction. It may be further contended that people whose access to IVF is denied could still retain their autonomy if they rationally repudiate their lower-order desire (to become parents) at their higher-level of desire (not harm their children or be bad parents), so that preventing them access to treatment may not be considered paternalism or breach of autonomy.[26] Moreover, there are situations in which we ought to persuade others when they have false or ill-considered views or to override autonomy where competing moral considerations, such as harm to others or requirement of scarce resources for which no funds are available. Finally, one can hold that the principle of autonomy competes with providers' ethical of beneficence and the latter should override the patient's autonomy when she makes irresponsible choices.[27] Under such an account, refusal of request to IVF is a simple case of passive paternalism.

A third way to evaluate the ethical implications of treating people's access to ARTs and fertility care differently and not in accordance with the principles of justice and equality may be in light of the moral rule of truth telling. Assuming that health providers enjoy professional autonomy to refuse IVF treatment on an unequal basis, a question may then arise as to what they should be able to tell their patients, and specifically how they should justify and explain the sources of their unwillingness to provide treatment.

Preventing access to fertility care on social grounds is not a regular case where physicians want to pursue a medical goal. It is more like refusal on moral or conscientious grounds. One can argue that while patients largely wish to be informed about their medical condition they may not necessarily want to know the social factors participating in decision-making. Moreover, the significant meaning of parenthood and the high likelihood that revealing the true motives for refusal would create much distress and emotional harm may diminish the patient's sense of rationality, her ability to deliberate effectively and, in effect her future autonomy.[28] Also, the rationales for truth telling seem not to apply either.[29] Revealing the true motives of refusal does not enable patients to be autonomous and make informed decision; it

---

[25]   C McLeod and S Sherwin, 'Relational Autonomy, Self-Trust, and Health Care for Patients Who Are Oppressed' in C Mackenzie and N Stoljar (eds) *Relational Autonomy: Feminist Perspectives on Autonomy, Agency, and the Social Self* (OUP 2000) 259-272.

[26]   Gerald Dworkin, *The Theory and Practice of Autonomy* (CUP 1988).

[27]   Edmund D Pellegrino & David C Thomasma, *For the Patient's Own Good: The Restoration of Beneficence in Health Care* (OUP 1988) 25, 32, 46-47.

[28]   Anita Natarajan, 'Medical Ethics and Truth Telling in the Case of Androgen Insensitivity Syndrome' (1996) 154 (4) *CMAJ* 568.

[29]   Micahel Devita, 'Honestly, Do We Need a Policy on Truth?' (2001) 11 (2) *Kennedy Institute of Ethics Journal* 157.

does not provide the foundation for physician-patient relationship (as the meaning of such disclosure is the termination of that relationship) nor does it create trust in the medical team (not specifically and not institutionally). To the contrary, there is much incentive to conceal the truth: hiding the truth protects physicians or their institutions from harm in the form of litigation or harm to their reputation, and allows them to avoid unpleasant confrontation with patients or their family. If this is so, the problem of how a physician should explain her refusal to treat the patient remains open.

Finally, another way to conceptualize the justice and equality question is to regard it as a question of justice and rationing. Under this perspective, one should query whether inequalities in access to IVF treatment and/or fertility care, specifically the exclusion of persons from access to such scarce and expensive medical services can be justified by a theory of justice. I will turn now to discuss and analyze this aspect of the justice and equality question.

2. The Justice & Rationing Question

Can people be excluded from access to fertility care based on non-medical criteria? Can we justify inequalities in access to IVF treatment?[30] There are two major difficulties when one thinks of these questions in light of the more general discussion of resource allocation and health rationing.[31]

Usually, need serves as the major basis for allocating resources in health care. However, need is usually determined by a burden of illness approach or the quantifying of "capacity to benefit", namely the requirement to demonstrate some health gain or an expected benefit to be obtained as a result of the resource allocation.[32] In each case needs are defined solely in terms of health and may not accord with what is important for people when they want to exercise their reproductive liberties thereby seeking resources for that purpose.

Another difficulty arising as a result of the application of the general idea of health rationing concerns the concept of health. Usually, the justification for allocating resources to health care has also to be with the concept of health, whatever this concept means. It does not follow from this, however, that health or ill-health are adequate ethical bases for allocating resources within health care but that they are necessary for such allocation to take place.[33] It follows from these two difficulties

---

[30]   Another important consideration, which will not be discussed in this article, is what inequalities we ought to reduce or prevent. Arguably, some inequalities will matter more than others, especially those that tend to sustain, compound, and reinforce inequalities in other aspects of life.

[31]   The article will assume that the justification for allocating resources to health care has to be health, whatever this concept means. It does not follow from this, however, that health or ill-health are adequate ethical bases for allocating resources within health care. Gavin Mooney, '"Communitarian Claims" As An Ethical Basis for Allocating Health Care Resources' (1998) 47 (9) *Social Science & Medicine* 1171.

[32]   AJ Culyer, 'Need: The Idea Won't Do – But We Still Need It' (1995) 40 (6) *Social Science & Medicine* 727.

[33]   Mooney (note 31).

that when one considers whether fertility care and ARTs more generally should be accessed to whoever needs them, one has to address first the question of whether these needs are classified as health needs. This may not be an easy task when one considers the act of reproduction, especially reproduction of adult women, single women or gays, who may otherwise by healthy but usually suffer from unequal access to fertility care.

A better way to address the justice and rationing question without necessarily involve the laden concept of need would be to investigate whether access to fertility care and ARTs can be justified under major theories of justice. In this article I wish to argue that despite strong intuition that denying a person access to the very means that would enable them to become parents is an unjust treatment of that person, most theories of justice would find it difficult to provide and support an argument for equal access to IVF treatment. I will turn now to discuss these theories.

3. Libertarianism

The job of justice, libertarians argue, is to protect individual liberty and property rights, not to bring about some patterned conception of distribution. Of course this is a problem when you don't acknowledge a citizen's right to health care, let alone the right to access fertility treatment.[34] In their view, like other welfare rights, the right to health care removes it from the political arena where negotiations are undertaken and compromise is struck, leading to the fact that policy decisions are not made by representative institutions but by courts whose rulings are handed down. As a result, social cohesion, democratic governance and individual freedom are undermined[35] and tremendous inefficiencies are generated.[36] Inefficiencies mostly occur when governments supplant competitive markets in making investment decisions relating to, e.g. health care, and in producing and delivering health-related goods and services.

Another way to frame the libertarian position would be to hold that rewards should be given to those who by virtue of skill, prescience, risk-taking and so forth determine for themselves what is worth and desired and take positive steps to satisfy these. Under such a view the individual has the freedom to express her

---

[34] Compare Sade who argues that medical care is neither a right nor a privilege: it is a service that is provided by doctors and others to people who wish to purchase it" Robert M Sade, 'Medical Care as a Right – A Refutation' (1971) 285 *NEJM* 285: 1288, 1289 and Goodman interpreting international and national laws to only create "an expectation that governments will promote better health care for their citizens, especially by facilitating access to basic health services". Timothy Goodman, 'Is There a Right to Health?' (2005) 30 *Journal of Medicine & Philosophy* 643, 652. The expectation for health cannot be compelled by law but depends on a market-based policy environment that offers incentives for private sector investment, production and innovation, ibid. at 659.

[35] Most disturbingly, the breach of individual liberty is made possible through the expansion of the power of governments to regulate, tax, hire and fire as a result of their increased responsibilities for funding and guaranteeing the entitlements secured by the welfare rights. Goodman, *ibid* at 650.

[36] Goodman, ibid.

wishes, select from a variety of competing options and dispose of them without coercing others.[37]

It follows that inequalities in access to fertility care and ARTs may be unfortunate, but not unfair, unless some intentional violation of another's liberty or property rights is responsible for the inequalities.[38] Priority setting should be a matter of individual choice among health plans or insurance programs in the market place and there is (and could) not (be) need for social agreement on what counts as minimum health, or in our case minimal access to fertility care.[39] Fertility care is thus viewed not as an entitlement but as a good provided through the market.[40] Reliance upon individual market choice is claimed to produce greater efficiency, to make individuals be accountable for different lifestyle choices and to avoid moral conundrums accompanying debates about morally contested choices like infertility treatment.

4. Utilitarianism

Under Utilitarianism the standard of justice depends on the principle of utility which demands that we seek to maximize overall good. The way benefits and burdens are distributed independently of aggregate welfare is thus irrelevant to Utilitarianism. Such a view is problematic since in some instances, health care delivery may go against calculations of societal advantage, like in the case of providing medical care for the aged or the disabled. Moreover, and regardless of the possible exclusion justified by Utilitarians, as Paul Ramsey noted, "we have no way of knowing how

---

[37] G Outka, 'Social Justice and Equal Access to Health-Care' (1974) 2 *Journal of Religious Ethics* 11, 19; Sade (note 34) 1289.

[38] Madison Powers and Ruth Faden, 'Inequalities in Health, Inequities in Health Care: Four Generations of Discussion About Justice and Cost-Effectiveness Analysis' (2000) 10 (2) *Kennedy Institute of Ethics Journal* 109, 110.

[39] As argued by Goodman, "access to health care cannot be a human right, since there is no shared understanding of what constitutes good health care. Patients differ in their health care preferences; medical culture and standards of practice vary from one location to another; available services and benefits change frequently with the introduction of new technologies; and physicians make independent clinical judgments about what their patients need. These and similar variables would make it virtually impossible for governments to anticipate and fund the costs involved in recognizing an individual right to health." Goodman (note 35) 655.

[40] One of the major criticisms to such a view holds that competitive health markets have many market failures as they are characterized by informational gaps, monopoly suppliers, unequal bargaining power and other deficiencies. This is mostly observed e.g. in the market for pharmaceuticals where due to patent protections competition is limited for a fixed period of time, price information about competing medicines is difficult to find and governments are perceived as more straightforward and reliant than market-based mechanisms to secure scientific innovations that contribute significantly to the lives and health of people. Arnold S Relman and Marcia Angell 2002. America's Other Drug Problem: How the Drug Industry Distorts Medicine and Politics. *The New Republic* (16 December 2002), available: http://healthcoalition.ca/archive/jan28-06.pdf. Goodman, *ibid* at 651-652. For a response to this criticism see Richard Epstein, 'Does America Have a Prescription Drug Problem? The Perils of Ignoring the Economic of Pharmaceuticals' Institute for Policy Innovation (October 7, 2004), available at: http://www.ipi.org/.

really and truly to estimate a man's societal worth or his worth to others or to himself in unfocused social situations in the ordinary lives of men in their communities.[41]

Specifically, the major obstacle for justifying equal access to fertility care stems from cost effectiveness analysis, especially the evaluation of benefits while these are usually measured in terms of expected health gains. In our context, is helping one to have another come into existence considered a health gain? If so, to whom? Is it the creature that is yet to exist, or is it the patient whose gain may not necessarily be considered "health" gain? Also, Can we estimate the exact costs associated with the social factors affecting future health expenditures of raising these children especially if they will suffer some social harm by being associated with "unwelcome" families?

One can argue that for some groups of people, their coming into existence will result in large expenditures of social resources over a lifetime and in minimal contribution to social utility. Under this and previous arguments, Utilitarianism will find it difficult to justify equal or any other access to fertility care or ARTs.

Allen Buchanan provides a pluralistic moral case for a legal entitlement to a decent minimum of health care resting on the non-rights based idea of enforced beneficence with the assurance that enough others will contribute to the one in need so that such benefit could be secured.[42] His theory provides a justification for coordinating charitable efforts by "focusing them on one set of services (for the needy – D.S.) among the indefinitely large constellation of possible expressions of beneficence", thereby ensuring that the decision to allocate resources to these services will become effective.[43] It follows that the scope and character of the list of services included in the decent minimum is a matter of collective choice, and so the decision which services to allocate and how should only be concerned with the fairness of such a procedure.

One of the major problems with this justification is that since it rests on a libertarian conception of voluntary and discretionary giving (to the needy), it does not provide a firm moral foundation for a minimum health care services for *all*, thereby allowing the benefactors to choose which of the needy they will help.[44] Under Buchanan's proposal only a limited part of the society will have access to this minimum health-care. If fertility care is included in Buchanan's list of minimum care, it is still not clear that everyone has equal access to it. Such an outcome depends on whether various categories of candidates for fertility care should be regarded as "needy" under his theory.

---

41   Paul Ramsey, *The Patient as Person* (Yale University Press 1970) 256.
42   Buchanan's argument is similar to the common justification for enforced principles requiring contributions towards public goods like national defence, energy conservation, etc.
43   Buchanan 2009 (note 18) 31.
44   Buchanan replies to this critique by narrowing its application to individual as opposed to collective beneficence only. In his view, in cases of collective beneficence, the rationales for the duty of beneficence support a nonselective policy, ibid 34.

5. Communitarianism

This theory regards the principles of justice as relative and pluralistic, deriving from various conceptions of the good and it emphasizes the responsibility of society to the individual or the responsibility of individual to society and the community.[45] Communitarians argue that the idea of free and rational choice of the individual is ontologically and epistemologically false and that the only way to understand the human behavior and the *telos* of man is to refer to individuals in their social, cultural, and historical contexts.[46] More specifically, they criticize the individualistic premise that the right is prior to the good meaning both that individual rights cannot be sacrificed for the sake of the general good and that the principles of justice (specifying these rights) cannot be premised on any particular vision of the good life.[47]

From a normative perspective, communitarians argue that individualism results in the impossibility of achieving a genuine community, neglects some ideas of the good life that should be sustained by the state and may justify unjust distribution of goods.[48] The community has an interest in the efficiency of the organization for which they are paying through taxes (health services), and of the ways in which resources are allocated. Additionally, the prospects for credible commitment by the community are greater than those of decision makers or politicians, since the former will be around longer than the latter.[49] The community or society as a whole[50] should decide how resources are allocated to different groups and their consumption by the preferences of members of the society.[51]

---

[45] Communitarians vary in their views as to what constitutes such community. Contrary to Michael Walzer who maintains that communities can encompass nations, Alasdair MacIntyre for example holds a relatively limited conception of community referring mostly to the family the tribe and the neighborhood rather than to the state or the nation. In his view, the state exhibits confusion in values and so one cannot ascribe a shared understanding of the good to the state. In Charles Taylor's view the community constitutes a common culture, including a common language that has the capacity to form independent moral convictions. For the purposes of this article the Shiell and Hawe's definition of community will be adopted: "Community means more than association or shared location. It also means more than the inclusion of interpersonal effects (externalities) in the individual's utility function. The intrinsic and not just the instrumental value of social relationships is important." A Sheill and P Hawe, 'Health Promotion Community Development and the Tyranny of Individualism' (1996) 5 *Health Economics* 241-2.

[46] Alasdair MacIntyre, *After Virtue: A Study in Moral Theory* (3rd ed University of Notre Dame Press 2007).

[47] Michael Sandel, 'The Procedural Republic and the Unencumbered Self' (1984) 12 (1) *Political Theory* 81.

[48] Shlomo Avineri and Avner de-Shalit, 'Introduction' In *Communitarianism and Individualism* (OUP 1992) 1-11.

[49] Mooney (note 31).

[50] For such a requirement to be fulfilled there will have to be a system of educating the citizenry as to setting social rules on informed basis. It also depends on some level of social homogeneity with the risk that minority groups will have their claims adequately acknowledged and promoted by the majority. Mooney, ibid 1174.

[51] ibid. There have been some attempts to establish mechanisms for community decision making in health-related issues through representatives in the UK [J Lenaghan, 'Involving the Public in Rationing Decisions: the Experience of Citizens' Juries' (1999) 49 *Health Policy* 45]; Australia [Medical Council, *Citizens' Jury: What's Fair in Health Care?* (Health Department of Western Australia 2001)]; Israel [N Guttman and others, 'What Should Be Given a Priority – Costly Medications for

Applying this theory to the question of whether one should enjoy from equal access to fertility care may raise some worries. How can we elicit community preferences with regard to reproduction qua community? Who are the representatives of the community whose opinions and values serve decision-making in discharging their responsibilities, especially with regard to private and intimate decisions relating to reproduction and family planning?[52] In addition, under such a view, to bring a child who in some cases will need tremendous support from society may be an irresponsible act and may not be justified.

On the other hand, it can be argued that providing equal access to reproductive technologies is vital to ensure the adequate functioning of society as a whole (by promoting the interests of all members of society) and it is the community traditions and practices themselves that should determine our commitment to equal access to health care and to fertility treatment specifically.[53] There may be pro-natalist communities where such access will support the culture of reproduction, while in other communities where the roles of family, childrearing and procreation receive less attention, equal access to fertility care will not serve as a necessary means to strengthen community life.

6. Norman Daniel's development of Rawls' principle of fair equality of opportunity

According to Norman Daniels, social resources should be allocated so to ensure that everyone can attain the normal opportunity range for his or her society, defined as "the array of life-plans reasonable to pursue within given conditions obtaining in a society."[54] Under this understanding, health care promotes, restores or provides surrogates for normal species functioning, the latter of which is important contributor for the attainment of the normal opportunity range.[55]

In his more recent book, *Just Health* having acknowledged that health needs are broader than the need for health care, and that normal functioning makes a significant but limited contribution to the range of plans of life which people can reasonably adopt (opportunity range), Daniels argues that the right to health should be construed "to characterize functionally the relevant, socially controllable actions, namely those that affect population health and its distribution", even if these actions

---

Relatively Few People or Inexpensive Ones for Many? The Health Parliament Public Consultation Initiative in Israel' (2008) 11 *Health Expectations* 177] and other countries.

52   Mooney Gavin, 'Communitarian Claims and Community Capabilities: Furthering Priority Setting? (2005) 60 *SScM* 247-255; Mooney (note 31). The citizens may be directly involved in decision-making only when it becomes apparent that the rules or principles for priority setting have been broken or not being adhered to. Mooney (note 31) 1174.

53   Michael Walzer, *Spheres of Justice* (Basic Books 1983).

54   Unlike Rawls whose conception of opportunity focuses on access to jobs and offices, Daniels' conception (inspired by Rawls) is broader and relates to all projects and set of life plans the people can reasonably adopt given their talents and skills.

55   Under this theory, a baseline assigned by the natural lottery of talents and skills is taken as a given and equality of opportunity is defined relative to all, regardless of their capabilities to pursue their life plans.

are not normally construed as health care services and even if they involve elements outside the health sector.[56]

However, there is much difficulty in regarding the state of being fertile as part of a person's health just as much as it is difficult to argue that infertility is a disease. Infertility treatment cannot be regarded as medical services devoted to restore normal (physical) functioning or cure disease conditions that involve a great curtailment of normal opportunity range under Norman Daniels' definition of health care[57] nor can it be construed to characterize those actions affecting population health and its distribution. One can even argue that allowing everyone to reproduce creates much burden on society, restricts the conditions for population health, such as food, shelter and environment and limits the distribution of health resources.

Also, even if the general criticism against Daniel's theory can be met (e.g. that health care is important not only because it contributes to attainment of normal opportunity range, that it may be difficult to know for whose perspective the array of life plans should be reasonable to pursue? etc.), the array of life-plans which all (or most) people in a given society can reasonably pursue will be determined in part by the availability and quality of health care in that society.[58] Furthermore, Daniel's theory does not tell us whether, in realities of scarcity, we should devote all resources to narrowing the distance between the opportunity ranges of the worst off and the normal opportunity range or divide resources among all who fall short of the normal opportunity range. The effect of Daniel's idea of normal opportunity range in our case thus depends on the question of whether new reproductive technologies are advanced in a specific society, whether the social views regarding them promote the idea that they should be allocated equally, and whether they are fully or partially financed by the state, so that if one desired to promote her life-plans through the use of these technologies, it would have been feasible. It follows that applying Daniel's idea here may not provide a *prima facie* justification for a *universal* right to access to IVF.

7. Robert Veatch's Egalitarianism

Egalitarianism rests on three basic premises determining the ethics of distribution. These include the assumption that human beings are of equal worth so that no human deserves a claim to more or less than an equal share of available resources; that natural resources have moral implications and have never been "unowned" and available for appropriation and use without conditions attached; and that human

---

[56] Norman Daniels, *Just Health: Meeting Health Needs Fairly* (CUP 2008) 145.

[57] Norman Daniels, *Just Health Care* (CUP 1985) 32. Compare Norman Daniels, 'Health-Care Needs and Distributive Justice' (1981) 10 (2) *Philosophy & Public Affairs* 146, 157 who argues that the biomedical model of disease and health, assumed by his theory, would still count infertility as a disease even though some individuals seek medical treatment to render themselves from being fertile.

[58] This is why Allen Buchanan argues that Daniel's principle requiring equal opportunity must be supplemented with a principle requiring that the opportunity range be maximized up to some limit or maximization of the opportunity range. Buchanan 2009 (note 18) 25.

beings have *prima facie* responsibility to use the resources to move society toward a distribution that is more equal.[59]

It follows that justice requires equality of objective net welfare over a lifetime for each individual, and that a "pragmatic derivative" of this principle favors a right to the health care necessary "to provide an opportunity for a level of health equal as far as possible to the health of other people".[60] In this regard, health care resources are regarded like any other natural resources but are unlike other social goods, so that they should be allocated equally and not according to need.[61]

Like with other theories of justice, the Egalitarian account of health distribution rests on the un-settled notions of health and disease which are difficult to apply in the area of reproduction. Even if one holds that fertility treatment should be regarded as treatment (also for healthy couples), one should wonder whether being a parent contributes to one's level of health as much as organ transplantation or preventive medicine do, so that it should compete with services contributing to one's opportunity to become healthy.

Additionally, according to this theory we must assure people of equal opportunity for welfare or advantage or at least assist or compensate people whenever they suffer a deficit in welfare not resulting from their own fault or choice (prioritarianism).[62] On the other hand, if one made certain choices and opted for a specific lifestyle that poses certain difficulties and risks in reproducing, it can be argued that others do not owe them assistance.[63] In our case, we should ask whether one's sexual orientation or marital status is a matter of choice for which his or her need of assisted reproductive technologies may still be justified? Of a similar concern: do one's poor socio-economic background or narcotic addiction result from one's own fault so that

---

[59] Robert M Veatch, 'Justice and the Right to Health Care: An Egalitarian Account' In TJ Bole and WB Bondeson (eds), *Rights to Health Care* (Kluwer Academic Publishers 1991) 83-102.

[60] An exception for this rule would be when the net welfare of the least well off would be increased by waiving their justice-based claim to health care. In this case, justice is sacrificed in order to act on the principle of autonomy. Hence, unlike Rawls' difference principle which is indifferent to the question of who favors inequality, egalitarianism permits inequality only as a matter of autonomy-based right of the least well off. Veatch, ibid at 100. Another exception would be the deontological principle of promise keeping. If others had been promised health care, then such a principle may serve as a check against the justice-based claim to health care.

[61] If care is distributed on the basis of need and people are permitted to trade for other goods until Pareto optimality is reached, there will be unequal health statuses. Although such a situation will be just since the less healthy will still have had their opportunities for health but traded them away, it will be difficult to distinguish between these people and those who are unhealthy and have not yet been compensated and in some cases, the first will still need a second round of care. Thus, from a practical reason it would have been a good idea to treat health care differently. Veatch, ibid at 92-93.

[62] Richard J Arneson, 'Equality and Equal Opportunity for Welfare' (1989) 56 *Philosophical Studies* 77; GA Cohen, 'On the Currency of Egalitarian Justice' 99 (4) *Ethics* 906.

[63] The emphasis on choice or responsibility is a response to social hijacking by persons with expensive tastes. The idea is to avoid the duty of assistance to those people who choose to cultivate such preferences and are not happy when these are not satisfied through making a consistent proposition about whoever makes risky lifestyle choices and expects others to assist them. Daniels, 2008 (note 56) 75.

she should not be entitled for a justice-based claim to fertility treatment? These are difficult questions to answer, and they go to the roots of what it means to be free.

Finally, Egalitarianism assumes that health is different than other goods and so trades in health should not be permitted. Even if reproduction is part of one's health, we would still want to allow people waive their right to reproduce as part of their autonomy and privacy or, alternatively, as part of the more general concept of justice demanding the improvement of the lot of the least well off or making them more equal to others in net welfare. The latter justification would permit to improve people's lot by trading something they desire less (a certificate for a number of IVF cycles) for something they desire more in the form of health resources (a certificate/coverage for high blood pressure drugs or polio vaccine to the presently healthy) or other social goods (food, shelter).[64]

It may also not necessarily be, as Egalitarianism assumes, that equal net welfare is best measured by equal resource consumption.[65] This is because in our case, if the net welfare which is at stake is parenting a child, then adopting or contracting with a third party to bring a child may serve as good alternatives for consuming IVF cycles. If this is the case, and if these alternatives are not health-care related, then allegedly one can trade them or completely waive them, if and the way she finds fit.

8. My thesis

It follows that major theories of justice would find it difficult to justify an equal access to fertility care and other assisted reproductive technologies. I wish to provide a basis for the claim that such access should be *prima facie* equal, by drawing on Martha Nussbaum's capabilities approach.[66] According to Nussbaum who follows Sen,[67] what matters from the point of view of justice or equality is not our primary social goods, since those with the least marketable skills and talents will be able to enjoy less their life plans than those with more marketable talents or skills,[68] but to give people an equal or at least a sufficient share of capabilities, namely those things a person can do (Sen) or are most important for people for what they are (Nussbaum).[69]

---

64 Egalitarians like Robert Veatch would acknowledge such criticism and argue that justice requires that people will get equal amounts of health care even if this means they are somewhat less well off on balance and that autonomy considerations justifying the free disposal of one's resources are illusionary since there never has been any "unowned resources" to be possessed as private property with regard to which people should exercise their autonomy. Veatch (note 59) 95, 99.

65 Veatch, ibid 96.

66 Martha C Nussbaum, *Women and Human Development: The Capabilities Approach* (CUP 2000).

67 Amartya Sen, 'Why Health Equity' (2002) 11 *Health Economics* 659. For the differences in their approach see Nussbaum, 2000 (Introduction, section III).

68 Norman Daniels provides a defence for the Rawlsian theory in this respect, arguing that the effects of the principle of equality of opportunity are mitigated by the difference principle requiring that inequalities in primary social goods like income and wealth be constrained so that they will advantage those with the worst prospects in life. Daniels, 2008 (note 56) 67-68.

69 The central question asked by the capabilities approach is not how satisfied Mr. X or How much in the way of resources is he able to command. Rather, it is "What is Mr. X actually able to do and to be? Nussbaum, see note 67 (In defense, aside note 65). In his recent book Norman Daniels ar-

Under such theory health is regarded as one of the most important conditions of human life and a significant constituent of human capabilities that we have to value. Therefore, an illness which is un-prevented and not treated because of social arrangements, as opposed to personal choice, has negative relevance to social justice.[70]

Nussbaum lists a specific list of ten basic and universal human capabilities that can be the object of an overlapping consensus among people who otherwise have very different comprehensive conceptions of the good.[71] These are: life; bodily health; bodily integrity; senses, imagination and thought; emotions; practical reason; affiliation; other species; play; and control over one's environment.[72]

On her view, each and every person should be assured – and has the right to demand- the development of an adequate or sufficient set of these basic capabilities.[73] Under this threshold approach, if people are systematically falling under the threshold in any of these core areas of capabilities, they are "fruitless, cut off, in some way but a shadow of themselves".[74] Such a situation should be seen as a situation both unjust and tragic, in need of urgent attention both nationally and internationally[75] – even if in other respects things are going well.[76]

Nussbaum's list conveys the message that certain functions are particularly central in human life so that their presence or absence marks the presence or absence of human life, and that, following Marx' reading of Aristotle, they distinguish humans form animals making them "truly human".[77] The purpose of her approach is to make

---

gues that the space characterizing those plans that people can reasonably adopt given their talents and skills coined "opportunity range" is the capability space defined by Sen. Daniels 2008, ibid 66.

[70] Sen (note 67). Such an understanding further calls for a distinction between health achievement and the capability to achieve good health (which may not necessarily be exercised). Sen (note 67) 660.

[71] This way, the list is set in the context of political liberalism and resembles John Rawls' idea of overlapping consensus. Nussbaum (note 67) Introduction, above note 8) and (In defence, above note 76). Yet, Nussbaum argues that the list should be viewed as a proposal put forward in a Socratic fashion, so that it remains open-ended and humble with the possibility of being contested and remade. In this sense, the list leaves room for a reasonable pluralism and cultural differences. Nussbaum note 67 (in defence above note 80).

[72] Nussbaum, ibid (in defence, above note 82-above note 85). Although one cannot satisfy the need for a specific component of the list by giving a larger amount of another one, Nussbaum argues that practical reason and affiliation stand out as of special importance since they both organize and suffuse all the other components, making their pursuit truly human. Nussbaum, ibid (In defence above note 88).

[73] Although not as her main object, Nussbaum's approach allows for a space within which comparisons of life quality (how well people are doing) are possible.

[74] Nussbaum (note 67) (in defence above note 91).

[75] ibid (In defence note 73).

[76] ibid aside note 65. This is not to say that the capabilities approach is a complete theory of justice and there are additional requirements of justice which are at place. To complement the discussion of the capability approach one also needs to discuss the appropriate role of the public sphere vis-à-vis incentives to private actors, the control of activities of the private actors by public sphere in the latter's pursuit of the capabilities, and more. Nussbaum, ibid (in defence, above note 73).

[77] Nussbaum, ibid (in defence, above note 69 and aside this page).

society pursue basic state of affairs in which persons are treated as each worthy of regard and are put in a position to live really humanly.[78]

It will be argued that access to fertility treatment and assisted reproduction may be justified by reference to six such basic capabilities mentioned in Nussbaum's list, two of which are of the most special importance. Moreover, while discussing the capability list, Nussbaum uses reproduction as an example of a "central human capability",[79] that may further support the main argument of this article.

a. Bodily health – Nussbaum specifically mentions reproductive health under bodily health and in one of her footnotes (fn 83) she also refers to a broad definition of reproductive health, proposed by the 1994 International Conference on Population and Development that includes, among other "having safe sex life and...the capability to reproduce and the freedom to decide if, when and how often to do so."

b. Bodily Integrity – under such a capability Nussbaum includes one's having opportunities for sexual satisfaction and for choice in matters of reproduction

c. Emotions- No doubt reproduction allow one to be able to have attachments to people outside oneself and to form human associations that are crucial for one's development.

d. Practical Reason – reproductive choices, especially the decision of whether to have children, with whom and under what circumstances, are central for "being able to form a conception of the good and to engage in critical reflection about the planning of one's life".

e. Affiliation – having children and making children with one's beloved enables one to "live with and toward others, to recognize and show concern for other human beings, engage in various forms of social interactions; imagine the situation of another and have compassion for that situation." Another form of the protection of this capability would be protections against discrimination on the basis of race, sex, sexual orientation etc. These forms of discrimination are very frequent when one is denied access to fertility care on a non-medical basis.

f. Play – it is with children and through child rearing that one is able to laugh, play and enjoy recreational activities.

Applying Nussbaum's theory to justify equal (and minimal) access to reproductive technologies and to fertility care not only avoids the problematic need to classify reproductive technologies under burdensome concepts such as medicine and health, but it also provides a more elaborate understanding of what Rawls called the primary goods, expanding this list of goods to also include social basis for "natural goods" such as health, vigor, intelligence and imagination.[80] Unlike other theories, especially those emphasizing functioning as the major goal of justice, it

---

[78] ibid (in defence, aside note 73).
[79] See especially, Nussbaum, *ibid* (above note 107, above note 108).
[80] ibid above (note 101).

does not push citizens into functioning in a single determinate manner, thereby precluding personal choices, nor does it deplete important functions such as play or love if they are carried out without latitude of choice or good will of their agent. These theoretical advantages have much force in the context of reproduction and reproductive technologies, that despite their requirement of medical assistance they all reside in the territory of personal choices, human dignity and personal respect.

Yet two main difficulties may arise while applying Nussbaum's theory to justify equal access to ARTs and fertility care. Both difficulties are more general possible criticism of her theory. First, it can be argued that such a view expands the goals for medicine from protecting normal functioning to reconstructing people in order to make their capabilities more equal. Such an expansion may result in difficulty to draw the line between treatments and enhancements,[81] since medicine will now have a duty to enhance the capabilities of those who function normally with less than equal capabilities.[82] While this criticism has much weight it assumes that the distinction between treatments and enhancements or between medical procedures done for therapeutic and non-therapeutic purposes is and should be firm and solid. It also presupposed that the medical profession is acting in a neutral environment and has no obligations to protect and promote the principles of justice and equality in the society. As argued elsewhere, such a distinction suffers from conceptual difficulties and may not be successfully justified neither under basic notions of medical ethics nor by revised goals of the medical profession.[83] One has to rethink the purposes of medicine in light of advanced uses of medical procedures in contexts which are different than healing or combating a disease.

Second, given that sets of capabilities may vary in many dimensions, a question may arise as to how one could judge when one set of capabilities is worse than another? Alternatively, how can one rank difference in or different expressions of capabilities? These questions are especially important in light of the attempt to apply Nussbaum's theory to access to fertility care since only six capabilities from her list may apply, while the other two seem to be irrelevant here. However, these questions call for the development of her more general theory as they indicate a theoretical and practical need to say more on the relationship between the capabilities in her list and the relative importance of any of the items. While this is a significant expansion of her theory, it may not serve as an obstacle to argue that since most of capabilities that are so central to human life may be enhanced through reproduction and reproductive choice, denying access to the means that make reproduction possible *prima facie* contradicts the maxim according to which persons should be treated as each worthy of regard and should be put in a position to live really humanly.

The questions of whether access to IVF and reproductive technologies more generally should be equal or not and what inequalities in access can be justified,

---

[81]   Another related distinction is between medical necessity and a thing which is not medical neces-
       sity.

[82]   Daniels 2008 (note 56) 67.

[83]   Daniel Sperling, 'The Therapeutic Triumph: Making Poor Claims and Offering a Revised Concep-
       tualization to Justify Embryo Selection' (2011) 18(3) *Ethical Perspectives* 407-440.

and on what grounds, will continue to occupy us theoretically and empirically. A starting and more promising point would be to apply Martha Nussbaum's theory of justice to justify equal access to the technologies. Resolving the tension created by the application of the principles of formal justice and equality to ARTs will also shed light on the more fundamental problems in health equity and rationing.

Chapter VII

NICE and the problem of 'postcoc prescribing' in the English National Health Service

Keith Syrett

Amongst the many controversies generated by the recent reforms to the National Health Service (NHS) in England has been a rekindling of anxiety as to so-called 'postcode prescribing'.[1] The situation of seemingly arbitrary geographical inequity in access to treatments and services which this phrase seeks to capture has presented a significant policy problem for government for at least the past two decades, since resource allocation within the NHS began to attain a more explicit character in the early 1990s. This Chapter seeks to identify the nature of the problem and the attempts which have been made to resolve it. It will then focus upon the debate which ensued as a consequence of the announcement by the present British Coalition Government of its intention to alter the role of the agency which undertakes technology appraisal guidance for the NHS, with a view to examining the significant part played by arguments of geographical inequity in shaping the eventual outcome of this debate.

1. An ongoing tension: universality and equity versus local provision and patient choice

The NHS in the United Kingdom (UK) was established on the basis of a principle of universality. Its chief architect regarded it as essential that it should seek to 'achieve as nearly as possible a uniform standard of service for all' and that an 'equally good service is available everywhere'.[2] This value feeds into other foundational tenets of the Service, including notions of equity and comprehensiveness, which have recently been accorded special status within an *NHS Constitution*,[3] to which those providing and commissioning care are legally obliged to have regard.[4] In turn, it is underpinned by the notion of social solidarity upon which most European health

---

[1] While the phenomenon of geographical inequity of access to healthcare exists elsewhere in the UK, the present analysis will focus upon the situation in England. It is worthy of note, however, that a different variant of geographical inequity from that described here – that between those seeking access to treatment on the NHS in England and those doing so *elsewhere in the UK*, as distinct from variations *within* the English NHS – arises as the consequence of health being a matter which is devolved to legislative assemblies in the other constituent countries of the UK.

[2] A Bevan (1945), quoted in C Webster, *The National Health Service: a Political History* (2nd edn, Oxford University Press 2002) 18.

[3] Department of Health, *The NHS Constitution for England* (Department of Health 2010).

[4] Health Act 2009, s 2(2).

systems are based and which the 'Dunning Committee', appointed by the Dutch Government to report on priority-setting in healthcare, defined as 'the awareness of a unity and a willingness to bear the consequences of it'.[5]

Yet a fundamental conflict, which has existed since its establishment in 1948, lies at the very heart of the NHS. While the Service is *national* – denoting that access to it is available to all in equal shares across the country – the management, purchase and provision of resources, including medical treatments and services, is carried out on a geographically localised basis. This powerful countervailing trend of devolution and decentralisation has various facets. In its simplest form, it is manifest in the means by which funds are allocated by central government on a differential basis to those locally-based bodies which are responsible for commissioning care to meet the health needs of their populations. The amount which is allocated is intended to enable each such local body to 'commission similar levels of health services for populations with similar need'.[6] This commitment to horizontal equity also implies vertical equity: that is, that not every local area will receive the same amount, since health needs will vary geographically. This is recognised in the resource allocation formula, which adjusts the share received (calculated initially by reference to share of the population of England) in accordance with the age distribution of the population, overall population health and levels of deprivation, and unavoidable geographical differences in the cost of providing services.[7]

Decentralisation, linked to policies to enhance supply-side efficiency and patient choice, has also been a key feature of central governmental policies relating to the structure of the NHS over the past two decades. In the early 1990s, the creation of the so-called 'internal market', in which the functions of purchasing and provision of healthcare were split in an attempt to enhance value for money, appeared to signal a further retreat from such centralised control as had ever existed in an NHS in which the autonomy of the medical profession has always been a fundamental characteristic. The relationship between purchasers and providers of care, each of whom gained increased freedom in the performance of their functions, was now to be governed by contract. The consequence was that differing 'menus' of treatments and service emerged across the country, as will be explored in the next section.

Although the Labour administration elected in 1997 sought – in seeming contrast to its neoliberal Conservative predecessors – to 'renew the NHS as a one-nation health service offering fairness and consistency to the population as a whole',[8] it simultaneously attempted to 'give clinicians greater control and flexibility over the resources they receive... giv[ing] GPs (general practitioners) the maximum choice about the treatment option that best suits individual patients, free from

---

[5]   Committee on Choices in Health Care, *Choices in Health Care* (Committee on Choices in Health Care, 1992) 15. See also Council of the European Union, 'Conclusions on common values and principles in European Union Health Systems' (2006/C 146/01).

[6]   Department of Health, *Resource Allocation: Weighted Capitation Formula* (7th edn, Department of Health 2011) 7.

[7]   ibid.

[8]   Department of Health, *The New NHS: Modern, Dependable* (Cm 3807, 1997) [7.1].

the constraints imposed by artificially distinct budget heading:
clinical and financial responsibility so that those who prescri
have control over the financial decisions they make.'[9] Subsequ
of 2000 rejected both 'command and control and market fragmenta..... , ...
that 'clinicians and managers want the freedom to run local services. They want to
be able to shape services around patient needs'.[10] The government endeavoured to
realise this vision through a policy of 'shifting the balance of power', which entailed
the establishment of Primary Care Trusts (PCTs) at the heart of the English NHS,
with responsibility for management of some 80% of the total NHS budget.[11] As Ham
observes, these reforms aimed to 'ensure that staff in close contact with patients
were able to influence how resources were used'.[12] Consequently, they carried the
potential to exacerbate geographical disparities in the allocation of those resources
in response to differing patterns of demand.

Devolution of power, responsibility and resource management to front-line
NHS staff was accompanied by a growing emphasis upon strategies and rhetoric of
patient choice. The central vision articulated in the *NHS Plan* was one of 'a health
service designed around the patient',[13] a principle taken further in *Delivering the
NHS Plan* (2002)[14] and *Creating a Patient-Led NHS* (2005). The latter spoke of the
need to 'anticipate what patients want... and to retain enough flexibility to respond
to individual needs', noting that 'this is different from the planned services of the
past – where clinicians and managers decided in advance what would be offered
to patients'.[15] Such policies, while intuitively attractive in so far as they privileged
individual autonomy, also threatened to undermine founding principles of universality and equity and to disrupt the collective allocation of resources:

> The principles underlying the NHS are collectivist, and are intended to secure
> access to healthcare services irrespective of the socioeconomic or demographic
> circumstances of the individual. The key to this system is that everybody
> be treated fairly given available resources. The system is unfortunately but
> inevitably resource-constrained, since the government can only target a pro-
> portion of the nation's wealth toward these services. If there were unlimited
> NHS resources, everybody's preferences could be satisfied fully, and it would
> be possible to allow everyone free, extensive choice. In reality, it is necessary
> to accept that the NHS cannot provide everything that each individual patient

---

[9]   ibid [9.8].
[10] Department of Health, *The NHS Plan: a plan for investment, a plan for reform* (Cm 4818-I, 2000)
      [2.31]-[2.32].
[11] Department of Health, *Shifting the Balance of Power: the Next Steps* (Department of Health 2002);
      National Health Service Reform and Care Professions Act 2002, s 2.
[12] C Ham, *Health Policy in Britain* (5th edn, Palgrave Macmillan 2005) 65.
[13] See Department of Health (note 10) chapter 1.
[14] Department of Health, *Delivering the NHS Plan: Next Steps on Investment, Next Steps on Reform*
      (Cm 5503, 2002).
[15] Department of Health, *Creating a Patient-Led NHS: Delivering the NHS Improvement Plan* (Depart-
      ment of Health, 2005) [5.36].

may want. Although an individual patient may gain greater satisfaction from being offered more choice, the opportunity costs of extending choice to this patient, arising from the reductions in resources available to other patients, may be detrimental to the overall social good. The individual patient is a poor judge of the institutional resource constraints, and thus the notion of choice and its individualistic underpinnings is fundamentally inconsistent with the collectivist NHS ethos... If we conclude that the system's founding solidarity-based principles remain relevant we might thus be better advised to place emphasis on protecting the decision-making capabilities of those imbued with social responsibilities, rather than be guided increasingly by individual patient choice.[16]

2. *Geographical inequities in access*

Prior to the establishment of the 'internal market' in the 1990s, most rationing of resources in the NHS – with the exception of the waiting-list – was carried out primarily by clinicians and was implicit in character, with allocative decisions being presented to patients as exercises of medical judgment.[17] The degree of clinical autonomy afforded to medical professionals (especially to GPs who functioned as gatekeepers of secondary (hospital) care), coupled with the mechanism for resource allocation outlined above, meant that, in practice, local variations in access to care were inevitable. However, such discrepancies remained largely obscured from public view and therefore did not create significant controversy.

The contractual nature of the purchaser/provider relationship in the 'internal market' both rendered rationing visible and raised the prospect of geographical differentiation. Purchasers of care (such as district health authorities and 'fundhold-ing' general practitioners) were obliged to publish plans and to enter into contracts specifying which services would be made available. As a consequence, it became apparent which services and treatments were *not* being provided, albeit that most of those which were excluded tended to be at the 'margins' of NHS care, such as tattoo removal, varicose vein surgery and reversal of sterilisation or vasectomy.[18] Furthermore, the obligation placed upon purchasers to respond to the health needs of *their* populations meant that it was possible for a treatment of service to be available in one locality and not in another. Where this occurred, access was (at least in some cases) dependent upon the apparently arbitrary consideration of where one lived; and, perhaps more importantly, there was public awareness of this fact. This phenomenon became known as 'postcode prescribing'.

In order to comprehend why this issue is controversial, it is useful briefly to probe the concept of equity in health policy. As Culyer notes, there is no universally

---

[16]   A Oliver and JG Evans, 'The paradox of promoting choice in a collectivist system' (2005) 31 *Journal of Medical Ethics* 187, 187.

[17]   See S Harrison and G Wistow, 'The purchaser/provider split in English Health Care: Towards Explicit Rationing?' (1992) *Policy and Politics* 123.

[18]   See R Klein, P Day and S Redmayne, *Managing Scarcity* (Open University Press 1993) 68-70.

accepted definition of the term, since 'any idea of "equity" must embody value judgments about what it is that makes for a good society'. However, it is clear that it connotes some notion of equality, which might itself have a variety of meanings, including equality of opportunity or equality of outcome.[19] Equity in the distribution of healthcare may be thought to be especially necessary because of its special moral importance. Upon one influential account, this derives from its capacity to restore normal species functioning, thereby correcting impairments to an individual's ability to pursue their preferred "plan of life" or "conception of the good".[20] If one considers that obligations of justice extend to all of the residents of a particular jurisdiction, then healthcare should be distributed in such a manner that no one is denied the possibility of restoration to full functioning (and, by extension, a chance to live the life they would choose) by restrictions on access to healthcare resources which are available to others within that jurisdiction. Put another way, geography – like class or religion – is an irrelevant or arbitrary characteristic in determining who shall have access to healthcare.[21]

This analysis, of course, returns us to the tension at the heart of the NHS which was outlined in the preceding section of this Chapter. Whether we consider geographically differentiated access to healthcare resources within a country to be inequitable will depend upon how far obligations of justice arising from spatial proximity can be said to extend.[22] In a society in which moral obligations are properly owed only to one's family or immediate neighbours, geographical distinctions in access to healthcare resources beyond the neighbourhood would be regarded as ethically unproblematic. It appears, however, that 'the nation is important psychologically to underwrite our behaviour, moral or otherwise' – perhaps because of the existence of shared cultural and moral understandings, or because the nation is an aspect of personal identity – and that it can therefore be argued that special obligations of justice are owed to our compatriots.[23] The existence of a *national* health service founded upon values of uniformity and universality serves to underline the significance of such obligations, with the controversy generated by instances of 'postcode prescribing' demonstrating that the countervailing trends

---

[19]   A Culyer, 'Equity – some theory and its policy implications' (2001) 27 *Journal of Medical Ethics* 275, 275.

[20]   N Daniels, *Just Health Care* (Cambridge University Press 1985) 49.

[21]   Arbitrariness or random allocation is well captured by the phrase which is most commonly deployed in the media to describe the phenomenon examined here: the 'postcode *lottery*'. This can refer to any geographical variation in provision of public services and is therefore wider in scope than the specific issue of access to treatments on the NHS which is the focus of the present discussion. For this reason, 'postcode prescribing' has been used here: however, for an analysis of other types of geographical variation in the NHS, including hospital admissions and overall expenditure on particular disease areas, see *inter alia* King's Fund, *Local Variations in NHS Spending Priorities* (King's Fund 2006) and J Appleby, V Raleigh, F Frosini and others, *Variations in Health Care: the good, the bad and the inexplicable* (King's Fund 2011).

[22]   For a discussion, see P Nortvedt and M Nordhaug, 'The principle and problem of proximity in ethics' (2008) 34 *Journal of Medical Ethics* 156.

[23]   D Hunter and A Dawson, 'Is there a need for global health ethics? For and against' in S Benatar and G Brock (eds) *Global Health and Global Health Ethics* (Cambridge University Press 2011) 85.

of decentralisation and localism which were previously identified are insufficient to displace the bonds of solidarity associated with citizenship.

The potential for geographical inequities to generate conflict and contestation, thus posing a significant policy problem for government, is demonstrated by two instances of litigation dating from the late 1990s. In *R v North Derbyshire Health Authority, ex parte Fisher*,[24] the health authority refused beta interferon treatment to a multiple sclerosis sufferer. The refusal was pursuant to a policy which it had adopted whereby funding for such treatment would only be provided to patients who participated in a randomised controlled trial of the drug. Because the date of a proposed national trial had been indefinitely postponed, this amounted in practice to a 'blanket ban' on funding for the drug and, as such, the authority had failed to demonstrate that it had taken proper account of the terms of government guidance the aim of which was to target the treatment at those patients who were most likely to benefit from it. The guidance issued by the government was not binding: the authority might therefore have been able to justify departure from it, had it provided a satisfactory explanation of why it had done so. However, the fact that neighbouring health authorities (which were not in a materially different financial position to North Derbyshire) had, despite initial reluctance, made arrangements to fund beta interferon in appropriate individual cases lent weight to the conclusion that the authority's policy of refusing funding was unlawful. Thus, while the existence of geographical inequity was not in itself decisive in the patient's favour (as must have been the case given that the statutory obligation placed upon health authorities is one to commission services to meet *local* needs), it nonetheless placed a significant burden upon the authority to justify an approach which was different from its neighbours, which burden it had failed to discharge.

'Postcode prescribing' was also evident in *R v North West Lancashire Health Authority, ex parte A, D and G*,[25] although again geographical inequity was merely one factor which contributed to the court's finding of unlawfulness. In this case, the health authority had determined that gender reassignment surgery should be placed low on its list of priorities for funding. The Court of Appeal acknowledged that it was open to an authority to prioritise funding in the light of limitations upon the resources available for provision of services and treatments to meet the needs of its local population. However, it determined that the authority had acted unlawfully because, despite making provision for circumstances of 'exceptional clinical need' which would justify gender reassignment surgery, such exceptional circumstances could never, in practice, be established because the authority had refused to accept that this form of treatment was effective. The authority had therefore unlawfully fettered its discretion. More pertinently for the present discussion, the finding of unlawfulness on this ground was supplemented by a second argument based upon the authority's failure to explain why it had departed from a significant body of medical evidence which regarded gender reassignment surgery as effective. In this

---

[24] [1997] EWHC Admin 675.
[25] [1999] EWCA Civ 2022; [2000] 1 WLR 977.

context, the court noted that other health authorities had adopted 'less restrictive policies' on funding the treatment, with at least 34 (of 41) authorities making some form of provision for it.[26] Once again therefore, in a situation of geographically differentiated access to a form of treatment, a legal obligation was imposed upon the authority to explain a deviation from the norm, in the absence of which the court drew the conclusion that a refusal to provide funding was unlawful.

Of course, these legal challenges to refusals by health authorities to provide funding represent only a very small proportion of the number of cases in which treatments or services which were available to individuals living in one geographical area were denied to those residing in another, albeit that they were – by definition – amongst the more controversial instances. That the issue was emerging as a significant policy problem is evident from criticism of variations between health authorities expressed by the parliamentary Select Committee on Health in 1995,[27] and a call made by two influential commentators for central government (rather than local health authorities) to determine which treatments were to be provided by the NHS.[28] The governmental response to such arguments was to claim that 'to draw up a national list of treatments which will and will not be provided would be an exercise fraught with danger'.[29]

This position did not change with the election of the Labour Government in 1997. However, the new administration did seek to address the problem of 'postcode prescribing' in ways which stopped short of a specification at national level of the 'basket' of NHS treatments and services, as will now be detailed.

3. Responses to the problem: the birth of NICE

Rudolf Klein, arguably the leading academic analyst of the changing political environment in which the NHS operates, has written perceptively of the paradox which existed within the Labour Government's policies for the NHS during the late 1990s.[30] Whilst on the one hand (and as outlined previously in this Chapter), the reforms devolved greater autonomy and power to local clinicians and managers, on the other there was a strengthening of techniques and instruments of central control. The latter strategy was necessary if government was to realise its objective of achieving a level of uniformity of provision and service across the country, an aspiration which included – but which was not restricted to – the elimination (or, at least, the mitigation) of instances of 'postcode prescribing'. Thus, in the White Paper issued in 1997, the Government 'committed itself anew to the historic principle of the NHS: that if you are ill or injured there will be a national health service there to help; and access to it will be based on need and need alone – not on your ability to

---

26   [2000] 1 WLR 977, 991.
27   Health Committee, *Priority Setting in the NHS: Purchasing* (HC 1994-95, 134-I) [113].
28   B New and J LeGrand, *Rationing in the NHS: Principles and Pragmatism* (King's Fund 1996) 70.
29   *Government Response to the First Report from the Health Committee* (Cm 2826, 1995) [4].
30   R Klein, *The New Politics of the NHS: From Creation to Reinvention* (5th edn, Radcliffe Publishing 2006) 206-08.

pay, or on who your GP happens to be *or on where you live'*,[31] and sought to 'renew the NHS as a genuinely *national* service', understood to mean that 'patients will get fair access to consistently high quality, prompt and accessible services right across the country'.[32] As these extracts make clear and as Klein observes, the policies 'can be seen as an attempt, for the first time ever, to apply the full logic of the values and constitutional principles that had shaped the NHS in 1948'.[33]

Two new mechanisms were of key importance in pursuit of the goal of enabling 'patients [to] get greater consistency in the availability and quality of services, right across the NHS'.[34] First, the National Institute for Clinical Excellence (NICE),[35] which came into being in 1999, was created to act as a 'single, national focus for appraisal of significant new and existing interventions'[36] through its technology appraisal function, and as a means of disseminating best practice in the management of particular conditions through its clinical guideline activity (with implementation of guidelines initially overseen by a separate Commission for Health Improvement).[37] Secondly, National Service Frameworks were established to offer national statements of standards and service models for major care areas and disease groups, based upon evidence. Their objective was 'to set clear quality requirements for care... based on the best available evidence of what treatments and services work most effectively for patients.'[38] Of these two, it is NICE which is most germane to the present analysis, since its work directly impacts upon access to treatments and services in the NHS, although its clinical guidelines also contribute to maintaining consistency in quality of care.

By far the most high profile and controversial function of NICE is its health technology appraisal role. Technology appraisals take the form of guidance and, as such, are not legally binding upon clinicians, who remain free to depart from the recommendations issued by the Institute if the circumstances of the patient so require. However, Directions which have been issued by the Secretary of State for Health to all PCTs and NHS Trusts require funding to be provided for technologies which are recommended by the Institute for use on the NHS (whether such

---

[31]   Department of Health (note 8) [1.5]. Emphasis added.
[32]   ibid [2.4]. Emphasis in original.
[33]   Klein (note 30) 207.
[34]   Department of Health (note 8) [7.8].
[35]   The Institute was renamed the National Institute for Health and Clinical Excellence on 1 April 2005 when it assumed the role of issuing public health guidance formerly exercised by the Health Development Agency. The Health and Social Care Act 2012, s 232, renames the Institute the National Institute for Health and Care Excellence, to reflect its assumption of a role in setting quality standards for the social care sector.
[36]   Department of Health, *A First Class Service: Quality in the new NHS* (Department of Health 1998) [2.11].
[37]   The Commission was abolished in 2004 and replaced by the Healthcare Commission, which itself was abolished in 2009. NICE now works with the Care Quality Commission, but primary responsibility for implementation lies with local NHS bodies, with assistance provided by the Institute. See 'Dear colleague' letter, 14 June 2004 and NICE, 'Benefits of Implementation', available at http://www.nice.org.uk/ search for: benefits of implementation (accessed 27 July 2011).
[38]   http://www.nhs.uk/nhsengland search for: National service frameworks (accessed 27 July 2011). See also NHS Executive, *National Service Frameworks* (HSC 1998/074, 1998).

use is unlimited or is restricted to certain classes of patient, certain conditions or under certain specified circumstances).[39] This has a crucial practical impact upon resource allocation. If NICE *recommends* that a particular intervention should be made available on the NHS, then funding must be found to provide it – albeit that a clinician is not obliged to prescribe it to a particular patient. This position is now underlined by the *NHS Constitution*, which accords to patients a 'right to drugs and treatments that have been recommended by NICE for use in the NHS, if your doctor says they are clinically appropriate for you'.[40] If, on the other hand, NICE *does not recommend* an intervention, or *recommends that its availability should be limited*, then it remains possible that the intervention will be funded either universally within a local area, or beyond the restricted classes of patient indicated by NICE. However, in practice, this scenario will occur relatively infrequently since scarcity of resources is likely to preclude funding for non-recommended interventions: commissioning bodies operating in financially straitened circumstances will almost inevitably prefer to divert their limited funds elsewhere. In short, therefore, the mandatory funding Direction translates into general availability on the NHS of treatments recommended by NICE, and general unavailability of those treatments which are not recommended (subject to arrangements for consideration of exceptional cases, which will be discussed below). There will also be a substantial intermediate category of treatments which are made available only to those who fall within the categories or conditions specified in the Institute's guidance.

It is important to note that the establishment of NICE constituted merely a partial amelioration of the problem of 'postcode prescribing'. Its contribution in this regard has been limited by a number of factors. First, as previously noted, recommendations contained in technology appraisals do not displace the clinical judgment of individual physicians, while clinical guidelines have only ever possessed an advisory status. This raises the possibility of continued local variation. Secondly, and relatedly, NICE has had some difficulty in ensuring that its guidance is implemented, particularly in respect of its clinical guidelines (which tend to be more complex in nature than technology appraisals, not least because they impact upon a broader range of health professionals).[41] The Institute has recently taken a number of steps to improve levels of implementation.[42]

However, the most significant limitation on NICE's capacity to ensure uniformity of access to treatments and services arises from the fact that it does not appraise every single intervention: indeed, it 'carries out appraisals on only a minority of new and existing licensed health technologies'.[43] There are two distinct aspects of this.

---

[39] Directions to Primary Care Trusts and NHS Trusts in England concerning arrangements for the funding of technology appraisal guidance from the National Institute for Clinical Excellence (NICE), 1 July 2003. Funding should normally be provided no later than three months from the date of the issuing of the guidance by NICE.

[40] Department of Health (note 3) 6.

[41] See J Chidgey, G Leng, T Lacey, 'Implementing NICE guidance' (2007) 100 *Journal of the Royal Society of Medicine* 448.

[42] See NICE, *Putting NICE Guidance into practice* (NICE 2009).

[43] King's Fund, *Briefing: NICE Technology Appraisals* (King's Fund 2008) 3.

First, the White Paper of 1998 which set out details of NICE's role in the NHS envisaged that the Institute would conduct appraisals of significant *existing* interventions.[44] Although certain treatments which were in existence at the date of the Institute's establishment have been covered (for example, beta interferon for multiple sclerosis), much of its work has tended to focus upon newly-developed technologies.[45] Crucially, the Institute does not have the capacity to appraise *all* existing technologies which are used within the NHS, and (except where the guidance is specifically directed towards the question of disinvestment of interventions)[46] does not provide advice upon which treatments should be displaced. Since government does not provide additional resources to enable the cost of funding NICE recommendations to be met, it is inevitable that disinvestment in existing treatments and services will have to take place if the funding obligation is to be honoured. Such decisions are taken at local level, raising the prospect that 'inconsistent decisions on which treatments to abandon will also lead to geographical variation... There is a danger that although medicines approved by NICE are adopted uniformly, the treatments, interventions, and services that are displaced will be selected haphazardly'.[47]

Secondly, geographical variation in access might arise in a situation where NICE has not appraised a particular new technology. This may occur because the technology has not been selected for appraisal by the Institute,[48] because it has not yet received a licence from the European Medicines Agency,[49] or because the appraisal process is ongoing.[50] While government has indicated that it is unacceptable to cite an absence of NICE guidance as the sole reason for non-funding of a treatment,[51] there remains the possibility of 'unexplained variation in the way local decisions are made on the funding of new drugs before the appraisal takes place, or where no guidance is issued.'[52] In order to minimise the controversy generated by this variant of 'postcode prescribing', the *NHS Constitution* contains a right 'to expect local decisions on funding of other drugs and treatments to be made rationally following a proper consideration of the evidence',[53] and a concomitant obligation to provide an explanation of a decision not to fund a treatment which a clinician

---

[44] Department of Health (note 36) and accompanying text.

[45] See Health Committee, *National Institute for Health and Clinical Excellence* (HC 2007-08, 27-I) [13].

[46] See Department of Health, *Selection Criteria for Referral of Topics to NICE* (2006).

[47] D Hughes and R Ferner, 'New drugs for old: disinvestment and NICE' (2010) 340 *British Medical Journal* 690, 690, 692.

[48] The final decision on which interventions should be appraised by the Institute rests with the Department of Health. The National Horizon Scanning Centre provides ministers with advance notice of new and emerging health technologies which should be appraised.

[49] For an example of this, see *R (on the application of Rogers) v Swindon NHS Primary Care Trust and Secretary of State for Health* [2006] EWCA Civ 392, discussed further below.

[50] NICE has frequently been criticised for the length of its appraisal process. Although an expedited process of appraisal for certain interventions was introduced in 2005, appraisal may still take between 9 months and two years: see Health Committee (note 45) [185].

[51] See Department of Health, *Good Practice Guidance on Managing the Introduction of New Healthcare Interventions and links to NICE Technology Appraisal Guidance* (Department of Health, 2006) 4.

[52] Department of Health, *High Quality Care for All: Next Stage Review Final Report* (Cm 7432, 2008) 43.

[53] Department of Health (note 3) 6.

has deemed appropriate for the patient. Legally binding Directions underpin the latter obligation,[54] and the Department of Health has issued guidance as to the processes which local decision-makers should adopt in situations where no positive NICE guidance exists.[55]

These procedural requirements extend beyond the provision of reasons for rationing decisions, to obligations to make arrangements for patients whose circumstances may be regarded as exceptional and who therefore warrant a departure from a general policy not to locally fund a particular healthcare intervention. The legal duty to cater for exceptionality thus represents another means through which access to treatment may vary from place to place. The degree to which variation in this context may be regarded as acceptable and uncontentious is likely to depend upon considerations of horizontal and vertical equity.[56] That is, it will be acceptable to treat patients unequally across geographical boundaries *if* the clinical needs which form the basis of a claim for exceptionality differ; by contrast, patients with the same clinical needs should be dealt with identically across geographical areas.

That such principles of equity have not always been upheld is apparent from a leading case relating to access to Herceptin (trastuzumab) for early-stage breast cancer. In *R (on the application of Rogers) v Swindon NHS Primary Care Trust*,[57] the applicant successfully challenged the decision of the Trust not to provide funding for the drug, which had not at that stage been appraised by NICE. The Trust had purported to allow for exceptional cases, but had also indicated (in a somewhat misguided attempt to give effect to guidance issued by the Secretary of State for Health) that resources were not to be considered as relevant to the decision not to fund. The Court of Appeal held that, in circumstances in which the Trust ostensibly 'had funds available for all women within the eligible group whose clinicians prescribed Herceptin',[58] the only rational means of determining who fell within the category of exceptional circumstances was on the basis of clinical need; yet the Trust had not provided any criteria for establishing what might amount to such clinical need. Effectively, therefore, it had operated a 'blanket ban' on access to the drug. As the court noted, this position differed from that adopted by a number of other PCTs elsewhere in the country:

> Many authorities and trusts have taken a different view from that of the PCT and have funded Herceptin treatment for all applicants in the eligible group. These include Cheshire and Merseyside; Greater Manchester; Hampshire and Isle of Wight; Leicestershire, Northamptonshire and Rutland; North and East Yorkshire and North Lincolnshire; Northumberland and Tyne

---

[54]   Directions to Primary Care Trusts and NHS Trusts concerning decisions about drugs and other treatments, 1 April 2009.

[55]   Department of Health/National Prescribing Centre, *Defining Guiding Principles for Processes Supporting Local Decision-Making about Medicines* (Department of Health 2009).

[56]   However, for further discussion see A Ford, 'The Concept of Exceptionality – a Legal Farce?' (2011) 19 *Medical Law Review* (forthcoming).

[57]   See note 49.

[58]   ibid [77].

and Wear; South West Peninsula; and South Yorkshire Health Authorities, together with Lancashire and South Cumbria Cancer Network; all Primary Care Trusts in Norfolk and in Northern Ireland; and many PCTs in London, Staffordshire, Cambridgeshire, Somerset and elsewhere. Other trusts have declined routinely to fund Herceptin treatment. It is not however clear on the evidence what, if any, role the cost of the drug and the treatment, has played in the policies of such trusts. It may be that some trusts have a policy similar to that of the PCT, whereas others take account of funding difficulties and apply a test of exceptional circumstances in deciding for which patients to provide funding for Herceptin treatment and for which patients not to do so.[59]

The conclusion which may be drawn from this is that women with identical clinical needs were being treated differently depending upon where they lived because not all PCTs understood or applied criteria of exceptionality in the same way. And while in this case the inequity was undoubtedly ameliorated once NICE issued guidance recommending that the drug be made generally available on the NHS,[60] it cannot be assumed that the interposition of the Institute always serves to eliminate all forms of variation which arise from the operation of a procedure to determine exceptionality. It should be noted that local decision-makers are obliged to consider exceptional circumstances even when NICE recommends that a particular intervention should *not* be available on the NHS. A survey conducted by the Rarer Cancers Forum indicated that there was significant variation in rates of PCT approval of requests for exceptional funding of drugs, certain of which relate to drugs rejected or restricted by NICE. Most notably, one Trust approved 96% of cases in which exceptionality was argued, whereas a neighbouring Trust approved none.[61]

4. Reforms to the NHS: the Coalition Government's proposals

The preceding discussion demonstrates that it would be mistaken to assume that the measures taken by the Labour Government between 1997 and 2010 had the effect of *solving* the problem of 'postcode prescribing'. However, it might be argued that, at least in two respects, the situation had improved. Firstly, the creation of NICE had provided a single, national, mechanism for approval of a significant number of the most high-profile, innovative and expensive new healthcare interventions, access to which would be likely to create the highest level of public interest and controversy. The mandatory funding attached to NICE guidance ensured that all PCTs in England were obliged to provide funding for access to such treatments, although clinical judgment was ultimately decisive in determining access in an individual case. Secondly, albeit latterly, procedures by which access decisions were made were harmonized in response to legal obligations to establish panels to

---

59   ibid [53]-[54].

60   NICE, *Trastuzumab for the adjuvant treatment of early-stage HER2-positive breast cancer*, NICE Technology Appraisal 107 (2006).

61   Rarer Cancers Forum, *Taking Exception* (Rarer Cancers Forum 2008) 26.

determine exceptionality claims and to provide explanations for decisions to refuse funding for treatments.

It was against this backdrop that the Coalition Government led by David Cameron announced proposals for radical reform of the NHS in England in its White Paper, *Equity and Excellence: Liberating the NHS*, in July 2010.[62] The document reaffirmed a political commitment to the values and principles of the Service, notably the 'social solidarity of shared access to collective healthcare'.[63] However, it also set out significant changes in the manner in which commissioning (*ie* purchasing) of healthcare for local populations was to be undertaken. PCTs were to be abolished and replaced by local consortia of GP practices created with a view to securing optimum healthcare outcomes for their patients and locality.[64] These would 'commission the great majority of NHS services for their patients', agreeing and monitoring contracts with providers such as hospitals, and would have responsibility for management of the commissioning budgets of constituent GP practices.[65] They would be supported by a statutory NHS Commissioning Board which, *inter alia*, would allocate funds to them 'on the basis of seeking to secure equivalent access to NHS services relative to the burden of disease and disability', would commission certain services directly (such as those provided by GPs themselves, as well as dentistry, maternity and national/regional specialised services including heart and liver transplants), would hold consortia to account, and would provide national leadership on commissioning, for example by designing model contracts and setting quality standards.[66]

The Coalition Government's stated purpose in devolving power and responsibility to general practitioners for the management of budgets was to reduce bureaucratic, top-down control, giving clinicians a greater degree of autonomy and bringing decision-making closer to patients. The latter objective connected to a central theme of the White Paper, partnership between patients and clinicians, expressed in the slogan 'nothing about me without me'.[67] It is clear, however, that the reforms were also designed to secure supply-side efficiencies:

> Primary care professionals coordinate all the services that patients receive, helping them to navigate the system and ensure they get the best care (of course, they do not deliver all the care themselves). For this reason they are best placed to coordinate the commissioning of care for their patients while involving all other clinical professionals who are also part of any pathway of care. Commissioning by GP consortia will mean that the redesign of patient pathways and local services is always clinically-led and based on more effec-

---

[62] Department of Health (Cm 7881, 2010). See now Health and Social Care Act 2012.

[63] ibid 7.

[64] GP consortia were subsequently renamed 'clinical commissioning groups', reflecting the fact that the membership would consist of more than general practitioners. See Department of Health, *Government Response to the NHS Future Forum Report* (Cm 8113, 2011) [3.14] and Health and Social Care Act 2012, ss 10, 25-28.

[65] Department of Health (note 62) 28-29; Health and Social Care Act 2012, s 10.

[66] Department of Health (note 62) 31-32; Health and Social Care Act 2012, ss 9, 23-24.

[67] Department of Health (note 62) 13.

tive dialogue and partnership with hospital specialists. It will bring together responsibility for clinical decisions and for the financial consequences of these decisions. This will reinforce the crucial role that GPs already play in committing NHS resources through their daily clinical decisions – not only in terms of referrals and prescribing, but also how well they manage long-term conditions, and the accessibility of their services. It will increase efficiency, by enabling GPs to strip out activities that do not have appreciable benefits for patients' health or healthcare.[68]

Given the objective of effective management of limited NHS resources, it might be thought that NICE would retain a key role in the reformed structure. Leaving to one side, for the present, the issue of geographical inequity, a centralised health technology assessment process such as that carried out by the Institute can be valuable for a government which seeks to keep a limit on health expenditure. This is because, in principle, the process of appraisal should permit disinvestment in ineffective and inefficient treatments and services, and enable greater oversight and control to be exercised over total expenditure than would be possible if *all* allocative decisions were taken at local level.[69] And, indeed, the White Paper did seem to envisage a continued central role for the Institute, stating that it would be placed on a 'firmer statutory footing, securing its independence and core functions'.[70] In particular, emphasis was placed upon NICE's role in the development of quality standards consisting of statements and measures which would act as 'markers of high-quality, cost-effective patient care'.[71] These would form the basis of commissioning guidelines set by the NHS Commissioning Board, with which local commissioners and providers would seek to comply in order to achieve improvements in health outcomes. That these proposals additionally denoted a continued commitment to minimising the problem of geographical inequity was apparently confirmed by the promise that 'together with essential regulatory standards, these [quality standards] will provide the national consistency that patients expect from their National Health Service'.[72]

Viewed from this perspective, the announcement, in November 2010, of radical changes to NICE's role from 2014 onwards was unexpected, albeit that the context in which those changes would take place had broadly been presaged in the White Paper.[73] The Government had announced therein its intention to replace the expiring Pharmaceutical Price Regulation Scheme – under which manufacturers are free to fix prices subject to a ceiling on profits made on NHS sales – with a system of 'value-based pricing' (VBP) for all new pharmaceuticals,

---

[68]   ibid 27.

[69]   However, it has been estimated that funding NICE technology appraisal recommendations cost the NHS £1,022 million between 2003 and 2007: see D. Batty, 'Q & A: How NICE works', http://www.guardian.co.uk/ search: medicine and health (accessed 27 July 2011).

[70]   Department of Health (note 62) 23. See Health and Social Care Act 2012, Part 8.

[71]   Department of Health (note 62) 23.

[72]   ibid 24.

[73]   In fact, the proposed change had first been announced in HM Government, *The Coalition: Our Programme for Government* (Cabinet Office 2010) 25.

designed to 'help ensure better access for patients to effective drugs and innovative treatments on the NHS and secure value for money for NHS spending on medicines'.[74] No mention was made of the Institute having a part to play in this process. However, as further details emerged of the proposed new pricing regime, a junior minister in the Department of Health commented that its introduction would render NICE's function of evaluating the cost-effectiveness of treatments 'somewhat redundant'.[75] The speculation to which this remark gave rise led a spokesperson for the Department to state as follows:

> We will introduce a new system of value-based pricing which will make effective treatments affordable to the NHS. Our plans will ensure licensed and effective drugs are available to NHS clinicians and patients. We will focus NICE's role on what matters most – advising clinicians on effective treatments and quality standards – *rather than making decisions on whether patients should access drugs that their doctors want to prescribe.*[76]

The clear implication of this (and the assumption which was drawn by the media)[77] was that, once VBP had been introduced, it would no longer be obligatory for clinical commissioning groups (which, by then, would have succeeded PCTs) to provide access to treatments which had been the subject of a positive technology appraisal. That is, the statutory Direction mandating funding for interventions recommended by NICE would be repealed. Instead, decisions on funding of treatments and services would be taken within locally-based commissioning groups, as noted by the (apparently unprepared) Chief Executive of the Institute in an e-mail to NICE colleagues:

> NICE will continue to undertake an independent and objective assessment of the benefits of new drugs. What will be different is that from 2014, it is likely that we will stop short of converting that assessment of therapeutic benefit and economic impact into a recommendation for use... Our appraisal will be available to the NHS and the public, *to help inform the decisions they take locally on the way the drug should be used...* I am sorry that speculation on the future of the appraisal programme has appeared without me being able to forewarn you. We were also taken by surprise.[78]

---

[74]   Department of Health (note 62) 26.

[75]   Earl Howe, 25 October 2010, quoted in http://www.healthpolicyinsight.com/ (accessed 27 July 2011).

[76]   1 November 2010, quoted in 'NICE to lose powers to decide on new drugs', available at http://www.bbc.co.uk/news/health (accessed 27 July 2011). Emphasis added.

[77]   See *eg* 'Drug victory for patients: "Penny-pinching" NICE stripped of power to ban life-saving drugs', *Daily Mail* (1 November 2010); 'NICE to lose powers to decide on new drugs', *The Guardian* (29 October 2010).

[78]   E-mail from Sir Andrew Dillon to NICE Appraisal Committee members, 2 November 2010, available at http://www.healthpolicyinsight.com/ (accessed 27 July 2011). Emphasis added.

The subsequent consultation document on VBP confirmed the proposed alteration in the Institute's role, albeit without explicitly spelling out that the requirement to fund recommended treatments was to be dropped. It stated that NICE would 'continue to have a central role, both in undertaking pharmacoeconomic assessments and in providing advice to the NHS on the relative clinical and cost-effectiveness of treatments',[79] but proposed that appraisal of the clinical and cost-effectiveness of a particular treatment should merely be a starting-point for establishing the value of a medicine. Other factors, such as burden of illness, therapeutic innovation and wider societal benefits were to be considered in the calculation of value and the reimbursement price which the NHS was prepared to pay.[80] In line with the earlier White Paper, the consultation document envisaged a shift in NICE's role, away from one in which it was effectively the decision-maker on access to new technologies in the NHS (subject to exercise of clinical judgment) to one which would 'increasingly focus on giving authoritative advice to clinicians on when and how the most effective treatments can best be used and on the development of quality standards which set out the standards the NHS should aim for in the treatment of certain conditions'.[81] That this shift connected to the broader objective of enhanced autonomy for general practitioners was made apparent by the document:

> For GP consortia in England, value-based pricing offers the opportunity of increasing access to medicines. GPs should have clinical freedom to determine their patient's *(sic)* need, or to commission through consortia for the more flexible use of drugs in secondary care... This approach reflects the Government's view that doctors are best placed to make clinical decisions, whilst being supported in their prescribing and commissioning roles by consortia and, importantly, by authoritative and expert advice from NICE.[82]

The precise shape of the 'value-based' model of pricing new pharmaceuticals, and NICE's part within it, continues to remain somewhat unclear at the date of writing. The Government's response to the consultation process, which was published in July 2011, acknowledged a 'lack of detail of some of the aspects of the VBP process', which it claimed was 'a consequence of carrying out a consultation at an early stage in the policy development process'.[83] However, it reiterated that 'NICE will have a central role in the VBP system including undertaking the planned pharmacoeconomic evaluation, in which is it is world leader.'[84]

---

[79] Department of Health, *A new value-based approach to the pricing of branded medicines: a consultation* (Department of Health, 2011) 5 (Ministerial Foreword).
[80] ibid [4.10-4.32].
[81] ibid [5.4].
[82] ibid [5.11].
[83] Department of Health, *A new value-based approach to the pricing of branded medicines: Government response to consultation* (Department of Health 2011) [5.141].
[84] ibid [5.148].

5. Responses to the proposals: the recurring spectre of 'postcode prescribing'

Despite some positive responses, notably from media outlets which had consistently criticised the Institute's work,[85] the proposals to remove NICE's powers to recommend or reject treatments and instead to allow local clinical commissioning groups to make decisions on what would be funded generated a substantial degree of criticism. Significantly, a powerful strand of this criticism was rooted in the language of geographical inequity, premised upon the belief that localising funding decisions on new health technologies would inevitably result in differential access across the country.

Thus, the Chair of the GPs' committee at the British Medical Association outlined a vision of 'busloads of sick people traversing the country based on rumours that another consortium is offering drugs that their local one isn't';[86] the Chair of the Royal College of General Practitioners opined that 'NICE protects us. I am absolutely convinced it needs to be strengthened, not reduced. I'm long enough in the tooth as a GP to have worked pre-NICE, I know what postcode lotteries are about and I'm very concerned',[87] adding that 'I don't understand why he [ie the Secretary of State for Health] is putting in a system that in Scunthorpe you can get a different service to Scarborough, when we've spent the last 60 years working against that';[88] while a group of consultant oncologists writing in the *British Medical Journal* argued that 'the plan to abolish the NHS funding of decisions made by NICE in favour of local decision making will result in even greater inconsistency of treatment across the country'.[89] Beyond the medical profession, the Chief Executive of Asthma UK commented that 'once they [NICE] have decided in favour of a new drug, or against it, you know that whether you live in Liverpool or Brighton you will be treated the same. In the future, GP consortia will make those decisions. That means, for a new drug... which is expensive but often life-changing – you might get it in West Sussex but not if you live over the border in East Sussex';[90] a *Financial Times* editorial urged the Government to 'Be nice when handling NICE',[91] defending the principle of a centralised body which would systematically assess therapeutic advantage and cost-effectiveness; while an editorial commentary in *The Guardian* newspaper warned that the impact of the reform would be to stimulate unmanageable levels of demand for expensive new treatments across the entire NHS: 'if one GP consortium offers an expensive but doubtful drug, the patients' group for that disease will make sure

---

85   See especially *Daily Mail* (note 77).
86   Dr. L Buckman, quoted in 'Fears that curbing NICE will bring chaos', *Financial Times* (7 November 2010), available at http://www.ft.com/ (accessed 27 July 2011).
87   Dr. C Gerada, quoted in 'Gerada hardens RCGP's stance on White Paper', *Pulse* (15 November 2010), available at http://www.pulsetoday.co.uk/ (accessed 27 July 2011).
88   Dr. C Gerada, quoted in 'Doctors warned to expect unrest over NHS reforms', *The Guardian*, 20 November 2010.
89   J Graham, S Guglani, S Elyan and others, 'Return of the postcode lottery' (2011) 342 *British Medical Journal* 69.
90   N Churchill, 'Postcode lottery or postcode democracy?', available at http://blog.asthma.org.uk/ search: postcode and lottery (accessed 27 July 2011).
91   8 November 2010.

all other patients demand it from their consortiums. This is not a postcode lottery, but a one-way escalator: whatever one offers, all must offer soon.'[92]

As for the Institute itself, its initial response – shaped to some degree by the surprise which was outlined in the preceding section – was conciliatory, reflective of a 'wait and see' attitude: its Chief Executive stating that 'we support moves to extend access to new treatments at prices which reflect the additional value to patients. NICE is the global leader in evaluating the benefits of new drugs and we anticipate being at the heart of the new arrangements.'[93] However, in its response to the consultation on VBP, NICE was more critical of the proposed downgrading of its role, drawing upon the geographical inequity argument and making an explicit connection to the provisions of the *NHS Constitution*:

> The current system for providing advice on the optimal use of new drugs to NHS organisations, prescribers and patients, which has the NICE technology appraisal process at its heart, contains three clear signals, which together provide an important mechanism for stimulating the consistent uptake of effective and cost effective new drugs:
>
> A clear recommendation for the optimal use of new drugs, from NICE, in the form of technology appraisal guidance and through quality standards;
>
> A Funding Direction, which required NHS organisations to make available the resources necessary to allow new drugs, recommended by NICE to be used;
>
> The provision in the NHS Constitution that provides a right for patients to have access to new drugs recommended by NICE.
>
> We believe that any new process for value-based pricing needs to retain these elements. This is because we know that even in recent years, during which the NHS has been receiving significant real terms growth, the application of the recommendations made by NICE has been uneven. The tight fiscal environment in which the NHS will be operating over at least the next 4 years, together with the proposed arrangements for commissioning NHS services will tend to increase, rather than reduce, the challenge of achieving consistent access to new treatments. We believe that there is a risk that patients and health professionals who want to use drugs made available under the new arrangements may find it difficult to do so unless the new arrangements retain these powerful, national reference points.[94]

Other respondents to the VBP consultation were equally exercised about the potential of the proposals to exacerbate geographical inequities in access to treatment.

---

[92] P Toynbee, 'Forget patients, Lansley is the servant of big pharma' (2 November 2010). See also 'Nobbling NICE will lead to a new NHS postcode lottery', *The Guardian* (4 November 2010).

[93] Sir A Dillon, quoted in 'NICE to lose powers to decide on new drugs', *BBC News* (1 November 2011), available at http://www.bbc.co.uk/news/ (accessed 27 July 2011).

[94] NICE, *Value Based Pricing: Response to the Department of Health consultation* (NICE 2011) [4]-[5], available at http://www.nice.org.uk/media/ (accessed 27 July 2011).

Significantly, disquiet was voiced by the full range of stakeholders involved in the process of health technology appraisal. For example, the Alzheimer's Society (which had previously participated in litigation against the Institute)[95] professed itself 'very concerned that removing the mandatory nature of NICE guidance will result in a return to the situation that occurred pre-NICE. Access to treatment depended on where one lived, not whether the treatment was cost and clinically effective. NICE has helped to remove that "postcode lottery". We do not feel the case has been made for making NICE guidance optional'.[96] Similarly, the Royal College of Nursing argued that 'the proposed system introduces significant risk with the removal of the mandatory status of NICE technology guidance. We feel that this has the potential to disadvantageously increase "postcode lottery" prescribing'.[97] Furthermore, the Association of the British Pharmaceutical Industry, referring to data which indicated that regional variations in access to certain cancer treatments persisted despite the Government's establishment of a special fund to facilitate access to drugs for the disease,[98] and observing that this situation would be likely to continue under VBP, called for 'consideration... to be given... to NICE guidance issued for medicines after 2014 carrying with it a mandatory implementation requirement'.[99]

The issue was also taken up in parliamentary committee debate upon the provisions of the Health and Social Care Bill, which gave effect to the Government's proposals for reform of the NHS in England. An MP from the opposition Labour Party asked: 'was the whole rationale of the establishment of NICE not to address the issue of the postcode lottery – drugs and therapies being available in one part of the country and not another? Will these changes not turn the clock back and make that situation more likely?'.[100] Another referred to the NICE response to the VBP consultation,[101] commenting that 'what NICE says is that clear steps have to take place at a national level to try to ensure that there is as small a postcode lottery as possible'.[102] Similarly, an MP from the governing Conservative-Liberal Democrat coalition argued that 'one benefit of NICE rules is that no PCT at the moment can refuse to deliver a treatment that NICE recommends. There is a possibility of that happening with the Bill, because if we change the function of NICE there will not

95   The Society appeared as an interested third party in *R (on the application of Eisai Limited) v National Institute for Health and Clinical Excellence* [2007] EWHC 1941 (Admin).
96   Letter from Alzheimer's Society (9 March 2011), available at http://alzheimers.org.uk/site/ (accessed 27 July 2011).
97   Royal College of Nursing, *RCN Response to Department of Health Consultation on a new value based approach to the pricing of branded medicines (England)* (Royal College of Nursing 2011) 5, available at thttp://www.rcn.org.uk/ (accessed 27 July 2011).
98   The Cancer Drugs Fund, launched on 1 April 2011, makes £200 million a year available for access to cancer treatments which have not been recommended or which have been restricted by NICE or which the Institute has not (yet) appraised. See Department of Health, *Guidance to Support the Operation of the Cancer Drugs Fund in 2011-12* (Department of Health 2011).
99   Association of the British Pharmaceutical Industry, *Value Based Approach to the Pricing of Branded Medicines: Consultation Response from the Association of the British Pharmaceutical Industry* (ABPI, 2011) 31, available at http://www.abpi.org.uk/ (accessed 27 July 2011).
100   PBC Deb (Bill 132) 29 March 2011, col 1169 (G Morris).
101   See note 94.
102   PBC Deb (Bill 132) (note100), col 1172 (L Kendall).

be approved standards in the same sense. That must produce a more uneven picture in terms of health outcomes.'[103]

Given the degree of disapprobation which was generated by the proposal to limit NICE's powers in respect of new treatments, it was scarcely surprising that the Government eventually reconsidered its position on this matter, while remaining committed to implementation of a form of VBP for new pharmaceutical products from 2014 onwards. The change in stance was first signalled in the response to the 'NHS Future Forum', an independent group of clinicians, patient representatives, voluntary sector workers and others which was established to oversee a 'listening exercise' in the wake of widespread criticism of all elements of the Coalition Government's intended reforms to the NHS. In this context, the Government committed itself to upholding all of the patient rights contained in the *NHS Constitution*, including that which guaranteed access to drugs and treatments recommended by NICE if a clinician considered these appropriate to prescribe to a patient.[104] Subsequently, in its response to the VBP consultation, the Government noted that a 'number of responses' had stressed the value of the mandatory funding requirement attached to NICE guidance,[105] and conceded that 'we understand the concerns about potential local variations in prescribing of drugs with a value-based price'.[106] Accordingly, it confirmed that it was its intention to 'maintain the effect of the funding direction in the value-based pricing arrangements, to ensure that the NHS in England consistently funds medicines with a value-based price. The NHS will be required to fund drugs already recommended by NICE, as well as drug treatments subject to the value-based pricing regime'.[107] An accompanying written statement issued by the Secretary of State for Health reiterated the need for geographical equity in access to treatment as a rationale for the change in position:

> We want the arrangements that we put in place from 2014 to ensure that NHS patients have consistently good access to effective, clinically appropriate medicines, wherever they live. The current funding direction requiring NHS commissioners in England to fund drugs and treatments in line with NICE's recommendations is designed to achieve this, and it is one of our key objectives for value-based pricing.[108]

6. Conclusion

The fact that the Coalition Government was eventually obliged to rethink its proposals to remove the mandatory funding Direction which attaches to NICE technology appraisal guidance demonstrates the considerable potency of equity as an enduring

---

[103] ibid, col 1174 (J Pugh).
[104] Department of Health (note 64) [2.5], [3.84].
[105] Department of Health (note 83) [5.168]. See above n.40 and accompanying text.
[106] ibid [5.164].
[107] ibid [5.142].
[108] HC Deb, 18 July 2011 vol 531, col 81WS.

foundational principle of the NHS. As this Chapter has shown, this principle has, particularly over the course of the past two decades, become primarily associated in public, political, media and (to some degree) legal discourse with values of uniformity and consistency in access to treatment, irrespective of geographical factors.[109] This is so notwithstanding the countervailing centrifugal trends of localism and clinical autonomy which – to a greater or lesser extent – have always been weaved into the fabric of the Service and which have recently been supplemented by strategies of a competitive or quasi-competitive nature which serve to strengthen horizontal purchaser-provider relationships rather than the vertical, hierarchical, unified model upon which the NHS is usually said to be based.

'Postcode prescribing' is, of course, a real-world issue which will inevitably generate distrust and dissatisfaction amongst those patients who are denied access to treatments which others, elsewhere, have received. Such sentiments may, in certain instances, reach such a profound level that local decision-makers are forced to confront a challenge to the legitimacy of their moral and legal authority to undertake resource allocation, as the instances of litigation examined in this Chapter demonstrate (although it is notable that, from a judicial perspective, geographical inequity merely serves as an underpinning for other, more legally persuasive, arguments of unlawfulness). However, perhaps more significant – because it is in this form that the greater part of the population will experience the phenomenon, driven by media reporting of it – is the function of 'postcode prescribing' as a political symbol or narrative which speaks to arbitrariness and unfairness of treatment in the NHS. As such, it both facilitates and constrains political action, as the story of NICE serves to illustrate.

The Blair Government constructed 'postcode prescribing' as a policy problem which demanded decisive action. This afforded it *justification* for implementing measures, notably the establishment of NICE, whose centralising nature might otherwise have generated intractable opposition within the NHS, especially from clinicians concerned as to intrusions on their autonomy as a consequence of the so-called 'cookbook medicine' character of clinical guidelines.[110] The Institute's function in minimising geographical inequity may also have served to soften the otherwise hard choices on access to treatments on the NHS which it was, in effect, required to undertake, rendering those decisions somewhat more publicly acceptable as a consequence.

By contrast, the discourse of geographical inequity proved to be an effective rallying-point for *opponents* of the reform proposals advanced by the Coalition Government, such as Labour Party politicians and representatives of clinicians who were concerned as to the possible consequences of assuming greater responsibility

---

[109]   Equity was also central to the debate on so-called 'top-up' fees in the NHS: that is, whether it was permissible to supplement publicly-funded care with privately-purchased treatment. For discussion, see K Syrett, 'Mixing Public and Private Treatment in the UK's National Health Service: a challenge to core constitutional principles?' (2010) 17 *European Journal of Health Law* 235.

[110]   For an early refutation of the 'cookbook medicine' argument, see D Sackett and others, 'Evidence-based medicine: what it is and what it isn't' (1996) 312 *British Medical Journal* 71.

for allocative choices.[111] However, ultimately more decisive was the fact that even those who might have been expected to be broadly supportive of a reduction in the Institute's role – such as pharmaceutical companies or patient groups which stood to lose out if NICE refused or restricted access to a particular intervention – professed fears relating to the arbitrariness which might ensure if NICE's functions were curtailed. Thus, confronted with opposition from the entire range of stakeholders in the process of technology appraisal, and further limited by the relative inflexibility inherent in a 'constitutional' commitment to universal access to NICE-recommended treatments, the Coalition Government was left with little choice but to abandon this aspect of its changes to the NHS.

In this instance, therefore, rather than providing an impetus to set the reform agenda, 'postcode prescribing' served significantly to restrict governmental policy space. That matters should develop in such a way might seem surprising to a casual observer of British politics, schooled in the notion of an overmighty executive branch which operates relatively unchecked by countervailing constitutional forces, albeit that a subscriber to a 'network approach' founded upon the 'post-parliamentary thesis... that policy change generally took place only when the relevant "policy community" agreed it was necessary and a consensus existed on the direction of change',[112] might be rather less shocked by the course of events. Yet most of all, this episode surely demonstrates the veracity of the oft-quoted remark that the NHS is 'the closest thing that the English have to a religion'.[113] Any erosion of that religion's foundational tenets – such as equity and universality – is apt to be highly controversial, and any government which interferes with them or is perceived to do so, as was the Coalition Government in the episode described in this Chapter, does so at a high political cost.[114]

---

[111]   See especially Dr. C Gerada (note 88): 'At worst, the negative impact for GPs could be patients lobbying outside their front door, saying, 'You've got a nice BMW car but you will not allow me to have this cytotoxic drug that will give me three more months of life'.

[112]   J Richardson, 'Government, Interest Groups and Policy Change' (2000) 48 *Political Studies* 1006, 1006. The 'post-parliamentary' thesis was first comprehensively advanced in J Richardson and G Jordan, *Governing Under Pressure: the Policy Process in a Post-Parliamentary Democracy* (Martin Robertson, 1979).

[113]   N Lawson, *The View from Number 11: Memoirs of a Tory Radical* (Bantam 1992) 613.

[114]   It remains to be seen whether the Coalition Government will incur long-term electoral unpopularity as a consequence of the highly controversial reforms to the NHS contained in the Health and Social Care Act 2012.

Chapter VIII

Re-balancing the Rationing Debate – Tackling the Tensions between Individual and Community Rights

Christopher Newdick

Health care is not just about the rights of individuals. It is part of a larger endeavour to secure optimum performance from finite funds for a community of patients and to do so fairly, safely and effectively. At a time of economic austerity, questions arise about affordability. Health economists refer to this as "opportunity cost" because choices to commit finite funds to particular purposes prevent those funds being available for other purposes. Inevitably, choices that favour the needs of individuals (what I call the "individualist" approach), tend to disfavour the needs of communities (what I call the "community" approach). My purpose is to discuss the limitations of the "individualist" approach to rationing and the need for clearer population-based objectives in health care. By itself, the individualist approach is not equipped to respond to the challenges presented by scarce resources, especially in the light of the increase in chronic, "life-style" diseases. I do not deny the importance of the individual perspective, but argue that we need to re-balance the debate.

Therefore, we should be more explicit about the public dimension of health care. However, the community-based approach presents problems of its own and there is a risk that it may undermine the legitimate clinical rights of individuals. Unless we get the balance right, the forces acting on health care costs will make the individualist approach unsustainable. By looking though s telescope, instead of a microscope, we highlight broader concerns and different objectives. This chapter considers examples from the English National Health Service (NHS), but the issues it raises are international in scope. Thus, we consider: (1 the individual rights model of substantive and procedural rights, (2 the community dimension of health care, (3 community interests and the politics of individualism and (4 population-based objectives and the tyranny of targets.

I. *The Individual Rights Model of Substantive and Procedural*

In the NHS, two systems emphasise individual rights, ie *substantive*, rights and *procedural* rights. Substantive rights guarantee access to the treatment itself. In the English NHS, substantive rights have been created by the National Institute for Health and Clinical Excellence (NICE). NICE is a national authority which makes recommendations to commissioners of health care. NICE exists because there are (currently) 152 Primary Care Trusts (PCTs) in England.[1] The Secretary of State is subject to a legal duty to "promote a comprehensive health service"[2] but this duty is delegated by regulations to each of them to perform on his behalf.[3] There is clearly a risk of unacceptable variations in local decision-making which, in a *national* health service, is unattractive. NICE introduces greater consistency between commissioners. Thus, recommendations in its *Technology Appraisal Guidance* (TAG) have mandatory legal effect so that the treatment must be made available by commissioners provided a doctor prescribes it.[4] This substantive duty is confirmed by the NHS Constitution and the duty upon commissioners to support funding is enforceable by individuals against PCTs in judicial review. Conscious of opportunity costs, NICE becomes more critical of the clinical evidence of effectiveness for drugs which cost more than £20,000 per Quality Adjusted Life Year (QALY) and is unlikely to support treatments costing more than £30,000 per QALY.[5] Thus, a number of expensive treatments for cancer have not been recommended because their costs are not justified by their limited therapeutic benefits.

This encourages consistency throughout the NHS and it can respond to general concerns about particular illness, such as cancer (treatments for which are frequently considered by NICE). However, with the exception of NICE, the NHS does not use a national list of approved treatments. Instead (as we have seen) it delegates to commissioners the duty to promote a "comprehensive" health service subject to their own discretion. One of the benefits of delegating this duty to local health commissioners is their ability to respond to local needs in consultation with their local communities.[6] Clearly, decisions made at national level tend to be detached from the concerns of local health commissioners and the stresses on their resources. Each of NICE's mandatory (ie substantive) recommendations carries opportunity costs which have consequences for other patients and there is a balance between consistency at national level and local responsiveness. Put another way, within finite resources, the greater the greater the number of treatments subject to substantive rights, the smaller the discretion that remains to local decision-makers. This brings us to the alternative mechanism for rationing health care; the procedural-rights approach.

Procedural rights are promoted at national level by the English, *NHS Constitution*. Procedural rights do not guarantee access to treatment. Instead, they guarantee a fair and transparent procedure by which the decision-makers are required to

---

[1]   From April 2013, The Health and Social Care Act 2012 will abolish PCTs and replace them with around 200 Clinical Commissioning Groups. The intention is to inject greater clinical influence into the commissioning process.

[2]   See National Health Service Act 2006, s 1.

[3]   Under the National Health Service (Functions of Strategic Health Authorities and Primary Care Trusts and Administration Arrangements)(England) Regulations 2002, SI 2002, No 2375.

[4]   See Secretary of States' Directions on the National Institute for Clinical Excellence 2003.

[5]   See generally, C Newdick, 'Evaluating New Technology in the English National Health Service in T Jost (ed), *Health Care Coverage Determinations – An International Comparative Study* (OUP 2005).

[6]   In truth, although it is easy to find single-issue pressure groups, finding genuine representatives of "public" interests is more difficult.

justify decisions. After years of denying that rationing was really necessary, the government promoted the NHS Constitution in the form of a statutory Bill of Rights for patients in 2010.[7] The ideas promoted by the NHS Constitution reflect over ten years of principles developed by judicial review cases.[8] Thus (other than the substantive rights supported by NICE), in allocating health resources, local commissioners must adhere to the procedural rights-approach promoted by the NHS Constitution. The procedural approach recognises that hard choices are inevitable and accommodate broader, community interests alongside the needs of individuals. Equally, it is heavily accountable to the individual. Actually, the Constitution is not wholly candid about the need for hard choices in health care. It says only: "The NHS is committed to providing best value for taxpayers' money and the most effective use of finite resources."[9] However, documentation which explains the Constitution confirms: "Like all public authorities, PCTs are required to operate within finite budgets and, therefore, have to prioritise some treatments over others according to the needs of local communities...[ ] Disinvestments should be considered along with investments."[10] "Disinvestment" recognises that, as in any system working within fixed financial allocations, choices that favour some may disfavour others. The NHS Constitution describes how decisions should be made according to transparent procedures. Promoting the principle of transparency, it says:

> ...each PCT must have in place arrangements for making decisions and adopting policies on whether particular healthcare interventions are to be made available for patients for which the PCT is responsible... Each PCT must compile and publish clear written information outlining the arrangements specified...[11]

Promoting accountability to individuals, it says that patients are entitled to know how those arrangements have been applied in their individual case.

> You have the right to expect local decisions on funding of ... drugs and treatments to be made rationally following a proper consideration of the evidence. If the local NHS decides not to fund a drug or treatment you and your doctor feel would be right for you, they will explain that decision to you.[12]

---

[7] "Each of the [NHS bodies] must, in performing its functions, have regard to the NHS Constitution [and] Each person who provides NHS services under a contract, agreement or arrangements [inc PMS and GMS] must, in doing so, have regard to the NHS Constitution" (Health Act 2009, s2).

[8] For the evolution of case-law in this area, see C Newdick, *Who Should We Treat? – Rights, Rationing and Resources in the NHS* (OUP 2005).

[9] *NHS Constitution*, Principle 1(6).

[10] *Defining Guiding Principles for Processes Supporting Local Decision Making About Medicines*, 3 and 14.

[11] Directions to PCTs and NHS trusts concerning decisions about drugs and other treatments 2009.

[12] *NHS Constitution*, Principle 2a.

This means that: "Where a PCT makes a decision to refuse a request for the funding of a healthcare intervention, where the PCT's general policy is not to fund that intervention, the PCT must provide that individual with a written statement of its reasons for that decision."[13] In addition, the right of explanation is supplemented by a further right of appeal because "PCTs should establish an appeals process for decisions made on individual funding requests, including clearly defined grounds of appeal, independent of the original process and open to patients and the public."[14]

Therefore, health service commissioners must have fair, reasonable and account-able systems for setting health priorities and be prepared to explain to individual patients the reasons for their decisions. Procedural rights insist that rationing decisions are taken within a fair and consistent framework of values capable of explaining why a particular treatment cannot be funded. Although they are pro-cedural only, they are certainly *enforceable* by individual patients. The legal power of procedural rights enables judicial review courts to "overturn" (but not reverse) a decision and to return it to the commissioner to be reconsidered in the light of the court's criticisms. In legal theory, the decision-maker may come to the same conclusion in respect of a particular case, provided the reasoning is defensible, but political and media pressure often mean that the decision is reversed. However, it stops short of creating substantive rights to particular treatment.

These generic procedural rights are given effect by local commissioners of health care (other than treatments subject to mandatory NICE guidance). Local commis-sioners may combine in consortia to use *ethical frameworks* to make decisions about treatments consistent with the NHS Constitution. For example, such a framework exists in the South Central region of the English NHS where nine PCTs have combined to adopt a single Ethical Framework which forms the basis of its advice to its PCT commissioners.[15] The ethical framework is applied to specific *treatments* to determine which should be recommended to local PCTs and which should be considered "low priority." Low priority means that the treatment will not normally be purchased by the commissioner unless the patient is judged to have exceptional circumstances which merit an exceptional response.[16] To preserve consistency in its approach, it considers the following criteria for decision-making, (a) evidence of clinical and cost effectiveness of the treatment, (b) equity and the principle of equal access for equal need, (c) the health care needs of the patient and their capacity to benefit from the treatment, (d) the cost of the treatment and its opportunity costs, (e) the sometimes countervailing needs of the community and (f) guidance from

---

[13] Direction to PCTs and NHS trusts concerning decisions about drugs and other treatments 2009.
[14] Defining Guiding Principles for Processes Supporting Local Decision Making About Medicines, 23.
[15] See http://www.berkshire.nhs.uk/ search: priorities, containing the South Central Ethical Frame-work and the 170 treatment recommendations made within it. The author is a founder member of the committee which commenced work in 1999. This accountability for reasonableness ap-proach is championed in N Daniels, *Just Health – Meeting Health Needs Fairly* (OUP 2008), chapter 4 and N Daniels and J Sabin, *Setting Limits Fairly – Learning to Share Resources for Health* (OUP 2008), chapters 3 and 4.
[16] Exceptional circumstances are considered below.

national institutions such as NICE, or the government.[17] This "procedural-individual" rights approach puts individual claims into a community context and, with proper procedural safeguards in place, can do so fairly and consistently.

Whether they are procedural, or substantive, decisions about affordability involve judgments which are not uniquely clinical. They involve distributive ethics which also engage a range of other views, including those of the public. Although one can attempt to put numbers against criteria to produce (what is called) a "balanced scorecard" which enables comparisons to be made, in reality, this is often no more than a guide because each numerical assessment requires judgment. Therefore, it is difficult to use a single scoring system to compare, for example, a need for mental health care as opposed to palliative care, or orthopaedic care and paediatric care. Different assessors may give different scores to identical situations. It is important that this system is not used as a crude utilitarian calculation which promotes aggregates of health benefit by ignoring individual need. Clinicians must be prominent amongst commissioning decision-makers to represent the patient-centred perspective as a counter-balance to broader, economic and managerial considerations. In this way, individual needs can properly be weighed against those of the community. The transparency of the NHS Constitution and local ethical frameworks recognise that we could spend more on the NHS, but choose not to. We prefer to value health care in a way that provides extensive, but not infinite access to treatment because we also value other non-health "priorities." These structures promote fairness, consistency and equality in the NHS in the hard choices created by this balance. Although the underlying purpose of making choices is to promote community interests, individual claimants are entitled to proper recognition as an expression of the humanity and compassion inherent in the health care system.

This brings us to the next question. In assessing the balance between individual and community rights, has English law put the fulcrum in the right place, or do community interests deserve greater weight?

2. *The Community Dimension of Health care*

Why is it important to keep the community dimension in health care in mind? Once we acknowledge that demand for care will exceed the resources we make available, the answer is obvious. Unless we engage fair and consistent *systems* for allocating scarce resources, the process is likely to become inconsistent and unfair and respond to patients unequally. The question is more urgent than ever. For the past 20 years,

---

[17]   The lawfulness of this approach was confirmed by the Court of Appeal in *AC v Berkshire West PCT and the EHRC* [2011] EWCA Civ 247, concerning the interaction of two policies on (a) transgender treatment and (b) cosmetic surgery. The former permitted transgender surgery but the latter excluded cosmetic surgery. The applicant was a male-to-female transgender patient who wished to have her breasts enhanced. Consistent with the cosmetic policy, the health authority refused the treatment in order to preserve consistency with other female patients with small breasts. The Court of Appeal upheld the lawfulness of the policy.

the response of government to increased demand has been additional investment; the funds invested in the NHS in the UK have increased steadily from about £24 billion in 1990 to about £110 billion today.[18] Now all that has changed. Additional investment is no longer available as a solution. Instead of responding to illness after it has arisen, more attention must be given to preventing people becoming ill in the first place. The point is made in the following extracts.

> In the future, we are likely to have more people living in poorer health and this presents a significant challenge for health services and wider society. Firstly, we have an ageing population, which partly reflects the huge progress that has been made in reducing mortality and extending lives. Many health conditions increase markedly with age, which will mean a considerable rise in age-related chronic conditions such as diabetes, dementia, blindness and arthritis. It will also mean a greater concentration of poor health, meaning more people living with multiple chronic conditions. It is expected that the number of people who have three or more long-standing illnesses will rise by 60% over the next 10 years.
>
> Secondly, several major diseases are expected to become more common in all age groups, reflecting changes in people's lifestyles. For example, higher rates of obesity will result in a higher incidence of chronic conditions such as arthritis and type 2 diabetes. There were an estimated 3 million people with diabetes in England in 2009; estimates suggest that the number of people with diabetes could rise to 4.6 million by 2030. There has also been a rapid rise in gastrointestinal diseases, particularly chronic liver disease where the under-65 mortality rate has increased 5-fold since 1970. Liver disease is strongly linked to the harmful use of alcohol and rising levels of obesity.[19]

Thus, demographic pressures and life-style choices will significantly increase the pressure on health care systems at a time when additional investment is unlikely.

The individual- rights approach (whether substantive, or procedural) is not designed to respond to this challenge. It is good at articulating the patient's voice, but it is not intended to address community interests or redress social inequalities in health status. Courts are not equipped to perform such a role. Public health certainly promotes sanitation, clean air and water, nutrition and tackling infectious diseases. But it also has an *ethical* dimension. Take heart disease, diabetes, cancer and the other diseases associated with today's more affluent life-styles. As in many countries, the burden falls disproportionately on the poorest classes. In any public health system committed to social solidarity, the presumption of equality is axiomatic.[20] Whilst inequalities in *private* income are largely acceptable, rights of access to *public* health funds to which we have all contributed are a different matter. Public

---

[18]   See *NHS Expenditure in England* (HC Library, SN/SG/724, 2009) www.nhshistory.net/ search: keywords.

[19]   *Our Health and Wellbeing Today* (HM Government 2010), para 3.6-7.

[20]   See *Fair Society, Healthy Lives* (The Marmot Review 2010).

health policy is committed to ensuring that all those it serves have equal access to health. As WHO recommends in *Closing the Gap in a Generation*, "In any country, economic inequality – including inequity in public financing – needs to be addressed to make progress towards health equity."[21] This commitment to social solidarity has a redistributive element which is no part of the "individual-rights" approach.

However, this ethical imperative also provokes difficulty because the poorest members of the community are at most risk of neglecting their health. This group is more likely to eat, drink and smoke to excess and fail to take sufficient exercise.[22] Accordingly, life expectancy in this community is shorter and the years spent suffering disability much longer. The cost of remedying these inequalities is also very high, not only because the response is multi-disciplinary and long-term (rather than a course of medicines or a stay in hospital). In addition groups in this category are more resistant to change. How should public health ethics respond to these stubborn inequalities? "Libertarians" may respond that this is the product of individual choice; that people are free to choose how they live, including the right to neglect their health. Provided they have equal *access* to health care when they are ill, it does not matter if they are more likely to *become* ill, even if this exacerbates inequalities in health.[23] By contrast, "egalitarians" may say this is not just about unrestricted choice because the poorest members of society are not entirely free with respect to these choices. Circumstances impose pressures on the lives of this group which are different from those that exist elsewhere. Whether it is the product of upbringing, education, housing, employment, or the pressures of time or money, it is not a mystery that larger numbers of those living in the most difficult circumstances tend to suffer the poorest levels of health. Exposed to a similar environment, surely we are all subject to the same risks. Egalitarians argue that basic principles of fairness and equality demand that more is invested here to redress these inequalities of health status.[24]

In England (and Scotland and Wales too), the Department of Health has given an "egalitarian" response which seeks to reduce health inequalities. There are number of ways in which it has done so. First, generic policies have been promoted without putting any special emphasis on particular groups. For example, targets have been set for reducing inequalities in infant mortality, smoking, obesity and teenage pregnancy.[25] Generic policies are effective in the sense that *aggregate* levels of health

---

[21]   *Closing the Gap in a Generation – Health equity through action on the social determinants of health* (WHO 2008) 120.

[22]   See *Health Inequalities* (HC 286-1, Third Report, 2008-09) 26. Within each social class, differentials of health status exist between gender (men worse than women), age (old worse than young) and ethnic sub-groups (South Asians worst), see *ibid*, 18 and 59. See also *Tackling Inequalities in Life Expectancy in Areas with the Worst Health Deprivation*, HC 186 Session 2010-11, 26.

[23]   The scope of the debate is discussed in C Knight and Z Stemplowska (eds), *Responsibility and Distributive Justice* (OUP 2010) and S Anand, F Peter and A Sen (eds), *Public Health, Ethics and Equity* (OUP 2006).

[24]   The debate is clearly discussed by S Holland, *Public Health Ethics* (Polity Press 2007).

[25]   See eg, *Enabling Effective Delivery of Health and Wellbeing* (DoH, 2010), 21. In *Healthy Lives, Healthy People – Update and Way Forward* (2011, HM Government), 5: "The bold changes... are a response to the challenges we face to the public's health. For example, two out of three adults

---

status improve and overall levels of morbidity and mortality fall. However, they are ineffective in reducing health inequalities; indeed, they may make them worse. The reason is that better off groups respond more readily to public health campaigns. Second, campaigns have been focused on particular groups by providing advice and assistance where it is most needed. For example, "Sure Start" children's centres tackle poverty by providing extended services to local schools, additional health care clinics or child care services, giving advice on parenting and helping parents back to work.[26] But this may produce only modest improvements in health status relative to better off groups and it is expensive in terms of resources. In truth, proportionately greater investment is required in this group to reverse inequalities in health status. The policy choice is between generic, or "group-specific" public health intervention. However, the latter presents its own opportunity costs. If policy-makers *disinvest* from the majority to narrow the inequality gap with a minority resistant to change, this could reduce *aggregate* levels of health status in the community as a whole. On the other hand, although there are short-term costs of doing so, group-specific intervention promises considerable longer term savings:

> If everyone in England had the same death rates as the most advantaged, a total of between 1.3 and 2.5 million extra years of life would be enjoyed by those dying prematurely each year as a result of health inequalities. They would, in addition, have had a further 2.8 million years free from limiting illness or disability. The estimated costs of these illnesses accounts, per year, for productivity losses of £31-33 billion and lost taxes and higher welfare payments in the range of £20-32 billion. The additional NHS healthcare costs in England are well in excess of £5.5 billion.[27]

English health policy understands these questions, but has provided far from conclusive answers. Indeed, the Department of Health has been criticised by the House of Commons Health Committee for its lack of progress in this area: "Having set an objective to tackle a complex and intractable problem, the Department did not set about its task with sufficient urgency or focus... was too slow in making health inequalities a priority, and set a performance measure that proved too blunt an instrument to target those in most need effectively."[28] No doubt there is sensitivity about government trespassing into people's private lives and of being labelled the "nanny state."[29] Also, the proportion of the total health budget invested in preventive

---

are overweight or obese; and inequalities in health remain widespread, with people in the poorest areas living on average 7 years fewer than those in the richest areas, and spending up to 17 more years living with poor health."

[26]   Sure Start schemes are described at: www.dcsf.gov.uk/ search: every child matters.

[27]   *Fair Society, Healthy Lives* (The Marmot Review 2010) 38.

[28]   *Tackling Inequalities in Life Expectancy in Areas with Worst Deprivation* (HC 470, Third Report of Session 2010-11) 5.

[29]   Interest is being shown in "libertarian-paternalism," see *Nudge – improving decisions about health, wealth and happiness* (Penguin Books 2009). However, this argument is framed firmly within the "libertarian" tradition in which individual choice is dominant. It does not claim to have a "com-

medicine and health promotion (ie policies likely to prevent illnesses in those most likely to suffer from them) is small. The UK spends about 3.6% of its entire health care budget on public health projects of this nature (which is more than many other EU member states).[30] Perhaps we are naturally drawn to prioritise the need to rescue those who are ill today, rather than reducing the burden of illness tomorrow. And, of course, public opinion may be less sympathetic to those who are perceived to be responsible for their own ill-health. On the other hand, the NHS will eventually absorb the costs of rapidly increasing rates of, for example, cardio-vascular disease and type 2 diabetes caused by obesity. So there are compelling reasons of economics (apart from social justice) to prioritise the challenge of health inequality now.[31]

3. Community Interests and the Politics of Individualism

What challenges confront these community-based objectives? Although the NHS Constitution and the procedural-rights approach are designed to balance individual and community needs, the voice of the individual is often more articulate and urgent. Inevitably, the circumstances of individual patients are sensitive and sometimes harrowing. From a personal point of view, many of us in similar circumstances would want access to the treatment. Yet, from a community perspective, "last chance" treatments may be largely untested, ineffective and expensive, and may divert resources from other patients on effective treatments. [32]Logically, by engaging the NHS Constitution, local commissioners might reasonably balance community and individual interests and decide that the cost of the treatment cannot be justified by its limited benefits, but the emotional tug of such a case is naturally immense.

Unsurprisingly, political pressure is often placed on commissioners to divert funding from other patients to fund the last chance treatment and get the story off the front pages.[33] Although the Secretary of State is not normally responsible for commissioning NHS services (because, as we have seen, the job is delegated to local commissioners), he or she is often a favourite target for the media when distressing stories are published about, for example, a patient suffering from a terminal illness who has a last chance for a new and expensive treatment. In one sense, commis-

---

munity" perspective. Some will doubt whether life-style diseases established over many generations will be amenable to such a policy. See J-F Menard, "A Nudge for Public Health Ethics: Libertarian Paternalism as a Framework for Ethical Analysis of Public Health Interventions?" (2010) 3 *Public Health Ethics* 229.

[30]   *The Government's Response to the Health Committee Report on Health Inequalities* (2009, Cm 7621), para 54. Figures taken from *Prevention and Preventative Spending* Health England Report No 4 (2009), 4. The European average is about 2.9%.

[31]   At present, no-one seriously suggests individuals should be coerced into healthy life-styles, although there is talk of "libertarian paternalism" and "stewardship." As the avoidable costs of ill health escalate and impacts on others, there may be discussion of more forthright paternalism in this area. See generally, *Public Health: Ethical Issues* (Nuffield Council of Bioethics 2007) chapter 1.

[32]   For a US perspective on last chance treatments, see N Daniels and J Sabin, (note 15) chapter 5.

[33]   See *Incentives for Prevention* (Health England Report No 3, 2009), 3 discussing the "politics" that can stand in the way of public health policies.

sioners with duties to promote community interests are less party-political than the Secretary of State. Perhaps because they are not elected, or directly accountable to the public, they are in a better position to resist pressure of this nature. Never the less, the Secretary of State may impose severe pressure to fund treatments whose opportunity costs commissioners consider not to be justified (the ultimate sanction being to dismiss commissioner board members from their posts).[34] Although these matters are not aired publicly, in many cases the PCT quietly backs down, funds the treatment and the cost is silently diverted from other patients. This represents the realpolitik of the balance of power between commissioners and the Secretary of State.[35] Often, therefore, the *politics* of rationing gives the rights of individuals priority over community interests.

Although in theory the courts endorse the procedural-rights approach to rationing, similar pressure is imposed by litigation. By their nature, rationing cases highlight the rights of individuals. And by *their* nature, lawyers are probably better at comprehending individual rights than more recondite "public," or "community" interests. Indeed, modern legal theory lauds individual and human rights as a bulwark *against* the state. This preconception in favour of individual patients is demonstrated by the principle of "exceptional circumstances."[36] Judicial review requires decision-making to be based on all the relevant considerations, which include the *exceptional* needs of the patient. For example, a last-chance, life saving treatment for a terminal illness may be refused under the general ethical framework because its cost is not justified by its benefits. However, in response to this general policy, individual patients are entitled to argue that their circumstances are so "exceptional" that they should be given exceptional access to funding. The difficulty is in knowing how readily the court should concede such claims. Too much willingness, and *litigants* will tend to get special consideration over others and this would be unfair. But if there is too little, the sense of compassion for individuals will be undermined. The strength and weakness of the judicial forum in these cases is that it focuses on the tragedy facing the individual, but can it also give adequate weight to the interests of others whose interests are unknown to the court?

Take the example of *Otley*. Mrs Otley suffered from lung cancer and had received NHS treatment for it. Unfortunately, it had not halted the disease and her condition became terminal. A new drug, *Avastin*, became available which was unlikely

---

[34] A Barrett and others "How much will *Herceptin* really cost?" (2006) 333 *BMJ* 1118. In one case in which a senior manager was held to have been unfairly treated, the court said: "As a bystander at the execution of Admiral Byng explained to Candide: "Dans ce pays-ci, il est bon de tuer un amiral de temps en temps pour encourager les autres." It seems that the making of a public sacrifice to deflect press and political obloquy, which is what happened to the appellant, remains an accepted expedient of public administration in this country," *Gibb v Maidstone and Tonbridge Wells NHS* [2010] EWCA Civ 678, [42], Sedley LJ.

[35] Although this does not represent the legal position because once statutory powers are delegated from central government to another statutory body, *all* the delegated powers are transferred to the delegee. See *Blackpool Corporation v Locker* [1948] 1 KB 349.

[36] See generally, C Newdick, 'Exceptional Circumstances: Access to Low Priority Treatments After the Herceptin Case' (2006) *Clinical Ethics* 205 and C Newdick, 'Judicial Review: Low-priority Treatment and Exceptional Case Review' (2005) 15 *Medical Law Review* 236.

to halt the disease, but might slow its progress and extend her life by a number of months. The PCT considered its costs and benefits and said that it could not afford to purchase the drug as a general policy. The patient argued that she had "exceptional circumstances." An eminent oncologist, Dr Karol Sikora, supported her case and the matter proceeded to judicial review. The court agreed that she was "exceptional" because she was relatively fit. She was young by comparison with the cohort of patients suffering from this condition. Her reactions to other treatment, in particular to Irinotecan plus 5FU had been adverse. Her specific clinical history suggested that her reaction to a combination of chemotherapy and Avastin had been of benefit to her. By comparison with other patients, she, unlike many of those the subject of the studies, had suffered no significant side effects from a cocktail which included Avastin. All of those points are fairly made by Professor Sikora...[37]

In one sense this supports a finding of exceptionality. However, it is highly individualistic. Doctors will naturally support their patients in these cases. But if each case were considered on this very personal basis, it would surely include large numbers of patients and defeat the logic of being "exceptional." If it is insufficiently robust to withstand individual claims, the *raison d'etre* for priority setting is undermined and the principle fails in its objective of promoting fair and equal resource allocation by preferring the articulate and litigious.

Therefore, we need a more consistent approach to exceptional cases. One proposal would be to have a hierarchy of persuasiveness against which new treatments could be assessed as follows: (a) well-conducted meta-analysis of several, similar, large, well-designed randomized controlled trials (RCTs), (b) a large well-designed RCT, (c) meta-analysis of smaller RCTs, (d) case-control and cohort studies (e) case reports and case series, (f) consensus from expert panels, (g) individual opinion.[38] Commissioners should use this to identify treatments for which there is reliable evidence of clinical and cost effectiveness. Cases should be considered in a way that does not simply reflect individual circumstances, but against a common framework and in a way that assesses whether the clinical merits of one person are so different to those of other patients that they should be regarded as "exceptional." *Otley* was not decided on this basis. As the judge said in Otley: "The one significant respect in which [Dr Sikora's] criticism may not be justified is that it may be the case that Ms Otley's prospects of long term survival may not be enhanced..."[39] Indeed, the drug could prolong Mrs Otley's life for a few additional months only.

The community-side of the rationing debate has also been undermined by litigation in the European Court of Justice (ECJ). Applying the principle protecting free movement of services between member states, it has developed a theory of *substantive* rights of access to treatment. Thus, it says, if a patient requires "normal" treatment which cannot be provided in the "home" state within a "reasonable time", the treatment may be obtained from a "host" member state, paid for by the patient

---

[37] *Otley v Barking and Dagenham PCT* [2007] EWHC Admin 1927; [2007] LS Law 593, para 20.

[38] See eg, *Supporting rational local decision-making about medicines (and treatments)* (National Prescribing Centre 2008) 42.

[39] *Otley*, at para 20.

and its cost reimbursed by the local health system. This individualistic approach favours those who are robust and wealthy enough to travel, but ignores those who are too frail, or poor to do so. It also ignores those denied care because younger, fitter and stronger patients who can travel may take priority in respect of funding.[40] The only exception to this principle is when there is a risk of "undermining the balance of a social security system." But while this may focus on *economic* stability, it has little to do with fairness, democracy, or equality, ie the ethical integrity of the system. Until recently, it appeared that the ECJ had simply not understood the implications for resource allocation of its individualistic approach to patients' rights.[41] However, in October 2010, in *Commission v France* the ECJ accepted the argument for balance between individual and community choices. Rejecting the Commission's claim that free movement principles protected individuals' right of access to expensive diagnostic testing in another Member State, it said:

> If persons insured under the French system could, freely and in any circum-stances, obtain at the expense of the competent institution, from service providers established in other Member States, treatment involving the use of major medical equipment corresponding to that listed exhaustively in the Public Health Code [ie "Scintillation camara, magnetic resonance imaging, medical scanner, hyperbaric chamber, cyclotron], the planning endeavours of the national authorities and the financial balance of the supply of-up-to-date treatment would as a result be jeopardised. That possibility could lead to under-use of the major medical equipment installed in the Member State of affiliation and subscribed by it or yet a disproportionate burden on the Member State's social security budget.[42]

This community-sensitive approach has also been endorsed by the European Directive on Cross-border Access to Healthcare which concerns the rights of EU citizens to obtain treatment in a "host" member state and to have the costs reim-bursed by the "home" health system. Despite strong opposition from the European Parliament (which argued for individual-substantive rights), the final version of the Directive created *procedural* rights. Thus, Directive 2011/24 of 9 March 2011 on the Application of Patients' Rights in Cross-border Healthcare confirms that, subject to the principles of non-discrimination justified by "planning requirements relating to the object of ensuring sufficient and permanent access to a balanced range of high-quality treatment," public health insurers may impose on patients wishing to obtain hospital treatment elsewhere in the EU

---

[40]   See Case C-372/04 *R(Watts) v Bedford PCT and the Secretary of State* [2006] ECR I-4325, para 103. For criticism of the shortcomings of the ECJ's reasoning in these cases, see C Newdick, 'Citizen-ship, Free Movement and Health Care: Cementing Individual Rights by Corroding Social Solidar-ity' (2006) 43 *Common Market Law Review* 1645.

[41]   See C Newdick, 'The European Court of Justice, Trans-National Health Care and Social Citizen-ship – Accidental Death of a Concept' (2008) 26 *Wisconsin International Law Journal* 844, discuss-ing the failure of the ECJ to consider these matters.

[42]   Case C-512/08 *Commission v France* [2010] ECR I-8833.

...the same conditions, criteria of eligibility and regulatory and administrative formalities, whether set at a local, regional or national level, as it would impose if this healthcare were provided in its territory. This may include an assessment by a health professional or healthcare administrator providing services for the statutory social security system or national health system of the Member State of affiliation... if this is necessary for determining the individual patient's entitlement to healthcare.[43]

Accordingly, member states "may provide for a system of prior authorisation for reimbursement of the costs of cross- border healthcare."[44]

Thus, procedural-rights systems are preferable for providing a fair, consistent and objective mechanism for balancing individual and community interests. Put another way, individual needs cannot be considered in isolation from the wider context of community interests. The precise balance between the two is a matter for effective political participation by all socioeconomic groups, assisted by the "procedural" approach discussed above.[45] In truth, the NHS has had limited success in engaging public opinion and this important subject deserves considerably more attention.[46]

4. Population-based Objectives and the Tyranny of Targets

Now we consider challenges that confront population-based objectives. We have noted how priority setting is often understood in terms of particular individuals and treatments, but that we should also focus on population-based outcomes. We have also discussed targets for smoking, obesity and teenage pregnancy and health care inequalities. In addition, in England, hospitals are subject to a regular "Health Check" in which they are assessed against a wide range of "target" standards which are reflected on a league table of comparative performance. These measures include waiting times for (a) hospital admission (18 week maximum), (b) care in accident and emergency departments (maximum of four hours) and (c) cancer treatment (maximum of two weeks from referral). The purpose of these objectives is to enhance health care efficiency.[47] These targets are intended to promote the interests of whole populations of people. In principle, therefore, there is much to be said in support of this approach and, indeed, for extending its focus to particular sub-groups, especially those at most socio-economic disadvantage. The following does not quarrel with the principle. Rather, it considers some of the unintended

---

[43] Art 6(1). Non-hospital treatment may be obtained on a substantive-rights basis.

[44] Art 8(1).

[45] See N Daniels, (note 15) ch 3, asking "When Are Health Inequalities Unjust?" and using Rawls' Difference Principle to assist his analysis.

[46] Regulation of public participation has been subject to rapid and destabilising change in the NHS. See C Newdick, *Who Should We Treat? – Rights, Rationing and Resources in the NHS* (OUP 2005), 211-17. Discussing the recondite nature of the subject, see A Fung, 'Varieties of Participation in Complex Governance' (2006) 66 *Public Administration* 66.

[47] Health Checks are now undertaken by the Care Quality Commission, see generally: http://www.cqc.org.uk/ search: annual health check.

consequences of these population-based policies for patients and reminds us again of the need for balance in assessing individual and community needs.

Take the example of waiting time targets. Undoubtedly, prioritising waiting times has been beneficial to NHS patients. But the benefit is not entirely risk free. The danger is of NHS managers regarding the "target" as the primary objective to be achieved even at the cost of good quality care for patients. The reason for this is that government treats the achievement of targets as a proxy measure of its own success in improving the NHS and hospital managers are subject to "performance management" by reference to, for example, the percentage of patients treated in time. Also, league tables are published and permit patients to compare hospitals and choose where to receive their treatment. Hospitals which achieve targets may be rewarded with additional funding and greater freedom from supervision by government and regulators. Failure, on the other hand, is taken as a sign of poor management and may lead to senior managers being dismissed from their posts. There is a danger that as rationing by *delay* declines, rationing by *dilution* may increase.

A number of examples demonstrate the risks. I do not say they are common; rather, they are not completely exceptional. First, consider the 18-week target for referral for treatment. Compare two patients: Patient A has been on the waiting list for 17 weeks and nearing the target limit. He has been waiting so long because his condition is not serious, is not getting worse and he would not suffer were he to have to wait longer than 18 weeks. Patient B has just been referred to hospital. She needs urgent treatment. Unless she is dealt with quickly, she will quickly deteriorate. Who should we treat first? Clinicians will say Patient B. Managers, however, may argue that the decision is not purely clinical because if Patient A misses the target, then the hospital will compare unfavourably in the league table and patients may choose to go elsewhere. Hospital revenue will fall, staff will not be appointed to the unit, or new equipment may not be purchased. Government and the regulator may subject the hospital to closer scrutiny and inspection. Such a case is said to have occurred in the Bristol Eye Hospital when less urgent, long-waiters, were treated before more urgent, short-waiters, in order to achieve the waiting time target. As a result, 25 patients may have lost their sight.[48]

Their difficulty is also highlighted by a report into Mid Staffordshire Hospital NHS Foundation Trust in respect of the treatment of patients between 2005 and 2009. The hospital was being encouraged to become a NHS Foundation Trust. This meant that it would be regarded as an example of excellence for the NHS with greater autonomy and less supervision by regulators. However, to qualify for foundation status, it had to demonstrate compliance with waiting time targets and robust financial governance. However, the targets distorted managerial and clinical judgment because the four-hour waiting time target for treatment in the Accident

---

[48]   See evidence of Dr Richard Harrad, Clinical Director of the Bristol Eye Hospital, to the House of Commons Public Administration Committee. See *On Target – Government by Measurement* (HC 62-1, 2003) para 52-3.

& Emergency (A&E) Department sometimes led to those with less pressing needs being given higher priority than those with most urgent need. As one report said:

> ... the care of patients had become secondary to achieving targets and minimising breaches. Doctors considered that the prioritisation of the patients with minor ailments led, on occasions, to a distortion of clinical priorities. Middle grade doctors told us that they were asked to work with patients in the "minor" side to push these patients through, although this was at the expense of more seriously ill or injured patients. They felt pressured to prioritise patients who were close to breaching the [four-hour A&E] target rather than prioritise by clinical need.[49]

Pressure to demonstrate financial stability meant that insufficient clinical staff were engaged to manage the hospital wards. For example, when patients arrived in A&E, "they were usually assessed by reception staff with no clinical training, before waiting in an area out of sight of the staff in reception. There was no regular check by nursing staff of the patients in the waiting room..." To give the appearance of meeting the target: "Patients were moved to the clinical decision unit to 'stop the clock', but were then not properly monitored since this area was not staffed."[50] These are examples from A&E, but inadequate staffing levels also led to harrowing accounts of some elderly patients being neglected in their beds because insufficient nurses were available to respond to their calls for assistance and some were left to soil their beds which led to increased infection and further illness. Thus,

> The trust stabilised its finances and successfully focused on becoming a foundation trust. However, it lost sight of what should have been its main priority: to provide high quality care to all of its patients. It took a decision to significantly reduce staff without properly assessing the consequences. Its strategic focus was on financial and business matters at a time when the quality of care of its patients admitted as emergencies was well below acceptable standards...[51]

Mid Staffordshire is not an isolated example. Comparable institutional pressures played a role in the circumstances surrounding Stoke Mandeville Hospital NHS Trust in 2006 and Maidstone and Tonbridge Wells NHS Trust in 2007. In both cases, hospital reorganizations had been undertaken to improve financial efficiency, but at the costs of standards of care. For example, in the Stoke Mandeville Hospital Report, the Healthcare Commission criticized unacceptable infection rates in the hospital. In Stoke Mandeville, "there was a lack of effective leadership, accountability and support for the control of infection. The director of infection prevention and

---

49 See the *Investigation into Mid Staffordshire NHS Foundation Trust* (Healthcare Commission, March 2009) para 49.
50 ibid 129.
51 ibid 134-35.

control had not persuaded the board to give sufficient priority to the control of infection in general and to the control of C. difficile in particular. The achievement of the Government's targets was seen as more important than the management of the clinical risk inherent in the outbreaks of C. difficile. This was a significant failing."[52] And, in Maidstone and Tonbridge Wells Hospital, principles of good clinical governance were overridden by targets relating to finance and access. The report noted that organisations "should not compromise patient safety by making decisions and taking actions that put some patients at risk."[53]

These examples arose from conscious choices to prioritise some objectives over others and to dilute the quality of care to patients. Local hospital managers and clinicians are surely be responsible for this failure. But the House of Commons Health Committee considered that government should also bear some responsibility. It said:

> the Government's overwhelming emphasis on hitting targets (particularly waiting-list and A&E waiting), achieving financial balance and attaining Foundation status did not help to improve failing Trusts – rather it compounded their failure. The failing Trusts, like Mid Staffordshire and Maidstone and Tonbridge Wells, clearly thought the Government was telling them that patient safety was a second-order priority.[54]

Naturally, government prefers to hear good news that the NHS is improving. To this extent, there are "institutional" pressures to report good statistical results and, indeed, for government to turn a blind eye to some of the unintended effects of targets. As commentators have remarked:

> ... there was no systematic audit of the extent to which the reported successes in English health care performance... were undermined by gaming and measurement problems... The audit hole can be interpreted by those with a suspicious mind (or long memory) as a product of a "Nelson's eye" game in which those at the centre of government do not look for evidence of gaming or measurement problems which might call reported performance successes into question... In the English NHS, "hard looks" to detect gaming in reported performance data were at best limited.[55]

This echoes theories of "regulatory capture" which explain how those subject to regulation may dominate the agenda and decision-making of regulatory agencies. However, in these examples, the "capture" appears to have been by government itself.

---

[52]   *Investigation into outbreaks of Clostridium difficile at Stoke Mandeville Hospital, Buckinghamshire Hospitals NHS Trust* (Healthcare Commission, July 2006) 6.

[53]   *Investigation into Outbreaks of Clostridium difficile at Maidstone and Tunbridge Wells NHS Trust* (*Healthcare* Commission, October 2007) 111, 113.

[54]   *Patient Safety, Sixth Report of Session 2008-09* (HC 151-I, 2009) para 300.

[55]   G Bevan and C Hood, 'What's Measured is What Matters: Targets and Gaming in the English Public Health Care System' (2006) 84 *Public Administration* 517, 530.

The problem has been described by Julian Le Grand in his metaphor of good intentions being turned bad in which noble "knights" are turned into selfish "knaves."[56] Put another way, systems created to improve standards, encourage patient choice and transparent competition in the interests of quality, may unintentionally encourage staff working under pressure to undermine clinical standards and, consequently, to spread distrust and cynicism amongst those they are intended to serve.[57]

These examples must be seen in context. The general quality of care available to NHS patients is good and I do not suggest that targets should abandoned. They are valuable for assessing the health care outcomes of large groups of patients and emphasising the community perspective of priority setting. However, they illuminate some of the *risks* of putting too much weight on crude targets of measurement if the net effect is to undermine, or distort the proper balance of priority setting.[58] The challenge now is to develop more sensitive and accurate measures of quality which are less prone to gaming and properly represent the experience of the community.

5. Conclusion

Rationing and priority setting systems may not be popular, but they are not terrible things. Ideally, with public support, they openly recognise that the investment we choose to make in a crucial part of our lives is not infinite. In public health systems, they express fundamental values about community, solidarity, equality and fairness. However, in answering one group of questions about individual rights and the sharing of health care resources, they also raise others, especially when systems seek to promote population-based objectives. I have emphasised some of the risks and benefits raised by the community-end of the *choices* debate and the need to respond to the challenges that confront us. Public investment in health care systems is unlikely to increase at a time when we are living longer, pharmaceutical and medical technology is becoming more costly, and the burden of chronic, "life-style" diseases is increasing. The remorseless economic logic of the position argues for a much larger community-based enterprise to reverse upward trends of mortality and morbidity. In this, health care services are not the only, or even the dominant actor.[59] In addition, it will need the co-operation of departments of education, housing, employment, town planning, the environment and private enterprise. We have discussed some of the difficulties of integrating public and private objectives in health care and probably raised more questions than answers. The public health logic of diverting finite funds from those currently receiving care to those who are not yet to fall ill raises immense problems of politics and ethics, but the need to

---

[56]   See J Le Grand, *Motivation and Agency- of Knights & Knaves, Pawns & Kings* (OUP 2006).

[57]   See also O O'Neill, *A Question of Trust* (CUP 2002).

[58]   "Fear of numbers" has been identified as a sign of "ethical collapse." See M Jennings, *The Seven Signs of Ethical Collapse – How to Spot Moral Meltdowns in Companies... Before it's Too Late* (St Martins' Press 2006).

[59]   See *Health Inequalities* (HC 286-1, Third Report, 2008-09), 26. It is estimated that 80-85% of variation in PCTs' mortality statistics are caused by socio-economic factors outside the control of health care, such as poverty, intelligence and ethnicity.

do so is inescapable. Unless we re-balance the priority setting agenda toward the community-end of the equation, current patterns of investment in health care will become unsustainable.[60]

---

[60]   "Public finances are likely to come under pressure over the longer term, primarily as a result of an ageing population... Government would end up having to spend more as a share of national income on age-related items such as pensions and healthcare. But the same demographic trends would leave government revenues roughly stable as a share of national income. In the absence of offsetting tax increases or spending cuts this would eventually put public sector net debt on an unsustainable upward trajectory...The UK, it should be said, is far from unique in facing such pressures." See *Fiscal Sustainability Report 2011* (Office for Budget Responsibility) para 4 and 5.

Chapter IX

Setting Limits on Health Care: Challenges in and out of the Courtroom in Canada and Down-under

Colleen M. Flood and Insiya Essajee

I. Introduction

Pressure to fund new drugs and technologies is placing an increasing strain on public healthcare systems, even though there is often limited evidence regarding their effectiveness. And with annual increases in healthcare spending already tending to outpace growth in GDP, this added pressure makes the issue of economic sustainability of our health care systems all the more urgent. Despite the pejorative connotations associated with the idea of rationing, few dispute that governments must exercise some sort of control over public healthcare spending; ultimately, some limits – or rationing – must be legitimate. This need to control spending can be overshadowed in public discourse by the hope and hyperbole accompanying new drugs and technologies. As a result, decisions by government to ration healthcare are perennially ripe for challenge in a variety of formal and informal settings. Frequently, decision-makers express concerns that explicit and transparent decision-making with respect to the limits of health care will be subject to both political pressures and judicial review. There are also concerns that any decision made setting a limit on health care can be characterized as "discriminatory". For example: refusing to fund Herceptin, a breast cancer drug, discriminates against women;[1] refusing to fund Prostate Specific Antigen screening and testing discriminates against men;[2] a decision to close a French language hospital discriminates against francophones;[3] refusing to fund in vitro fertilization treatments discriminates against the infertile;[4] and refusing to fund sex-reassignment surgery discriminates against transsexuals.[5]

In this chapter, we examine the trend towards more explicit rationing, characterized by identifiable decision-makers and transparent processes, as well as the informal and formal means used to challenge decisions limiting healthcare.

---

[1]   *Walsh & Ors v. Pharmac and Anor* (2008) HC.WN CIV 2007-485-1386 [3 April 2008] online: http://www.pharmac.govt.nz/ [*Walsh*].

[2]   *Armstrong v. B.C. (Ministry of Health)*, 2008 BCHRT 19 [*Armstrong*].

[3]   *Lalonde v. Ontario (Commission de restructuration des services de santé)* (2001), 56 O.R. (3d) 577, aff'g (1999), 181 D.L.R. (4th) 263 (Ont. Div. Ct.) [*Lalonde*].

[4]   *Cameron v. Nova Scotia (Attorney General)* (1999), 204 N.S.R. (2d) 1, 177 D.L.R. (4th) 611 [*Cameron*].

[5]   *Ontario Human Rights Commission & Hogan and others v. Ontario* (2006) HRTO 32 [*Hogan*].

While the paper focuses primarily on the Canadian context, we also consider rationing and challenge trends in New Zealand and Australia in order to offer points of comparison and enhance our analysis. We start by looking at how rationing operates in these three healthcare systems and the differences between and arguments surrounding implicit versus explicit rationing. We observe a trend towards more explicit rationing, particularly with respect to funding decisions for new drugs and technologies. We then proceed to explore challenges against rationing decisions in each of the three countries. First, we consider examples of how healthcare decisions are challenged through informal means – such as patient advocacy groups applying political pressure through the media – in order to explore whether more explicit rationing is likely to result in greater politicization of the process, by providing clear decisions that politicians feel pressured to intervene with and over-rule. Second, we look at formal challenges that have been raised – before the regular courts and before human rights tribunals – in order to study the susceptibility of explicit rationing to judicial review. With respect to both informal and formal challenges, we also consider how claims that decisions are discriminatory are likely to fare.

Our analysis illustrates that although explicit rationing does provide clear decisions that are vulnerable to informal challenge and politicization, it also helps to foster a dialogue about both the need to ration and the importance of evidence-based decision-making. Our review of formal judicial challenges indicates that courts are largely sensitive to the fact that difficult rationing decisions must be made, and when presented with the clear evidence and transparency characteristic of explicit rationing processes, are inclined to find decision-making processes fair and the decisions themselves to be reasonable. Thus, while the politicization of healthcare rationing is problematic, explicit rationing may nevertheless help to encourage discussion about the need and method of rationing. This in turn ensures that decision makers are held "accountable for the reasonableness of their decisions",[6] and serves to legitimize evidence-based decisions before both the public and the courts.

2. The Spectrum of Rationing

A distinction is frequently drawn between explicit and implicit healthcare rationing. Explicit rationing is characterized by publicly stated decisions denying a particular treatment or service. By contrast, implicit rationing is characterized as far more opaque; rather than clearly disclosing decisions to limit healthcare coverage, implicit rationing is instead felt through long wait times,[7] or staffing and equipment shortages. An important difference between the two forms of rationing is the ability to point to an accountable decision-maker. Whereas explicit rationing involves an identifiable party who takes responsibility for the decision, with implicit rationing

---

[6]   N Daniels, JE Sabin, 'Accountability for Reasonableness: an Update' (2008) 337 (a1850) *BMJ* 903.
[7]   J Manning, R Paterson, 'Prioritization': Rationing Health Care in New Zealand' (2005) 33(4) *JLME* 681 n. 16.

a patient may struggle to access the services or treatment they need, but it is not as clear who is responsible or why access is limited (it's simply "the system").

Critics of explicit rationing, worried about the influence that patient groups, the media and the public may exert on politicians, express concern that making decisions transparent opens them up to politicization and can result in an inappropriate allocation of resources. As an alternative to explicit rationing, this camp argues that expert providers are best left to allocate resources across various medical needs, but within the parameters of an overall budget.[8] These critics also argue that implicit rationing may help to prevent black and white categories or one-size-fits-all approaches to allocating resources across a range of needs.

In contrast, advocates for explicit rationing note the importance of a certain level of democratic participation. Even in situations where the extent of explicit rationing merely involves imparting that a rationing decision was made and the basis for it, this nevertheless allows for informed approval or critique. Furthermore, they argue that these processes help to foster consistent, and by extension, principled decision-making. Decisions that are made openly spawn a "case law" which can be referred to during subsequent decision-making.[9]

In reality, every health care system employs a mix of approaches along a spectrum from explicit to implicit rationing. In order to illuminate this spectrum, below we review how decisions to limit or restrict high cost drugs and technologies are being made in Canada, New Zealand and Australia.

Canada

The Canadian system requires public funding for most hospital and physician services pursuant to the *Canada Health Act*. As all "medically necessary" hospital and "medically required" physician services must (in theory) be publicly funded, historically access has been largely limited through implicit rationing. This has resulted in, for example, growing concerns about access to physicians, wait times etc. However, there are some examples where explicit rationing has been adopted, particularly in times of economic recession. For example, the decisions of Ontario's Health Services Restructuring Commission, established in 1996, led to the closure of 37 hospitals and 6 provincial psychiatric sites.[10]

In contrast to hospital and physician services, governments across Canada take a more explicit approach to decision-making regarding public coverage of prescription drugs. To provide some context, the escalating cost of drugs is one of the most pressing contemporary issues in Canada. Inflation-adjusted per capita expenditure on pharmaceuticals in Canada increased 338% between 1975 and 2006,

---

[8]   SMR Lauridsen, MS Norup and PJH Rossel, 'The Secret Art of Managing Healthcare Expenses: Investigating Implicit Rationing and Autonomy in Public Healthcare Systems' (2007) 33 *JLME* 704.

[9]   N Daniels, 'Accountability for Reasonableness in Private and Public Health Insurance' in A Coulter, C Ham (eds), *The Global Challenge of Health Care Rationing* (OUP 2000) 105.

[10]   D Sinclair, M Rochon and P Leatt, *Riding the Third Rail; The Story of Ontario's Health Services Restructuring Commission*, 1996-2000 (Montreal: Institute for Research on Public Policy, 2005) 2-3.

compared to a 51% increase for hospital care, and 98% for physician services.[11] With respect to access, prescription drugs attract significantly more private finance than do hospital and physician services. However, while 75% of Canadians finance prescription drugs through private insurance,[12] the poor and the elderly, the most high cost and high volume users, are covered by provincial (public) health plans.[13] As a result, public healthcare bears a disproportionately high share of the prescription drug costs, and in 2009 was estimated to amount to almost 40% of total Canadian pharmaceutical expenditure.[14]

There is a distinct lack of consistency across provinces/territories with respect to public funding for prescription drugs. Determinations of public coverage for prescription drugs are explicitly made by 18 distinct provincial, territorial and federal formularies across the country.[15] In an effort to harmonize the decisions made by these various formularies, a central review entity, the Common Drug Review (CDR), was founded in 2003.[16] However, provincial drug plans are not bound by the CDR's recommendations, and substantive harmonization has yet to be achieved.[17] A 2004 study examining access to cancer drugs in Canada concluded that there is no substantial agreement between provinces on cancer drug listings, and that it "matters where you live" in terms of what drugs, particularly new ones, Canadians have access to.[18] Provincial variation in coverage enhances the potential for the decisions to be challenged as a patient may fail to be persuaded it is just and fair that a particular drug, although available in Alberta, is not similarly available in Ontario.

---

[11] S Morgan, 'Challenges and Changes in Pharmacare: Could Social Insurance Be the Answer?' in CM Flood, M Stabile and CH Tuohy (eds) *Exploring Social Insurance: Can a Dose of Europe Cure Canadian Health Care Finance* (McGill-Queen's University Press 2008) 199.

[12] V Demers and others, 'Comparison of provincial prescription drug plans and the impact on patients' annual drug expenditures' (2008) 178 (4) *Can. Med. Assoc. J. (CMAJ)* 405.

[13] JP Gregoire and others, 'Inter-Provincial Variation in Drug Formularies' (2001) 92:4 *Canadian J Public Health* 307.

[14] Canadian Institute for Health Information, 'Drug Expenditure in Canada, 1985 to 2009' (2010) <http://secure.cihi.ca/cihiweb/> (accessed July 24, 2010).

[15] M Tierney, B Manns, 'Optimizing the use of prescription drugs in Canada through the Common Drug Review' (2008) 178 (4) *CMAJ* 432; SG Morgan and others, 'Centralized Drug Review Processes in Australia, Canada, New Zealand, and The United Kingdom' (2006) 25(2) *Health Affairs* 337-347.

[16] ibid Morgan.

[17] Moreover, before a drug can be submitted to the CDR for approval, Health Canada (a federal entity) must first determine whether a new drug meets quality and safety standards of the *Food and Drug Act*, R.S.C., 1985, c. F-27 as am. While Health Canada's decision does not employ economic evaluation, it does place pressure on both provincial and private drug insurers to list the drug. Thus the provinces have what Nauenberg and others call the "Herculean task" of convincing their populations that, while approved as beneficial by Health Canada, a drug will nonetheless remain unlisted on the provincial formulary. E Nauenberg, CM Flood and PC Coyte, 'A Complex Taxonomy: Technology Assessment in Canadian Medicare' in TS Jost (ed), *Health Care Coverage Determinations: An International Comparative Study* (Maidenhead UK, OUP 2005) 57.

[18] D Menon, T Stafinski and G Stuart, 'Access to Drugs for Cancer: Does Where you Live Matter?' (2005) 96 (6) *Canadian J Public Health* 454; AH Anis and others, 'A Dog's Breakfast: Prescription Drug Coverage Varies Widely Across Canada' (2001) 39:4 *Medical Care* 315; Gregoire (note 13).

New Zealand

In contrast to Canada, New Zealand has been more explicit about the need to ration hospital and physician services.[19] Priority setting is largely the responsibility of twenty-one district health boards (DHBs), which are responsible for the delivery of a wide range of publicly-funded health and disability services. There is also a National Health Committee whose role it is to advise the Health Minister on "[t]he kinds, and relative priorities, of public health services, personal health services, and disability support services that should, in the NHC's opinion, be publicly funded".[20] Although DHBs must take into account existing national priorities,[21] they have discretion over funding decisions at the district level.

As in Canada, explicit rationing is most employed vis-à-vis prescription drugs. However, unlike Canada, prescription drugs in New Zealand are covered by a universal public plan (i.e. 100% of New Zealand citizens are covered by the public plan (which imposes very low co-payments) compared to just 25% of Canadians covered by a variety of provincial public plans.[22] The Pharmaceutical Management Agency (Pharmac) determines what drugs will be included in the public plan, and unlike formularies in most countries, rations within the confines of a capped centrally-set budget (Pharmac 2010) – thus making very clear that to spend money on one drug (and one class of patients) has the effect of limiting the ability to fund other drugs and other patients. Pharmac receives clinical advice from the Pharmacology and Therapeutics Advisory Committee (PTAC), which reviews all drug submissions. In order to make listing decisions, Pharmac, which operates within a fixed budget, assesses the PTAC's recommendations in light of cost-effectiveness criteria. Pharmac does not directly regulate prices, but encourages price competition on the part of drug companies through competitive processes (e.g. tendering for supply) and negotiating reduced prices in exchange for sole supply contract status for the New Zealand market. Although stunningly successful in controlling overall pharmaceutical expenditures whilst ensuring supply, obviously Pharmac must make choices at the margin and openly acknowledges the difficulty of rationing: "[d]ecisions...inevitably [include] particular judgments about the needs, rights and privileges of the many against the needs, rights and privileges of the few".[23] In terms of the potential for politicization of decisions it is important to note that Pharmac, whilst it works closely with the Ministry of Health, remains at arms length from the government, and so to some extent is shielded from political pressure. It is, however, a Crown Entity, and

[19] R Paterson, 'The Patients' Complaints System in New Zealand' (2002)21(3) *Health Affairs* 72; Manning and Paterson (note 7).
[20] National Health Committee, 2010, 3.1a. Available at http://www.nhc.health.govt.nz, search terms reference.
[21] Manning and Paterson (note 7).
[22] Demers and others 2008 (note 12) 405.
[23] New Zealand, PHARMAC, Paper for Public Consultation, 'How Should High Cost Medicines be Funded?' (December 2006) www.pharmac.govt.nz/ (accessed June 24, 2010).

thus accountable to the New Zealand Parliament for its actions. Its performance is also scrutinized by Parliament's Health Select Committee.[24]

Australia
Australia's health care system is a complex mix of public and private financing.[25] Within this mix the federal government plays a central role in funding and administering both physician services and prescription drugs,[26] in both cases rationing explicitly. First, decisions to list new medical services and technologies on the Medical Benefits Schedule (MBS), the public formulary, are made by the Minister for Health and Ageing based on the recommendations of the Medical Services Advisory Committee (MSAC) (Australian Government Department of Health and Ageing). MSAC evaluates new services and technologies by "assessing their safety, effectiveness, and cost-effectiveness, while taking into account other issues such as access and equity".[27] MSAC may also recommend delisting items already on the MBS, but has not yet done so[28] reflecting the reality that once services are publicly funded it is very difficult in a political sense to remove them.

As is the case in New Zealand, funding decisions for prescription drugs are made in the context of a federal insurance plan that covers all Australians, the Pharmaceutical Benefits Scheme (PBS). As with medical services, PBS listing decisions are made by the Minister of Health and Ageing based on recommendations from the Pharmaceutical Benefits Advisory Committee (PBAC), which conducts both economic and drug utilisation assessments.[29] In fact, Australia was the first nation to require eividence of cost-effectiveness – in addition to quality, safety and efficacy – as part of the drug approval process.[30] If the Minister accepts PBAC's recommendation, the drug is referred to the Pharmaceutical Benefits Pricing Authority (PBPA), an independent statutory body that conducts price negotiations

---

[24] New Zealand, PHARMAC, Media Release, "Herceptin (trastuzumab)" 2008 http://www.pharmac.govt.nz/ search: herceptin (accessed June 24, 2010).

[25] J Hurley and others, 'Parallel Private Health Insurance in Australia: A Cautionary Tale and Lessons for Canada' (2002) 3 IZA Discussion Papers 515 http://ftp.iza.org/; J Glover, S Tennant, and S Duckett, 'The Geographic Distribution of Private Health Insurance in Australia in 2001' (2009) 6 (19) *Aust New Zealand Health Policy online* http://www.anzhealthpolicy.com/; SJ Duckett, 'Living in the parallel universe in Australia: public Medicare and private hospitals' (2005) 173 (7) *CMAJ* 745.

[26] GP Marchildon, 'Canadian Health System Reforms: Lessons for Australia?' (2005) 29:1 *Australian Health Review* 105.

[27] Australia Medical Services Advisory Committee, Australian Government – Department of Health and Ageing, 'Funding for new medical technologies and procedures' (2005) online: <http://www.health.gov.au/> (accessed October 4, 2011). Australia Victorian Government Department of Human Services – Metropolitan Health and Aged Care Services Division, Future directions for health technology uptake, diffusion and disinvestment in Victorian public health services. (2007) http://www.health.vic.gov.au/ (accessed July 6 2010).

[28] ibid.

[29] Morgan (note 16).

[30] RS Taylor and others, 'Inclusion of Cost Effectiveness In Licensing Requirements of New Drugs: The Fourth Hurdle' (2004) 329 *BMJ* 972-975;TJ Jackson, 'Health Technology Assessment in Australia: Challenges Ahead' (2007) 187 (5) *Medical Journal of Australia* 262.

with the drug manufacturer, and then advises the Minister.[31] With the government as the single buyer of medicines, Australia's pharmaceuticals scheme, like New Zealand's, enjoys what economists call "monopsony power" – an increased ability to "negotiate the terms and price of reimbursement" of a pharmaceutical".[32] Until recently, PBAC only required Cabinet approval of listings for new drugs that would cost the government $10 million or more. However, spurred by cost concerns in February 2011, the Ministry of Health announced that from thenceforth, all new drug listings would have to be approved by the Cabinet.[33]

A trend towards explicit rationing
What can be seen over time in the three countries is a gradual move from rationing implicitly, with a heavy reliance on physicians' decision-making, to a greater reliance on explicit rationing. In particular, explicit rationing is used when determining the prescription drugs and therapies to be included in public insurance schemes.[34] Furthermore, it is interesting to note the increasing use of more nuanced forms of explicit rationing, for example approving public funding for new drugs or therapies but only for specific sub-populations of patients and/or conditions ("special authorities").

The embrace of explicit rationing, particularly with respect to new drugs and therapies, raises two important questions. First, is more explicit rationing likely to result in greater politicization of the process, by providing clear decisions that politicians feel pressured to intervene with and over-rule? Second, are explicit rationing decisions more vulnerable or less vulnerable to being overturned through formal challenges before the courts? To put it another way, on the one hand, being more transparent potentially increases opportunities for those disaffected to challenge the decision; on the other, it may be more difficult if its rationality or reasonableness is clear.

---

[31] A Biggs, 'The Pharmaceutical Benefits Scheme – an overview' (2003) online: Parliament of Australia – Parliamentary Library http://www.aph.gov.au/ search in archive (accessed October 4, 2011).

[32] BJ O'Brien, 'Cost-effective Prescribing: Trying to Hit the Target in Ontario and Australia' (2002) 25 (6) *Australian Prescriber* 128. (See also concerns over the effect of Australia-United States Free Trade Agreement on the PBS: T Faunce and others, 'Assessing the Impact of the Australia-United States Free Trade Agreement on Australian and Global Medicines Policy' (2005) 1:15 *Globalization and Health*, http://www.globalizationandhealth.com/; KJ Harvey and others, 'Will the Australia–United States Free Trade Agreement undermine the Pharmaceutical Benefits Scheme?' (2004) 5 *MJA* 256.

[33] Australian Broadcasting Corporation, 'Changes to the Pharmaceutical Benefits Scheme' (18 April 2011) http://www.abc.net.au/ search stories (accessed 2011 June 20).

[34] The different approach to prescription drugs and medical services is puzzling. In part, it may be explained by regulations requiring clinical trials before approving pharmaceuticals as safe for distribution, which results in more data to support judgments about inclusion in the public basket. There is no similar requirement for medical services. Another reason may be the availability of patents for drug innovation as opposed to services, spurring more drugs being introduced to health care markets.

3. Patients, politics and the media: Challenging rationing informally through the media and political processes

One approach that can be taken by those dissatisfied with healthcare rationing is to challenge decisions through informal means. For example, patients suffering from a particular disease or condition may form Patient Advocacy Groups (PAGs), which campaign to raise awareness and may lobby governments to gain access to particular services or medications. Using the media is also a powerful way of drawing attention to services or treatments that are not being funded, and garner public support that in turn can create political pressure to overturn a decision.

A common feature of informal challenges is to highlight the harrowing plight of a specific patient. The story of a patient's struggle is both emotional and familiar, portraying an individual facing up to a large, uncaring bureaucracy. Framing the dynamics of decision-making as pitting the plight of individuals against each other or against larger societal interests creates fertile ground upon which to challenge rationing decisions.

Allegations of discrimination are a common feature of informal challenges to rationing decisions. Examples of challenging rationing decisions on the basis of discrimination have included claims: that refusing to fund Herceptin, a breast cancer drug, discriminates against women;[35] that refusing to fund Prostate Specific Antigen screening and testing discriminates against men;[36] a decision to close a French language hospital discriminates against francophones;[37] refusing to fund in vitro fertilization treatments discriminates against the infertile;[38] and that refusing to fund sex-reassignment surgery discriminates against transsexuals.[39] Both patients' stories and discrimination claims are powerful and persuasive, and can foster public pressure to overturn decisions.

Below, we examine some examples of informal challenges that have been launched in Canada, New Zealand and Australia. In doing so, we explore the concern that explicit rationing exposes decisions to politicization, and reflect upon the impact of challenging rationing informally.

Canada
Kidney Cancer Canada, a support organization which actively "advocates for access to new treatments",[40] is an example of a very influential Canadian PAG. In 2007, the Common Drug Review (CDR), which provides recommendations to provinces regarding what drugs to publicly fund, advised against listing the kidney cancer

---

[35]   *Walsh* (note 1).
[36]   *Armstrong* (note 2).
[37]   *Lalonde* (note 3).
[38]   *Cameron* (note 4).
[39]   *Hogan* (note 5).
[40]   Kidney Cancer Canada. Homepage (2010) http://www.kidneycancercanada.ca/ (accessed June 24, 2010)

treatment Nexavar.[41] While the Ontario government would likely have followed the CDR recommendation absent PAG action, upon meeting with KCC representatives, it examined additional data beyond that provided by CDR, and the decision was made to list the drug on Ontario's formulary.[42] Furthermore, following continued KCC action, a 2009 amendment resulted in the federal government also increasing access to Nexavar through removal of pre-existing conditions on its safe use in advanced/ metastatic renal cell carcinoma in patients who had failed or proved intolerant to prior systemic therapy.[43]

The campaigning and lobbying following the Ontario Health Services Restructuring Commission's 1997 decision to close a French-language hospital provides another example of influential informal challenges. Within 24-hours of the Commission's decision to close Hôpital Montfort, the only full-time French hospital in Ontario, Gisèle Lalonde, the former mayor of an area serviced by the hospital, formed the lobby group "S.O.S. Montfort".[44] S.O.S. Montfort organized a 10,000-person rally in Ottawa and collected 126,000 signatures protesting the closure. In response, the Commission reviewed its decision, and proposed a new plan that allowed the hospital to remain open but severely limited the services offered. As discussed in more detail below, S.O.S. Montfort went on to pursue the case through formal court challenges, eventually succeeding in 2001 to ensure continued full-time French service at the hospital.

A further example of a successful informal challenge in Ontario was public pressure that led to a decision by the government in March 2011 to change its policy that the breast cancer drug Herceptin, used to treat tumours with the HER-2 receptor, would only be funded for patients with tumours greater than 1 centimetre in size. This pressure arose as a result of a highly publicised complaint by a breast cancer patient to the Ontario Ombudsman, which prompted the Ombudsman to initiate a systemic investigation into the reasonableness of the decision to restrict funding for Herceptin.[45] Adding to this pressure was the fact that patients with small tumours were able to receive Herceptin in British Columbia, Alberta and Saskatchewan and on a case-by-case basis in Quebec, Manitoba and Newfoundland. Part of the problem was that there was a knowledge gap: while the Ontario government only had evidence to support the use of Herceptin in patients with tumours larger than 1 centimetre, this was primarily because clinical studies only enrolled patients with tumours greater than that size, which was principally done in order to expedite

---

[41]   Canada, Agency for Drugs and Technologies in Health, CEDAC Final Recommendation on Reconsideration and Reasons for Recommendation: Sorafenib (Nexavar – Bayer Inc.) (Common Drug Review, 2007) http://www.cadth.ca/ (accessed June 24, 2010).

[42]   Kidney Cancer Canada (note 40).

[43]   D Maskens, "Important Health Canada Update Regarding Nexavar for mrcc." http://www.kidney-cancercanada.ca/ (accessed June 24, 2010).

[44]   G Lalonde, 'French-Language Services: A Matter of Language, Equity and Health – The Montfort Hospital Experience' (2005) *Ontario Health Promotion E-Bulletin* http://www.ohpe.ca/ (accessed June 24, 2010).

[45]   CBC News 'Ontario to expand cancer drug access' (2011) CBC News, http://www.cbc.ca/news/ search for herceptin coverage (accessed 2011 June 20).

the studies. However, there was mounting evidence from other jurisdictions that small HER-2 positive tumours had a high risk of recurrence, and that Herceptin should be used for tumours under 1 centimetre in size.[46] The change to Ontario's policy involved the development of an "Evidence-Building Program" (EBP) for cancer drugs, which would provide funding on a "time-limited basis" for drugs with "evolving, but incomplete evidence of [their] benefits" so as to allow Cancer Care Ontario to "gather real-world data about their efficacy and cost-effectiveness" in order to determine whether permanent changes to the drug's funding should be made. In May 2011, Herceptin became the first drug covered by the EBP, ensuring public funding for patients with tumours smaller than 1 centimetre.[47]

New Zealand

The informal challenges against limited funding for interferon beta and Herceptin in New Zealand both illustrate the susceptibility of explicit funding decisions to politicization. In the case of interferon beta, a treatment for patients with multiple sclerosis, Pharmac had twice recommended against funding on the basis that the benefit for patients was low relative to the cost of the drug.[48] However, in 1999, after a long campaign by the MS Society of New Zealand,[49] the incoming Labour government honoured an election pledge to provide more access to the drug.[50] The (then) Minister of Health, Annette King, directed the Health Funding Authority to instruct Pharmac to fund beta interferon, explaining that, "[w]e made this pledge during the election campaign, and it was a decision supported by the health select committee which heard compelling evidence that the previous Government took little notice of".[51]

In the case of Herceptin, a breast cancer treatment, Pharmac's 2007 decision to fund only nine weeks of treatment[52] was aggressively challenged by patients seeking twelve months of treatment as recommended by the manufacturers. The decision spurred extensive pro-Herceptin campaigning, including Herceptin charities, awareness campaigns, art shows, etc.[53] In 2008 the High Court heard a challenge to both Pharmac's process of decision-making and the reasonableness of the decision itself. The court ordered Pharmac to undertake a broader consultative process

---

[46]   L Priest, 'Ontario to expand access to breast-cancer treatment' *Globe and Mail* (21 March 2011) http://www.theglobeandmail.com/ (accessed 2011 June 19).

[47]   CBC News (note 45); Ontario, Cancer Care Ontario, 'Cancer Drug Funding and Administration in Ontario: Background information' (2011) http://www.cancercare.on.ca/ (accessed 2011 June 21).

[48]   C Masters, 1999. 'MS patients welcome move to fund drugs' *New Zealand Herald* (27 December 1999) http://www.nzherald.co.nz/ (accessed June 24, 2010).

[49]   H McNaughton, N Kayes, and K McPherson, 'Interferon beta, PHARMAC, and political directives: in the best interests of people with multiple sclerosis?' (2006) 119:1232 *The New Zealand Medical Journal* 1939.

[50]   JP Raftery, 'Paying for Costly Pharmaceuticals: Regulation of New Drugs in Australia, England and New Zealand' (2008) 1 *MJA* 26.

[51]   New Zealand Government. 1999. Press Release: Beta-Interferon http://www.beehive.govt.nz/ (accessed June 24, 2010).

[52]   Pharmac 2008a, http://www.pharmac.govt.nz/ search: media Herceptin.

[53]   S French, S., 'Campaign art – taking Herceptin to the stage' (2008) http://www.stuff.co.nz/ (accessed June 24, 2010).

than it had originally done.[54] Following the court's directive Pharmac undertook broader consultations but after weighing this information it once more decided to only provide funding for nine weeks of treatment.[55] Despite this, in December 2008 the newly elected Prime Minister John Key announced that the National-led government, based on a pre-election promise, would ensure a twelve-month course of Herceptin for eligible breast cancer patients.[56]

New Zealand's experiences with interferon beta and Herceptin reveal how governments of all political stripes may be tempted to promise overturning controversial explicit rationing decisions to garner political support during election campaigns. However, the relative rarity of this behaviour in New Zealand (just twice in the last 10 years, which is infinitesimal relative to the volume of decisions made) suggests that *once in power* governments understand that absent fair rationing processes the floodgates will open for unmanageable increases in spending.

Australia

In 2006 PBAC made recommendations denying funding for Gardasil, a vaccine against strains of the human papillomavirus that can lead to cervical cancer,[57] and limiting Herceptin coverage to early-stage breast cancer patients. The subsequent response both demonstrates how the media can be used to bolster informal challenges, and illustrates how decisions can be overturned through government intervention.

Gardasil received a negative recommendation from PBAC in November 2006.[58] Two days later, in response to public and patient demands, the Australian Prime Minister intervened, personally announcing that the drug would be subsidized upon negotiation of the price with the manufacturer.[59] Following his announcement, there was heavy reporting of the discussions between PBAC and the vaccine manufacturer, and a group of MPs petitioned the government to request that PBAC review its decision.[60] By the end of November, PBAC had held a special meeting to address the issue, and decided to reverse its decision against recommending Gardasil for listing.[61]

---

54   Walsh & Ors v. Pharmac and Anor HC WN CIV 2007-485-1386 [3 April 2008] http://www.pharmac.govt.nz/ (accessed on January 2, 2012).
55   Pharmac 2008a (note 52).
56   New Zealand Government, Media Release 2008. 'Government Honours Herceptin Promise' (10 December 2008 http://www.beehive.govt.nz/ (accessed June 24, 2010); New Zealand, Ministry of Health, Cancer Control in New Zealand: Herceptin (2008) http://www.moh.govt.nz/ (accessed June 24, 2010).
57   T Abbott, Minister for Health and Ageing Media Release, ABB149/06 'PBAC Advice on Gardasil' (8 November 2006) http://www.health.gov.au/ (accessed June 24, 2010).
58   ibid.
59   M Haas, 'Government Responses to PBAC Recommendations' (2007) *Health Policy Monitor* http://hpm.org/survey/ (accessed June 24, 2010).
60   ibid.
61   ibid.

Similarly, in 2006, PBAC approved listing Herceptin, but only for some early stage breast cancer patients.[62] Although the government accepted PBAC's recommendation to limit Herceptin funding, in response to public demands it established a special, separate fund for Herceptin, administered by Medicare Australia, the national insurer.[63] As with Gardasil, the initial decision limiting Herceptin funding was followed by significant media coverage of patients with breast cancer. A study on the media influence of Herceptin funding in Australia shows that the media's invocation of the "rule of rescue" – the "psychological imperative...to rescue identifiable individuals facing avoidable death without giving too much thought to the opportunity cost of doing so" – was dominant, while little was reported on Herceptin's side-effects, drug industry pricing, and absolute survival rates, which are much more modest than the increase in improvement rates (e.g. some amelioration in tumour size etc.).[64]

Informal challenges and politicization
These brief case studies from three jurisdictions illustrate the power of both media and public advocacy in challenging explicit decision-making. Two major, related, concerns arise with respect to these kinds of challenges; first, the over-politicization of rationing decisions, which may result in opportunistic support for a particular funding decision by a political party in order to gain or maintain power; and second, the gradual prioritizing of treatments and services for conditions that are common enough to mobilize a patient advocacy group (PAG), or are currently receiving significant media attention.

These concerns, in turn, invite an inquiry into the composition and funding of PAGs and media-based advocacy campaigns. Pioneer PAGs in the 1960s were associated with seeking greater regulatory controls and with an activist anti-corporate stance, but many now resemble corporations and are not opposed to cooperating with pharmaceutical companies.[65] Indeed, most "high profile" disease advocacy groups in Canada rely on funding from pharmaceutical companies for their operation; a relationship lacking any regulatory framework.[66] These relationships raise questions about hidden agendas, as PAGs may become a medium through which drug companies promote their product.[67] Furthermore, the greater attention being paid to vocal PAGs raises a concern that the needs of patients who are unable to secure support – either financial backing from pharmaceutical companies or public advocacy from the media and general public – may not be appropriately prioritized.

---

[62] Australian Government – Department of Health and Ageing, 'Fact Sheet: Listing of Herceptin on the PBS' (2006) http://www.health.gov.au/ (accessed June 24, 2010).

[63] Haas (note 59).

[64] R MacKenzie and others, 'Media Influence on Herceptin Subsidization in Australia: Application of the Rule of Rescue' (2008) 101 *Journal of the Royal Society of Medicine* 305.

[65] H Lofgren, 'Pharmaceuticals and the Consumer Movement: The Ambivalences of 'Patient Power' (2004) 28:2 *Australian Health Review* 228.

[66] E Johnson, 'Promoting drugs through patient advocacy groups' (2000) *CBC News* http://www.cbc.ca/ search: consumers, drugmarketing (accessed June 24, 2010).

[67] ibid.

Thus, while informal challenges can be a legitimate method of drawing attention to real needs in society, they should not override decision-making processes that attempt to allocate resources fairly across a population. Generally, the story pitched by the media presents suffering patients battling an uncaring bureaucracy. This story, which forms the crux of the patient power initiative, also problematizes it. Although every story of suffering elicits sympathy, every public system must nevertheless have some limits or else be unsustainable. Resources spent on the sad plight of one individual are by necessity resources that cannot be spent on other needs that may ultimately save more lives or otherwise bestow more health.[68] In order to withstand informal lobbying that prioritizes the needs of those who benefit from political connections, industry backing and the emotional appeal of media patient stories over others who objectively have more serious health needs amenable to treatment, a system must be embedded throughout with thoughtful principles and processes. Moreover, the extent to which politicians are able to overturn rationing decisions should be restricted by, for example, devolution of this decision-making power to arm's length agencies.

These concerns regarding the susceptibility of explicit rationing to informal challenge seem to counter our thesis that more explicit decision-making is preferable. Nevertheless, there are three reasons why we continue to argue that a greater emphasis on explicit decision-making is preferable. First although there have been a small number of high-profile informal challenges to explicit decision-making that have resulted in political intervention, given the total volume of decisions, the proportion of those overturned is relatively small. Second, with respect to drug funding decisions, explicit rationing may in fact be the only feasible option. Whereas access to health care services can be rationed implicitly by, for example, reducing the number of hospital beds or physicians and leaving clinicians to prioritize patients within the confines of limited resources, one cannot limit the supply of drugs in the same way. Moderating the supply of prescription drugs is essentially only possible by limiting particular brands or classes of drugs and controlling prescribing behaviour. Third, as use of explicit rationing increases, it carries the potential to raise awareness about both the need to ration, and the importance of evidence-based – rather than emotional – decision making. Arguably, strong and robust decision-making processes – at arm's length from politics – may over time foster public confidence in the fairness and reasonableness of the decisions. Explicitly acknowledging healthcare rationing may not only encourage a far more robust, albeit difficult, discussion about how resources should be allocated, but also help legitimize funding decisions in the eyes of the public, whereas shielding rationing and decision-making processes through implicit rationing can prevent informed public participation.

---

[68] C Newdick, *Who Should We Treat?: Rights, Rationing, and Resources in the NHS* (Oxford: OUP 2005).

4. Legal Challenges in Canada: Four Observations

As explicit rationing is increasing, challenges to government decisions regarding health care allocation are becoming more frequent. Decision-makers fear that, persuaded by patient claims of unfairness and/or discrimination, courts and human right tribunals will overturn their decisions.

In order to explore how courts and tribunals are dealing with these challenges, we examine formal challenges to rationing decisions in Canada, as well as the leading cases from Australia and New Zealand. More specifically we surveyed constitutional and administrative cases challenging limits on publicly funded health care in Canada between 1990 and 2009. To assess the differences between how courts and human rights tribunals respond to such challenges, we also reviewed relevant decisions made by human rights tribunals across Canada during the same time period. The 1990s witnessed an effort by Canadian provinces to reduce healthcare costs by limiting funding under provincial insurance plans.[69] Thus, we decided to examine cases dating back to 1990, focusing on challenges launched by the patients themselves, in order to capture how formal challenges were being made and responded to during a period where healthcare rationing was increasing across Canada. In general, the majority of the cases we encountered challenged explicit rationing decisions, which, being clearer and associated with an identifiable decision-maker, are naturally more amenable to formal challenge than implicit decision-making. However, although they were not as prevalent, we also reviewed challenges against implicit rationing i.e. limited access in the form of long wait times etc.

The cases and tribunal decisions reveal several important trends that we explore in more detail below. First, we note that although allegations of discrimination may have resonance in public opinion (i.e., in informal challenges), such allegations are frequently hard to sustain before courts and tribunals. Second, challenges to the substance of an administrative decision are less likely to succeed than those which identify flaws in the reasoning process employed by the decision makers, for example, by identifying factors that were overlooked. One cannot simply invite the court to revisit the same chain of reasoning followed by government decision makers and substitute a different conclusion. Very often, courts will, by way of remedy, outline the factors that need to be integrated into the decision-making process, and remit the matter to government decision-makers for reconsideration. Third, courts and tribunals repeatedly acknowledge the need for, and complexity of, rationing decisions in healthcare. Consequently, although courts and human rights tribunals will review decisions on reasonableness, they start from a stance that is highly deferential to expert government and healthcare bodies, acknowledging the court's comparative lack of expertise on issues of allocation. Fourth and finally, all of these observations highlight that explicit rationing may result in clear decisions that are more vulnerable to a formal court or tribunal challenge, but this is offset

---

[69]   O Madore, 'The Canada Health Act: Overview and Options' (2005) Library of Parliament Publications List, Economics Division http://www2.parl.gc.ca/ (accessed July 25, 2010).

by the fact that explicit decision-making also attracts greater deference from courts and tribunals. Viewed optimistically, one might expect that the move toward explicit rationing would give rise to a kind of virtuous circle: clear, evidence-based decisions invite judicial review, but that review is itself mostly deferential to the evidence and expertise of planners; courts intervene only where the *process* of decision-making is found lacking. In this way, judicial review may actually reinforce the selling points of explicit rationing, fostering transparency and accountability without usurping the authority of health-care decision-makers. All of this may in turn have a positive spill over into broader public discourse, where informal challenges are levelled against rationing decisions. Courts and tribunals can serve an important watchdog function over agencies charged with making rationing decisions – pushing for fairness, transparency and accountability, and thereby strengthening public trust in the system. Whether and to what extent this optimistic scenario plays out is largely a function of how courts and tribunals exercise their power. Where a rationing decision is based on clear evidence, there is a need for deference. But where the decision-making process is lacking in fairness or transparency, courts and tribunals must be ready to intervene.

a. Courts do not necessarily find discrimination claims persuasive

Formal challenges alleging discrimination rely on legal instruments that protects citizens' rights, such as constitutional rights or human rights acts prohibiting the government from acting or providing services in a manner that is discriminatory. However, even when discrimination is made out prima facie, provisions in the relevant rights-protecting legislation generally further shield a law or decision. For instance, s. 1 of the *Canadian Charter* states that rights are guaranteed "subject only to such reasonable limits prescribed by law as can be demonstrably justified in a free and democratic society."

As healthcare funding decisions tend to group people and can readily be cast as distinctions drawn on the grounds of disability, alleging discrimination can be both appealing and seemingly straightforward. However, it is clear that courts and tribunals are not overly persuaded by claims of discrimination. Our review included twelve cases alleging discrimination, of which six were unsuccessful. In four of these unsuccessful cases, the courts and tribunals concluded that the funding decisions were not discriminatory, but were instead based on evidence and expert advice concerning the effectiveness or necessity of the treatments at issue.

Although discrimination was, in fact, made out in two of the unsuccessful cases, *Cameron v. Nova Scotia*[70] and *Ontario Human Rights Commission & Hogan and others v. Ontario*,[71] the funding decisions in both were justified by the need to prioritize and make decisions about how healthcare funding should be allocated. For example,

---

[70]   *Cameron* (note 4).
[71]   *Hogan* (note 5).

in *Cameron v. Nova Scotia*,[72] a couple successfully claimed that denying provincial funding for intra-cytoplasmic sperm injection (ICSI), a specialized in vitro treatment, discriminated against the infertile. However, the court ruled that the government's funding scheme was justified under s. 1 of the *Charter*. The court said of the specialized in vitro fertilization procedures that, "in the order of priorities...having regard to costs, the limited success rate and the risks do not, at this time, rank sufficiently high to warrant payment for them from public funding" and that "this [was] the real explanation why these procedures were considered not medically necessary".[73] The court in *Cameron* is frank in acknowledging the difficulties of rationing, but recognizes it as valid and necessary.[74]

Cameron can be contrasted with another case – this time before a human rights tribunal – involving access to ICSI treatment: *Buffett v. Canadian Forces*.[75] Unlike *Cameron*, *Buffet* was ultimately successful in challenging the lack of funding for ICSI by alleging discrimination. Mr. Buffet claimed that the Canadian Forces' (CF) coverage policy, which provided IVF treatment for infertile female members, discriminated against men by failing to also provide ICSI. The Canadian Human Rights Tribunal found that there had been discrimination, and that funding should be provided to allow "the couple the opportunity to conceive and have a child that is biologically theirs,"[76] thereby allowing both Mr. Buffet and his wife, who was not covered by the CF plan, to receive infertility treatments. The Tribunal dismissed CF's claim that the financial burden posed undue hardship, finding a lack of evidence and that the costs presented had been inflated.[77] At judicial review, the Federal Court found that the tribunal had mischaracterized the services as enabling a couple to have their own children, instead of simply as infertility treatments, and referred the case back to the Tribunal.[78] Finally, in 2008, the Tribunal ordered that as long as CF provided IVF funding for females, that males should receive funding for ICSI.[79]

The comparison of *Cameron* and *Buffett* highlights a distinction between alleging discrimination through the *Charter*, as done in *Cameron*, versus other human rights legislation, as in *Buffet*. Each has different tests for when a rights infringement can be justified. In order to justify a *Charter* rights breach, the government must meet the requirements set out in the *Oakes* test: that government have a "pressing and substantial" objective and that the measures being used to achieve this objective

---

[72] *Cameron* (note 4).
[73] ibid 87.
[74] "The evidence makes clear the complexity of the health care system and the extremely difficult task confronting those who must allocate the resources among a vast array of competing claims." *Cameron* at para. 234. "[I]n the development of the policy the responsible decision makers must make trade offs in a constrained health care system. Having regard to the costs, the limited success rate and the risks, they are not yet ready for acceptance as insured services." *Cameron* at para. 239.
[75] *Buffett v. Canadian Forces*, 2007 FC 1061 [*Buffett*]. ("Buffet" refers to the Federal Court decision).
[76] ibid 48.
[77] ibid 101.
[78] ibid 48.
[79] ibid 4.

are proportionate.[80] By contrast legislation such as the *Canada Human Rights Act* or the *Ontario Human Rights Code* merely requires demonstrating that the claimant's rights cannot be accommodated without "undue hardship" for the defendant. Thus claims relying on human rights legislation may have a greater chance of success than *Charter* challenges.

Overall while discrimination claims may seem appealing to litigants because of the ability to identify oneself as disadvantaged by aligning oneself with an identifiable group, courts and tribunals appear well attuned to the distinction between discrimination on its face and discrimination in substance. Although vulnerable and identifiable groups may not be able to access certain treatments, this may be both a necessary and inevitable result of fair healthcare rationing and prioritization. As explicit decision-making grows, so too will the volume of decisions that are potentially contestable, but as rationing bodies become more open and transparent, with clearer guidelines and processes, the relative risk of a successful challenge seems likely to decline.

b. *Substantive challenges in administrative law infrequently overturn decisions*

Canadian administrative law decisions are broadly divided between cases of *substantive review* and cases being reviewed for *procedural fairness*. Procedural fairness concerns the plaintiff's right to a fair process (right to be heard) before an impartial decision-maker. If a fair process is not followed the decision may be remitted back to the decision-maker to follow that process before reaching a decision. In contrast, where substantive review is undertaken, courts scrutinize the actual reasoning of government decision-makers charged with making rationing decisions. A central preoccupation in cases involving substantive review, is with the amount of deference due to government decision makers (i.e., will the courts defer where a decision is merely *reasonable*, or must the decision be *correct?*). However, as we discuss below, even when reviewing the substance of a decision a court generally refers the issue back to the decision-maker in question with orders to, for example, take into account a particular factor that had been omitted in the original consideration. Consequently, by the remedies awarded in administrative law, courts generally exhibit a significant degree of deference to governmental decision-making, particularly in rationing decisions.

Among the successful administrative law challenges reviewed, only one stands out as a categorical reversal of a decision reached by a rationing body: *Stein v. Québec*, a 1999 judicial review of a decision denying funding for treatment obtained outside of Canada.[81] *Stein* involved a patient, who, after undergoing treatment for colon cancer, discovered that the cancer had spread to his liver. Although his doctors urged immediate treatment, the patient's operation was cancelled three times because of hospital overcrowding. In order to avoid further delay he sought and obtained

---

[80]   Oakes test, [1986] 1 S.C.R. 103.
[81]   *Stein v. Québec (Tribunal administratif)* [1999] RJQ 2416 181.

surgery in New York, but was subsequently denied reimbursement by the Régie de l'Assurance-maladie du Québec. Ultimately, the reviewing court concluded that requiring Stein to continue to wait for surgery in Montreal was "irrational, unreasonable and contrary to the purpose of the *Health Insurance Act*, which is designed to make necessary medical treatment available to all Quebecers,"[82] and ordered the Régie to accept Stein's claim for coverage.[83] However, in other cases where a patient's life is arguably in jeopardy courts have recognized that rationing of care may be justified on grounds of resource limitations. *Flora v Ontario Health Insurance Plan*, like *Stein*, also challenged a decision denying funding for treatment obtained outside of Canada.[84] After being diagnosed with liver cancer and learning that he was not a suitable candidate for a liver transplant, Mr. Flora sought treatment in England. The Ontario Health Insurance Plan (OHIP) refused to reimburse the cost of his treatment, and Mr. Flora appealed the decision first to the Health Services Appeal and Review Board,[85] and then to the court. The Board confirmed OHIP's decision, explaining that the treatment was not considered acceptable for someone of Mr. Flora's condition in Ontario, and thus need not be insured.[86] At the Divisional Court, Mr. Flora argued that the standard of review of the Board's decision was correctness, in other words, the court should not defer to the Board's findings but rather ask whether or not the court would have reached the same result.[87] The Divisional Court, however, chose to emphasize that the question before the tribunal was largely one of fact and that "on judicial review, [the court] should not substitute its opinion on the sufficiency of the evidence for that of the statutory tribunal."[88] It also emphasized the relative expertise of the Board on issues of resource allocation in health care.[89] Thus the court concluded that deference was warranted to the Board's decision, the proper standard of review was reasonableness,

---

[82] ibid 32.

[83] ibid 44.

[84] *Flora v. Ontario Health Insurance Plan* (2007), 83 O.R. (3d) 721, 219 O.A.C. 142.

[85] Several provinces in Canada have established administrative tribunals where individuals may appeal decisions of their provincial public health insurance administrators. Some of these (Alberta and British Columbia) are limited to hearing claims about funding for out-of-country treatment. In contrast, Quebec's tribunal hears claims on any governmental decision. Ontario's HSARB, in turn, is comprehensive in its jurisdiction concerning health care related claims; it covers appeals under fourteen different statutes. However, most of the appeals fall under the *Health Insurance Act* and most of these appeals relate to funding for out-of-country treatments. W Lahey, 'Medicare and the Law: Contours of an Evolving Relationship' in J Downie, T Caulfield, and CM Flood (eds) *Canadian Health Law and Policy* (4th ed., Markham: LexisNexis, 2011); C Pitfield, CM Flood, 'Section 7 'Safety Valves': Appealing Wait Times Within A One-Tier System' in C Flood, K Roach, and L Sossin (eds) *Access to Justice, Access to Care: The Legal Debate over Private Health Insurance* (Toronto: University of Toronto Press 2005) 477. Under s.28.4 of regulation 552 of the *Health Insurance Act*, out of country treatments are covered under OHIP if, the treatment is generally accepted as appropriate for a person in the appellant's medical circumstances and the treatment is not available in Ontario, or there is a delay in getting the same treatment in Ontario that would lead to death or irreversible tissue damage.

[86] Flora (note 84) 6.

[87] ibid 49.

[88] ibid 61.

[89] ibid 63.

and in applying this standard held that the Board's decision was reasonable. This finding was upheld at the Ontario Court of Appeal.[90]

As mentioned, in many instances where plaintiffs achieved courtroom successes via substantive review, the court will not order a that given therapy be funded but will instead order decision-makers to reconsider the case, attending to considerations that were initially overlooked. Thus in *Lalonde*,[91] area residents challenged the Ontario Health Services Restructuring Commission's decision to downsize the only francophone hospital in the vicinity. The court sided with the plaintiffs, finding that the Commission had, in its deliberations over the closure, failed to give due attention to the impact on cultural and language rights. The matter was remitted to Ontario's Minister of Health to re-evaluate the decision, this time giving due weight to francophone rights. This left the Ministry latitude to go forward with the downsizing. The issue was never reconsidered, as a new provincial government came to power and opted to expand the hospital with financial support from the federal government. In *C. (C.) v. Ontario Health Insurance Plan*,[92] the plaintiffs sought treatment outside of Canada without prior approval that the province would reimburse the costs. The Ministry refused reimbursement, and the Health Services Review and Appeal Board upheld that decision, claiming that the relevant legislation did not allow for retroactive approval. The Ontario Superior Court sided with the plaintiffs, finding that the 'doctrine of necessity' dictated that exceptions be made in some cases, for example, where the urgency of a situation does not allow the patient time to seek prior approval. As in *Lalonde*, there is an emphasis on improving the quality of decision-making here (as opposed to telling the Board what it has to do): having explained the reasoning process that should be followed, the question was remitted to the Board for reconsideration.[93]

It is difficult, of course, to assess overall trends from the relatively small pool of cases in this area. Insofar as rationing decisions have invited judicial review under administrative law, though, it appears that the courts respect the judgement and authority of rationing bodies. It is true that the increasing explicitness of rationing decisions allows courts to more easily identify overlooked considerations (e.g., the issue of minority rights in *Lalonde*). Yet it is rare for courts, in these cases, to reconsider the matter themselves, and enforce a final decision on the rationing question at issue. This practice of handing matters back to rationing bodies for reconsideration exhibits deference on the part of courts vis-à-vis decision-makers. We turn now to consider the deference of courts and tribunals more broadly.

c. The deference of courts and tribunals

Third, we note that when bringing an action challenging the government's health care allocation decisions, the claimant must face courts and tribunals that are

---

90   *New Brunswick (Board of Management) v. Dunsmuir*, 2008 SCC 9 at para 62.
91   *Lalonde* (note 3).
92   (2009) 246 O.A.C. 115.
93   See also *Delisle v. Canada* 2006 FC 933; *Segal v. Ontario Health Insurance Plan* (1994) 77 O.A.C. 31.

traditionally deferential to the government, and more specifically, to the expertise of its particular decision-making bodies.[94] For example, even though the court in *Stein* ultimately overturned the decision, it highlighted the need for caution and deference when reviewing a decision from a specialized tribunal such as the T.A.Q.,[95] and emphasized that the decision would need to be "manifestly unreasonable or irrational" in order for the Court to intervene -- it just so happened to find in the *Stein* case that the decision was indeed irrational![96]

Furthermore, in *Armstrong v. B.C.*, one of the unsuccessful discrimination cases, the B.C. Human Rights Tribunal stated that it "should be reluctant to second guess decisions made by experts within the scope of their specialized judgment, as long as that judgment is exercised in a non-discriminatory manner."[97] In this case, the claimant asserted that a decision not to fund prostate cancer screening tests discriminated against men particularly since public funding was available for women for mammograms and pap smears. The Tribunal dismissed Mr. Armstrong's discrimination claim after re-framing the issue as a question of what tests are "determined to be medically necessary, based on sound epidemiological and public health considerations,"[98] and stressed that it was the cancer's behaviour, not the sex of the person the cancer attacks, that informed the funding decision.

The courts and tribunals openly acknowledge that they are not well equipped to assess complex pharmaco-economic and clinical findings or second-guess expert recommendations. This deferential stance corresponds to the trend identified above that claimants seem to have had far greater success by pointing to procedural problems with respect to how a decision was made, rather than challenging the rationing decision itself.

d. Rationing as an important objective

Finally, both the courts and tribunals repeatedly recognize healthcare rationing as an important objective. In *Cameron*, discussed above, the court explained that the high costs and limited success of in vitro fertilization warranted denying public funding.[99] Additionally, the necessity of rationing was raised by the Supreme Court of Canada in *Auton v. British Columbia*.[100] *Auton*, another one of the unsuccessful discrimination cases, challenged British Columbia's decision not to fund a new Lovaas applied behavioural therapy for autistic children. The Supreme Court found that the government is not obligated to fund all treatments, only those that are

---

[94]   See: *Irwin Toy Ltd. v. Quebec* (Attorney General), [1989] 1 S.C.R. 927.

[95]   *Stein* (note 81) 18.

[96]   ibid 23. Since this case the law regarding standard of review has been substantially revised. In the 2008 case *Dunsmuir v New Brunswick* the Supreme Court of Canada ruled that there would only be two standards – reasonableness and correctness – rather than the three standards that existed when *Stein* was decided.

[97]   *Armstrong* (note 2) 370.

[98]   ibid, para. 356.

[99]   *Cameron* (note 4) 87.

[100] *Auton (Guardian ad litem of) v. British Columbia (Attorney General)*, 2004 SCC 78 *Auton*.

medically necessary, and that the decision did not violate equality rights guaranteed by the *Charter*.[101] The court accepted that it was permissible for the government to deny Lovaas treatment funding because of "financial concerns and competing claims on insufficient resources,"[102] and the "emergent and controversial nature of this therapy."[103]

The need to ration has also been acknowledged by various Canadian tribunals. In 2006 the Human Rights Tribunal in *Ontario Human Rights Commission & Hogan and others v. Ontario* upheld a decision to discontinue funding for Sex Reassignment Surgery (SRS).[104] Hogan challenged the Ontario government's 1998 decision to delist SRS from the provincial schedule of benefits.[105] The Tribunal majority found that the decision to delist this service was not discriminatory, but rather "was integral to the cost-cutting means to preserve the health care system for the long term."[106] As well, in *Armstrong*, the B.C. Human Rights Tribunal pointed to the B.C. *Medicare Protection Act*'s preamble that, "[t]he people and government of British Columbia recognize a responsibility for the judicious use of medical services in order to maintain a fiscally sustainable health care system for future generations".[107] Here, the Human Rights Tribunal framed the government's decision to not provide the PSA test funding as an act of explicit rationing supported by recommendations of a relevant expert committee.

Ultimately, faced with insufficient evidence to significantly counter the cost-effectiveness and clinical data of experts, claimants rely on the idea of unfairness backed by their disheartenment with a rationing process that leaves certain people without public funding for medical treatment. While able to fuel patient power in settings outside the court, this strategy does not usually take the claimant far in terms of a legal argument. *Armstrong*, for instance, questioned the reliability of scientists who employ cost-effectiveness studies, calling them "money crunchers" who make decisions with the help of calculators and science rather than their hearts. Mr. Armstrong had given an interview on national radio prior to the trial, asserting that there is a consensus amongst practicing physicians – whom he deemed "men out on the field" – that prostate screening tests should be publicly funded; yet in the court setting, he did not have any evidence to back this claim. In *Cameron*, as the claimant couple argued their case, they relied on an idealized view of what Canada's comprehensive Medicare system should look like, saying "that Medicare coverage is ascertained by reference to principle, not by a mere list. The principle is that there

---

[101]   ibid at para 5.
[102]   ibid at para 60.
[103]   ibid at para 11.
[104]   Hogan (note 5).
[105]   SRS had been funded by OHIP only under the condition that the patient had completed a two-year program at a specialized clinic and been recommended for the surgery. Those who completed the program were most often not recommended for the surgery. The operations were furthermore all performed outside the province and often outside the country.
[106]   *Hogan* (note 5) 92.
[107]   *Armstrong* (note 2) 341.

is universal comprehensive (in the sense of all-inclusive) Medicare."[108] Similarly, *Flora* argued that if something is potentially beneficial, as the liver transplant was for him, that it should *a priori* be publicly funded.

Rejecting the idea that Canadians' healthcare access should be based on "a mere list" formulated by cost-minded bureaucrats prevails in unsuccessful attempts to challenge formulary listings and expert-body decisions. Yet the courts seem largely aware of and immune to this sentiment of "unfairness", and without something more substantive to back up such claims, generally find that provinces have "a pressing and substantial objective to sustain the health care system."[109] As the court stated in *Hogan*, "[i]ndividuals or groups will assert the need for benefits from the public purse", yet it is up to the government to make the difficult decisions of health care allocation and the courts must in turn be deferential to that.[110]

5. Challenges to Rationing Down-Under: Cases From New Zealand and Australia

We now turn to a number of cases that challenge healthcare rationing decisions in New Zealand and Australia. The results of these cases align with several of the trends we identified above when examining formal challenges in Canada. Once again, we observe that courts may be more comfortable reviewing a challenge to decision-making procedure rather than the decision itself, while showing a deferential approach to expert decision-making bodies, and recognizing that healthcare rationing is an important objective.

Two cases *Walsh & Others v. Pharmac*[111], from New Zealand and *Hagar, Morrish and Marinaro v. the Minister for Health and Family Services and the Commonwealth of Australia*,[112], from Australia, both highlight the effectiveness of challenging a healthcare rationing decision by targeting decision making *processes* rather than the decision itself. *Walsh*[113] was a challenge launched by eight breast cancer patients, dubbed the Herceptin Heroines, against Pharmac's decision to provide Herceptin funding for only nine weeks instead of twelve months. The claimants sought judicial review using a "scattergun approach,"[114] employing "[a]lmost every cause of action or ground for review known under administrative law".[115] Despite the varied claims, the Court found that Pharmac had failed at only one point in its decision-making process namely to adequately consult with affected parties regarding a preliminary decision, and ordered a re-determination of that decision with proper consultation.[116]

---

[108] *Cameron* (note 4) 101.
[109] *Hogan* (note 5) 103.
[110] ibid at para. 104.
[111] *Walsh* (note 1).
[112] *Hagar*
[113] *Walsh* (note 1).
[114] ibid 25.
[115] ibid 21.
[116] ibid 206. The 9-week funding decision remained intact as the judge found none of the grounds challenging it were made out. *Walsh* at para. 216.

After engaging in comprehensive consultation,[117] Pharmac once again decided against funding Herceptin for 12 months, explaining that: "it is only right to feel compassion for breast cancer sufferers...but [Pharmac's] role is to not favour one group ahead of any others. Our task is to look hard at the evidence for different treatments and make the best possible decisions to improve New Zealand's health outcomes overall from within the funding available".[118] It should be noted that, although the court in Walsh ordered a redetermination of the decision based on procedural errors, it acknowledged that it lacked the medical and economic expertise necessary to closely assess the decision itself.[119] However, as mentioned earlier Pharmac's victory was relatively short-lived as a newly elected government overturned its decision, forcing it to fund Herceptin for 12 months. Similarly, in *Hagar*,[120] victory for the decision-maker (the Minister for Health) was short-lived. In this case four male complainants alleged that limiting funding for Calcitriol, an osteoporosis drug, to post-menopausal women discriminated against men. After the Australian Human Rights and Equal Opportunity Commission concluded that the decision discriminated against men, the Commission's decision was reviewed and set aside by the Federal Court.[121] The court found that the Commissioner erred in making his decision without hearing evidence about how the Calcitriol listing was determined, which may have included medical effectiveness and cost rationales. Even although the Commission's decision was overturned, nonetheless, PBAC did decide in the end to provide funding for men to access both Calcitriol as well as another osteoporosis drug, Didrocal.[122] Thus, both *Walsh* and *Hagar* suggest that while courts may be deferential to the process of decision-making, the politics surrounding the decision can change the ultimate outcome of the decision.

Additionally, courts in New Zealand and Australia tend to defer to rationing decisions particularly if portrayed as being "clinical" decisions rather than resource allocation decisions.

In New Zealand, the 1990s saw two high-profile challenges against decisions to withhold dialysis treatments. In the first, South Auckland Health, a decision to deny dialysis treatment for 76 year-old James McKeown was challenged at the Human Rights Commission on the basis of age discrimination. Mr. McKeown's family claimed that the decision denying dialysis, based on the guideline that "persons over 75 years are not likely to be accepted into a...dialysis program," breached the *Human Rights Act* 1993. In response to the complaint, and possibly

---

[117] "This included seeking new advice from PTAC and its cancer treatments sub-committee, revising the budget impact and the cost-utility model for Herceptin (both concurrent 9 weeks and 12 months), as well as undertaking wide consultation which included face to face meetings with breast cancer patients and oncologists." (Pharmac, 2008a) (note 52).

[118] New Zealand, PHARMAC, 'Herceptin Funding' Inpharmation (2008b) http://www.pharmac. govt.nz/.

[119] *Walsh* (note 1) 28.

[120] *Hagar* (note 112).

[121] *Australia v. Human Rights Commission* (1997), 47 ALD 235 at 260.

[122] Human Rights and Equal Opportunity Commission, Media Release, 'Sex Discrimination Commissioner welcomes listing of osteoporosis drug for men' (1 August 1999) HREOC http://www. hreoc.gov.au/.

pressured by a media campaign surrounding the issue, South Auckland Health ordered a reassessment excluding age considerations, Mr. McKeown was approved for treatment, and the case was never pursued at the courts. However, a few years later, a similar challenge, *Shortland v. Northland Health Ltd.*,[123] was launched against a decision to discontinue dialysis for 63-year old Rau Williams. Unlike South Auckland Health, this decision was challenged through the courts. The guidelines used to determine dialysis eligibility outlined that there "must be the ability to cooperate with active therapy". Williams, however, suffered from dementia, and was unable to administer the treatment. Ultimately, the High Court stated that the decision was based solely on clinical judgement – with no element of cost considerations – and dismissed the appeal, demonstrating how courts, typically deferential to expert decision-making, are even more so to decisions cloaked as "clinical". However, without a resource consideration, there was no need to deny the treatment, which could have been administered with the aid of a home nurse, or by allowing in-hospital treatment.[124]

In the Australian case of *Pfizer Pty Ltd v. Birkett*,[125] we also see recognition that healthcare rationing is a necessary and important objective. This case involved a challenge to a decision not to list Sildenafil, more commonly known as Viagra, on Australia's PBS. Sildenafil had been rejected twice on the basis that there was no evidence that it was more effective than a comparable drug already being listed, and that "[g]iven that the condition to be treated is not life threatening, the overall cost to the PBS...was difficult to support."[126] Pfizer argued that PBAC should not have considered overall costs, but instead focused on medical issues.[127] The Federal Court dismissed the appeal, stating "it is clearly relevant for the PBAC to consider...the overall cost of the drug."[128] Furthermore, the court made clear that "[a]ny consideration as to whether a drug should be declared a pharmaceutical benefit must have regard to the type of condition for which it is indicated. It goes without saying that funds will more readily be directed towards subsidising drugs which treat serious, debilitating or life-threatening conditions over those which treat minor conditions only."[129] Here, the court clearly recognized the need to consider costs and the importance of priority setting when making healthcare funding decisions, concerns that were raised repeatedly by Canadian courts and human rights tribunals.

---

[123]   *Shortland v. Northland Health Ltd* [1998] 1 NZLR 433 (C.A.).
[124]   Manning and Paterson (note 7) 681.
[125]   *Pfizer Pty Ltd v. Birkett* (2000) 171 ALR 427 (F.C.)
[126]   ibid at para. 30.
[127]   ibid 68.
[128]   ibid 81.
[129]   ibid 95.

6. Conclusion

Amidst competing views about healthcare rationing techniques, our examination of healthcare decision-making in Canada, New Zealand and Australia nevertheless reveals a shift – particularly pronounced for drugs and technologies – from implicit to explicit rationing. As new drugs and technologies are a major contributor to escalating healthcare costs, it is crucial to understand how and why funding decisions are made, as well as what the repercussions of those decisions will be.

Despite the evident importance of fairly rationing healthcare, decisions limiting access to treatment are often difficult and controversial. We have seen how citizens who are reluctant to passively accept rationing decisions, are increasingly likely to challenge such decisions both in and out of the courtroom. A major concern associated with explicit rationing is that it will facilitate these challenges by producing clear, stated decisions that can be contested and politicised, as was the case with the decision denying twelve months of Herceptin funding in New Zealand (*Walsh*). Even following the High Court ruling, when Pharmac once again decided to deny twelve months of funding for Herceptin, media attention and patient lobbying led to an election promise to provide it, ultimately fulfilled by an incoming National government.[130] The way the decision denying Herceptin funding was swept up by the media and used to garner political support showcases the risk that even principled, evidenced-based decisions can be overturned because of media attention and political agendas.

The increased risk that explicit rationing is more vulnerable to judicial challenge was also evident in our examination of three countries. Almost all of the cases we studied involved challenges against explicit decisions denying funding for a particular drug or treatment, decisions that are far more exposed than the indirect impact of implicit rationing as there is a clear and identifiable decision-maker and decision that can be challenged. However, delving deeper revealed that while explicit decisions may be more vulnerable to formal legal challenge, the clear evidence and transparency typical of explicit rationing also helped legitimize the decisions before courts and tribunals. Not only did courts start from a stance deferential to expert decision-makers, but they repeatedly recognized healthcare rationing as an important, albeit difficult, objective. Correspondingly, courts expressed reluctance to overturn evidence-based rationing decisions themselves, but were more willing to review decision-making procedures and processes. While many of the challenges alleging discrimination or challenging the reasonableness of a rationing decision lacked enough evidence to overturn a decision made based on medical and economic considerations, those that targeted procedural errors or factors that needed to be considered (e.g. respect for minority language rights) were more far more successful.

Our analysis reveals that despite producing decisions more vulnerable to challenge, explicit rationing also enables an understanding and dialogue about both the need for rationing, and how healthcare-funding decisions should be made. While

---

[130]   Pharmac 2008 (note 52).

the risk of politicization is clearly troubling, we also see that courts are receptive to the transparent processes associated with explicit rationing. Although decisions denying healthcare treatment will always be difficult, explicit rationing may help to foster an important dialogue about the need to carefully allocate healthcare resources, and promote public confidence in the decisions that do so.

Chapter X

The special moral status of health care. On market forces, equal treatment, and having a say

Martin Buijsen

1. Introduction

The economic crisis will affect the health care system in the Netherlands as well. The Netherlands Bureau for Economic Policy Analysis (CPB) concluded that drastic measures are needed to curb the increase in health care spending. The government will only be able to reduce its budget deficit, and prevent the national debt from exploding, by making relatively most savings in this area.[1] This was concluded, too, in the broad reconsideration reports drawn up by official working parties at the request of the former Cabinet.[2] It would seem that the Netherlands is facing important choices on health care issues.

Prior to the parliamentary elections of 9 June 2010 it was already clear that politics had taken good note of this message. Regrettably, the solutions from that quarter are no other than the hackneyed solutions of old. Once again the necessity of higher co-payment is brought up, a renewed plea for raising the insurance premiums is made, the scope of the collective health insurance package is again up for debate ... An then, it is no surprise that right-wing politicians are making a case for more competition in health care, whereas their colleagues at the other end of the political spectrum favour a stronger state presence.

Without intending to wave aside the seriousness of the possible consequences of the credit crunch, I should like to point out that scarcity of resources in health care is far from a new phenomenon. Financial tightness in this sector is of all times; the response on the side of politics is not. Although the above-mentioned measures have been considered possible solutions for some time already, they nevertheless testify of a different way of thinking about economic choices. For this way of thinking, which gives priority to efficiency, and to which also the shifting of public responsibilities to the private sector seems to be inherent, does generate its own moral problems of alienation, inequality, and exclusion.

---

[1] Centraal Planbureau, *Economische Verkenning 2011-2015* Document no. 203 (Den Haag 2010) 48-54.

[2] See the reports *Brede heroverwegingen curatieve zorg* (werkgroep 11) and *Brede heroverwegingen langdurige zorg* (werkgroep 12), Den Haag, April 2010.

2. Health care: a supreme good

Although in those days policy-makers hardly seem to acknowledge this quality, health care has a special moral status. Health care is not just a service (or 'product'). From where does it derive this status?

There are goals which the practical mind recognizes as goals in itself: goals that are desirable, but whose desirability fails further logical reasoning. We cannot imagine any condition they could derive their 'goodness' from. Their 'goodness' is a matter of course. Health is one of these goals, and so are knowledge and friendship, which are good 'by itself/themselves' (or intrinsically). The thesis that 'health is a desirable good' (i.e. one to save, protect, or restore), is one of those obvious practicalities that as the most basic reason for action form the starting point of each and every practical reasoning.[3]

Other than the 'goodness' of health, that of health care is purely instrumental. The latter, after all, derives its 'goodness' from that of health, and gains in value as it becomes more effective in relation to health.[4] And there is no doubt that present-day health care can achieve a great deal. In fact, it can make the difference between life and a premature death, between minor, temporary physical harm and a severe, chronic handicap. Clearly, it is health care that largely accounts for the higher life expectancy achieved in the past decades.[5]

But of course all this does not go to say that every practical choice that benefits health is morally right. Also a choice for health can be immoral. After all, the choice for a course of action that saves, protects, or restores health may at the same time be detrimental to other goods, also goods that are desirable of themselves, too. What is morally right, or not, will depend on the moral norms that are guiding in dilemmatic situations. Choices made in such situations are (in part) embodied in positive law. The identification of health as an intrinsically valuable human good explains the special normative stature that positive law assigns to health care.

3. Health care as a human right

Positive law reflects the special moral status of health care in several ways. For one, in being acknowledged as a human right. The Netherlands is a party to many international treaties declaring that any individual has the right to necessary (preventive, curative, rehabilitative, and palliative) health care.[6] It is up to the individual State parties, however, to define what is regarded as necessary. In the Netherlands, all collectively financed care is regarded as necessary. The government, then, is obliged

---

3   The intrinsic good of health is convincingly argued in R George, *In Defense of Natural Law* (Clarendon Press 1999) 45-48.

4   See JP Mackenbach, *Ziekte in Nederland. Volksgezondheid tussen biologie en politiek* (Elsevier health care 2010) 213-218.

5   *ibidem.*

6   See for example article 12, second paragraph under d, of the *International Covenant on Economic, Social and Cultural Rights*, New York 16 December 1966, Trb. 1978, 178.

to see to it that the services providing necessary health care are equally accessible to everyone, not only geographically, temporally, informatively and qualitatively, but also financially.[7] Notably the latter requirement rests obviously on a degree of solidarity that is not to be underestimated.

Of old, certain human rights are considered as second-rate in the Netherlands. Classic freedom rights are 'hard', whereas social fundamental rights, such as right to health care, education, housing, social benefit, et cetera, are not. Typical of the Dutch way of dealing with the human right to health care, prior to the 2006 health care system reform the policy-makers looked at length at the European rules and regulations regarding the common market, but hardly at those that relate to health care as a human right.[8] In this country it is still not understood that also acknowledging this kind of human rights reflects the internationally accepted standard of respect for human dignity.[9] Not recognizing an individual's right of health care is a breach of this individual's dignity, not less worse than restricting someone's classic freedom rights, e.g. freedom of speech. In this sense, social fundamental rights are not at all second-rate human rights. Moreover, internationally we have done away with the idea that such rights are merely 'programmatic' rights, rights that only involve commitments from the side of the state.[10]

4. Fairness in health care

Moreover, the special moral status of health care is evidenced by a quite specific idea of fairness, which as well is contained in positive law. The notion that fairness is closely intertwined with the concept of equal treatment is widely accepted.[11] The right to equal treatment (or non-discrimination) is therefore also a human right.[12] With regard to necessary health care, international treaty provisions refer to equal access.[13] But what then do 'equality' and 'equal treatment' mean in this context? And what then does 'inequality' mean in relation to this? It goes without saying that discrimination is quite unjustifiable in health care, too.

Discriminatory grounds in antidiscrimination provisions are typically worded negatively and non-limitatively. Article 1 of the Constitution of the Netherlands confirms this, by stating that 'all persons in the Netherlands shall be treated equally in equal circumstances'. Discrimination on the grounds of religion, belief, political

---

[7]   Committee on Economic, Social and Cultural Rights, *General Comment No. 14*, accepted on 11 May 2000. UN documents E/C.12/2000/4, 11 Augustus 2000, marginal refs. 12 en 17.

[8]   Legislative proposal on the Health Insurance Act, *Kamerstukken II* 2003/04, 29 763, nr. 3, p. 20 ff..

[9]   In the preamble of almost every human rights treaty, human dignity is identified as the core value to be cherished.

[10]   See for example F Coomans (ed), *Justiciability of Economic and Social Rights. Experiences from domestic systems* (Intersentia, Antwerpen 2006).

[11]   DD Raphael, *Concepts of Justice* (Clarendon Press 2001) 5-6.

[12]   See for example article 14 of the *European Convention for the Protection of Human Rights*, Rome 4 November 1950, Trb. 1951, 154, most recently emended by Trb. 1994, 165.

[13]   See for example article 3 of the *Convention for the Protection of Human Rights and Dignity of the Human Being with regard to the Application of Biology and Medicine*, Oviedo 4 April 1997, ETS No. 164. (not yet ratified by the Netherlands) (*Biomedicine Convention*)

opinion, race or sex or on other grounds whatsoever, the article continues, shall not be permitted.[14]

In view of the special moral status of health care, equal treatment in relation to the fundamental right to health care is consistently defined positively and limitatively (even exclusively). In health care there is only one ground that justifies making a distinction between individuals. Both in international law and in the field of medical ethics it is clearly argued that in this context the only justifiable distinction is the distinction that can be made on the grounds of differences in objective, i.e. based on medical criteria, need of health care.[15] Put simply: more need, higher on the waiting list, treated sooner; less need, lower on the list, treated later. Within the context of health care, any distinction based on other criteria would in principle boil down to discrimination. And seeing that also equal treatment is a recognized human right, violation of that right as well would equate to violation of the dignity of the person affected by it.

One of the consequences of the introduction of market forces in health care has been the stealthy importation of merit criteria.[16] In many cases there is nothing wrong with allocation on the grounds of merit. In athletics it is taken for granted that the one gold medal goes to the fastest runner. And in science, too, it is no more than fair that scarce research resources should go to the best researcher. In the context of health care, 'fairness' according to international law and medical ethics does not have this meaning. However, in the new Dutch health care system, which is based on marketisation, it has indeed acquired that meaning unnoticed. Today, making 'informed' choices may gain earlier access to better health care. The one who is able to make a sensible choice – because he has access to information (on quality of the service provided by the health insurer, on quality of the health care purchased by the insurer, on the own future health and care needs), because he can afford a higher policy excess, because he can take out an expensive non-contracted care policy – does definitely all right for himself. But in matters of health and health care not everyone is gifted with that degree of 'sensibility'. This is the very area where such inequity is out of place.[17]

Markets are often thought to be morally neutral. This is not the case. True, markets are functioning anonymously and do not openly and purposefully discriminate, but they are far from being morally neutral instruments of distribution. Markets

---

[14] Constitution of the Kingdom of the Netherlands of 24 Augustus 1815, *Stb.* 1815, 45, most recently emended by law of 22 Augustus 2008, *Stb.* 2008, 348 (Constitution).

[15] See for example the *Explanatory report* to the *Biomedicine Convention*, Nos. 24 en 25.

[16] Martin Buijsen, 'De betekenis van solidariteit in de gezondheidszorg' [The meaning of solidarity in health care], in Martin Buijsen, Wim van de Donk en Nicolette van Gestel (red.) *Marktwerking versus solidariteit? Op zoek naar nieuwe evenwichten in de publieke dienstverlening* (Valkhof Pers 2007) 65-98.

[17] Of course, also under the 'old' system people with knowledge and connections were able to procure better care for themselves. That was a known fact, but the normative framework actually did not allow for another response than indignation. The system reform resulted in a change. Making informed choices is considered commendable. The citizen who does not receive the best care is to blame himself. He should have been 'more informed'.

tend to reflect general social inequities rather than doing away with them.[18] After all, not everyone can get hold of a grand mansion on the housing market. And only the happy few will be able to buy that pricey Mercedes on the automobile market. Many people, for that matter, do not even have access to these markets. If merit should be the dominant principle of distribution outside the domain of health care is, which is definitely the case in our society, and if there unequal treatment between people should be justified by differences in merit, the health care domain –once this has been 'marketized' – is bound to embrace this principle. Marketisation carries with it that inequities that occur elsewhere (on the labour market, for example), and perhaps can be accepted there, are imported into a domain where in principle they cannot serve to justify differences in treatment.

All this does not imply, however, that other criteria are not at all relevant when it comes to health care distribution. In fact, it is inevitable that they should bear significance. And this is something that also by definition is not unfair. But 'sneaking in' those criteria through the back door is unfair indeed, as it truly would be to the detriment of the individual, needier fellow human being.

5. Moral ambiguity

Other criteria are being sneaked in through the back door in many ways. Although the legislation that lies at the basis of the system reform forbids risk selection (the barring of sick individuals by basic health care insurers) and premium differentiation (charging higher premiums to sick individuals by the same health insurers),[19] it does happen but goes unnoticed. There are many smuggling routes.

For one, everyone must be accepted to a basic insurance plan, and everyone is expected to pay the same nominal premium for the same insurance product, irrespective of his or her health status or -risks. In 2009, however, the Dutch Council of the Chronically ill and the Disabled (CGR) drew the attention to a quite ingenious basic insurance construction. Certain health insurance companies had come up with the idea that students could opt for the € 500 legal maximum of voluntary policy excess. Added to the € 155 compulsory policy excess, the total policy excess amounted to € 655, against which these companies obviously could offer a considerable premium reduction. As a next step they worked out that these insurees could re-insure the risk of unexpectedly having to cough up the policy excess to the maximum account, namely via very cheap supplementary health insurance schemes from the same companies. This scheme enabled students to save up to 30 percent of their total health insurance costs.[20]

---

[18] According to L Fleck in *Just Caring. Health care rationing and democratic deliberation* (OUP 2009) 148.

[19] Article 3 of the Act of 16 June 2005, *Stb.* 2006, 79, on a social insurance plan for medical care for the entire population, most recently emended by Adjustment of 30 September 2009, *Stcrt.* 2009, 15178. (*Health Insurance Act*)

[20] See for example *Algemeen Dagblad* (Daily newspaper) of 21 Juli 2009.

This seemed to be an excellent arrangement for people who are known to be liable to be squeezed for money. Was there any reason to assume that things were not well with a construction like this? According to Mr. Klink, Minister of Health, Welfare and Sport, there was no reason at all. Being asked whether a Rabobank construction possibly violated the prohibition of premium differentiation, he replied negatively. The minister pointed out that the applicable Health Insurance Act in fact provides for one exception to this prohibition: in the case of a so-called collectivity, members are entitled to a reduction of maximally 10 percent. In addition he made clear that Interpolis, the health insurer contracted by Rabobank, does not adjust the premium for its insurance product to factors related to the person of the candidate-insuree, such as age, health status, et cetera. That would indeed be inadmissible, said the minister. Nevertheless, as it was not Interpolis but rather Rabobank that had opted to take out a collective insurance for a specific target group – students – it was still allowed. And as long as the collectiveness-based reduction on the basic insurance scheme does not exceed 10 percent, nothing was wrong with the arrangement. Furthermore, because the reduced premium for the supplementary health insurance scheme and the re-insuring of the policy excess via that scheme fell outside the scope of the same Health Insurance Act, the minister stated this was neither a matter of prohibited risk selection. The minister wisely left unanswered the question whether such constructions eventually would allow the solidarity element to erode.[21]

However, the policy excess was re-insured through a supplementary health insurance scheme from the same health insurer, for no more than a few euros per month. The minister omitted to mention that this insurance scheme was a straightforward non-life insurance, to which the Health Insurance Act indeed does not apply, whereas the regular insurance law laid down in the Civil Code obviously does. The latter does not preclude premium differentiation and risk selection. What is more, it is the very essence of non-life insurance. For young and usually healthy people it was relatively easy to take such an insurance scheme, but things were different for people with a less favourable risk profile (the chronically ill, elderly). As far as those are not barred anyway, they will have to pay a considerably higher premium. Therefore, the chronically ill or elderly person who also is less able to opt for an high policy excess, does not to an equal degree have access to a supplementary health insurance scheme with which – when it comes to the pinch – also necessary health care can be financed. Because necessary health care also financially should be equally accessible to everyone, this situation is unfair.[22]

The following anecdote illustrates that the system is clearly struggling to retain an eye on the morals of health care. In 2008 it became known that the *Kennemer Gasthuis* hospital, Haarlem, offered patients preferential treatment at extra cost. This concerned necessary care. This hospital had teamed up with an intermediary

---

[21]   *Kamerstukken II* 2008/09, 3047, p, 6422.
[22]   Martin Buijsen, 'Teloorgang solidariteit in de zorg dreigt', in (2009) 4 *Tijdschrift voor health care en ethiek* 101-103.

agency –Quality Medical Services (QMS) – which sent patients, usually as commis-sioned by employers in small- and medium-sized companies who like to have their employees back to work soon. At the price of € 900,- these patients were treated without the usual waiting time. The hospital and the treating specialist shared this amount of money. The hospital director justified the arrangement by pointing out that it did not harm other patients. Only patients who did not require emergency care – the arrangement was restricted to relatively simple knee- and hip operations – were eligible for preferential treatment. Also, the surgeons worked longer hours (in the evenings and weekends) to attend those patients.[23]

A few years ago, anyone would unhesitatingly have labelled such a type of prefer-ential care as discriminatory and unfair.[24] Not now. Judging from his commentaries in the press the hospital director was unaware of any wrongdoing. He said he could not but conclude that the new system stimulated initiatives like these. And indeed, the Health Insurance Act does not specifically prohibit such arrangements. In his turn the minister did not dare pronounce in advance on the admissibility of the arrangement. Eventually the authorities, through the same minister, pronounced against the arrangement, but not until advice had been received from the Dutch Health Care Authority (NZa), one of the many supervisory bodies in Dutch health care. This advice in its turn was based on an interpretation of the Act that even the most experienced health lawyer failed to grasp, and moreover included the urgent request to the minister to consider whether commercial care mediation could perhaps be a future option.[25] In this affair, there was hesitation, vagueness, and ambiguity all round.

For that matter, the Haarlemmer hospital director's train of thought was not all that strange. For several years earlier, in 2006, it had become known that the health insurance company *Zorg & Zekerheid* (Z&Z) had entered into a comparable arrangement with the *Diaconessenhuis* hospital at Leyden. This concerned cataract operations: also collectively financed, necessary health care. Z&Z had agreed with the hospital to finance such operations when performed after office hours, but not without stipulating that this extra capacity would be exclusively used for the own clients, who thus would receive preferential treatment. The hospital board argued they could accept this treatment inequity because also cataract patients not insured with Z&Z could benefit from the arrangement. True, not as much as the Z&Z-policyholders, but still... After all, cataract patients with a basic policy from Z&Z no longer were placed ahead of them on the waiting list for treatment within office hours. While this argument was to no avail to the director of the *Kennemer Gasthuis*, the board of the Leyden Hospital did get away with it however. The then minister of health, Hans Hoogervorst, simply concluded that this is nothing but

---

[23]   See *Nederlands Dagblad* (Daily newspaper) of 13 November 2008. See also Martin Buijsen, 'Onge-lijke behandeling in de Nederlandse gezondheidszorg. Te rechtvaardigen of niet?', in (2009) 10 *Nederlands Juristenblad* 609-614.

[24]   M Buijsen, 'De handigste verzekeraars dringen voor', in *Trouw* (Daily newspaper) van 25 maart 2006.

[25]   *ibidem*.

the way of the market. And also the umbrella organizations of health care insurers and hospitals considered this a 'logical consequence of marketisation'.[26]

The remarkable thing about this event was that minister Hoogervorst was informed about it by an outraged NP/CF: the umbrella organization of patient associations that at the time had warmly supported the system reform. In its turn the NP/CF had been alerted to the arrangement via one of its complaints lines. A patient who was waitlisted for treatment in the *Diaconessenhuis* hospital noted that she was moved down on the waiting list, not so much because the other patients needed surgery more badly, but rather because they were insured against this type of basic care elsewhere.

Obviously, it would not have been amiss for the NP/CF as a genuine consumer organisation to point out to the person involved that she could opt for the Z&Z-policy, too. For that would have been fully in agreement with its belief in the virtue of freedom of choice.[27] But at the end of the day the belief in the abstract good of freedom of choice made way for the concrete experience of discrimination. Obviously there were plenty of reasons to put into perspective the moral significance of being able to choose a basic care policy.

The idea of equality that is inherent to the human right to health care appears to lose its unambiguity nationwide in the Netherlands. Differences in the access to health care services are increasingly defended on other grounds than medical necessity. It is not exactly clear what the criteria are. They emerge from the practice of health care, do hardly or not at all meet with consensus and appear to provide little moral guidance. With regard to equal treatment the unambiguity of the human right seems to have made way mainly for ambiguity and uncertainty.[28]

6. Collective choices and having a say

Fairness in health care can be addressed in a different manner as well. Where 'fairness' at the gates of the system has the meaning of equal treatment (or rather: of treatment 'as an equal'), it has not this meaning where choices about the use of collective resources within health care are made. What will go to preventive care? What amount of resources to curative care? How much to chronic care within the framework of the Exceptional Medical Expenses Act (AWBZ)? Fairness is then not so much interwoven with equality but rather with having a say.

What health care has in common with other goods is that it is scarce. Health economists will tell that the demand of health care always far exceeds the supply. Thus there will always be people requiring necessary care who nevertheless do not

---

[26] As appears for example from the NPCF-brochure *Zorgconsumentenwet*, NP/CF, Den Haag 2006.

[27] U Reinhardt, 'Rationing Health Care: What It Is, What It Is Not, and Why We Cannot Avoid It', in S Altman and U Reinhardt (eds), *Strategic Choices for a Changing Health Care System* (Health Administration Press 1996) 63-99.

[28] Note that the arrangements described in this section have been taken up by the media and have led to questions in Parliament. These types of unequal treatment have been subject to discourse. It is unknown what types of unequal treatment have been left out of view.

have access to it for lack of resources. This is inevitable. Is has been said therefore that health care is always subject to rationing.[29] Not only in strictly government-regulated systems, but also in systems that have accommodated for market forces. After all, the essence of the concept of rationing lies not so much in the fact that the good in question is being distributed but rather – and I repeat – that people have no access to it.[30] Also it is not true that rationing is always unfair. This need not be the case at all. The question that presents itself for each and every health care system is the following: who where on what grounds in which way makes decisions on rationing?

Apart from being inevitable in health care, rationing is also always more or less visible, and decisions on rationing can be more or less traceable, more or less transparent, more or less knowable, and more or less explicit. Owing to the abundance of parties, the changeability and the dynamic nature, rationing via the market strongly tends to be implicit.[31] Indication of the real reason for an unfavourable rationing decision (lack of resources) will then be held back, or it will be concealed. In a system of implicit rationing, the 87-year-old man who would gain several months of life with an artificial heart at the price of several tonnes would hear from his doctor, for example, that such an intervention for him would be medically futile. Naturally, this is a lie.

Inherent to implicit rationing is the piecemeal, less coordinated production of rationing decisions, on account of which also the risks of arbitrariness and injustice are more real. In a system of implicit rationing the individual with a lower socioeconomic status will inevitably fall victim to inequity soonest. And I repeat, in the context of health care this is a violation of human dignity.

In a system of explicit rationing, however, a patient will be told indeed why the scarce collective resources are not used to his benefit and why others have a stronger claim on those resources. In such a system the inevitable 'trade-offs' are explained. Going back to the example above: no wildly expensive artificial hearts for the elderly, but programs for the vaccination of newborns may be suitable options. In a system of explicit rationing, rationing decisions are the result of comprehensive, systematic, rational and above all, transparent deliberation; they are visible, verifiable, and at the end of the day ideally also legitimized in a democratic manner. [32]

Health care being a scarce good, for the distribution of which other criteria than need inevitably need to be considered, such as age in the example, it follows that fundamental choices in health care must be made in the full view of the public – with the best possible continual involvement of the public. Notably because – and I repeat again – it such a special good. Regrettably, in the Dutch system the 'who where in on what grounds in which way' of making choices is almost completely obscured from view. This can largely be ascribed to the large number of parties involved (the Package Advisory Board PAC, the Health Care Insurance Board CVZ,

---

[29]   *ibidem.*
[30]   L Fleck (note 18) 95-97.
[31]   *ibid.* 10-11.
[32]   *ibid.* 11.

the Minister, watchdogs such as NMa (the Dutch competition authority) and NZa, the medical-scientific associations, the health care insurers, et cetera).

Another contributing factor is the phenomenon that many of these parties, in so far they are governmental bodies, are operating on the basis of just a few legal powers that offer a very great deal of policy freedom. The Dutch Health care Authority NZa occupies a unique position in the regulatory apparatus in the Netherlands. The amount of policy rules yearly issued by this independent agency is virtually unparalleled. In a manner that can hardly be legitimized the rise in volume policies of such organisations obscures the view on the law, while problems in effect seem to be lacking any moral dimension on account of the technicity of the policy response. Policy-making suggests that there are no longer moral questions at all. Everything seems to have become implementation.[33]

And finally, because the implementation of the new health care system has been entrusted to private health care insurers, with or without profit motives, many rationing decisions are more and more taken behind the closed doors of the boardrooms of companies.

In the past period, Dutch health care has developed into such an unfathomable institutional complex, that it manages to mystify even those who are in the know.

7. Alienation and degeneration

As a system (the building of hospitals, conducting medical-scientific research, the schooling of care providers, et cetera.) health care is the fruit of enormous social efforts. Health care systems can hardly be accused of being the product of a clearly identified something or someone. Also the Dutch system of health care is not such a product. Nevertheless, the most recent system reform has achieved that only few people are still willing to maintain that health care 'belongs to us all'. As public engagement with the system is limited to the pure self-interest of the prudently choosing 'care consumer', health care has become alienated from the public, so that all sorts of blind forces have hijacked it.

The holding structures which health care executives currently rigging up, assisted by batteries of expensive consultants, and devouring millions of euros, are as breathtaking as mind-boggling. For example, the needy *Vlietland* hospital at Schiedam has spent much time in setting up a construction to ensure a constant patient flow with the help of the regional health care insurer DSW and local general practitioners and AWBZ-care institutions. Regrettably the advisors failed to realize at an early stage that one of the watchdogs, in this case the Dutch Competition Authority (NMa), might well come up with obvious fundamental objections against this unfortunate plan. The possibility of rest competition on the relevant local and

---

[33] The Health Care Market Regulation Act (WMG), which forms the basis for the activities of the NZa, does not contain norms of material right. It is only mentioned that the NZa should give priority to 'the general consumers' interests'. (art. 3 paragraph 4). The content of this interest, and the manner in which this interest should be served, are subject of policy.

regional 'care markets' thus became quite theoretical.[34] Manipulating consultants, legal pie in the sky, and health care robbed of another million euros. Constructions like these seem to be predominantly instilled by institutional survival struggle and self-interest. They do not testify to a great deal of consideration for the special character of care provision to people in need. Likewise, it is hardly a matter of prudent use of scarce collective resources.

The individual care provider, too, feels no longer 'at home' in the sector. Not only can others (institutional directors, health care insurers) apparently more easily encourage him to work according to norms that in fact are not his, as the events in the *Kennemer Gasthuis* and the *Diaconessenhuis* hospitals showed; more in general we could say that he finds himself increasingly in an environment of organised distrust –entangled in a tightly spun web of bureaucratic accountability. Performance indication reports – essential for pricing – have cut up his work in product units, with an alarming increase in the administrative load as a result.[35] The corresponding loss of productivity is severe. Absolutely pernicious are the consequences for the self-image and morality of the care provider. Not the one who knows his job but rather the one who is an expert in administration is seen as a good care provider. Pursuing a career and securing management positions run the risk of becoming synonymous in health care.[36]

Perhaps it is indeed out of this time to call it a vocation, but a health care professional does have very special responsibilities. For the very reason that – I repeat again – health care is such a special good. However, where care providers increasingly appear to be willing to put in extra effort provided this is financially remunerated, even if this (like the specialists of the *Kennemer Gasthuis* hospital demonstrated) boils down to discrimination, simply fulfilling the duty of care seems no longer to be that obvious. The doctor who turns his back to a patient in need because his shift has ended, the doctor who in his leisure time does not attend to a neighbour with heart failure, the doctor who refuses to provide medical necessary care to an uninsured illegal immigrant because the financing is such a hassle, the doctor on holiday who refuses to look at wrist fracture of a fellow tourist .... The doctor who 'was not there' has regrettably become a regular appearance before the disciplinary judge in the past few years.[37]

---

[34] See the conclusion of the NMa executive board of 18 February 2010 in case 6669/*Coöperatie Vlietland – Vlietland ziekenhuis*.

[35] The number of Diagnosis Treatment Combinations (DBCs) has since the introduction of this methodology on 1 January 20005 risen to 30,000. Efforts are being made to get a grip on this development. See the program "DBCs on the road to transparency", available on http://www.werkenmetdot.nl (accessed on Mach 1, 2012).

[36] Witness the rise of all kinds of management educational programs, academic or not, specifically aimed at the health care sector. There is great interest for these programs, increasingly also from health care providers.

[37] To such an extent even that the National Public Prosecutor's Office, dissatisfied with the relative light sentences imposed by the judge, requested the author to identify possibilities to start a penal procedure in those cases. Art. 255 of the Penal Code (abandonment of those in need) could be relevant here. A quite typical verdict is that by the Regional disciplinary board for health care of 24 June 2009, in case 0187. At this time of writing the appeal verdict was still awaited.

8. What to do?

The recent history of health care in the Netherlands is a classic story of alienating and gradually increasing injustice. Socio-economic health inequity is on the rise again. [38] The life expectancy of people with a low socio-economic status is falling behind and it is not difficult to imagine that a distributing system of health care that more and more is based merit clearly cannot prevent this development. The time has come for politics to become aware once more of the special moral status of health care. The human rights law testifies to that status. According to that law the individual who needs care, is no more than an individual with a medical problem. Regarding the distribution of health care, differences in the treatment of people can therefore only be justified on the grounds of needs differences. If the use of other distribution criteria should be inevitable – and that is the case: health care is always subject to rationing –, then this should be subjected to prior, transparent, democratically legitimized decision-making.

Financial scarcity is of all times. Lack of resources does not need to be in the way of policy that aims to give the citizens a say again. To achieve that Dutch health care will again really 'belong to us all', we must thoroughly democratise it first of all. The citizen who actually is involved in making choices in health care, who in fact knows where for what reasons what collective decisions are made, will really be more ready to accept rationing decisions that are disadvantageous to him personally. Should we succeed in transforming this process into a permanent social debate, as is the case for example in the United Kingdom,[39] we will be making a decisive step into the direction of a really sustainable system of health care.

Moral ambiguity seems to have become an essential characteristic of our system. The Dutch government would do well therefore to confirm unambiguously in national legislation the special moral status of health care.

---

[38] According to the joint recommendation of the Council for Public Health and Health Care, the Education Council and the Council for Public Administration to the Minister of VWS. See *Buiten the gebaande paden*. Advies over een intersectoraal gezondheidsbeleid (RVZ 2009) 5.

[39] The UK *National Institute for Health and Clinical Excellence* (NICE) continually instigates social debate on choices to be made in health care.

Chapter XI

Rationing Health Care: an economic perspective

Alan Maynard and Karen Bloor

1. Introduction

Fiscal austerity after the 2008 banking crisis has fuelled renewed consideration of rationing in health care. In the British context, seven years of unprecedented growth in NHS expenditure doubled the budget and now is to be followed, in almost biblical fashion, by seven years of austerity.[1]

The English Coalition government is planning funding increases of 1.2 per cent over the next four years. Even if this marginal growth is in addition to inflation proofing, it will be difficult to deal with demand increases arising from the effects of technological change and the ageing of the population.

In the Netherlands, health care reform has focused on the introduction of "managed care" or competition amongst insurers. This has led to oligopsony or few buyers of health care as insurers merged. These purchasers or demanders of health care have had little impact on the efficiency of providers.[2] Consequently insurance premia continue to grow and rationing issues are ubiquitous and translated into policy concern about expenditure inflation.

So once again rationing is back on the policy agenda, not just in England and the Netherlands but around European and other health care systems. But how is rationing in health care defined? Williams defined rationing as occurring "when somebody is denied (or simply not offered) an intervention that everyone agrees would do them some good and which they would like to have".[3]

What principles should inform health care rationing, and consequently determining who will live in what degree of pain and discomfort and who will die? This is the subject of the first section of this paper. Then we ask the question could health care systems be incentivised to be more efficient and mitigate the need to ration? In the final section we offer an answer to this 'productivity challenge' and predict a return to the ubiquitous problem of how best to make difficult social choices in all

---

[1]   A Maynard, A Street, 'Seven years of feast, seven years of famine: from boom to bust in the NHS' (2006) 322 *BMJ* 906-908.

[2]   K Okma, TR Marmor, and J Oberlander, 'Managed competition for Medicare? Sobering lessons from the Netherlands' (2011) 365, 4 *NEJM* 287-289.

[3]   A Williams, 'Intergenerational equity: an exploration of the 'fair innings' argument' (1997) 6 *Health Economics* 117–32, quoted in A Maynard and K Bloor, *Our Certain fate: rationing in health care* (Office of Health Economics, London 1998).

public and private health care systems, with continuing debates about who should live when all must die.[4]

2. The principles of rationing

Should access to care be determined by the patient's ability to pay or by "need", and what is the role of social values in determining access to health care?

a) Rationing by ability to pay

Patients can pay for health care in private markets out of pocket and by buying insurance cover. Insurance may be sold to consumers on the basis of individual actuarial risk or through some group or community pooling of risks.

Consumers' ability and willingness to pay for insurance is related to their income and their health status. The ability to pay for insurance of poor people is less than affluent citizens due to both income and health differences. Ageing and chronic disease increases actuarial risk, inflates premia costs and reduces access to insurance. Thus, for example, retirement in Chile, the USA and South Africa generally reduces access to private insurance and leaves citizens dependent on the pubic health care system.

There are several ways of mitigating these problems. Firstly access to insurance membership can be made by groups with the premium set to average risk and the good risks cross subsidising the poor risks. An extreme form of this approach is a monopoly insurer with comprehensive coverage, like the UK's National Health Service.

Alternatively governments may oblige private insurers to set premia equal to community risks and to take all comers who are prepared to contribute. The former Liberal government in Australia took this approach when it introduced expensive tax subsidies. They sought for ideological reasons to favour the more affluent, and encourage them to increase the use of private insurance. The opportunity cost of this policy in terms of tax revenue forgone exceeds two billion Australian dollars.[5]

Private insurance has several weaknesses, some of which are shared by publicly funded schemes. The first of these is moral hazard. Once insurees have coverage they have no incentive to be economical in their use of health care facilities. In a fee for service reimbursement system this leads to expenditure inflation as providers exploit their ability to induce demand and meet often unnecessary patient demand e.g. they are free to over diagnose and treat.[6] This behaviour is a product not only

---

[4]   VR Fuchs, *Who shall live? Health, economics and social choice* (World Scientific Publishing 1998) 3.

[5]   J Hall and A Maynard, 'What can Michael Howard learn from John Howard?' (2005) 330 *BMJ* 357.

[6]   HG Welch, *Over-diagnosed: making people sick in the pursuit of health* (Beacon Press 2011); U Reinhardt, 'Table manners at the health care feast: regulation versus the market', in D Yaggy and WG Anlyan (eds), *Financing Health Care: competition regulation* (Ballinger Publishing Company 1982) 13-33; U Reinhardt, 'Divide et Impera: protecting the growth of health care incomes' (2012) 1 *Health Economics* 21.

of the payment system but also of the agency relationship: because of the asymmetry of knowledge between provider and consumer, the former (the agent of the patient) is freer to make choices which may be therapeutically ambiguous or even unnecessary but which generate income for clinicians and their team.

A second problem with insurance is adverse selection. Individual patients know more about their health status than insurers and consequently those patients who feel there are at a greater risk of needing care will tend to purchase more comprehensive insurance packages. Their use of such benefits will inflate premia and drive out low risk patients from these insurance schemes. With bad risks driving out good risks, risk spreading is reduced and insurance markets fail. With wealth and ill health inversely related this worsens distributional equity.

Another problem associated with private insurance markets is that the benefit package may be ambiguous and is always finite. The literature offers many examples of attempts to define a "basic benefit package". For example, the Obama reforms will provide Federal government subsidies for previously uninsured consumers to buy insurance. This requires definition of a basic package which will be Federally funded.

Making access to health care dependent on unregulated ability to pay has clear distributional consequences: access to care is unequal and clearly favors the rich. In addition, such systems offer no incentives to providers to be efficient. These problems can be mitigated by subsidies, risk pooling and other forms of regulation of the supply side of the health care market. These interventions may provide better functioning of private insurance schemes but they are contentious as they run counter to the ethos of insurance advocates who prefer the elusive rhetoric of "free markets".

A good example of the need for and complexity of more efficient regulation of insurance markets is Enthoven's advocacy of managed competition over many decades.[7] Forms of managed competition have been adopted in Colombia and (publicly financed) in the Netherlands and are currently under discussion in Ireland.

Enthoven's proposals involve a high degree of regulation of insurance markets. He diagnoses the problems of US health care as being an unavoidable product of perverse incentives i.e. fee per item reimbursement of providers and cost unconscious choices of care by patients. To remedy these market failures Enthoven proposes the use of price competition in a highly regulated market. All citizens would be covered, with the disadvantaged subsidised to purchase a basic package of care, and the more affluent able to buy more cover. Insurance premia would be community rated and insurance cover would be provided by competing health plans with community rating and adjustment for risks. Providers' efficiency would be made more transparent with investment in quality data to inform patient choice.

These ambitious and logical proposals have been advocated for over 35 years. Their adoption in the Netherlands in 2006 was focused on creating competition

---

7   AC Enthoven, 'Shattuck lecture: Cutting costs without cutting quality' 1978, 298 *NEJM* 1229-1238; AC Enthoven and R Kronick, 'Consumer choice health plan for the 1990s' (1990) 320 *NEJM* 94-101; AC Enthoven, 'Reforming Medicare by reforming incentives' (2011) 364 *NEJM* e44.

on the demand side i.e. between competing insurers, although this is in the context of an internal market, with public finance, rather than in the context of a private market. Much effort was put into devising a risk equalisation scheme formula to ensure "level playing field" competition between competing insurers.[8] The benefits of this work appear to be modest. Insurers have merged, producing an oligopsony. There has been little effect in terms of moderating expenditure inflation and the improving efficiency of the supply side of the market.[9]

Rationing by ability to pay in insurance markets creates concerns about access to care. Managed competition proposals may mitigate such concerns in principle but in practice the translation of highly regulated price competition into practice has proved elusive in the USA and Columbia. This is epitomized by the current political and policy debate about the Obama health reforms in the USA.

b) Rationing by need

With the price mechanism rejected as a rationing device in most developed countries health care systems, the usual alternative prioritisation device is "need". Have need-based health care systems proved any better at controlling expenditure inflation and improving efficiency than their public and private insurance rivals?

In the UK the founding legislators of the NHS in 1946 declared that the new service "imposes no limitation on availability, e.g. limitation based on financial means, age, sex, employment or vocation, area of residence or insurance qualification". Such open criteria for access to care were re-iterated by Prime Minister Margaret Thatcher in 1983: "the principle that adequate health care should be provided to all, regardless of ability to pay, must the foundation of any arrangements for financing health care". Tony Blair when Prime Minister added to this chorus of free at the point of use health care: "the NHS will get better every year so that it once again delivers dependable high quality care- based on need, not ability to pay. The current Prime Minister, David Cameron, has pledged like Thatcher that "the NHS is safe with us".

Such political rhetoric buys votes but what are the real implications for rationing health care? A simple set of questions have to be answered i.e. who is to get what at whose expense?[10]

In tax-financed systems of health care like the UK and Sweden, rationing devices include creating queues and obliging patients to wait for elective procedures such as hip and knee replacements, hernia repairs and cataract removal. This is achieved by limiting staffing and facilities. In other publicly financed systems, and often where expenditure is higher and social insurance may be the dominant funding model, like in Germany and France, demand controls may be less obvious but they still exist.

---

[8]   W van de Ven, R van Vliet, and LM Lamers, 'Health adjusted premium subsidies in the Netherlands' (2004) 23, 3 *Health Affairs* 45-55.
[9]   Okma (note 2).
[10]   A Williams, 'Priority setting in public and private health care systems' (1988) 7 *Journal of Health Economics* 173-83.

All these publicly financed health care systems face many problems similar to those of insurance based health care systems. Providers of health care, be they clinicians, managers or the pharmaceutical industry, have an incentive to create demand for their services; the income they generate from trading provides them with employment, income and profits. The incomplete nature of the evidence base in medicine enables them to create demand even though their payment incentives, unlike fee for service in insurance systems, have a muted effect on demand creation. As in insurance markets the asymmetry of knowledge between the "expert" provider and the ill informed user facilitates activity and expenditure inflation.

The benefit package in needs based systems should be determined by evidence of the relative cost-effectiveness of competing interventions. This principle is difficult to translate into practice because of the paucity of evidence of effectiveness and cost effectiveness. NHS systems offer "comprehensive" benefit packages which means that interventions may be of dubious usefulness but continue to be used.

Investments in health technology assessment and guidelines development is now considerable across all health care systems.[11] However the impact of these investments on clinical decisions is less than clear. Ideally evidence-based information should improve the average compliance with "best practice" and reduce dispersion around the mean. Unfortunately an absence of investment in audit, peer review and efficient incentives means that variations in clinical practice remain resistant to change.

As a consequence, need-based systems exhibit similar problems to insurance based systems i.e. inefficient provision of health care and expenditure inflation. Whether the health care system is based on private insurance or Bismarck or Beveridge social finance, supplier induced demand preserves price and quality taking by insurers and government agencies. Is it possible to undermine provider power and make public and private purchasers price and quality makers through determined and more aggressive contracting?

3. Can we resolve rationing pressures by addressing medical practice variations?

Prior to having to make difficult rationing decisions it is desirable to identify and reduce provision of clinical interventions of low value, and unwarranted variations in clinical practice.[12] There are two aspects to this. Firstly about 50 per cent of common procedures used in health care systems internationally have no evidence base in terms of effectiveness, let alone cost effectiveness. The "guesstimates" that support this contention are shown in Figure 1.[13]

---

[11] M Drummond, 'Twenty years using economic evaluations for reimbursement decisions: what have we achieved?' *Journal of Health Policy and Law* forthcoming 2012.

[12] J Appleby and others, Variations in Health Care, Kings Fund, London 2011.

[13] BMJ 2011, Clinical Evidence Handbook, BMJ Evidence Centre.

FIGURE 1. *Levels of effectiveness*

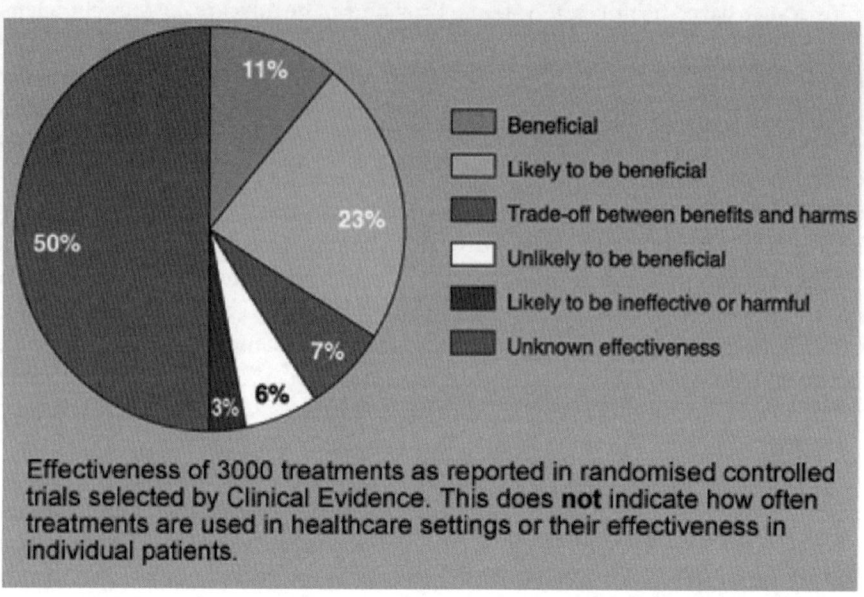

Effectiveness of 3000 treatments as reported in randomised controlled trials selected by Clinical Evidence. This does **not** indicate how often treatments are used in healthcare settings or their effectiveness in individual patients.

Source: Reproduced from Clinical Evidence

The interventions in the large, left hand segment of the pie chart should be evaluated. However there is opposition to this for ethical reasons (is it ethical to randomise patients for a treatment in common use?) and because of the conservatism of the medical profession ("we have always used this procedure and we know it works!"). More evaluation of these unproven but widely used interventions might produce savings which could ease the difficult task of rationing.

All industries are characterised by large variations in productivity. For instance across US manufacturing industry Syverson has reported that "a plant in the 90th percentile of the productivity distribution may makes almost twice as much output with the same measured inputs as the 10th percentile plant".[14] He notes that such dispersions in productivity are universal, but tend to be smaller in the USA than elsewhere. Surprisingly this broader literature on productivity variations has failed to impact on the variations debate in medical care.

For many decades, researchers have investigated variations in clinical practice. In 1939 Glover showed large variations in tonsillectomy rates in England.[15] Forty years later Bloor and his colleagues found similar variations in tonsil and adenoid rates with groups of professionals divided into camps favouring surgical action or

---

14 C Syverson, 'What determines productivity?' (2011) 49, 2 *Journal of Economic Literature* 326-64.
15 A Glover, 'The incidence of tonsillectomy in school children' 1938, 31 *Journal of the Royal Society of Medicine* 1219-36.

watchful waiting.[16] Both Glover and Bloor's group emphasised the role of medical opinion rather than evidence in determining clinical choices.

Subsequently a voluminous literature around practice variations has developed and is epitomised by the work of American researchers at Dartmouth Medical School in the United States. For nearly 40 years Jack Wennberg has been exploring practice variations using US Medicare data. An overview of this work is set out in a recent book.[17]

The Wennberg thesis is that unwarranted differences in health care delivery, defined as variations that cannot be explained due to illness prevalence, medical evidence and patient preferences, are considerable and can be reduced to free up resources to mitigate expenditure inflation and the need for rationing. He notes that the "chaotic patterns of clinical practice undermine the profession's assertion that clinical evidence and medical ethics determine the utilisation of health care".

Wennberg and colleagues such as Elliot Fisher have collaborated to create the Dartmouth Atlas of Health Care that maps clinical variations across the USA.[18] They have shown a threefold variation in clinical activity by dividing the US into 306 referral areas. They conclude that the variations are correlated with differences in the availability of hospital beds and specialist clinicians, and that US Medicare is a supply driven system.

They offer a variety of remedies for these variations which they assert would save 30 per cent of Medicare spending if conservative, 'safe practices' were adopted by high activity areas. Their solutions to this "waste" from unexplained variations involve increasing patient participation in clinical choices, reform of the payment systems for hospitals and clinicians, workforce planning that favours the production of primary care physicians rather than specialists and improved systems of performance feedback to clinicians and hospitals. Such reforms, along with the adoption of integrated health care as epitomised by the Mayo clinic would, the Dartmouth group assert, save $700 billion.

These assertions were influential in the design of the Obama health care reforms, which assumed that Dartmouth type savings would fund part of the expansion of insurance in the USA. But the savings are disputed by many. Cooper summarises the critique of the Dartmouth work succinctly and his view is that the Dartmouth estimate of 30 per cent savings of the US health care budget is unreasonably high.[19] Firstly he points out that Medicare savings potential cannot be generalised to other parts of the US health care systems, such as Medicaid, private insurance and the Veterans Administration.

Cooper's primary criticism, however, is that the Dartmouth 306 referral areas average out very disparate income characteristics, with affluent metropolitan areas having within them areas of acute poverty. It is poverty, asserts Cooper, that is the

---

16   MJ Bloor, GA Venters, and ML Samphier, 'Geographical variation in the incidence of operations on the tonsils and adenoids' (1978) Sep 92 (9) *J Laryngol Otol* 791-801.
17   JE Wennberg, *Tracking Medicine: a researcher's quest to understand health care* (OUP 2010).
18   http://www.dartmouthatlas.org/ (accessed on January 2nd, 2012).
19   See numerous posts on http://buzcooper.com/.

major determinant of variation in activity, with the relationship being non linear and much skewed by the very poor with complex chronic conditions. Cooper concludes that high use of facilities and care is a product of clusters of poor, unhealthy residents in the Dartmouth areas i.e. high levels of activity are a product of need and are not indicators of waste. For a review of this debate, see Physicians for health care reform.[20]

Other critics of the Dartmouth atlas have focused on the definition of efficiency used, which focuses on resources used rather than costs and outcomes; an assumption that would only be reasonable if all hospitals had the same outcomes. Furthermore the Dartmouth cost calculations use estimates of resources used in the two years before death and these are then attributed to the hospital which admits the patient. As Bach points out, costly sub-acute care means that patient contact with the admitting hospital may be quite limited.[21] Each of these issues is rejected by the Dartmouth group as can be seen in the Bach versus Skinner and others debate.[22]

The potential of the Dartmouth approach to produce large savings is thus much debated even in the US, and the potential for savings in other less supply-led systems is likely to be less. Despite the long history of the variations literature, savings from this source do appear more theoretical than actual. This has serious implications for policies such as the funding of the Obama health reforms (how can these be achieved without large increases in government expenditure which the US Congress will not countenance?), and for UK efforts to save and recycle up to £20 billion of funds over four years to meet growing patient demand. Even if these substantial and perhaps optimistic savings can be made, this at best mitigates the urgency of rationing policy. However in current circumstances the rationing debate will remain in all health care systems.

Overall, although there appears to potential for savings from reducing unwarranted variations in health care, it seems after forty years that simply highlighting variations is insufficient to drive change. A more recent development has been the use of 'pay for performance' (P4P) incentive systems (P4P) to reduce unwarranted clinical practice variations.[23] Both the Dartmouth group and its critics favour reform of payment systems as a means of reducing variation and productivity differences but is there an evidence base to support the plethora of P4P policies being used increasingly in numerous health care systems?

---

[20]   Physicians for Health Care Reform: commentaries and controversies, buzcooper.com (accessed October 12th, 2011).
[21]   J Skinner, D Steiger, ES Fisher, 'Looking back, moving forward' (2010) 362, 7 *NEJM* 569.
[22]   BP Bach, 'A map to bad policy: hospital efficiency measures in the Dartmouth atlas' (2010) 362, 7 *NEJM* 569; J Skinner, D Steiger, ES Fisher, 'Looking back, moving forward' (2010) 362, 7 *NEJM* 569.
[23]   J Bernstein, JD Reschovsky, and C White, 'Geographical variations in health care: changing policy directions' (2011) National Institute for Health Care Reform, Policy Analysis, 4 April.

4. Pay for performance incentives: help or hindrance to rationing policy?

Pay for performance incentives are increasingly proposed as a panacea to reduce the waste inherent in un-evidenced clinical practice variations. These devices could if implemented cost effectively could mitigate rationing pressures in all health care systems. There is great interest and experimentation internationally in the use of P4P incentive schemes. The evidence base, however, is limited with major unanswered questions of design and implementation.

A number of issues need to be clarified by improved policy design and evaluation to determine the relative effectiveness and cost-effectiveness of investing in changed incentives:

a) *Who* should be incentivised? Should the focus of P4P incentives be demand side decision makers i.e. consumers, or supply side decision makers such as hospitals and clinical teams? The literature on both demand and supply side targets for P4P interventions is considerable.[24] Reducing demand for health care by prevention, for example by incentivising weight loss and reducing population obesity levels, could in principle mitigate the need for harsher rationing practice, such as restricting bariatric surgery to the most severe cases. This may also involve financial transfers to disadvantaged populations, where behaviours like obesity and smoking are more prevalent, although it risks 'rewarding' unhealthy behavior in these populations. On the supply side, is it more efficient to incentivise individual decision makers (mainly doctors) or incentivise organisations to improve efficiency? Studies such as the EBOR trial have shown that the costs of persuading doctors to reduce prescribing of inefficient products can swamp any savings.[25] At hospital level, studies of organisational incentives have shown some effect on outcomes[26] but have yet to demonstrate cost-effectiveness, and again could cost more than they save.

b) *What* should be incentivised: activity and/or outcomes? Ideally any evaluation of a P4P intervention should address its cost and its effect. The latter often predominantly uses activities measures e.g. adherence to a practice guideline such as treating patients with aspirin and beta blockers after an acute myocardial infarction (heart attack). Activity measures should ideally be complemented by outcome information i.e. does the incentive change health outcomes? Outcome measures are generally weak, with a focus on inpatient or 30 day mortality. Slowly there is increasing investment in patient reported outcome measures (PROMs). In the English NHS the evolving PROMs programme initially covered hip and

---

[24] E.g. M Grossman, N Mocan (eds), *Economic Aspects of Obesity*, National Bureau for Economic Research, Chicago 2011; J Cromwell and others, (eds), *Pay for Performance in Health Care: Methods and Approaches* (RTI Press 2011).

[25] JM Mason and others, 'When is it cost-effective to change the behaviour of health professionals?' (2001) 286, 23 *JAMA* 2988-2992.

[26] RM Werner and others, 'The effect of pay-for-performance in hospitals: lessons for quality improvement' (2011) 30, 4 *Health Affairs* 690–8.

knee replacements, hernia repairs and varicose vein surgery using a generic quality of life measure[27] and specific measures (e.g. Oxford hip score). These patient reported instruments are used before and after these surgical procedures and illuminate gains (or not!) in physical and psychological functioning resulting from health care. The extension of PROMs to six chronic conditions in England means that in time outcome measurement in P4P experiments may be more comprehensive.

c) What interventions alter behaviour: financial or reputational incentives? Improving activity and outcome performance with comparative data may make hospitals, clinicians and their teams alter their behaviour and improve patient care and costs. Policies such as the UK general practitioner quality outcomes framework (GP-QOF)[28] and the US Premier hospitals incentive system[29] use explicit financial incentives to motivate change. QOF has been demonstrated not only to improve performance in primary care, but to reduce inequalities in primary care delivery.28 However in scrutinising and validating claims for these rewards the systems use comparative performance data that affect reputation. Separating out the effects of financial rewards from reputational effects is consequently very difficult when both motivations are used simultaneously to change behaviour.

d) What works best: penalties or bonuses? The implicit bias in favour of bonuses in the literature has been rationalised with arguments such as it is easier to develop incentivise gains rather than losses. However Adam Smith (1759) argued that the avoiding a loss might spur people into action better than a reward:

> "Pain . . . is, in almost all cases, a more pungent sensation than the opposite and correspondent pleasure. The one almost always depresses us much more below the ordinary, or what may be called the natural state of our happiness, than the other ever raises us above it."[30]

The work of behavioural economists over the last three decades has reinforced this contention with further analysis and empirical data.[31] The preference for using bonuses is complicated by schemes such as the US Premier hospitals initiative using bonuses for high performers and penalties for poor performers with difficulties in separating out their relative effects in terms of changing mean performance and reducing dispersion in activity and outcomes.

e) What is the right size of incentive? The UK GP-QOF used large incentives and altered the activity compliance of practitioners and reduced dispersion. The US Premier hospitals scheme used relatively small incentives of one to two

---

[27] EQ5D: http://www.euroqol.org. (accessed on 5th January 2012).

[28] E.g. T Doran and others, 'Effect of financial incentives on inequalities in the delivery of primary clinical care in England: analysis of clinical activity indicators for the quality and outcomes framework' (2008) 372 *Lancet* 728-736.

[29] Werner (note 26).

[30] A Smith, *A Theory of Moral Sentiments* (CUP 2002) 1759.

[31] D Kahneman, A Tversky, 'Prospect theory: an analysis of decision making under risk' (1979) 42, 2 *Econometrica* 263-91; N Ashraf, CF Camerer, G Loewenstein, 'Adam Smith, behavioural economist' (2005) 19, 3 *Journal of Economic Perspectives* 1131-45.

per cent increases in tariff to produce mean and dispersion changes. Further experimentation is needed to determine whether low or high tariffs work best, and when diminishing returns set in.

f) What is the best duration for such incentives? The use of bonuses makes the use of P4P expensive and raises the nice issues of how long does the "treatment" have to be applied and when stopped are the benefits permanent or temporary?

g) How do incentives affect non incentivised activities and institutions? There is a risk that incentivising one set of activities and outcomes will lead to neglect of other important types of patient care. Doran and others report no evidence of such opportunity costs for the GP-QOF.[32] However the QOF was developed during a period of rapid real increases in NHS expenditure. In the current period of fiscal imbalance and austerity, other services may be affected by incentivising particular services.

h) A final and crucial aspect of P4P incentive schemes is the need to focus not merely on their effectiveness but on their cost effectiveness. As ever what is effective may not be cost effective but what is cost effective is always effective. The evaluations of innovative work on P4P programmes have tended to ignore the issue of cost and focus myopically on effectiveness. Decision makers require comparative cost effectiveness data to inform their investment choices.

Whilst the quantity of P4P experiments is proliferating rapidly, the evidence base remains incomplete and contentious.[33] To the extent that the contested amount of clinical practice variations is amenable to change using P4P interventions, the conclusion must be that the benefits are uncertain and unlikely to mitigate the ubiquitous challenges of rationing.

5. *Rationing rules OK?!*

The rationing of health care is universal with its form varying between public and private health care systems and between different clinical teams. The production and use of evidence of cost-effectiveness is central to these rationing processes. Have governments addressed these issues in their rationing policy statements and has increasing investment in health technology assessment made rationing more efficient?

---

[32] T Doran and others, 'Effects of financial incentives on incentivised and non-incentivised clinical activities: a longitudinal analysis of data from the UK Quality Outcomes Framework' (2011) 342 *BMJ* d3590.

[33] E.g. A Maynard, 'The powers and pitfalls of pay for performance' (2012) 21 *Health Economics* 3-12; J Cromwell and others (eds), *Pay for Performance in Health Care: Methods and Approaches*, (RTI Press 2011).

a. Government rationing policies: some historical examples

During the late 1980s and the 1990s, during times of constrained public expenditure and increasing health technological innovation, some governments attempted to set out rationing mechanisms to control the allocation of resources amongst patients competing for care. The current need for fiscal austerity around the world may create an environment where health care rationing policies are again at the forefront of public debate. It is useful to review earlier experience and learn from the challenges faced.

In 1987 State legislators in Oregon, USA were faced by the twin problems of expenditure inflation and incomplete Medicaid coverage of the poor. Medicaid is a Federally subsidised programme governed, part funded and delivered by the constituent States of the USA. The immediate political crisis that precipitated intense policy debate was the death of a seven year old boy, Coby Howard, who was not covered by Medicaid and was denied a life saving bone marrow transplant which couldhave saved his life.

The Oregon legislators decided to offer a basic Medicaid package of care to all Oregonians below the Federal poverty line. By restricting the interventions that were available, they aimed to increase the population that was covered, an objective similar to the current Obama proposals. Determining the basic package to be offered in Oregon required a prioritised list of diagnostic procedures and treatments. Intensive debate resulted with public consultations through telephone interviews of citizens and town hall meetings across the state. These expressions of public preferences together with estimates of the effectiveness of competing interventions led to the production and debate about priority lists over the period 1990-97.[34] The final list was then costed to determine affordability and a line was drawn in the list below which items were to be excluded from the Medicaid package.

The effect of this prolonged process of debate was that prioritised items did not reflect cost effectiveness but economic value "watered down" by local public preferences. To fund the list, expenditure increased.

More recently, Oregon legislators were again faced by competing demands and the need to ration Medicaid benefits amongst competing poor citizens. Their novel response was to ration by lottery: 30,000 places in the Medicaid programme were allocated amongst 90,000 on the waiting list for coverage. As Baicker and Finkelstein showed, this allocation process created substantial cost inflation, like the original Oregon experiment and potentially like the Obama health care reforms.[35]

---

[34]   T Tengs, 'An evaluation of Oregon Medicaid rationing algorithms' (1995) *Health Economics* 171-81; T Bodenheimer, 'The Oregon health plan: lessons for the nation; first of two parts' (1997) 337 *NEJM* 651-55.

[35]   K Baicker and A Finkelstein, 'The effects of Medicaid Coverage: learning from the Oregon experiment' (2011) 365 *NEJM* 683-5.

In 1988 in the Netherlands, the Dunning report was published, proposing a "funnel with four sieves" or criteria to prioritise care.[36] The criteria were:

- necessary care
- effectiveness
- efficiency
- individual responsibility

All of these criteria are problematic. Who, using what criteria, can determine what is "necessary"? If the criteria used are effectiveness and efficiency, both criteria are necessary but not sufficient i.e. what is effective may not be cost effective, and but what is efficient may not be "equitable". The latter concept is evident in all health care systems but is excluded from explicit consideration in the Dutch criteria e.g. it may be inefficient to maintain the life of very low birth weight babies but because new life is highly valued by society, its values over-rule narrow economic criteria.

Similar ambiguities are evident in the attempts of other governments' attempt to ration health care by defining "core" or basic packages e.g. the 1992 New Zealand Core Services Committee[37] and priority statements from the governments of Norway,[38] Sweden,[39] and Finland.[40] Essentially, a flurry of activity around defining what should be a 'basic package' of care, in a number of countries, was largely unsuccessful. As outlined by the chair of the New Zealand Core Services Committee:

'A'yes/no' or 'in/out' list approach is just too simplistic. It would either have to be so broad and lacking in definition as to be meaningless, much the situation the Committee inherited, or its explicitness would make it too arbitrary and inflexible resulting in people being unfairly excluded from services. Either way it would fail.'[41]

b) The emergence of health technology assessment

The failures of governments to create basic packages of health care, and continuing debate about rationing elsewhere[42] were precursors of recognition for increased investment in the production of evidence about effectiveness[43] and cost effectiveness.

System for evaluating the cost-effectiveness of new technologies, with a focus on new pharmaceutical products, emerged in Australia and in Ontario, Canada, over

---

[36] Netherlands Ministry of Health, Welfare and Cultural Affairs, Changing health care in the Netherlands, Rijswijk, September 1988.

[37] DC Hadorn, and AC Holmes, 'The New Zealand priority criteria project: an overview' (1997) 314 *BMJ* 131-4.

[38] Report of the Lonning Committee, Guidelines for priority setting in the Norwegian health service, Oslo 1987.

[39] Swedish Health Care and Medical Priorities Commission, No easy choices: the difficult priorities of health care, Ministry of Health and Social Affairs, Stockholm 1993.

[40] National Research and Development Centre for Welfare and Health, 'From values to choice: report of the working group on health care prioritisation', STAKES, Helsinki 1995.

[41] L Jones in: Core Services Committee. The core debater 3. Wellington, New Zealand; October 1994.

[42] Eg, B New (ed) *Rationing: talk and action in health care,* Kings Fund and BMJ Publishing Group, London 1997.

[43] http://www.cochrane.org (accessed on January 2nd, 2012).

the late 1980s and 1990s. This has since been emulated in many other countries. These systems aim to ration new technology, by restricting its reimbursement from public funding using a cost-effectiveness 'fourth hurdle' following assessment of safety, effectiveness and manufacturing quality. In practice they have been useful in changing culture in health policy and highlighting the need for economic evaluation as well as clinical evaluation, but they have not contained overall health care costs, and have not addressed care that is routinely provided in health care systems, as they focus almost exclusively on new interventions.

In England, Wales and Northern Ireland the National Institute for Clinical Excellence (NICE) was established in 1999 to provide "mandatory" advice one new technologies (primarily pharmaceuticals) and to create clinical guidelines.[44] In Scotland the Scottish Medicines Consortium offers advice on pharmaceuticals and the Scottish Inter-collegiate Guidelines Network provides recommendations on appropriate treatment regimes.

These British systems face challenges identical to those in the Netherlands, Scandinavia, Canada, and Australia e.g.:

i) What threshold should be used, above which government agencies should advice no reimbursement or provide an intervention? NICE uses a cut off of around £30,000 per quality adjusted life year (QALY). However routine rationing decisions in the NHS are estimated to typically use a cost per QALY cut off considerably less than that used by NICE.[45] Are thresholds essentially arbitrary or can they be evidence based?

ii) There is a paucity of data about both benefits and costs, which often necessitates complex modelling. Also the measurement of costs and benefits may be narrow. Thus NICE is required to analyse costs to the NHS only, thereby ignoring costs to carers and other non public sector providers. Benefit estimation typically ignore benefits to carers e.g. possible changes in their burdens.

ii) Typically pharmaceutical producers are very anxious to get approval and market their new drugs. This means that clinical trials may have inadequate sample sizes and short follow up periods.

iii) Technical issues have also emerged, e.g. as cost and benefits may accrue over time future accruals have to be adjusted to take account of time preference. What rate should be used? Initially NICE used a six per cent discount rate for both costs and benefits. Since then they have shifted to differential rates with current proposals being one and a half per cent for benefits and six per cent for costs. The logic of this and its effects on cost per QALY calculations is contentious.[46]

iv) Distributional issues: Economists leadership in the advocacy of technology assessment has led to a simple focus on maximizing health improvements from a limited budget. This concern with efficiency gives equal weight to health improvements or the production of quality adjusted life years (QALYs). Should QALYs be

---

[44]   http://www.nice.org.
[45]   S Martin, N Rice, PC Smith, 'The link between health care spending and health outcomes in the new English Primary Care Trusts', Research paper 42, Centre for Health Economics, York, 2008.
[46]   Hutton/HEC 2012.

weighted equally regardless of to whom they accrue? It is apparent from health care choices that QALYs accruing to some recipients are of higher value than QALY gains for other members of society. For instance in many countries doctors deploy inefficient methods to keep low birth weight babies alive. This inefficiency reflects social values and has clear opportunity costs, i.e. it denies other patients potentially efficient care. Economists such as Williams have put forward the "fair innings argument" which suggests that once an elderly person is past some age and even if they could benefit from efficient interventions, higher priority should be given to the possibly inefficient treatment of young citizens who due to chronic disease are unlikely to get a "good innings". If policy is focused on reducing health care and health inequalities perhaps QALYs accruing to the poor and disadvantaged should be weighted more than QALYs received by middle class groups? Whilst debates about these issues are extensive they have minimal effects on the recommendations of technology appraisals and the consequent allocation of resources amongst competing patients.

The large investment in health technology in many countries begs the question: has this improved the efficiency of resource allocation, better known as rationing? This question is very difficult to answer as there are few studies of the effects of e.g. NICE technology appraisals and guidelines on what clinicians do.

Do they ignore or follow such advice? Whilst Sheldon and others have shown some adherence to NICE material, evidence on this issue is noticeable by its scarcity.[47] Practitioners conclude that they believe that economic evaluation has impacted favourably on the way in which scarce health care resources are used but proof of this contention needs urgent substantiation.[48]

6. Conclusions

Thirty years ago Williams asked whether economic evaluation in health care was an "insidious poison in the body politick".[49] He concluded that it was an essential guide to resource allocation or rationing in health care. During the subsequent decades there have been considerable advances in both the methodology and use of techniques of economic evaluation.[50]

The focus of this work has been the improvement in the efficiency of the use of health care budgets. But social preferences may include objectives other than efficiency. This is epitomised by the three criteria put forward by Williams:[51]

47   TA Sheldon and others, 'What's the Evidence That NICE Guidance Has Been Implemented? Results from a National Evaluation Using Time Series Analysis, Audit of Patients' Notes, and Interviews (2004) 329 *BMJ* 999.

48   M Drummond, forthcoming 2012, 'Twenty years using economic evaluations for reimbursement decisions: what have we achieved?' *Journal of Health Policy and Law* (note 11).

49   A Williams, 'Cost benefit analysis: bastard science and/or insidious poison in the body politick' (1972) 1, 2 *Journal of Public Economics* 199-225.

50   MF Drummond and others, *Methods for the economic evaluation of health care programmes* (3rd edn, OUP 2005); MF Drummond (note 11).

51   Mimeo 1996, quoted in Maynard and Bloor, 1998 (note 3).

- to treat equals equally and with due dignity, especially when near to death;
- to meet people's needs for health care as efficiently as possible (imposing the least sacrifice on others);
- to minimise inequalities in the lifetime health of the population.

The latter quality in rationing may involve weighting QALYs in terms of who gets them. For instance a decision maker concerned with the health of the poor\might advocate increased weighting for QALYs accruing to the disadvantaged. Williams favoured discrimination against the elderly, arguing with fellow pensioners that they had had a "fair innings" and that even though their treatment might be efficient, it should be foregone to fund the inefficient treatment of younger cohorts who had not had a fair innings.[52] This advocacy exemplified Williams' concern not just about the traditional focus of economists on efficiency but the need to weight this with equity in life time health.

The application of these principles is dominated by health technology agencies that emphasise efficiency and often ignore equity issues. This is a product of legislative design and a political emphasis on "value for money" or efficiency. Whilst the need for equity weights is accepted at a level of principle, its impact on policy choices appears to be limited.

How is the debate about rationing to be taken forward? Firstly it has to be accepted that it is universal and affects all health care systems. Whilst the word "rationing" may be avoided by policy makers, clinicians and their teams, they accept that their role is to allocate scarce resources and prioritise patients. They prefer to do this implicitly but resourcing difficulties are making opportunity costs ever clearer.

The way forward will involve continuing investments in developing the methods and applications of economic evaluation in health care. As the evidence base about the effectiveness and cost-effectiveness of medicine improves, some resource savings may be made from the use of at present tentative knowledge of the effects of pay for performance incentives on clinical practice variations. These efficiency gains may be more modest than anticipated by the Dartmouth approach and will take some time to be acquired. In the meantime rationing will be ubiquitous and contentious but hopefully more evidence based.

---

[52] A Williams, 'Intergenerational equity: an exploration of the fair innings argument' (1997) 6 *Health Economics* 117-132.

Chapter XII

Rationing Health Care: Balancing equity and efficiency[1]

Werner B.F. Brouwer and Frans F.H. Rutten

1. Introduction

Rationing relates to the activity of allocating available resources to different uses, ends and/or beneficiaries. Commonly, in this context, there is scarcity, implying a greater demand for than availability of these resources, which means that the allotted portion of resources is normally less than the desired or needed portion. Rationing therefore inherently relates to 'painful' choices. People may receive less of some good than they had hoped, wanted or needed. This is more painful when the importance of the allocated good is greater. Hence, it need not surprise that rationing of health care is a rather contentious subject. Some countries even try to avoid the word rationing all together in the context of health care and prefer to label rationing choices as 'priority setting'. Nevertheless, the outcomes of and difficulties related to such choices do not diminish when a different label is used. These difficulties are emphasized by Maynard (1999) who indicates that rationing *'takes place when an individual is deprived of care which is of benefit (in terms of improving health status, or the length and quality of life) and which is desired by the patient.'*[2] Rationing thus involves arduous choices: who gets what and why? In the health care sector, such choices sometimes involve life and death decisions. It need not surprise, therefore, that a landmark publication in the field of health economics, dealing (also) with this topic, was titled *'Who shall live?'*.[3]

In the context of having to make such choices, people may not instinctively turn to economists for assistance or even guidance. To some extent, that has to do with misperceptions regarding the discipline of economics. Some people tend to equate economists with the cynic as Oscar Wilde defined him: *'A cynic knows the price of everything but the value of nothing.'* Economists are then seen as people more interested in saving money than in saving lives, or more focused on the costs of health care than on the benefits it generates. Nothing could be further from the truth. Economists care about (health) benefits as much as they care about costs. And the reason why they care about costs in the first place is that these costs can

---

[1]   Acknowledgements: We are grateful to Elly Stolk and Job van Exel for useful comments on an earlier version. The usual disclaimer applies.
[2]   A Maynard, 'Rationing health care: an exploration' (1999) 49 [1-2] *Health Policy* 5-11.
[3]   VR Fuchs, *Who shall live? Health, economics and social choice* (World Scientific, New Jersey 1998).

be viewed as benefits foregone (for instance in other patients). Hence the term 'opportunity costs' is used by economists. Spending resources on one intervention or patient means that you cannot spend it on another intervention or patient. Moreover, economics is concerned with the allocation of scarce resources over alternative uses, and the efficiency *and equity* implications of such allocations. A core concept in economics is that of scarcity: resources are limited while wants and needs are unlimited. Therefore, setting goals and decision rules is required in order to determine what to do 'best' with available resources. In that sense, the avoidance of the word 'rationing' or even the denial of the need to ration (health care) can be seen as inherently 'uneconomical'. Rationing is omnipresent and unavoidable, and the question is merely *how* to ration efficiently and fairly. And it is exactly this question that lies at the heart of the economic science.

Therefore, economics may prove to be of great assistance in the difficult area of rationing health care. The growing interest in and use of economic evaluations in the context of rationing decisions in the health care sector may illustrate the assistance economics can offer, also in practice. Obviously, it should be recognized, also by economists, that the issue of rationing cannot and should not be fully addressed from one disciplinary angle, including the economic angle. It is pivotal that insights and concepts from philosophy, ethics, law and other disciplines are combined with those from economics in order to come to better and more defensible rationing mechanisms and processes across the globe.

In this contribution we will highlight some developments in the field of economic evaluation, especially highlighting attempts that have been made to combine the goals of efficiency (put simply: health maximization from a given budget) and equity (put simply: a fair distribution of health and health care) in the process of decision making. The emphasis is on the Dutch situation, but the lessons that can be drawn transcend the Dutch situation. We do not attempt to be exhaustive in any sense. For instance, rationing may take different forms and take place at different levels. In some countries, the health care system is organized in such a way that ability to pay importantly determines the allocation of health care resources. Then, rich individuals may receive more health care than poorer ones, ceteris paribus. In other countries, this influence of ability to pay may be banned and a distribution of collectively funded resources on the basis of 'need' may be more common. Within such systems some countries may ration relatively implicitly (e.g. through limiting supply and therefore waiting times, on which priority may be determined at a decentralized level), while other countries may be more explicit, for instance rationing the basic benefits package based on economic evaluations. Here, we focus especially on the latter aspect.

2. *Economics and economic evaluation*

Economics is concerned with choices regarding the use of available resources. In order to make judgments about what use of resources would be 'best', it is clear that some evaluation framework is required. Boadway and Bruce (1984) indicate that '...

the welfare economist wishes to determine the desirability of a particular policy – not in terms of his or her own values, but in terms of some explicitly stated ethical criteria'.[4] The central objective in welfare economics therefore is to provide and use such an explicit ethical framework for making meaningful statements about whether certain events, policies and interventions improve welfare. In this context, welfare is not defined in some narrow way (like GDP or income), but as a broad measure of wellbeing or 'happiness', commonly labelled 'utility' by economists. The framework with which welfare economists work tries to facilitate decisions that result in an optimisation of welfare, considering both efficiency and equity. Many difficult questions arise in this context, from the definition and measurement of welfare and utility, to the definition and 'measurement' of equity,[5] but practical tools and concepts have been developed over the years that, while clearly not perfect, have proved quite helpful. The most prominent tool is that of economic evaluation.

Economic evaluations are a form of applied welfare economics. They are based on the notion that the underlying goal of action is to improve social welfare. Given that it is not easy to determine whether social welfare actually improves, as it commonly involves winners and losers and welfare ('happiness') changes are difficult to compare between individuals, a number of assumptions are required to come to a practically applicable tool. The idea behind the common tool of economic evaluation is that social welfare improves if the value of the benefits exceeds that of the costs (so that winners could *compensate* losers and still some gain would be left; the so-called Kaldor and Hicks criterion). While this tool may not fully match welfare economic theory,[6] it has gained quite some popularity. The traditional form of economic evaluation is that of cost-benefit analysis, in which both costs and benefits are expressed in monetary terms. The decision rule on which this evaluation is based can be expressed in a more formal way in equation (1).

$$\sum_{t=0}^{t} \frac{v_t \Delta g_t - \Delta c_t}{(1+r)^t} > 0 \qquad (1)$$

In equation (1), v_t denotes the value per unit of some good g at time t, Δg_t indicates the change in the quantity of good g at time t, and Δc_t denotes the change in costs at time t. The term $v_t \Delta g_t$ thus denotes the monetary benefits at time t. Since people and societies commonly attach less weight to costs and benefits in the future relative to current ones, costs and benefits are discounted and r indicates the discount rate (i.e. the rate at which future costs and benefits are depreciated). If, for simplicity's

---

[4]   R Boadway and N Bruce, *Welfare economics* (Basil Backwell 1984).
[5]   See for example WBF Brouwer and others, 'Welfarism vs. extra-welfarism' (2008) 27 (2) *Journal of Health Economics* 325-338.
[6]   See, e.g., Boadway (note 4); J Hurley, 'An overview of the normative economics of the health care sector' in AJ Culyer and J Newhouse (eds), *Handbook of Health Economics* (Elsevier Science 2000).

sake, we consider a program yielding costs and benefits only in the current year (t=0) equation 1 simplifies to:

$$v_t \Delta g_t - \Delta c_t > 0 \qquad (2)$$

Equation (2) can also be written as:

$$v_o \Delta g_o > \Delta c_o \qquad (2')$$

This equation (2') states that the benefits should exceed the costs of an intervention, the Kaldor and Hicks criterion. Equivalently, this equation can be written as:

$$\frac{\Delta c_o}{\Delta g_o} < v_o \qquad (2'')$$

This expression indicates that the costs incurred to produce one additional unit of some good should not exceed the value of that good. The intuition behind this is simply that if the costs incurred to produce one additional unit of some good exceed the value of one unit of that good, then more welfare is sacrificed than gained. In what follows we will use the above equations (therefore implicitly using an intervention yielding only current costs and effects as example).

Economic evaluations in the health care sector especially relate to this final expression, as will be highlighted in the next section.

3. Economic evaluation in health care

Economic evaluations are becoming more important in rationing decisions in the health care sector. Such evaluations always consider a change, i.e. a choice between two or more alternatives. In health care, choices often relate to health care interventions, often comparing a new intervention with an old one (like current 'usual care'). Such interventions may be new pharmaceuticals, new surgical procedures, new psychotherapy, some preventive measure, etc. By calculating the costs and (health) effects of the old and the new intervention, it is possible to calculate the amount of additional costs required and the amount of additional (health) gained. With that information, the left hand side of equation (2'') can be calculated. This is shown in figure I.

FIGURE I. *A graphical representation of an economic evaluation*

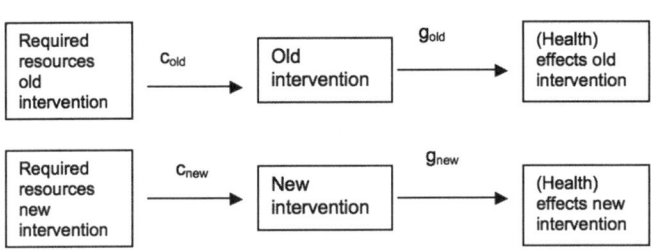

Once the costs of the old and new intervention (c_{old} and c_{new}) and their (health) effects (g_{old} and g_{new}) have been calculated, the difference between them can be determined: c and g, respectively, for all relevant years and then discounted and aggregated. Obviously, if a new intervention is both less costly (saving resources) *and* more effective, it dominates the old therapy and can be implemented without difficult choices. Likewise, if it is more costly and less effective, it is dominated by the old therapy and should not be implemented. Typically, however, a new intervention will be more expensive and more effective than the old one. Then the difficult question needs to be addressed whether the additional health gains justify the additional costs. (The same question arises when an intervention costs less but also produces less health, by the way.) We will return to this question later.

In the field of health care, it is uncommon to directly measure and capture health gains in monetary terms. Therefore, a cost-benefit analysis, the traditional form of economic evaluation, is not frequently used. This appears to be related to the difficulty with and aversion against expressing health in monetary terms. It is more common to express health gains in non-monetary units. This means that in health economic evaluations the emphasis in measuring 'benefits' is not on the full expression $v_o \Delta g_o$ in equation (2), but only on go. That is the difference in health gains between the old and the new intervention. The results are commonly expressed as the left hand side of equation (2"):

$$\frac{\Delta c_o}{\Delta g_o}$$

Thus, the additional costs of the new compared to the old intervention are divided by the additional health gains of the new compared to the old intervention. This end-result is normally called the incremental cost-effectiveness (or cost-utility) ratio, the ICER. It indicates the incremental costs per unit of health gained. Hence, in common economic evaluations, the monetary value of health gains is not alluded to in any direct sense. This aspect typically (and often implicitly) enters the discussion only in the decision making phase, as highlighted further in the next section.

How health gains are expressed distinguishes two main types of health economic evaluations: cost-effectiveness analysis or cost-utility analysis. In the former, health effects are expressed in so-called natural units, that is, clinical outcomes such as hip-fractures avoided, life years gained, percentage blood pressure lowered, event free life years gained, etc. While such outcomes may relate well to clinical practice and be meaningful within specific disease areas, they also suffer from some limitations. First of all, some 'natural units' may be considered intermediate outcomes rather than actual endpoints. For instance, a lower level of cholesterol is especially relevant if it results in fewer health problems (e.g. heart attacks or even deaths). However, the relationship between intermediate outcomes and relevant health outcomes may not always be clear (or linear). Secondly, using natural units may be helpful when making choices *within* a specific disease area (e.g. should we use drug A or B to lower blood pressure?), but makes comparisons *across* disease areas rather difficult. Hence, cost-utility analysis was developed and is commonly seen as the preferred type of economic evaluation.

In a cost-utility analysis, health effects are expressed in generic, preference-based outcome measures, labeled as Quality-Adjusted Life-Years (QALYs). QALYs basically can be seen as a measure of health, combining both length and quality of life. One year lived in the state 'perfect health' gets a value of 1, whereas one year in the state 'dead' gets a value of 0. Other health states are given values based on preferences measured in patients or, more commonly, the general public. Different techniques exist to derive such preferences, all with their own advantages and disadvantages, but a popular method is the time trade-off method (TTO). In a TTO, people are typically asked to indicate how many years lived in perfect health they consider to be equivalent to 10 years in some poor health state X. The idea obviously is that the worse health state X is, the fewer years in perfect health people require to be indifferent between the two options. The value of the imperfect health state X can subsequently be expressed as a number between 0 and 1, that is, expressed in relative terms in comparison to the value of perfect health (1) and dead (0). For instance, if someone is indifferent between 4 years in perfect health and 10 years in state X, the value of X can be expressed as $4/10 = 0.4$ (since living 10 years with value 0.4 equals living 4 years in perfect health with value 1). Although much can be said about methodological (and related normative) issues here, for instance regarding discounting, this falls outside the scope of this chapter. It does need noting that people may perceive some health states to be 'worse than dead'. These states then receive a negative value.

Using QALYs, two things can be achieved (at least in theory) that are difficult when expressing health gains in 'natural units'. First, the allocation of health care resources across disease areas is now facilitated, since different health states and diseases can be compared in terms of their QALY impact. Second, it allows resources to be allocated within the broad health care sector in such a way that the resulting allocation yields the most 'preference weighted' health possible. This broad comparability of interventions in terms of costs and health outcomes, without resorting to monetary valuations, has undoubtedly contributed to the popularity of cost-utility analysis.

4. Use of economic evaluations in health care

This popularity may be inferred from the increase in cost-utility analyses published in the scientific literature and the fact that cost-utility analysis appears increasingly used in the context of making (rationing) choices in the health care sector. These choices can take place on different levels. In many cases, economic evaluations will inform national decisions regarding funding or reimbursement of diverse health technologies. For instance, in England and Wales, where the National Institute for Health and Clinical Excellence (NICE) operates, NICE may restrict funding of specific technologies within the NHS. In doing so, it importantly relies on cost-utility analyses to establish which interventions offer most health per invested pound. Likewise, in the Netherlands, the Dutch Health Care Insurance Board (CVZ) judges whether certain technologies should be reimbursed as being part of the basic benefits package. The latter defines the minimal coverage under the compulsory health insurance for all Dutch citizens. Cost-effectiveness plays an increasingly important role in that process as well. Cost-effectiveness information can also be used at 'lower' levels of decision making, for instance at the level of an insurer or hospital, or when creating medical practice guidelines informing doctors about the most cost-effective strategy for diagnosis and treatment. Then, economic evaluations can be used to determine optimal treatment paths in different circumstances.

Regardless of the level of decision making, however, it must be acknowledged that the current way in which cost-effectiveness and cost-utility analyses are performed, cannot fully guide allocation decisions. The first reason for this is that such analyses, also from a theoretical perspective, are incomplete, as they ignore the issue of the monetary value of the health gains. Indeed, current economic evaluations, as indicated above, 'simply' produce an ICER. Decision making (or the full economic evaluation) requires this ICER to be judged against a relevant threshold, as shown in equation (2"). It needs noting that the nature of this threshold is issue of debate. Most notably, it has been argued that in the context of health care systems operating under a fixed budget, the threshold can be taken to represent the marginal cost-effectiveness of current programs in the health care sector. Put differently, it represents the efficiency of current programs in the health care sector that would need to be terminated if the new program is to be financed. Indeed, if the budget is fixed, spending money on a new intervention implies that some existing intervention needs to be sacrificed in order to free resources for the new intervention. Hence, the health gained with the new intervention comes at the expense of foregoing the health gained through the replaced intervention. Obviously, all other things equal, replacing current programs is not optimal *unless* the new programs produce more health.[7] Here, the notion of opportunity costs and the notion that the price of health is health foregone become obvious again.

---

[7] See e.g. H Gravelle and others, 'Discounting in economic evaluations: stepping forward towards optimal decision rules' (2007) 16 (3) *Health Economics* 307-317.

Here, we take the conventional position that the threshold should represent the monetary value of health gains. That is, it represents how much other consumption (education, infrastructure, private consumption, etc) a society is willing to sacrifice in order to obtain one additional unit of health. This implies that, in order to make a final decision, this threshold needs to be known.

Unfortunately, to date relatively little is known about the monetary value of health gains. Existing overviews present very broad ranges[8] and the validity of such estimates can be doubtful.[9] Moreover, countries appear to differ regarding the level of cost-effectiveness they consider to be acceptable. In the UK, for instance, values between £20,000 and £30,000 per QALY have been mentioned as threshold (albeit not very explicitly). In the Netherlands, a threshold of €20,000 was often mentioned. As will be discussed below, this has changed more recently into a range from 0 to €80,000 per QALY, but even that broad range is not well-founded.[10] Many questions regarding the nature and height of the threshold remain, therefore, hampering making rationing decisions based on cost-effectiveness information. Therefore, more attention should be devoted to deriving better estimates of the threshold value, also considering what this threshold should represent and how it should be derived. Some of these questions are crucial, not only for rationing, but also in the dialogue between economists, philosophers and ethicists. It needs noting that any exercise to express the value of health in monetary terms may be viewed as 'unethical' by some. However, it is pivotal to stress here that having and using a threshold not only protects other patients from unlimited resource use by one group of patients (as the price of health gains in one group is the health foregone in others!) but also protects the broader society against sacrificing more welfare (which may involve less education, less social security or less disposable income) than is gained through health care. Not having any (idea about the) threshold in that sense certainly can also be seen as 'unethical', as it may result in welfare losses and in inconsistent and unfair decision making.

Another, yet related, issue that deserves noting here is that cost-effectiveness alone, especially as currently operationalised as an ICER, cannot fully guide societal decision making. This relates to the point that cost-effectiveness normally is not the sole criterion on which rationing decisions should be made. To illustrate this, we will highlight the Dutch decision making framework first and some cost-effectiveness results next. Both indicate that the currently dominant way of performing economic evaluations misses out on important social values and principles regarding a fair distribution of health gains.

---

[8] See for a further discussion: K Claxton and others, 'Discounting and decision making in the economic evaluation of health care technologies' (2011) 20 (1) *Health Economics* 2-15.

[9] See e.g. RA Hirth and others, 'Willingness to pay for a quality-adjusted life year: in search of a standard' (2000) 20 (3) *Med Decis Making* 332-342; A Bobinac and others, 'Willingness to pay for a QALY: The individual approach' (2010) 13 (8) *Value in Health* 1046-1055.

[10] A Bobinac and others, 'Get more, pay more? An elaborate test of the validity of willingness to pay per QALY estimates' (2012) 31 (1) *Journal of Health Economics* 158-168.

5. Getting equity in the equation: the Dutch discussion

The discussion on principles that should guide rationing decisions has been especially stimulated in The Netherlands by the report of the Committee on Choices in Health Care (also known as the Dunning committee), published in 1991.[11] This Committee recognized the growing need to ration health care, given the increasing health care expenditures and the increase in medical technology. The Committee indicated that this called for being selective in terms of the care funded under the national health insurance scheme, i.e., the care included in the basic benefits package. It indicated that in order to be eligible for inclusion, health technologies should meet four different criteria. The decision framework, based on these four criteria, was depicted as a funnel with four sieves (the four criteria): necessity, effectiveness, cost-effectiveness and 'own responsibility or payment', as shown in figure 1.

FIGURE 1: *The Funnel of Dunning.*[12]

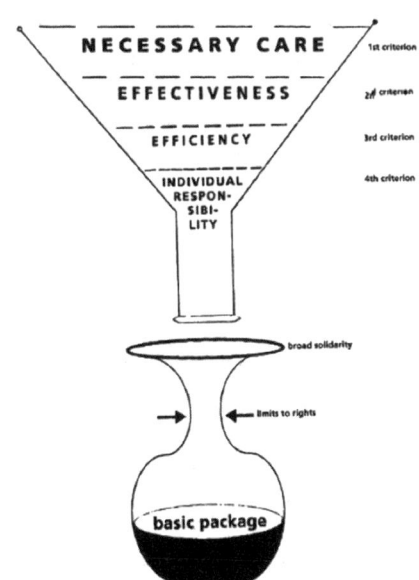

The idea behind this funnel was that the criteria could be addressed sequentially. Only if an intervention was considered necessary, it would be evaluated in terms of the criterion of effectiveness, and so on. The funnel was well received and stimulated much debate and research in this area. Its practical use was somewhat

---

11   WBF Brouwer, *The basis of the package* [in Dutch] Inaugural lecture, Erasmus University Rotterdam 2009.

12   Committee on Choices in Health Care. Report 'Kiezen en delen' [in Dutch] Rijswijk, Netherlands: Ministry of Welfare, Health and Cultural Affairs 1991.

limited, however. This mainly related to the first and fourth criteria, as well as to the sequential approach suggested.

The criterion of necessity mainly concerns the severity of the underlying problem and whether the problem would justify a claim on solidarity.[13] However, there was no clear definition of what exactly constituted necessity or how it might be measured. This made it difficult to decide when something would be labeled 'necessary' and especially when an intervention could be deemed 'unnecessary'. Given the sequential approach adopted, only if something was considered 'unnecessary' it would not go through to the second criterion of effectiveness. Without a clear and measurable operationalisation and some cut-off point between necessary and unnecessary, the criterion was of little practical use – although theoretically relevant. The final criterion of 'own responsibility and payment' also remained difficult to operationalise, since it was unclear, for instance, when something would be sufficiently cheap not to impose too much financial burden on patients, or when patients could be held responsible for their own health care costs. This resulted in a situation in which especially the criteria of effectiveness and cost-effectiveness were (increasingly) used in practice. These also became more influential in the context of rationing decisions regarding the content of the basic benefits package. Their use subsequently spurred the debate, however, about the decision criterion implicitly underlying these two remaining criteria. This could be summarized as follows: a more cost-effective intervention should be favored over a less cost-effective intervention. Put differently, the overall aim of the health care sector was to produce as much health as possible from the available budget. Although such an aim may perhaps not sound unreasonable, this notion became difficult to sustain. It turned out that especially the fact that the first criterion (necessity) was not used in practice, resulted in difficulties.

This can be illustrated by Table 1, as presented in Stolk and others.[14] Therein, the outcomes of a number of Dutch cost-utility studies are summarized. As can be seen, some interventions, such as the surgical correction of congenital anorectal malformation in newborns, were relatively cost-effective with an ICER of less than 3,000 dollars per gained QALY. Other interventions provide much less health per dollar invested, such as lung transplantations. If one would allocate resources on the basis of cost-utility, the interventions listed low in Table 1 should receive priority. The reason for this is that they produce most health per dollar spent. When considering spending a fixed budget and assuming that the interventions in Table 1 are the only available interventions, one would 'fill' the basic benefits package with interventions starting at the bottom of Table 1 and move up until the budget is exhausted. The interventions high in the Table are then less likely to be funded. When judging the ICERs against some fixed threshold, say $40,000, a similar allocation of resources results: all programs with a higher ICER than this threshold

---

[13] EA Stolk and others, 'Rationalising rationing: economic and other considerations in the debate about funding of Viagra' (2002) 59 *Health Policy* 53-63.

[14] College voor Zorgverzekeringen (CvZ), The practice of managing the basic insurance package 2 [Pakketbeheer in de praktijk 2 – in Dutch] CVZ, Diemen 2009.

value would not be funded. (This, by the way, also stresses the importance of having a justified threshold – if the threshold would be set at $50,000 more interventions would be funded and performed, while a lower threshold would result in a more restrictive judgment of interventions.)

TABLE 1. *Outcomes of Dutch studies in terms of incremental cost per QALY*

Intervention	Comparator	$/QALY[a]
GM-CSF in elderly with leukaemia	Daunomycine cytosine	235 958
EPO in dialysis patients	Conservative treatment	139 623
Lung transplantation	Conservative treatment	100 957
End stage renal disease management	No treatment	53 513
Heart transplantation	Conservative treatment	46 775
Liver transplantation	Conservative treatment	44 566
Didronel profylase	Conservative treatment	32 047
PTA with stent	PTA	17 889
Breast cancer screening	No screening	5147
Viagra	Androskat	5097
Surgical correction of congenital anorectal malformation	No treatment	2778

Source: Stolk and others (note 13)

An allocation of resources on the basis of cost-effectiveness information results in efficiency in the sense that it, broadly speaking, ensures that the most QALYs are produced with available resources. When looking more closely at Table 1, one may doubt, however, whether such an allocation is in line with societal preferences and fairness principles. Indeed, not everyone would agree that Viagra should be more eligible for funding than heart transplantations, *even though it may produce more health per dollar*. Moreover, not all would agree that prevention of osteoporosis (with didronel) would be more eligible for funding than lung transplantation, *even though it may produce more QALYs per dollar*.

In the Netherlands, especially the discussions regarding the funding of Viagra caused a fundamental debate about these issues.[15] It resulted in the awareness that a prioritization of interventions on the basis of cost-effectiveness does *not* reflect societal values well. Regardless of the exact height of the threshold, even the rank-order of interventions is not in line with societal preferences. The implicit assumption underlying common cost-utility analysis that 'a QALY is a QALY no matter who gets it', appeared to be at variance with societal preferences for a fair distribution of health and health care. Put differently, people, on average, do not consider erectile dysfunction or heart failure to be similar in terms of 'necessity' and 'therefore' attach different weights or values to the gains in both contexts. A QALY is not a QALY. For society, the value attached to a QALY is not independent of the context in which this QALY is gained. Thus, the first sieve of the funnel of Dunning re-entered the debate. The discussion on necessity was reframed in terms of 'severity of illness' and linked to the debates on a fair distribution of health and

---

[15]   Stolk (note 13).

health care. Note that these aspects do not imply that QALYs are 'wrong' in some sense, but simply that in societal decision making more is important than only the maximization of health.

6. Equity weighting and flexible thresholds

The Dutch discussions regarding the funding of Viagra illustrated that striving for efficiency (in the sense of producing most QALYs with available resources) is not the sole goal of health policy. People commonly do not consider the resulting prioritization as desirable. They may especially consider the resulting choices or prioritizations to be 'unfair'. Indeed, fairness or equity is another important goal of health policy. Efficiency and equity have been noted as the twin goals of health policy before.[16] People do not only care about the amount of health gained, but also about the way in which it is distributed. 'A QALY is not a QALY', therefore, but some QALYs may be deemed more important, or put differently, more valuable, than others. Numerous empirical studies have indicated that people weight QALY gains differently when they are gained in different circumstances or different beneficiaries. For instance, QALYs gained in people with more severe diseases (i.e. those causing larger health losses) are normally preferred to QALYs gained in people with milder diseases (i.e. those causing smaller health losses). Moreover, QALYs gained in younger persons are often preferred to those gained in older individuals.[17] This literature normally describes these preferences in terms of 'equity weights'. Some QALY gains receive more weight than others in decision making. This implies that people are willing to forego larger health gains in elderly in order to gain less health in children, since the latter health gains receive more weight. One can equivalently say that some QALY gains are considered more 'valuable' from a societal viewpoint than others. We are willing to pay more for health gains in young people than for those in older persons.

Without recognizing these societal preferences for a fair distribution of health and health care, economic evaluation risks to promote choices that are not justifiable or sustainable. In terms of the decision rules of economic evaluation, it simply implies that equation (2") needs to be adjusted in order to allow different values (or weights) to be attached to different values:

$$\frac{\Delta c_o}{\Delta g^i_o} < v^i_o \qquad (3)$$

Equation (3) indicates that the costs made to produce one QALY of type i (where type refers to the 'relevant equity characteristics' of the gained QALY) should not exceed

---

[16] ibid.
[17] ibid.

the value of that type of QALY. Hence, there no longer is one specific threshold value for all QALYs gained, yet this threshold becomes context specific. It is important to stress that this is equivalent to having one threshold yet using 'equity weights' and multiplying g with these 'equity weights'.[18] The latter approach appears to be taken in the UK, where under specific conditions, particular life prolonging interventions may be funded even though they do not meet traditional standards of acceptable cost-effectiveness.[19] Then, it can be calculated what additional weight the QALYs gained through such interventions would need to receive in order to meet the common threshold. Obviously, when multiplying g with a number larger than 1 (i.e. giving more weight than 'normal'), the incremental cost-effectiveness ratio lowers and, hence, cost-effectiveness improves.

In the Netherlands, rather than working with weights, a flexible threshold was proposed. This threshold would increase when the intervention was deemed more 'necessary', hence reintroducing the first criterion from the funnel of Dunning. This concept of necessity thus referred to the context in which QALYs were gained, i.e. to the equity characteristics of the gained QALYs. This is shown in Figure 2.

FIGURE 2. *Increasing threshold with increasing necessity*

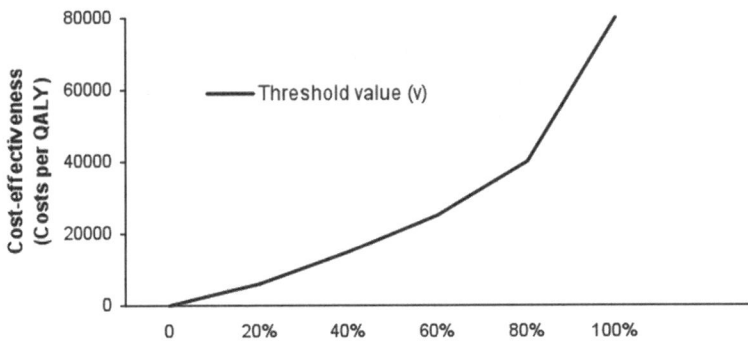

Figure 2 indicates that the threshold becomes less restrictive when the necessity of intervention increases. Note that information on the height and shape of the curve is currently lacking, so the model depicted in Figure 2 is especially a decision model giving direction to subsequent decisions.

Obviously, a crucial question is how to determine whether an intervention is more 'necessary'. (This again is an example of an issue where more interaction between economics and philosophy could be very fruitful.). In the literature three

18   See for example: Maynard (note 2).
19   See for an overview: P Dolan and others, 'QALY maximisation and people's preferences: a methodological review of the literature' (2005) 14 (2) *Health Economics* 197-208.

dominant approaches may be distinguished: the fair innings approach, the severity of illness approach and an approach one may label as 'empirical ethics'.

The fair innings approach was prominently advocated by Alan Williams.[20] This approach was based on the notion that all human beings are entitled to some 'normal' or 'fair' health achievement during their lives. People who fall short of achieving this 'fair innings' are relatively disadvantaged in health terms and, therefore, more entitled to health improving interventions than people who have already had their fair innings in life and, so to speak, are living on 'borrowed time'. As Van de Wetering and colleagues explain, adopting a fair innings approach implies that '*QALY gains in people who have had their fair innings should be valued lower than QALY gains in people who are expected to get less than their fair innings. Thus, the equity weights depend on the expected lifetime QALY total, therefore also considering past health losses and age is a key element (as proxy for lifetime health achievement), resulting in higher weights for QALY gains in relatively young persons and lower ones for those in relatively older persons.*'[21]

The severity of illness approach considers the current and future health losses occurring due to some illness.[22] A prominent (but not the only) operationalisation of severity of illness is the prospective health approach. In this approach the expected health profile of a person in the case of no treatment determines their priority for treatment (all other things equal). As Van de Wetering and others (2012) explain: '*This aligns with an alternative definition of need, namely, expected ill health over the remaining years of life. Prospective health considers the expected health (including death) in future years in the case of non-intervention and distributes QALY gains initially to those with the worst prognosis if left untreated.*'[23] QALY weights thus are used to give more priority to those with the poorest health prospects. To illustrate, in such an approach a person faced with almost instant death, will receive highest priority. This aligns well with the well-known Rule of Rescue.[24]

Both the fair innings and the prospective health approach are based on clear notions on what determines 'need' or 'necessity' and, therefore, on what basis priority setting should take place. A third stream that can be distinguished does not start from an equity principle, but rather considers what (a representative sample of) the general public considers to be a fair distribution of health gains. We shall call this approach 'empirical ethics' here. The principle here therefore may be considered to be directed at the process of deriving weights (in a 'democratic' fashion), rather than at the outcomes or content of the weights. In such an approach, unlike the former two approaches that both seek to base equity weights only on health characteristics of the potential beneficiaries, numerous factors could be taken

---

[20] L van de Wetering and others, 'Balancing equity and efficiency in delineating the Dutch basic benefits package using the principle of proportional shortfall' *European Journal of Health Economics*, in press.

[21] NICE: Appraising life-extending, end of life treatments (2009).

[22] A Williams, 'Intergenerational equity: an exploration of the 'fair innings' argument' (1997) 6 *Health Economics* 117-132.

[23] Van de Wetering (note 20).

[24] E Nord, 'Concerns for the worse off: fair innings versus severity' (2005) 60 (2) *Soc Sc Med* 257–263.

into account, including aspects like culpability (e.g. responsibility for own illness, lifestyle) or having dependents (e.g. young children).

In the Dutch situation, a choice was made for a specific operationalisation of the severity of illness approach, labeled proportional shortfall.[25] The underlying principle here is that those patients who lose the greatest *proportion* of their remaining health expectancy due to some illness in case this illness remains untreated should receive priority. The higher the proportion of remaining health lost due to some illness, the higher the priority the treatment of these patients is given. Put differently, the higher the proportion of health lost due to some illness, the more necessary treatment is considered to be. By using remaining QALY profiles with and without the disease, it is easy to express this necessity as a number, ranging from 0% (nothing lost) to 100% (all remaining health lost). By using proportions, also elderly can receive high priority. In fact, people facing the loss of all remaining health (e.g. immediate death), will all receive a necessity score of 100%, regardless of age. It needs noting that this feature of proportional shortfall also can be seen as a weakness, since many people will judge preventing a loss of all remaining 80 years of a 3 year-old to be more important than preventing a loss of all remaining 3 years of a 80 year-old.[26]

This way of quantifying necessity, albeit imperfect, helped to operationalise the first sieve from the funnel of Dunning and to give more systematic attention to necessity. While the current way of doing this may not be without problems, it can be seen as a useful starting point for further discussions on necessity, both on a conceptual level as well as on the level of rationing decisions dealing with specific interventions. Note that the developers of the notion of proportional shortfall stressed its limitations and did not intend it as capturing all relevant elements of necessity or as a substitute for a clear deliberative process weighing all relevant aspects in a more qualitative way. In the Netherlands, such a process is now institutionalized in the 'appraisal phase' of the decision making process. In this phase, all quantitative information regarding the health technology, potentially including a preliminary conclusion based on this 'assessment phase' (using Figure 2) is weighed and balanced with less or non-quantifiable considerations. In that sense, the saying *not all that can be counted counts, and that not all that counts can be counted*, is a very important one.

Using the concept of proportional shortfall, Figure 2 can be made more practically useful. This model allows Viagra, despite favorable cost-effectiveness, to be left out of the basic benefits package (as being located on the left hand in Figure 2) while lung transplants, placed on the right hand side in that same figure, may be included, despite unfavorable cost-effectiveness. Thus it leads to choices in health care that combine the twin goals in health care policy of efficiency and equity, which can be considered as a significant step forward.

---

[25]   Van de Wetering (note 20).
[26]   J McKie and J Richardson, 'The rule of rescue' (2003) 56 (12) *Soc Sc Med* 2407–2419; DC Hadorn, 'Setting health care priorities in Oregon' (1991) 265 (17) *JAMA* 2218–2225.

The evidence on preferences in the population or among policymakers on equity weights, also related to severity of illness, is growing. An aspect still largely under-explored is that of the value of health. While rationing as a topic may already be contentious, estimating (or setting) a monetary value for health gains is even more controversial. But, as indicated above, it is necessary, because not having such a threshold increases the risk of arbitrary, suboptimal and harmful decisions. The Dutch Health Insurance Board (2009) wrote that in evaluating cost-effectiveness the Board uses an 'indicative range' from about € 10,000 for a low necessity to about € 80,000 per QALY for very high necessity.[27] Gaining one QALY may cost € 10,000 in the former case, therefore, but even € 80,000 in the latter (implying relative equity weights of 1 and 8 respectively). These figures do not have a sound basis, however, and more research and debate seems necessary in order to arrive at a better justification of the model.[28]

An interesting question here is what value the threshold should represent. Much current research aims to derive individual valuations of own health gains. This does not seem to relate well to the fact that these values ultimately should reflect societal valuations also reflecting notions of equity. Commonly, the valuations used capture equity considerations such as the fact that a QALY of a poor person intrinsically is not worth less than that of a rich person. This also raises questions regarding how to obtain relevant valuations in empirical research.[29] Fruitful multidisciplinary co-operation is conceivable in this area, if not necessary!

7. Towards a multidisciplinary future of rationing?

This paper has provided an overview of some of the developments and issues related to health care rationing using economic evaluations. As indicated, it has not attempted to be exhaustive in any sense. It highlighted the current state of affairs in The Netherlands, which may be exemplary for other countries as well, if nothing else in terms of the relevant issues to be addressed. Many other relevant issues could have been addressed and should be addressed in future (multidisciplinary) research. These issues range from who should provide the QALY scores for health states between dead and perfect health to be used in health care decisions (patients or the general public), to which elements should be considered in weighting QALY gains for reasons of fairness. And from how to make decisions in sectors where health improvement (as measurement in terms of QALYs) may not be the main aim of health care (e.g. long term care, palliative care), to how the process of health care decision making can be developed further in such a way that all relevant considerations are given due attention.

---

[27] EA Stolk and others, 'Proeftoetsing iMTA model', in WGM Toenders, Vervolgonderzoek breedte geneesmiddelenpakket [in Dutch] Amstelveen: College voor Zorgverzekeringen 2002; EA Stolk and others, 'Reconciliation of economic concerns and health policy: illustration of an equity adjustment procedure using proportional shortfall' (20040 22 (17) *Pharmaco Economics* 1097-1107.
[28] See for an elaborate discussion: Van de Wetering and others (note 20).
[29] College voor Zorgverzekeringen (note 14).

It seems that multidisciplinary co-operation in the context of health care rationing is crucial in moving forward. It is clear that such co-operation is required in determining who is most deserving in priority setting, i.e. in determining who is worse off. It appears that there are no 'right' answers in this context, and, therefore, it is important to be transparent, to be conscious of the limitations of any chosen principle, to construct balanced deliberative processes to weight other arguments, and so on. A transparent and accountable appraisal phase needs to be part of a full decision process in the context of explicitly rationing care through limiting entitlements. If such appraisal is done by a committee then the constitution of such committee in terms of a balance of interests and a fair representation is vital, an area that seems understudied so far. Moreover, attention needs to be given to (fair) implementation of decisions. Typically, interventions are necessary, effective and cost-effective for certain groups of patients (and not for others). This means that rationing decisions need to be tailor-made. This can, for instance, be achieved through developing practice guidelines based on the rationing principles discussed here above. This would promote that the care actually given in practice is necessary, effective and cost-effective. Unfortunately, most guidelines focus on effectiveness and are not developed using the rationing criteria discussed here (necessity, effectiveness and cost-effectiveness). Without the required instruments to implement in a tailor-made fashion, however, rationing decisions will be inherently 'blunt'.

Quantifying specific aspects of rationing decisions helps to improve decisions and can make them more transparent and consistent. However, it is naïve to assume that a full, prescriptive, quantitative framework resulting in 'optimal' decisions and guidelines will ever be found. Improving what we measure, how we measure it and how we interpret what we measure should go hand in hand with more deliberation on the normative choices underlying the decision making framework and a further development of the decision making process. This again requires multidisciplinary co-operation.

Concluding, given the growing gap between technological opportunities and available resources, a transparent and scientifically sound way of making decisions on rationing becomes increasingly important. Denying the need to ration health care is to deny scarcity of resources and risks non-optimal, arbitrary and potentially harmful decisions. Our *joint* effort cannot avoid painful decision, but can ensure that the inevitable rationing decisions are justifiable and accountable.

Contributors

Karen Bloor is a Senior Research Fellow in the Department of Health Sciences, University of York. Her research focusses is the economics of health policy, in particular the productivity of the physician labour force, the role of financial and non-financial incentives on medical workforce behaviour, the regulation of the pharmaceutical industry and rationing

Werner Brouwer (1972) is a Professor of Health Economics and Chairman of the institute of Health Policy & Management (iBMG) of the Erasmus University Rotterdam. He obtained an MSc in Economics (1996) and a Ph.D in Health Economics (1999) from the same university. His research interests are broad and cover for instance the methodology of health economic evaluations, the link between economic evaluation and health policy, and public health economics. He has published extensively on these topics.

Martin Buijsen (1963) is professor of Health Law at the Erasmus School of Law and the Institute of Policy and Management of Health Care (Erasmus University Rotterdam). He studied law and philosophy before obtaining a Ph.D at Erasmus University. Martin Buijsen is founder of the Institute of Law and Health Care at Erasmus University. His research extends to all areas of health law. He is especially interested in issues relating to access to health care.

Norman Daniels, Ph.D, is Mary B Saltonstall Profesor and Professor of Ethics and Population Health in the Department of Global Health and Population at Harvard School of Public Health. His most recent books include *Just Health: Meeting Health Needs Fairly* (CUP 2008); *Setting Limits Fairly: Learning to Share Resources for Health* (2nd edn., OUP 2008); *From Chance to Choice: Genetics and Justice* (CUP 2000); and *Is Inequality Bad for Our Health?* (Beacon Press 2000). His current research is on justice and health policy, including priority setting in health systems, fairness and health systems reform, health inequalities, and intergenerational justice.

Insiya Essajee. After obtaining her Honours Bachelor of Arts and Science from McMaster University in 2007, she went on to pursue her J.D. at the University of Toronto. While attending law school, Ms. Essajee participated in the Health Equity and Law Clinic, and received the John Yaremko Award in Human Rights and the Judy LaMarsh Prize in Feminist Analysis of Law for her academic performance. After completing her J.D. in 2011, Ms. Essajee articled with the Ontario Human Rights Commission

André P. den Exter (1966) is a lecturer in Health Law at the Institute of *Health Policy and Management, Erasmus University Rotterdam. The title of his dissertation was Health care lawmaking in Central and Eastern Europe. Review of a Legal-Theoretical Model* (EUR

2002). His research and teaching activities include: access to health care, pharmaceutical law, international and European health law. He (co)edited several books and wrote various articles on health legal issues.

Leonard M. Fleck, Ph.D, is Professor of Philosophy and Medical Ethics in the Center for Ethics and Humanities in the Life Sciences, College of Human Medicine, Michigan State University. He is the author of *Just Caring: Health Care Rationing and Democratic Deliberation* (OUP 2009) as well as more than 90 articles and book chapters on a range of issues in health care ethics, health care policy, and social and political philosophy. He is co-editor of a forthcoming collection of essays titled *Toward Fair Rationing at the Bedside* (OUP).

Colleen M. Flood is a Canada Research Chair at the Faculty of Law, University of Toronto and is cross-appointed to the School of Public Policy and the Institute of Health Policy, Management & Evaluation. From 2006-2011 she served as the Scientific Director of the Canadian Institute for Health Services and Policy Research. Her primary areas of scholarship are in administrative law, comparative health care law & policy, public/private financing of health care systems, health care reform, and accountability and governance issues more broadly.

Carina Fourie is a Research Fellow at the Department of Philosophy and the Institute of Biomedical Ethics, University of Zurich. After completing her Ph.D in Moral and Political Philosophy at University College London, she conducted research into occupational health. At present she is combining her research interests of philosophy and health. She is particularly interested in social justice, equality and health, and is currently working on applying the capabilities approach to health, and on assessing the ethical implications of Diagnosis-Related Groups in Swiss hospitals.

Frances M. Kamm, Ph.D is Lucius Littauer Professor of Philosophy and Public Policy, Harvard Kennedy School, and Professor of Philosophy, Harvard University. She is the author of *Creation and Abortion; Morality, Mortality, vols. 1 and 2; Intricate Ethics; Ethics for Enemies: Terror, Torture and War, The Moral Target: Aiming at Right Conduct in War and Other Conflicts* (forthcoming) (all from Oxford University Press), and numerous articles on normative ethical theory and on practical ethics. She serves on the editorial boards of Philosophy & Public Affairs, Legal Theory, and Utilitas, and on the Faculty Advisory Committee of the Edmond J. Safra Ethics Center. She has been a fellow of the Guggenheim Foundation and the Center for Advanced Studies in the Behavioral Sciences, Stanford, and is a fellow of the American Academy of Arts and Sciences.

Alan Maynard is Professor of Health Economics in the Department of Health Sciences and Hull-York Medical School, University of York, England. His research focusses is the economics of health policy, in particular the productivity of the physician labour force, the role of financial and non-financial incentives on medical workforce behaviour, the regulation of the pharmaceutical industry and rationing.

Christopher Newdick is the Professor of Health Law at the University of Reading, UK. He is the author of *WHO Should We Treat? - Rights, Rationing and Resources in the NHS* (OUP 2005) and co-editor of *Law and Ethics in Intensive Care* (OUP 2011). In addition to his research, he has served on the UK government's Medicines Commission and has advised the National Prescribing Committee. He is a consultant to health care purchasers in England and is a legal advisor to the South Central Priorities Committee which advises health care purchasers in England on setting health care priorities for local populations of people.

Jean-Marc Piret (1960) is Associate Professor of Philosophy of Law at the University of Rotterdam Law School and at the (Flemish) Free University of Brussels. Jean-Marc Piret published on different topics of legal philosophy such as the ethical and philosophical aspects of *wrongful birth* and *wrongful life claims*. Most recently he wrote articles about just war theory, the "war" against terrorism; on the extraterritorial scope of the U.S. constitution and on torture.

Frans F.H. Rutten, Ph.D, is professor of Health Economics at the Erasmus University Rotterdam and was head of the department of Health Policy and Management in 2002-2007. In 1988 he founded the institute for Medical Technology Assessment and was managing director in 1988-2000. His research interests include the methodology and application of economic evaluation of health care programs and medicines, health policy and global health issues. He chaired the organising committee of the second iHEA World Conference on Health Economics in Rotterdam, June 1999, and served as president of the international Health Economics Association (iHEA) in 2001-2002.

James Sabin is Clinical Professor in the Departments of Population Medicine and Psychiatry at Harvard Medical School. He directs the ethics program at Harvard Pilgrim Health Care, a not-for-profit regional health plan in Massachusetts, New Hampshire, and Maine. He is a member of the American Medical Association Council on Ethical and Judicial Affairs.

Daniel Sperling is a senior lecturer in the Federmann School of Public Policy and Government and Braun School of Public Health & Community Medicine, the Hebrew University of Jerusalem where he teaches courses on bioethics, public health ethics, health law and health policy. He holds an LL.B and B.A.(Philosophy) from the Hebrew University of Jerusalem and LL.M (Collaborative Programme in Bioethics) and S.J.D. from the University of Toronto. Dr. Sperling is the author of *Posthumous Interests: Legal and Ethical Perspectives* (CUP 2008), *Management of Post-Mortem Pregnancy: Legal and Philosophical Aspects* (Ashgate 2006) and other numerous articles in his area of interests.

Keith Syrett is Professor of Law at Cardiff University, UK. He is the author of *Law, Legitimacy and Rationing: a Contextual and Comparative Perspective* (CUP 2007) and has written extensively on the relationship between law and the rationing of healthcare both in the United Kingdom and elsewhere. He is a Solicitor of the Supreme Court of England and Wales, Secretary of the British Association for Canadian Studies, a

Fellow of the Royal Society of Medicine and a member of the editorial board of Medical Law International.

Index

A

ability to pay 26-27, 88, 137, 210-212, 226
access to health care 70, 119, 122, 159, 183, 204, 210, 211, 243
accountability
 for reasonableness 15, 17-19-23, 156
appraisal phase 239, 241
assessment phase 239
assisted reproductive technologies (ARTs) 111
autonomy
 breach of 116

B

blanket ban 136, 141
bodily integrity 8, 95, 126

C

Canada Health Act 173, 184
care consumer 206
causative Principle 55-56, 59-61, 63
citizen's council 15, 20
collective choice 120
cost
 benefit analysis 223, 227, 229
 effectiveness analysis 13, 15, 120, 230
 utility analysis 94, 230-231, 235

D

death
 brain death 97, 99-101, 103, 105
 definition 97-99, 101-103, 105, 109
 panels 22, 35
democratic deliberation 8, 10, 26-27, 30-32, 35-38, 41, 45, 201
directive on cross-border care 164
disability-adjusted life year (DALY) 14
disability co-morbidity 57
discrimination 18, 28, 37-38, 47, 53-62, 113, 127, 164, 178, 184-187, 190, 193, 195,
 199-200, 204, 207, 224